NATURE SHOCK

JON T. COLEMAN

9/20

# Nature
# Shock

GETTING LOST IN AMERICA

Yale UNIVERSITY PRESS    NEW HAVEN AND LONDON

Published with assistance from the Louis Stern Memorial Fund, and from the income of the Frederick John Kingsbury Memorial Fund.

Yale University Press books may be purchased in quantity for educational, business, or promotional use. For information, please e-mail sales.press@yale.edu (U.S. office) or sales@yaleup. co.uk (U.K. office).

Set in Scala and Scala Sans type by IDS Infotech, Ltd.
Printed in the United States of America.

Library of Congress Control Number: 2019957742
ISBN 978-0-300-22714-7 (hardcover : alk. paper)

A catalogue record for this book is available from the British Library.

This paper meets the requirements of ANSI/NISO Z39.48-1992 (Permanence of Paper).

10 9 8 7 6 5 4 3 2 1

# CONTENTS

Acknowledgments    vii

Introduction: Want to Get Lost?    1

1  Brutal Symmetry    13

2  Helpful Woods and Violent Waters    52

3  Children of the Revolution    93

4  Homing    134

5  Dead-Certain Mental Compass    171

6  Keep Your Head    211

7  Male Pattern Trail Loss    242

Epilogue: Disconnect    285

Notes    297

Index    331

## ACKNOWLEDGMENTS

In the coming pages, I write about the transition from relational space to individual space in the North American interior. I argue that, while we mostly dwell in individual space today, the relational lingers in the age of smartphones, satellites, and GPS. I offer the production of this book as evidence of the continued potency of relationships. Without the help of many people, I would not have finished. I alone am to blame for the final product, but I thank the following for pushing me to figure out what I wanted to say and for giving me the courage to say it.

I wish to acknowledge the Simon Guggenheim Foundation and the College of Arts and Letters at the University of Notre Dame for the yearlong fellowship leave that got this project rolling. I also want to thank the Huntington Library for a short-term research fellowship as well as the expertise and friendship of Peter Blodgett. I have had the pleasure to work with two incredible research assistants: Danae Jacobson and Madelyn Lugli.

Thank you to my colleagues who read the manuscript in various states of readiness, especially to Patrick Griffin, Darren Duchuk, Thomas Tweed, Jake Lundberg, Dan Graff, and Ted Beatty. Thanks as well to the Notre Dame graduate students in environmental and western American history who listened patiently to my elevator pitches about a "getting-lost" book—Danae Jacobson, John Nelson, Lindsey Wieck, Bethany Montagano, Felicia Moralez, Courtney Wiersma, and Craig Kinnear. Lisa Adams at the Garamond

Agency must have read a dozen versions of the book proposal. I am grateful for her feedback and her patience. Thanks to Dan Gerstle for suggesting a book about getting lost in America over breakfast many years ago. Jean Thomson Black at Yale University Press has shepherded this book through the publishing gauntlet. I appreciate her expert guidance and steadfast belief in the project. I want to thank the anonymous readers Jean solicited. Thanks as well to Michael Deneen, Elizabeth Sylvia, Susan Laity, Robin DuBlanc, and the many editors and media wranglers at Yale University Press.

For the past six years, I have worked in an academic office, a strange habitat for a scholar used to solitary confinement. Thanks to my officemates: Christina Ryan, Kevin Vaughn, Jaime Pensado, Alexis Miller, Lisa Gallagher, Nell Collins, Morgan Wilson, David Smiley, and Leslie Lestinsky.

Lastly, I want to recognize my family. My mom, Barbara Coleman, is an inspirational elder, game for whatever life brings. I admire her and love her greatly. John and Cally Gilbert have treated me like a son for over twenty-five years. I appreciate their love and support. My children, Harry and Louise, have gone from eye-rolling teens to young adults in the span of the writing of this book. I am lucky to have kids who embrace the world with humor, grit, and compassion. I dedicate this book to Annie Gilbert Coleman. When early drafts nearly drove me to despair, Annie held me together. A brilliant historian, she read and listened as I fumbled around in the dark, trying to puzzle a way forward. She remains my North Star. I steer by her light.

NATURE SHOCK

# Introduction

IN OCTOBER 2017, THE LUXURY TRAVEL company Black Tomato launched a bewilderment service, Get Lost. For a fee starting around $20,000, the company agreed to drop clients somewhere inhospitable. True adventurers could "roll the dice" and let travel consultants pick their outing from among "some of the most remote, unfettered destinations imaginable," like the jungles of Guyana, the steppes of Mongolia, or the tundra of arctic Svalbard. Those wanting more say could select a target region among polar, coastal, jungle, mountain, or desert options. Black Tomato offered training sessions and gear-selection appointments with qualified outfitters in the months leading up to departure. Once inserted into the wild, clients were "closely tracked" by an "experienced operations team." They carried satellite phones as a safety precaution, and Black Tomato's business partner, what3words, provided navigational technology far superior to off-the-shelf GPS devices. Clients who progressed through monitored check points eventually arrived at journey's end to reap their reward, "a truly one of a kind celebration and send off, something deeply personal and indulgent."[1]

Hiring a Get Lost concierge promised to make you a better person. A vacation filled with unexpected difficulties jarred clients out of their stressful lives and forced them "to disconnect, engage in the moment and push themselves to achieve a sense of satisfaction." The company's website told potential customers that "by starting with the feeling of being genuinely lost, you will set out (under the distant watch of a dedicated support team) to find your inner steel, beliefs and passion." Cofounder Tom Marchant told *Vogue* that he hoped to free clients from the "connected world" and help them rediscover "what it's like to travel authentically, restoring an important sense of self-discovery." Black Tomato bet heavily on the truism "Sometimes you need to get lost to find yourself."[2]

Examples of the getting-lost cure abound in the digital age. They run the gamut from the state of Montana's tourist slogan "Get Lost" to the DVD series "Get Lost: Your Guide to Finding Love," a ten-week Bible study for single women. If the freneticism of contemporary life is the problem, then getting lost has become a metaphor for slowing down, chilling out, and cultivating wellness. The prescription, however, deserves a historical warning label. Losing yourself to find yourself is a modern cliché parading as ancient wisdom. The notion that getting lost could be a healthy last resort in a modern world surfaced in the United States in the nineteenth century and became widely accepted in the 1960s. Before that, getting lost horrified most everyone. Communities rallied to find the lost, and observers likened the experience to going insane. Of course, we too send rescue teams after missing persons, yet we long to be lost even as we sound alarms when people are. When we talk about getting lost, what do we really mean?[3]

Black Tomato's marketing suggests a contemporary definition lacking in moral seriousness, true consequence, and historical continuity. When a travel agency orchestrates your discombobulation and an extraction team monitors your every move, can you genuinely be lost in the same way a Spanish conquistador was lost, a runaway slave was lost, or a backcountry hiker was lost? Probably not. Yet for all its slick packaging, Black Tomato harkened back to the past even as it promised to solve some very twenty-first-century problems like feeling besieged by too much information. Black Tomato imagined clients finding their true selves in bespoke isolation. Wanderers explored their psyches while hidden service professionals supported them with high-tech equipment. Neither side of this equation, the search for renewal in solitude or the surveillance, violated nature or history. The company sold a brand of individualism that traces back to the Enlightenment. The practice of spying on people to keep them from getting lost has an even longer history. Before eighteenth-century humans imagined free individuals roaming in space, they envisioned spaces as hierarchical communities. They conceived of space through kinship, and they kept track of one another primarily with their own eyes. Early moderns built relational spaces, and they spied on one another to stay connected and to prevent one another from escaping. The promoters of individual space concealed their prying behind impersonal technology. Still, we shouldn't judge them too harshly for their hypocrisy. According to scientists, when it comes to making spaces, human beings cannot help but make them together.[4]

Navigation space is shared space. It's a comingling of actual geography and a mental project involving many people. Humans reach out to one another, directly or empathetically, to build mindscapes that defy absolute space. Societies, writes cognitive psychologist Barbara Tversky, imagine what individuals cannot perceive alone. Groups cobble together composites from "different views, different encounters, different modes, from experience, from maps, from language." Mathematicians, physicists, and engineers can conjure abstract spaces outside the entities contained in them. Navigating humans reverse this perspective: they mull the entities and mangle the spaces. They bend, rotate, elongate, and mash space to make and remember connections. Such spatial cognition distinguishes humans, whether they cherish personal freedom or value communal attachment, as a species that resides in the world, in communities, and in their heads.[5]

Normally, this tripartite citizenship harmonized: social constructions, mental maps, and physical geographies lined up. But every so often the realms failed to synchronize, ejecting heads into outer spaces that defied imagination.[6]

Freefalls over unfathomed cliffs tore some minds loose from their moorings, inducing what I will call nature shock, a malady that combined stampeding emotions and wiped memories. In 1873, Charles Darwin pondered the abrupt disarrangement of "very old and feeble persons." He suspected that the "strong distress" they exhibited when they "suddenly found out that they have been proceeding in a wholly unexpected and wrong direction" proved that "some part of the brain" was "specialized for the function of direction." He guessed right. The point of origin for nature shock was neither a thicket of pines nor a dreary fen but rather the seahorse-shaped section of the medial temporal lobe. Spatial thoughts reside in the hippocampus, the region in the brain also dedicated to memory and emotion.[7]

A week after Darwin posted his observations on the mammalian sense of direction in London's science journal *Nature*, Henry Forde, a reader from The Walk, Lyme Regis, a hamlet of seaside cottages on England's southern coast, sent in his own brush with unhinged rovers. Years ago, he wrote, while traveling in the "wild parts of the State of Western Virginia," he had heard that "the most experienced hunters of the forest-covered mountains in that unsettled region [were] liable to a kind of seizure." The hunters became convinced they were headed in the wrong direction and "no reasoning nor pointing out of landmarks by their companions, nor observations of the position of the sun" could "overcome this feeling." They described the emotion as "a general sense of dismay and 'upset.' " Forde ended his letter with a query: what caused grown men, wilderness experts, no less, to fall into the same "sudden derangement" that attacked the old and the insane?[8]

Damaged or diseased hippocampi may explain why the elderly and the mentally ill strayed, but nature shocked brains up and down the social ladder and across the spectrum of health. The burly mountaineers were up against more than haywire neurology. The social and cultural construction of space unraveled alongside misfiring brain cells. The West Virginians crossed a biological, environmental, and social point of no return. It scared them senseless.

In this book about nature shock I argue that over the course of five centuries, North Americans traveled from relational space, where people navigated by their relationships to one another, to individual space, where people understood their position on earth by the coordinates provided by mass media, transportation grids, and commercial networks. The best vantage point to see this transition and thereby understand its consequences is on the edge of those spaces where people sometimes got terribly lost. Nature shock exposed the illusions of individual space—that persons could liberate themselves in spaces outside of human connection—and nature shock illuminated the dark recesses of relational space, where human connections often meant slavery and violence. Nature shock, I argue further, revealed neither a clear divide nor a revolutionary break between relational and individual space. Instead, one way of seeing the world blurred into the other, and we can spot remnants of relational space in the ways people navigate environments to this day.

What caused North Americans' spatial cognition to change? During the nineteenth century, transcontinental voyagers stretched impersonal networks of surveillance (newsprint and the U.S. mail) to stay in contact with friends, relatives, employees, and business partners. With the help of the federal government, steam transportation, and mass media, they accidentally created individual space in the service of relational goals. By the early twentieth century, the relational justifications had withered while impersonal networks grew both more extensive and less visible, creating imaginative openings for individuals to seek freedom alone in nature.

Observers often blamed nature for shocking people. Henry Forde, for instance, thought that the West Virginia hunters got turned around because they had tracked feral prey in the "wild parts" of an "unsettled region." To him, the hunters belonged to a line of American frontiersmen who battled wildernesses, who cleared them of edible and noxious creatures, who prepared the ground for civilization, and who sometimes got lost in the process. The notion of the wilderness presupposed a location outside human control where nature existed, if not untouched, then barely so. This, however, was never the case. The American wilderness was bespoke from the start. Mountains, deserts, prairies, swamps, and forests confused people, but their opacity had more to do with the quirks of humanity and the vagaries of history than with these spaces being outside the realm of imagination or manipulation. Many of the sites seen as wilderness were Native American farmlands, hunting grounds, buffer zones, and sacred spaces. It took acts of martial aggression and feats of mental acrobatics to empty them.[9]

Historians have written extensively about the shifting of wilderness definitions. In 1967, Roderick Nash published *The Wilderness in the American Mind*, in which he traced an arc of environmental thinking from the New England Puritans' fear and loathing of the wilderness to post–World War II Americans' veneration of untouched nature, culminating in the Wilderness Act of 1964. The law defined the wilderness as a federally owned parcel of undeveloped land of at "least five thousand acres" in "primeval condition" lacking "permanent improvements or human habitation." Wilderness areas cordoned off nature and history, giving modern Americans a chance to break free from landscapes dominated by their "works." Search-and-rescue groups, volunteer organizations that increased in number with the popularity of outdoor recreation in the postwar United States, drew wider boundaries around the wilderness than federal legislators or environmentalists. For them, any ecoregion "essentially undisturbed and uninhabited" qualified as wild. The site need not be scenic or untrammeled, it just had to be confusing and lightly supervised.[10]

Geographic expanses dedicated to the appearance of vacancy, wilderness areas, national parks, state parks, and undeveloped private holdings diminished home-field advantages. Tourists ventured into them to disrupt their everyday travel patterns, to relieve themselves of work commutes and trips to the grocery store. Wilderness ecoregions separated urbanites from their cars, inspiring an array of muscle-powered outdoor exertions from kayaking to ice climbing, but walking, rebranded as hiking, was the sport most likely to get you terribly lost.[11]

Pedestrianism abetted getting lost throughout American history. Walkers metabolized their own energy stores to move, and their bodies drew them into potential conflicts with supplies, habitats, and other humans. Hauling food to fuel journeys weighed pedestrians down. They burned energy to shoulder calories and packing either too much or too little could lead to danger. Walkers could abandon self-provisioning and live off the land. But hunting and gathering in unfamiliar environments absorbed tremendous amounts of energy for uncertain payoffs, and the pursuit of wild calories was in itself a good way to get lost. Walkers could conscript bearers or hire guides to lift their food and pilot their courses, yet this strategy fostered dependency on the strength, cooperation, and judgment of others, which opened a host of human resource problems. What if the laborers rebelled or the guide proved unreliable or unbearable?[12]

None of these complications necessarily produced nature shock until something unforeseen happened. And seeing poorly, along with bipedism, was a critical precondition for nature shock. Forests blocked sightlines and bombarded navigators with multitudes of landmarks. Open spaces with unending views triggered similar reactions: seeing everything felt like seeing nothing. Nighttime and storms cut visibility and contributed to getting lost. Unforeseen accidents and disasters befell humans in all spaces and historic eras, but walking into a setting and a scenario that tricked or occluded visual perception was a shortcut to a panic attack.[13]

The final key ingredient for nature shock was the assertion of power, and wildernesses were never free from politics. In the nineteenth century, government officials, property owners, and conservationists cleared wildernesses of their original inhabitants before they reintroduced the spaces as pristine. Getting lost proliferated during similar acts of trespass throughout American history. Entering someone else's land on foot or on horseback and being stricken by the unforeseen: that was one of the original and most enduring recipes for going astray in the continental interior.[14]

Evidence of getting lost accumulated in documents of conquest and recreation, disclosing the connection between the two. My sources include conquistador narratives, local frontier histories, personal correspondence, newspaper articles, outdoor magazine articles, and the memoirs of hikers and climbers who sought to find themselves in the wilderness. There were no archives dedicated to lost persons writ large, no rows of boxes labeled "antique lost persons: a cross-section." I hunted for examples in letters and journals and found a few. I located many more in digitized materials. The records, I soon discovered, not only explained the history of nature shock in North America, they propelled it. Starting in the 1850s, American publishers adopted steam-powered presses, escalating their output of books, newspapers, and magazines. These documents joined a flood of mail crossing the continent on trains, in stagecoaches, and aboard steamships. Promotional materials and personal correspondence drew invaders into the American West and changed how they perceived the region's indigenous residents, its wildlife, and its environments. Industrial information constructed new spaces out of old ones. Indian spaces, for example, became recreational wilderness areas. Individuals traveled to the wilderness to escape society and follow their own path. Some of them got lost.[15]

The sources shaped the history of nature shock, and they shape the experience of reading this book. The chapters track the changes in North American spatial cognition in this order: chapters 1 and 2 depict relational space; chapters 3, 4, and 5 chart the uneven and incomplete transition from relational to individual space; chapters 6 and 7 explore individual space. Early chapters are more anecdotal and fractured while later chapters, which rely on magazine articles and other mass media, yield a more coherent depiction of generic minds lost in recreational nature. Ironically, more individuals appear in the book's early section. Relational navigators were obsessed with other people while the inhabitants of individual space focused more on interior psychology and impersonal networks.

Human beings imagined and built spaces together. They shared regions, landmarks, paths, nodes, centers, and peripheries. Since they bent space in concert, the power that structured their relations contorted their projections. Powerful men got lost in bunches, and one of the reasons for their overrepresentation tracks back to seeing. Human beings struggled to navigate environments when their vision failed. That's why blizzards and setting suns often precipitated bouts of geographic dishevelment. Poor visibility, however, blocked more than a wayfarer's point of view. Fog and nightfall blinded comrades, kin, and neighbors as well. Communities looked after their constituents in the spirit of solidarity and love, but also to exert control and enforce discipline. Power organized surveillance. Marginal and exploited members of communities were observed more intently than principal ones. Fewer eyes watched the watchers, making hunters, explorers, lumberjacks, soldiers, surveyors, treasure seekers, and wilderness trekkers susceptible to disappearance. Their social privilege became a spatial liability when they stole out of sight when no one was looking.[16]

Yet even though the archives netted more of them, white men never monopolized getting lost. Native American hunters and war captives suffered bewilderment, as did African American men and women seeking to escape the surveillance regimes of slavery. Mothers and daughters broke free from the restrictions placed on their mobility to enter landscapes that spun them dizzy. Children with developing hippocampi and elderly persons in the throes of dementia wandered away throughout American history. Animals got lost too, dragging those who would surveil them into danger. Agrarian parents sent children to retrieve grazing livestock only to lose the kids as well as the cows in swamps and forests. Social relationships constructed spaces, and spaces tested social bonds.[17]

Nature shock exposed the limits of minds, spaces, and communities. Lost persons toed up to the edge of society and sanity. They reached the ends of their spatial imagination and peered into the abyss. What they saw rattled them. I chronicle their journeys into the continental interior of North America. I seek to understand why relational space gave way to individual space and why North Americans continue to reckon with their tangled desires to be surrounded and alone, to belong and to be free.

Well-oriented people litter American history. They star in stereotypical American endeavors like trailblazing, lighting out, freedom seeking, and road tripping. I am after the sideshow performers, the strays who stumbled around, made hasty decisions, and sometimes perished only to be buried in unmarked graves. The befuddled drifters represent a side of the human condition obscured by the impressions left by the army of pathfinders.

The alternative course they set leads into the continental interior. In this book, I intentionally forgo minds lost at sea and disoriented in the bays or inlets near the coast. Oceans may be the most difficult environments for humans to navigate and the shipwrecked sailor might count as the archetypal lost soul. I stay away from nautical catastrophes for a couple of reasons. Ocean travel proved so daunting that civilians turned to captains, navigators, and crews to plot courses for them. The chain of command and a hierarchy of expertise made getting lost in the open ocean less democratic than getting lost on land, a catastrophe that was open to lubbers of all ages and sexes across the demographic range. Closer to shore, smaller vessels and shallower waters freed nonspecialists to misdirect their own dinghies, yet coastal disappearances retained their maritime flavor. Drowning in a sunken boat was its own genre of environmental horror and a liquid death its own kind of lost. Besides, while puny in comparison to vast stretches of oceans, the continental interior of North America expands prodigiously when you add the inner spaces of human minds to its miles.[18]

I also downplay getting lost in cities and suburbs. A few baffled urban tourists will appear near the end, but for the most part I look for lost people in so-called wildernesses. This decision reflects the current state of the interior. In a 2008 training manual, search-and-rescue expert Robert Koester summarized the present geography of getting lost. Based on the findings of the International Search and Rescue Incident Database, a statistical compendium housing 50,692 lost-person reports from the United States and around the world, Koester found that 68 percent of lost-person episodes occurred in areas categorized as wilderness. Rural sites accounted for 14 percent, with cities (9 percent) and suburbs (2 percent) trailing behind. The loopy layout of suburban America might torment navigators looking for an address in mazes of Meadowlark Circles and Woodland Hill Drives, but the wilderness brought thousands of unlucky visitors to extreme locational perplexity.[19]

In this book, the wilderness starts as a willful blunder, a misperception colonial Euro-Americans applied to Native American territories to clear them for religious epiphanies and agricultural settlement. By 2008, when Koester published his search-and-rescue manual, the wilderness was assumed to be not only an empty space but an ingrown one as well. Recreationists and their attendants in the tourist industry understood nature preserves as therapeutic retreats from modernity. People hiked trails to heal. To find themselves, they moved out of cities and suburbs and ventured into spaces of exertion or reflection. One of the histories I trace is how the overinformed brain became the trailhead for the North American interior and how leisure wildernesses came to serve as venues for therapeutic loneliness, places to disconnect from communities for mental health.

The interior of this book unfolds chronologically, yet I will not move through it in a straight line. If spaces can stretch, collapse, tumble, and flatten, then the place to experience space is in the loose setting of literature rather than the linear confines of a map or the organized cells of a database. In the folklore of disorientation, lost people traveled in circles. To capture their bewilderment, and reorient American history around new landmarks as well as refresh old signposts, I roam around.[20]

I embark from a coast, the Gulf of Mexico side of Florida in 1539, in search of an early modern version of getting lost in the continental interior. Spanish subjects bound in religious and masculine hierarchies fumbled their way through the forests and the swamps inhabited by a variety of Native peoples. The invaders measured the earth by their station in society. They inhabited relational space. Who they were told them where they were. They could not fathom cutting personal ties to achieve a state of independence in free space away from other humans, for that was a nightmare scenario, and in most cases, a criminal offense. The edge of nature shock appeared where relationships failed or were torn asunder.

Early moderns viewed the world in relationships, and when they left the coast and entered the interior, they took care to form new social bonds to replace the ones they severed. This vision was shared by Europeans and Native Americans alike, and it underwrote the tensions and possibilities when the groups came together. Relationships torn apart by violence or interrupted by distance terrified everyone, and once they had their ties broken, these humans scrambled for replacements.

The American Revolution incited attempts to break free from relational space. Frontier parents sent their offspring on frightening missions to locate stray livestock in the name of inculcating republican independence. The edge of nature shock surfaced on the dark boundaries of agrarian communities. The rhetoric of individual self-mastery obscured the persistence of communal surveillance. Relational space remained strong throughout the eighteenth and nineteenth centuries. Neighbors came together to rescue neighbors from nature shock. They patrolled the boundaries of social spaces and extended their reach through the media. Local histories and newspapers asserted frontier communities' ascendancy over interior spaces, denying the continued presence of Native Americans and rejecting their long tenure over the trans-Appalachian territories now claimed by the United States. Poems about lost white children appeared in newspapers alongside advertisements for runaway slaves. The press extended the authority of white male heads of households, masters who countered accidental bewilderment and planned escapes with the speed of print. Independence belonged to these few men, and they constructed imagined, social, and material spaces to enhance their freedom while limiting the mobility and self-determination of everyone else.[21]

The United States acquired vast new territories. It became a continental nation as it industrialized. The nation built a transportation network and surveillance infrastructure that drastically extended its reach and velocity. Americans fought wars of conquest against the Indian nations in the interior, and they fought a Civil War among themselves to consolidate their country. The violence diminished rival sovereignties and terminated regional independence. The nation that emerged was more coherent, at least on the map. But the family, community, and cross-cultural relationships that defined the relational spaces of the interior seemed to unravel in the push toward uniformity. When railroads and then automobiles sped travelers through landscapes, Americans increasingly imagined that something was wrong with their modern spaces. More power did not bring progress, some thought. It fostered drift, as bodies, hearts, and minds scattered due to information overload and soul-crushing homogeneity. The edge of nature shock migrated outward and inward as Americans imagined and monetized wilderness spaces of individual freedom, escape, and disconnection.

There are no maps in this book, for I do not want to suggest, even subliminally, that graphic renditions of space stand apart, much less above, other conceptions. Psychologists have tested human beings' spatial cognition, and scholars across disciplines have studied their representations. They arrive at a similar conclusion: when it comes to space, people constantly cheat. They stretch, edit, and rearrange actual spaces in their heads and in their representations. They pick and choose scales, regions, landmarks, and time zones. They distort, and they simplify. Whether rolled up or imagined, maps have served the interests of their makers. And mostly they have done this well.[22]

I mull the edges where social, geographic, and cognitive space frayed, where navigation failed, and where people got terribly lost. These shocking episodes congregated in specific terrains, locations where humans saw poorly and misremembered landmarks. Yet the edges formed neither a continuous frontier line nor a contiguous wilderness area. They emerged at different times and in different formulations. For most of North American history, the edges were relational and spaces fell away when ties were severed. In individual space, people actually dreamed of disconnection even as they relied on infrastructures of impersonal surveillance. Their edge appeared when the signal died. The outer limits of any society depended on the perspectives of the people who ventured along them. One society's fringe could be another's home. The edges' shifting outlines made locating them on maps impossible; therefore, I follow the tracks of wanderers as they approached them. Not every discombobulated person in this book crossed over an edge into nature shock. I observed and wrote about many who came close in order to comprehend the few who traveled too far.

In the end, I side with Black Tomato. I think you should consider getting lost. It may turn out to be good for you, though not for the reasons most often given today. Getting lost does not move us closer to nature or bring us to our authentic selves. It offers no relief from the onslaught of information or the speed of modernity. Rather, nature shock teaches about the inadvisability of going back and the treacherousness of proceeding forward. It reveals the moral murkiness that always infused spaces. An infuriating blend of mutual responsibility and horrific oppression, true fondness and wretched cruelty, marked communities in the past and thus colored the spaces they made. Wherever we are headed, there is no future in going it alone—nature shock proves that much. Together, we will construct the spaces that will rise to meet our feet. By looking into the history of a navigational glitch that became a fantasy of disconnection, we might see our fraught communities in a new light, as assets to call upon instead of burdens to cast aside.

# CHAPTER ONE

# Brutal Symmetry

HERNANDO DE SOTO DIED IN GUACHOYA on the banks of the Mississippi River. Before his fever took him, the conquistador, who had rampaged through parts of what would become Florida, Georgia, South Carolina, North Carolina, Tennessee, Alabama, Mississippi, Louisiana, and Arkansas, confessed his sorrow for "leaving [his men] in so great confusion as he was doing in a land in which they did not know where they were." His departure unhinged his followers: "the danger of being lost in that land, which stared all of them in the face, was the reason why each one himself had need of consolation and why they did not visit him and wait upon him as was fitting." They buried the body at night near the village gate and then, in a panic, dug it up, filled the shroud covering it with sand, and tossed the bundle into the river. Upon their arrival in 1539, the invaders had announced to everyone they met that de Soto was immortal. The men fumbled around in the dark with a ripening corpse to preserve that illusion.[1]

De Soto was neither the first nor would he be the last Spanish conquistador to cross over an imperceptible North American edge and fall into nature shock. Over a decade earlier, Álvar Núñez Cabeza de Vaca, the royal treasurer of a 1527 expedition under the command of Pánfilo de Narváez, witnessed the disintegration of his invading army. After landing in La Florida, Narváez's company struggled to find food, locate treasure, conscript labor, and woo allies. The Florida Natives harassed the men and their horses as they stumbled through swamps and thickets. In desperation, Narváez ordered the expedition's steeds killed for meat and their stirrups and crossbows melted to forge ax heads to chop timber. The men built several rafts and cast off into the Gulf of Mexico, only to become separated from one another. Cabeza de Vaca wound up naked, wrecked on the coast of a space that would become Texas. He watched his comrades die from cold and hunger. Salvation arrived in the form of slavery. He and three others were taken captive by the Han and the Capoque. The survivors successfully traversed relational space. They left their own social order to assume lowly positions in Native hierarchies.[2]

Cabeza de Vaca resurfaced years later with a remarkable story, which he published in 1542 in the form of a *relación* to his king. He launched his narrative on a note of confusion and vulnerability: "[I] bring to Your Majesty an account of all that I was able to observe and learn in the nine years that I walked lost and naked through many and very strange lands." Cabeza de Vaca recounted the pain and hardships he endured, but he also recalled the many relationships he formed. In his last few years, he and his companions traveled from village to village in the role of religious healers, accompanied by a caravan of indigenous admirers. Cabaza de Vaca wrote to advance a peaceful vision of conquest. He represented the possibilities of relational space, the chances for humans to cross over territorial and cultural lines, to switch allegiances and languages to form new ties and understandings. This form of conquest required incredible suffering and a frightening drop in status. Cabeza de Vaca struggled to convince the crown and his fellow colonizers to follow his example.[3]

Hernando de Soto chose a bloodier path. Instead of collaboration, he fostered destruction. Yet his entrada was no less relational than Cabeza de Vaca's. Relational space could yield horrific brutality as well as surprising acceptance.

Hernando de Soto oversaw an epic disaster that splattered viscera across the maize-growing Mississippian chiefdoms of the humid Southeast. He planned a conquest on the scale of Cortés or Pizarro, but he searched in vain for wealthy lords like Montezuma and Atahualpa, finding a string of lowercase *micos,* or chiefs, instead. The best they could do was placate him with corn, with bearers for his equipment and provisions, and with baskets of burnt pearl beads. Many of them headed fortified towns, and some of them ruled over constellations of neighboring villages. One of them was so physically impressive the Christians thought him a giant. Even at their most resplendent, however, the Mississippian chiefdoms merely echoed the massive kingdoms de Soto knew from Mexico and Peru. The resemblance drove him to his death. He marched toward the glimmer of a city ever on the horizon.[4]

De Soto has turned into a mirage himself. No accurate depiction of his expedition has survived. Four narratives described the journey, but the geographic information contained in them, all written after the fact, has tormented archeologists and historians for centuries. In 1935, the United States Congress passed a joint resolution to establish a commission to locate de Soto's route and recommend the placement of historical markers in observance of the four-hundred-year anniversary of the expedition. The commission scoured the written record and the archeological data to produce maps, tables, and a four-hundred-page report. Led by Smithsonian anthropologist John R. Swanton, the committee members visited field sites and walked sections of what they thought might be the trail. Yet Swanton took care to lower expectations about the accuracy of their conclusions. The commission could not settle the question of where de Soto and his men went. "No such finality," he warned, "will ever be attained."[5]

The need to locate de Soto in individual space—space that can be measured by odometers and exits between rest stops—says more about joint-resolving societies that commune with the past through placards erected along roadsides than about the one to which de Soto belonged. His obsessions ran more toward people than places. His final words bemoaned the interpersonal rupture caused by his passing. Without him, his men were lost, shocked. Overcome with despair, they turned inward and let de Soto die alone. The interpersonal complexity of the interior overwhelmed their navigational skills, which were relational rather than technological. The Christians landed with a compass and a quadrant, yet they kept their way-finding instruments stowed for the duration of de Soto's command, unpacking them only months after his death to recross the Gulf in home-made rafts.[6]

De Soto and his entourage had been traveling without a clear idea of their location for over three years. Why did it take so long for them to feel lost? The timing of de Soto's breakdown corresponded with the duration of the relational spaces he and his followers constructed. Groups tailor their surroundings to make and remember connections, and different cultures foreground different sets of links. De Soto focused his sights on the tight circle of Christian men whom he considered his equals and rivals. He measured himself against them, and these calculations positioned him in the world. They were his location.

De Soto was a person fixated on other people, but that did not make him a people person. De Soto and his men kidnapped, tortured, and murdered. They targeted local leaders, seizing micos to ransom for food and safe passage. They questioned prisoners, and once they heard about a promising destination, they forced captives from one village to guide them to the next. They enslaved hundreds of Indians. Some they hoped to keep and take home; others they held for shorter intervals, forcing them to carry their gear and their plunder while in their country. Coercion skewed their geographic knowledge. Informants lied to get rid of the Christians. They made stuff up, withheld details, and professed to know more than they did. De Soto and his men, however, were alert to their deceptions. Indeed, hidden information excited them.

The Mississippians organized the most productive maize-growing river valleys in North America to suit their economic, cultural, and political requirements. They constructed space to conform to their religious cosmologies, and they marked and defended territories. Whatever label we apply to their political geographies, be it chiefdom, kingdom, nation, or empire, there is no doubt that the Mississippians conceptualized, managed, and manipulated space on a scale equal or superior to the transatlantic foreigners who stumbled into their creations. The Christian interlopers traveled down indigenous roads; they trespassed across indigenous territorial lines; and they barged into indigenous settlements laid out by indigenous architects. They most certainly did not bring order to an empty void or a trackless wilderness. In the humid Southeast, the invaders' spatial conceptions met and converged with Native spatial conceptions. The result was apocalyptic.[7]

The Christians disemboweled, hanged, and lit their fellow humans on fire. The Mississippians fought back, slaughtering the interlopers when they had the chance. The violence laid bare seething antagonism, and by rights a spatial diagram of the combatants' mutual understanding should reveal sharp opposition rather than Venn overlap. Yet for all their differences, these enemies inhabited similar head spaces. They both measured territories in kinship and allegiance, and they arranged these relationships into social hierarchies. They both equated seeing with power, and they constructed spaces so that those in authority could see more than subordinates. They parsed space into cardinal directions and invested cosmic meaning in the spaces below and above them. They both enslaved people they considered outside their social orbits to enhance their labor pool and expand their spiritual power.[8]

The Christians and the Mississippians inhabited small-scale, face-to-face societies riven with local and regional divisions that nonetheless retained the potential for stunning outbursts of unity. In the Southeast, archeologists have tracked the ebb and flow of the set of cultural beliefs, social arrangements, farming practices, architectural styles, and artistic motifs that came from Mesoamerica, spread up the valley of the main stem of the Mississippi River, and then seeped into drainage corridors throughout the Southeast. The people living under the influence of the so-called Southeastern Ceremonial Complex grew maize, erected earthen mounds, and decorated pots and jewelry with suns and snakes. Some micos ruled hierarchical social orders of thousands of people gathered into cities. The largest settlements, like Cahokia, on the east shore of the Mississippi River, opposite the patch of ground that would hold St. Louis, boasted populations of between six thousand and forty thousand, and bound adjacent communities into tribute-paying empires.[9]

Cahokia represented the prize for which conquistadors lusted, but by the time de Soto landed on Florida's western shore the great city had been abandoned for centuries. The Mississippian empires came and went, just like empires elsewhere in the world. Fragmentation counterbalanced aggregation. When rulers died, droughts struck, or rivals invaded, populations dispersed to re-form clans, grow maize, erect smaller mounds, and decorate with suns and snakes. The complex could accommodate a variety of groupings. The ability to go small or large underwrote the Mississippians' success in creating a malleable culture that endured for eight hundred years.[10]

De Soto entered at a moment when most Mississippians preferred smaller-town living. He encountered a few chiefdoms where a dominant ruler oversaw a home village as well as a handful of neighboring towns within a day's travel, but mostly he found communities enjoying their isolation from one another.

A student as well as a sponsor of interpersonal conflict, de Soto understood fragmentation. Divisions of class, family, region, and rank shot through his invading army. His country was a recent agglomeration of independent principalities, and his followers included men from Portugal and Africa. Calling them "Spaniards" overestimates their political unity. Christianity and masculine honor proved stickier glues than nationality at this time, yet faith and male chauvinism wrecked as many relationships as they cemented. The men's subservience to a global Catholic Church and their adherence to a masculine code of honor did not keep de Soto's invasion force from threatening to break apart on a regular basis.[11]

De Soto kept his army together by moving its disparate parts toward a golden city that lay just out of sight. The Mississippians could not help but promote his vision. Like the Christians, they conceived of space in terms of relationships, but their relationships trailed off at regional boundaries on purpose. The Christians dealt with their own fractious relationships by asserting the universality of their God, their church, and their honor. They wanted the Mississippians to see that a single hierarchy encompassed the earth, binding the Western Hemisphere together under Spain's command. The Mississippians' strategic isolation clashed with the Christians' desire for unification. This difference eroded the common ground of relational space and explained the brutality of their encounter. When forced to talk about space, to give directions to foreigners holding knives at their throats, Mississippian captives improvised to stay alive. They bluffed, giving the appearance of knowing more about geographies outside their home territories than they actually did, or they confessed, explaining as best they could how their knowledge faded at political drop-offs. Either way, they cleaved space into realms of the seen and the unseen. These representations of space accidentally fed the Christians' zeal to find hidden treasures and truths. They pressed forward, tormented by visions dredged up by the tortures they inflicted on others.

Experiencing nature shock in relational space required social fracture as well as geographic confusion. De Soto suffered nature shock when he lost sight of the coast, not with his senses, for that happened in the first months inland, but rather in his mind's eye. To stay mentally oriented, he deployed horses and riders to circle back to his ships anchored in the Gulf of Mexico. The boats connected him to Cuba, the Spanish Empire, and the domains of Christendom. The equine line of communication tethered him and his men to the world they knew, a world they thought they were revealing to the benighted Indians of La Florida. In their estimation, it was the Mississippians who were lost.

De Soto set his fall in motion when he severed the line to the coast to reach Cofitachequi, a city rumored to possess vast wealth. The person spreading the rumors was a Mississippian named Perico. The servant of Mississippian traders, Perico spoke several languages and boasted travel experience beyond the self-imposed bubbles of the chiefdoms. Perico led the Christians to the border of a wooded no-man's-land between the realms of Cofaqui and Cofitachequi. There, he became agitated and suffered a nervous collapse. He began foaming at the mouth; the Christians believed him possessed by a demon. Perico snapped out of his trance, but he never regained his bearings. The expedition wandered for days, finally happening upon Cofitachequi by chance. They found a complex chiefdom ruled by a formidable woman mico. Still, it was no Tenochtitlan. They packed the singed pearl beads the Lady of Cofitachequi offered them and roamed back toward the Gulf coast and the ships they would never see again.

Though a fiasco as a woodland guide, Perico did show the Christians the way forward. He escorted them to the edge of relational space and revealed to them the terror that awaited in Guachoya, the place where de Soto's vision would fail, and the bonds orienting him would dissolve.

## COASTS AND INTERIORS

De Soto and his compatriots perceived La Florida as a coastline with an interior. The coast offered psychological comforts and material opportunities. Coasts lent themselves to gazing. Eyes on the shore, rather than boots on the ground, launched de Soto's campaign: "On Whitsunday, May 25, they sighted the land of Florida." On the coast, the Christians could see for miles from the security of their ships. The invaders delighted in the combination of an open view and a protected vantage point. Captains stationed lookouts in crow's nests to scan horizons, and pilots dropped weights on strings to sight murky bottoms. The ships represented the height of Christians' visual power. As long as they remained on board, they were the masters of all they surveyed.[12]

Pulling within view was as close as many expeditions wished to come to La Florida. Numerous ships visited the coast, but before de Soto, only three groups—the Ponce de León, Narváez, and Ayllón expeditions—ventured inland. Florida drew its first incursions when disease and slavery decimated the Native population on the island of Hispaniola, and the colonial overlords sent out their fleets to the Bahamas to find replacement workers for their plantations. Several voyages overshot the islands and landed on the isthmus protruding from North America. The raids bred animosity. Violence, mistrust, and deception colored the coastline. The ships kept their distance for they were unwelcome. To preserve their view and their sensations of power, the crews kidnapped beachcombers and withdrew to the open water. Most had no taste for territorial conquest. The sight of the ocean, the way home, kept them out of the interior.

Pilots explored coastlines and contributed their observations of bays, inlets, and beaches to the readings of the sun, the stars, and the magnetic poles that facilitated ocean travel in the sixteenth century. Eyes traced the land's outline, sextants measured longitudinal distance, knotted ropes tied to logs chronicled speed, and compasses registered direction. All these tools brought ships to La Florida and La Florida into contact with sailing routes that encircled the globe.

Beyond the coast, La Florida's wetlands, forests, and unrelenting flatness obscured the land. Views were scarce, so humans built them. Communities erected earthen pyramids and topped them with abodes for the micos that symbolized their connection to the Upper World of the sky and the sun. The micos enjoyed the combination of sweeping vistas and a secure refuge, a pleasure they denied those underneath them. Seeing underscored power. In relational space, the mico surveilled the people and the surrounding landscape while the people looked up to him and through him to the sky. When de Soto conquered his first town, the coastal settlement of Uzita, he took the focal point for himself. He seized the hut on the top of the town's pyramid for his quarters. He ordered his troops to cut down all the woods within a crossbow's shot of the town to improve the sight lines.

Yet even from the high ground, de Soto could not observe all that he wanted: "The land was swampy and in many places covered with very lofty and thick woods." His success hinged on securing Natives who knew the land, not the physical layout so much as the relationships of kinship and allegiance that organized its people and through them the region's material resources. To move beyond the surf, he needed human go-betweens. The coastal slave raiders captured guides and interpreters. De Soto landed with two, taken during an exploratory mission sent to find a suitable port for the main fleet. The prisoners escaped soon after he landed. The Floridians resisted being pressed into service. Whenever they could, they declined to share space with the invaders. De Soto ordered his men to bring him more.

The Christians used force to make the relationships that would move them through the country.[13]

Captain Baltasar de Gallegos captured a man from Uzita hiding in the woods. He ordered the man to guide his cavalry to a town they had heard about six leagues (close to a dozen miles) inland. The exploration party spent "most of the day without a road and lost," its reluctant escort "drawing them always in an arc toward the seacoast with the design of coming upon some swamp, creek, or bay in which to drown them, if possible." Gallegos only discovered the guide's "iniquity" after he spotted the topsails of the fleet over the trees and figured out that they had been hugging the coast instead of marching inland. After Gallegos threatened to kill him, the guide shifted course and led his captors eastward. On a main road, they ran into a diplomatic entourage from Mocoso, a neighboring chiefdom, hustling to the sea to curry favor with the Christians. Gallegos ordered his men to hunt them down and enslave them. The group from Mocoso scattered at the sight of soldiers with spears charging on horseback. Cornered by a lancer, one heavily tattooed savage dressed in a loincloth unexpectedly professed his adoration for the Virgin Mary to escape a skewering.[14]

### THE INTERPRETER OF NATIVE RELATIONAL SPACE

The man was Juan Ortiz, a young nobleman from Seville who had sailed from Cuba to La Florida with Pánfilo Narváez in 1527. He remained on the ships while Narváez went ashore at the head of an army intended to establish his and Spain's control over the lands from Florida to northern Mexico. The fleet shadowed the three-hundred-soldier invasion force until Narváez ordered the ships to proceed to their destination, the Río de los Palmas. Narváez knew letting his ride home bob over the horizon was a risky move, and several members of the expedition told him so, including the royal treasurer, Álvar Núñez Cabeza de Vaca, yet none of them comprehended the monumental scale of his bad decision. The fleet's pilot had misjudged the drift caused by the gulf current, and the inlet they believed forty miles away was actually thousands. Narváez and his men passed into the interior, thinking they were just north of the Mexican frontier. Once the sailors realized the gravity of the error, they returned to Cuba and then circled back to Florida's coast to try to find the expedition. Ortiz volunteered to go ashore, and after a hostage-swap ruse orchestrated by a local mico sick of being raided and abused, he and three others were escorted to Uzita.[15]

Narváez had set the stage for Ortiz's thrashing months before when he took it upon himself to teach Uzita's leader, a mico named Hirrihigua, to respect his authority. As a result, Hirrihigua glared down a gruesomely incomplete nose when Ortiz and his companions appeared before him. He was a political, military, and religious headman who, like his fellow micos throughout the Southeast, believed that he possessed a special connection to the sky vault and the vault's star feature, the sun. The sun ruled the Upper World, a spiritual realm of clarity, purity, and perfection. Through his relationship with the Upper World, the mico brought order to the grittier Middle World, where humans struggled with the realities of hunger, war, and disease. Narváez had defaced a representative of an unblemished space when he clipped Hirrihigua's nose. He sowed extreme discord when he ordered his dogs of war, greyhounds and giant mastiffs, to tear one of the mico's wives to pieces.[16]

Ortiz and his mates were going to suffer in the open, for all to see, to restore order to a universe knocked off kilter by Narváez's brutality. Hirrihigua announced a day of festivities and his people lined Uzita's plaza. Guards pushed the naked captives into the square. The villagers launched arrows at the men, who sprinted from side to side, begging the onlookers to save them. The mico interrupted the pageant once to issue a warning not to kill the foreigners too quickly. After a lengthy bout of running and screaming, arrows thunking into torsos and blood gushing from puncture wounds, three of the Christians lay dead. Ortiz was spared when Hirrihigua's wives and daughters pleaded for a show of mercy.

Ortiz clung to the outer rim of the relational space of a coastal Floridian society. He was a war captive, a homeless stranger without rank or kin. He languished in the plaza like a restless ghost. The town flourished on the periphery of Mississippian influence. The bayside dwellers exploited marine resources and the abundant fisheries where fresh-water estuaries met the sea. They did not grow maize like the Mississippians to the north, and while the bay fed them well, the populations of their towns never reached the heights of the farming chiefdoms. Dried maize stored for years, feeding many people and supporting echelons of elites and warriors, whereas catfish rotted in hours. The transience of their food supply combined with the strands of Mississippian material culture they adopted inspired a fusion of homegrown traditions and imported practices. The coastal Floridians established chiefdoms and ranked members into hierarchical clans. They built mounds and cleared plazas, though their architecture bore only "superficial resemblances to the Mississippian mound centers." Their mounds were smaller, maxing out at twenty feet, and the flat-top earthen structures revealed their taste for oysters and mussels. The coastal Floridians mixed empty shells in with the dirt to strengthen their earthen structures. They heaped the dingier halves and worked the finer specimens into ornaments, sending pearled masterpieces inland to trade for prestige items the bay could not provide, such as mica discs and copper ear spools.[17]

Ortiz's interlude on the plaza introduced him to an abbreviated, beach version of the Southeastern Ceremonial Complex. The Uzitans were out to abuse him, not enlighten him, so it's doubtful that anyone took the time to explain the way things worked to a prisoner who spoke a foreign language. To a certain degree, Ortiz didn't need human tutors. The space communicated Mississippian ideas, which were relational and therefore scrutable.

He survived the initial round of torture, but more awaited. Hirrihigua tormented Ortiz from his perch on the mound. He ordered the captive to run laps around the circumference of the plaza for days on end. The plaza was another design element the coastal Floridians borrowed from the Mississippian mound centers. The plazas represented the shared space of the community. The multifunctional public square hosted religious ceremonies, sporting events, and political spectacles—like the torture of war captives. While the mounds stretched to the sky and the upper realm of the sun, the plazas brought collective minds down to earth. Plazas embodied the Middle World where humans lived out their lives struggling to balance the order of the sky and the chaos of the Under World. Neither a void nor an empty lot, the plaza was an architectural counterpoint to the mound's structural mass. The mounds and plazas bound micos and followers to each other through a mutually recognized cosmos. The pyramids and plazas re-created the upper and middle realms and displayed their relation. Ortiz's jogging around the lip of the plaza signaled his peril. Stolen from his own society, he was being ritually dangled off the edge of another.[18]

A few days into Ortiz's marathon, Hirrihigua signaled for a bonfire to be lit and the captive roasted over the coals on a spit. The flames licked Ortiz until, once again, one of the mico's daughters interceded to spare him—and set him up for yet another excruciating test. Hirrihigua sent him into the forest to guard Uzita's ossuary. The corpses rotted in the open on ceremonial platforms. When the flesh fell from the bones, the remains would be interred according to the corpse's rank. Micos and the dead of the leading clans entered mounds surrounded by copper ornaments, pearl beads, and other prestige goods, while those of the lower orders were buried under houses and in cemeteries without religious treasures to exalt them. Ortiz was instructed to stand watch through the night to keep wild animals from stealing the corpses. One evening, he fell asleep and a predator dragged a dead child into the forest. It was at this moment, of all the many disorienting and depressing low points he endured, that Ortiz "considered himself lost." Certain the lapse would end him, he charged after the beast and killed the man-eater in a thicket with a lucky toss of a spear.[19]

If Uzita's mound symbolized the Upper World of the sky and its plaza the Middle World of the earth, then the ossuary represented the lower realm of darkness and chaos. A defining feature of the Under World was its gloom. Living humans strained to see into it. The murky bottoms of rivers contained passages from the middle to the lower realms. Monsters emerged from the wet gateways to prowl the earth. By contrast, birds filled the Upper World, and the Mississippians celebrated keen-eyed predators like peregrine falcons, sparrow hawks, and bald eagles. The Under World hosted stranger beasts: water cannibals, the Water Cougar, and the Uktena, a frightening mishmash of deer, serpent, and fish parts. A species of confusion, the Uktena embodied the Under World's biological and spiritual rowdiness.[20]

Ortiz battled a shape-shifting animal that night in the charnel plot. Some accounts described it as a large canine; others said it was a big cat. If it was a panther, then Ortiz met the Southeast's mascot of bedlam. Panthers could see at night, which associated them with the Under World. Unlike hawks or eagles, which leveraged daylight to spot prey, cougars pounced on victims in the dark. Their screams sounded human, like a woman crying in the distance. Solitary animals, panthers withdrew from human observation, enhancing their mystery and their reputation for pandemonium. Whatever animal Ortiz killed, it won him respect. Hirrihigua called him back from his night patrol and treated him better for a time. The duel with the creature in the darkness inched Ortiz closer to a place in the Middle World.[21]

But in the end, Hirrihigua could not stand Ortiz. Try as he might, the mico could not suppress his ire. He set a date for the villagers to congregate and kill him in a shower of arrows. The night before the execution one of the mico's daughters pulled Ortiz from imminent destruction one last time. She arranged for a guide to escort the prisoner beyond the borders of Uzita.[22]

Ortiz hiked to another coastal chiefdom six leagues away, traveling a path that connected the towns. The Floridians cut and maintained wide trails through brush and wetlands. The Christians called them roads. Like the fishers and oyster diggers in Uzita, the residents of Mocoso were not full-blown Mississippians. They borrowed Mississippian architecture and ceremonies while holding onto their own culture. (For example, they decorated their clay vessels with etchings that distinguished their pots from those made by the Mississippians to the north.) The inhabitants of Mocoso constructed a shell and dirt mound and cleared a plaza, but they grew no maize, the leached soils along the bay being too poor to sprout the grain. Hirrihigua and the mico of Mocoso may have been brothers. They both paid tribute to an even more formidable relative who ruled a larger town further inland known as Urriparacoxi. Congregations of chiefdoms made up regions—territories of humans bound loosely together through kinship, environments, material cultural, and political affiliations. Ortiz would have recognized the layout. Roads, regions, and kinship territories were in his spatial grammar as well. However, despite the familiarity, Ortiz was not prepared to travel alone in the space between chiefdoms. No one survived alone in spaces between communities. Human relationships connected paths, towns, and regions, and Ortiz had severed his nebulous ties to a social hierarchy when he left Hirrihigua's domain.

Ortiz followed a path to a town, arriving at the outskirts of Mocoso at dawn. His appearance set off a panic. Men notched their bows and threatened to kill him. Ortiz begged for his life, but his words meant little because the town's security detail did not speak the language used in Uzita. His life could have ended there had not the ruler of the chiefdom that bore his name—Mocoso was both a place and a person—seen advantage in the gibbering stranger. Instead of shooting him or chasing him away, he welcomed Ortiz into his house on top of the town's earthen mound. Ortiz stayed with Mocoso for nearly a decade. His old clothes fell apart, and he put on new ones. Tattoos crept over his arms. He learned the language spoken in Mocoso's town and forgot most of his Spanish. Mocoso fielded requests from Uzita and other towns to turn the captive over, but he refused to let him go. In 1539, word reached Mocoso that a very large expedition (six hundred men and 230 horses) had come ashore at Uzita. The cacique sent

Ortiz to them with an escort as a peace gesture. It was this group that met Gallegos's cavalry.

The Christians welcomed Ortiz back into the fold with "much joy." What a stroke of good fortune! Here was an interpreter disinclined to bolt at the first opportunity. However, he was also scantily clad, exotically painted, and barely understandable. He had been speaking Mocoso's language "for so long," wrote the expedition's royal factor, Luys Hernández de Biedma, the only eyewitness to author his own history of the de Soto entrada, "that he was among us more than four days before he could join one word with another." What convinced Biedma, de Soto, and the rest that Ortiz was one of them and not a traitor who had converted to Floridian culture after eleven years away?[23]

Ortiz's social background as the scion of a noble family eased his reentry. His high rank lowered suspicions. Bred to be a gentleman, he knew how to comport himself even when words failed him. His many humiliations may have confirmed his honor instead of besmirching it. He had suffered mightily in the eyes of his countrymen, losing his weapons, his armor, and his Spanish vocabulary. He looked and lived like a savage, yet those who surveyed his pitiable state wanted to believe that his nobility adhered inside him. De Soto filled his expedition with recruits from high-placed families. To them, Ortiz may have portended what they hoped lay ahead of them: a test that would confirm the durability of their honor. De Soto encouraged this interpretation of Ortiz's return. He welcomed him, trusted him, and outfitted him in fine clothes, "some good arms, and a beautiful horse." Ortiz kept the blades and the steed, but he ditched the pants, finding them unendurable.[24]

His aversion to britches should have tipped the Christians off that all was not right with Ortiz. He proved loyal to his invading countrymen, serving as de Soto's guide, interpreter, and chief interrogator. But captivity had damaged his usefulness. Imprisonment in the Florida towns introduced Ortiz to three new realms, the Upper, the Middle, and the Under Worlds, and taught him the value of serving a mico like Mocoso, a force of stability who balanced the purity of the sky with the chaos bubbling up from underneath. Ortiz traveled from the plaza to the ossuary to the top of the mounds. Yet his cosmic journey carried him only to the brim of Mocoso's chiefdom. He knew the Mississippians' universe better than he knew their neighborhoods.

## THE CHRISTIANS' SPATIAL VISION

The plan was to use Ortiz to escape the coast. He would help, in Biedma's words, "penetrate the interior." Many of de Soto's men turned out to be vile rapists, so the penetration Biedma had in mind may have been a sex crime. Given how the invaders associated sight with power, the assault would also be visual. Ortiz would help the Christians peer into the continent. With all his experience, he would seem an ideal headlamp, but for the fact that in eleven years he had ventured no farther than the immediate surroundings of two bayside chiefdoms. He hadn't actually seen that much. "He knows little of the land," wrote Biedma, "and had neither seen nor heard of things only twenty leagues away." He spoke two languages, the dialects used in Uzita and Mocoso, which made him handy, but the Christians would need further interpretive help to communicate in the many tongues that lay ahead. To locate treasure, to make the expedition pay, de Soto would have to travel far beyond Ortiz's limited horizons.[25]

Ortiz's chief value turned out to be his talent for weighing information gathered from captives. He interrogated prisoners and collected routes and destinations. He advised de Soto on which reports to follow. He paid as much attention to an informant's behavior and appearance as he did to the forests and paths around him. The Christians trusted guides who knew their social place. Deference and fidelity counted more than orienteering skill. The primary inquisitor and judge of captives' decorum, Ortiz was neck-deep in the worst atrocities committed by the expedition. De Soto cut off guides' hands, arms, and noses; he fed them to his dogs; he burned them alive—based on his interpreter's social readings. Ortiz, more than anyone else, decided if captives were guilty of forgetting their place and getting the Christians lost.

De Soto chased down and chained Indians to ask the same questions. Was there a great lord ahead? Did he rule many people and towns? He wanted to find large settlements, on the assumption that sizable populations brought together resources from across vast spaces. He hoped to locate a transregional economic system, a distribution network that consolidated flakes of gold, bits of silver, and pecks of maize into centralized stockpiles.

A veteran of the conquests of Panama and Peru, de Soto was good at finding and taking other people's stockpiles. In Peru, he specialized in matching his small cavalry force against armies that outnumbered him by thousands. He was a master of bluster and brutality. When he reached the

Incan capital, he spurred his horse straight at the man in charge, the Sapa Inca Atahualpa, reining in the steed at the last second to let the animal blow snot and sweat over the sovereign emperor, who returned the macho posturing by keeping his eyes frozen in the middle distance. De Soto's behavior teetered along edges. He adhered to traditions of warfare that valued personal displays of bravado, but he was a maximalist, and to the Incas (and to some of his own countrymen) he was hard to take. The Incas struggled to defend their empire against his brand of warfare. De Soto's colleagues got rid of him as soon as the opportunity arose.

Francisco Pizarro and his clique shouldered the junior conquistador out of Peru. De Soto thought his victories earned him a plum appointment. Instead he was given a mayoral post. He quit the colony, took his ducats, and sailed for Spain, where he converted his wealth into prestige. He married Dona Isabel de Bobadilla, daughter of the prominent conquistador Pedrárias Davila, and, on the king's invitation, joined the venerated military Order of Santiago. De Soto spent his Peru earnings to secure personal connections. At court, he financed a display of status, employing "servants, including a mayordomo, grand master of ceremonies, pages, equerry, chamberlain, footmen, and all the other servants requisite for an establishment of a gentleman." Entourage in place, he surrounded himself with noble allies, all up-and-coming gentlemen fighters like himself, such as Juan de Añasco, Luis de Moscoso Alvarado, Nuño de Tovar, and Juan Rodriquez Lobillo. These men contributed their own fortunes to the North American conquest. De Soto gave a share of his Peru earnings to King Charles in the form of a loan. De Soto skimmed the wealth from the Incas and used it to turn himself, a man born to a modest noble family in the Spanish backwater of Extremadura, into a transatlantic power.[26]

Still, the personal connections that empowered De Soto also limited the force he could exert. Although a military outfit, De Soto's expedition did not operate like a modern army with a clear chain of command. He managed people in a world without nation-states. There was no central power that could finance expeditions across an ocean, no government to disperse and coerce subjects over long distances. "Spain" was a recently united collection of independent territories, and just as his predecessors had done, Charles V subcontracted the conquest of his domains in the Western Hemisphere. De Soto's venture included notable men from across the Iberian Peninsula. He recruited wealthy men with connections. The lines of genealogy and royal favor oriented the invasion more than any map, and keeping interpersonal squabbles among the nobles to a minimum would define de Soto's leadership. The Spanish crown pitched in legal sanction and titles to help him. King Charles V made de Soto the governor of an island, adelantado of Narváez's old grant, and the marquis of any new lands he might discover, but to move over six hundred men with provisions from Spain to Cuba to the mainland, de Soto relied on his own wealth as well as the contributions of his "followers," who often behaved more like partners. For example, Vasco Porcallo de Figueroa, the Cuban grandee de Soto appointed the expedition's "Captain General," left in a huff after a few weeks spent on the coast looking in vain for large populations of Indians to enslave and send back to Cuba to work his mines and plantations.

De Soto topped a hierarchy of gentlemen, servants, and slaves that could fracture at any time. He kept them together through displays of ferocity—he perpetrated violence on others and bore hardship himself—and promises of spectacular payoffs. The gentlemen agreed to cohere in pursuit of fortunes they could turn into relations of power: servants hired, wives courted, slaves enchained, and royals befriended. Relationships were the means and the ends of conquest.

The Indians stood outside the network of personal ties. For the moment. The Christians planned to convert them, bringing them into the fellowship of believers. Converting the heathens to the true religion was the primary justification for transatlantic journeys. But while it was easy to declare intentions, it was much harder to forge actual relationships. What if Indians refused to join? What if they fought back, ran away, or faked cooperation? How patient was a conquistador supposed to be? One thing was sure—they could not be left alone. No one existed outside of personal connections, a premise of human existence the Indians shared. All humans lived in networks of kinship, allegiance, and servitude. You were more likely to encounter a witch, a water cannibal, or a demon in 1539 America than you were to find an independent person. The Indians, however, placed geographic boundaries on their relationships, whereas the invaders' affiliations covered the globe. Christianity welded humanity together, an unbearable idea to many Natives, who were accustomed to keeping their enemies at a distance. The politics of separation and conversion collided when de Soto invaded the interior.

De Soto landed with paperwork intended to clarify his ideas about space and relationships. He read aloud from the "Requerimiento," a short legal document written in Spanish that set the conditions for peace. No one translated the passage for onlookers, if indeed there were onlookers. Sometimes conquistadors mumbled the words into spaces void of representatives from the communities they intended to impress, like on board their ships before they disembarked or into the underbrush onshore where only lizards heard the instructions. If communicating across cultures was the point, then the "Requerimiento" was the definition of an empty gesture. The document legalized conquests; it did not enhance understanding.

De Soto explained about the church and how authority flowed from it to secular monarchs. One God made the earth, he said, which he gave to Adam and Eve and all their children and their children's children. The job of ruling over the proliferation of humans fell to Saint Peter, founder of the Christian Church. The pontifical descendants of Peter bequeathed the subduing and governing of newly discovered territories to the crowns of Portugal (Africa and Brazil) and Spain (the Americas). De Soto asked his audience, if there was one, to ponder the organizational chart he outlined. They should feel free to discuss the implications among themselves—he had just slipped La Florida the news that the Christian God, through the pope and his kings, ruled everyone, including them.[27]

Vassals from the start, the Indians could only accept the prearrangement or suffer war and enslavement. The "Gentleman from Elvas," an unidentified Portuguese member of the expedition, later recalled a first encounter with a Mississippian mico. He described a fanciful exchange that captured the spirit of the "Requerimiento" from the Iberians' perspective. The mico spotted de Soto and his army and recognized their authority immediately: "Very exalted and very mighty and very excellent Lord. . . . The first thing I beg of your Lordship is that with my person and land and vassals, you do as with a thing of your own: and secondly, that you tell me who you are, whence you come, wither you go, and what you seek, so that I may better serve you." In this dreamy re-creation, it was plain to see that de Soto and his men radiated power, and the Indians responded by volunteering their obedience, their provisions, and their labor. In exchange, they wanted to learn from the newcomers. They begged to know how the Iberians came to be so impressive. "Funny you should ask," fantasy de

Soto might have responded. "I have brought teachers, the ones over there in the black robes, to instruct you." And so, the curtain would close on the "Requerimiento" ideal: a harvest of bodies, stockpiles, and souls triggered by the appearance of a visibly excellent and mighty lord.[28]

## SLAVERY AND RELATIONAL SPACE

The coastal slave raids ended any chance of this fiction becoming real. The groups living near the bays left their homes and hid in swamps and forests, disrupting the very notion of first encounters by refusing to participate in the rituals that would establish relationships with the invaders. Their disobedience gave de Soto his excuse to "enter forcefully against" them and "subject [them] to the yoke and obedience of the Church and his Majesty." The news of the Christians' belligerence traveled faster than they did. Word spread from the coastal towns of Uzita and Mocoso to the residents of the inland Timucuan chiefdoms. Seeking to avoid the strangers whenever possible, they abandoned their towns and stayed out of sight.[29]

Practiced at kidnapping Indians during shoreline raids, de Soto traveled with iron cuffs, collars, chains, and packs of hounds trained to stalk and attack human beings. The Christians planned on hunting Indians down and dragging them into first encounters against their will. Forced relationships started in Uzita and continued in the interior, with Ortiz interviewing detainees, pestering them with the same questions: Was there a great lord ahead? Did they know about cities with gold and other treasures?

In contrast to the coastal chiefdoms, the Timucuan settlements erected fewer mounds. They grew some corn, but their towns were even less Mississippian, at least architecturally, than those on the Gulf. Indeed, the Timucuans fended off a powerful northern neighbor, the Apalachees, a "complex" Mississippian chiefdom. With extensive maize fields and two ceremonial mound centers, one of which boasted seven pyramids, the Apalachee region was ruled by a mico who commanded tribute from numerous villages. The Apalachees raided the Timucuans for slaves and traded with the coastal chiefdoms for shells. The Apalachees' wealth showed in the impressiveness of their earthworks and the expanse of their trade network, which stretched from southern Florida to the Mississippi River.

The Timucuans withdrew in the face of the mounted soldiers bristling with spears and leading dogs of war. Escape and avoidance were effective strategies to counter the advantages of speed and leverage their horses and lances gave the Christians in battle. But retreats exacted spiritual costs. Leaving settlements meant leaving spaces organized to summon the power of the cosmos. When they fled mounds and plazas, communities severed their physical connections to the Upper World, the source of their purification and order. The inhabitants of chiefdoms arranged their built environments to reflect their place at the center of the world. Whether they erected mounds or not, chiefdoms pivoted around an axis mundi, often symbolized by a pole planted in the middle of plazas. Pushed into hiding, driven to the outskirts, refugees abandoned the physical manifestation of their shared identity. The sacrifice hit elites especially hard. Micos, and the powerful clans from which they emerged, based their social position on their proximity to spiritual centers. They resided on the tops of the pyramid, the bones of their ancestors buried beneath them, propping up their authority. Lower-ranking clans and slaves with no kin inhabited the edges of communities, near the ditches and wooden palisades that defended towns. When attacks came, the lower ranks absorbed them. De Soto's appearance shook the hierarchy, rearranging political and spiritual space as communities scrambled into peripheries to protect themselves.

For captured Indians, the chains and the dogs further transformed home landscapes, turning their territories into strange and unmanageable spaces. Dragging chains altered distances by extending the time it took to run and hide. Spaces grew impossibly large. The best protection against mounted adversaries was concealment, but not only did chains make it difficult to reach cover by disrupting strides and getting caught in the underbrush, they revealed positions with their clanks.

Enslavement ignited physical and psychological trauma. De Soto tortured relationships as well as bodies when he caught and immobilized people. He displayed hostages in the open for hiding family and friends to see. Captives pulled kin from places of concealment. Leaders and loved ones watched their people suffer from refuges in swamps and woods, and they abandoned their hiding spots, and their spatial advantage, to save them. Micos left the woods and submitted to meeting the invaders face to face. First encounters came after long bouts of mental anguish and bodily torment.

In the fall of 1539, marching north into Florida's interior to confirm rumors of a wealthy town, De Soto's army entered the Timucuan chiefdom of Uzachil. The place was deserted. The residents, reported Elvas, had heard about the invaders, how they chained and executed the people they met, and they wanted no part of them. De Soto sent two captains into the countryside to hunt the residents of Uzachil down. They came back with "a hundred head, among Indian men and women." The captives were divided up and enslaved: "These Indians they took along in chains with collars about their necks and they were used for carrying the baggage and grinding the maize and for other services which so fastened in this manner they could perform." The incident inspired Elvas to comment on the reactions of Indian captives to bondage. Some rebelled, killing their guards and escaping with their chains. Others tried to rid themselves of the metal collars first, filing the irons at night with rocks. However, the Iberians did not intend the chains to be permanent. As days passed and distances from homes lengthened, masters unlocked women and children: "A hundred leagues from their land, having become unmindful, they were taken along unbound." Along with their captors, the enslaved traveled into the unknown.[30]

It took a hundred leagues to reach the edge of relational space in sixteenth-century Florida. A Spanish league could measure anywhere from two to four miles; therefore, the sense of being centered, of being enmeshed in a community at the axis mundi, could fade in two weeks spent marching fifteen miles a day, an average clip for a walking human. Captives reached the limits of their mental maps and confronted a choice: risk nature shock or forge relationships with their captors. Elvas's testimony suggested that most selected the latter. After a hundred leagues, he reported, captives became "unmindful" of their connections to their homes and the chains came off. They did not run. Instead, they "learned the language of the Christians." The speed of their conversion impressed him, but he shouldn't have been surprised. In relational space, transferring loyalties, even if that meant entering the lowest rungs of an alien social order, was a better option than proceeding untethered into unknown space. Individuality was unfathomable and slavery preferable to isolation. Cabaza de Vaca and Juan Ortiz made the same choice as the captives from Uzachil. Separated from kith and kin, they opted for spots in indigenous societies. They both learned Native languages and forgot their own. When de Soto's crew found Ortiz, for every Spanish word he uttered, he "would say another four or five in the language of the Indians." Navigating relational space, staying anchored and in bounds, sometimes meant leaving a home and a language.[31]

### THE BOY WHO KNEW THE WAY

De Soto marched into the Apalachee territories in October 1539. He found a mound center "where a lord of all that land and province lived." The mico of Anhaica housed the leaders of the expedition. Elvas toured the fields surrounding the capital. Planted with "abundant maize, pumpkins, beans, and dried plums," the fields appeared "better than those of Spain" and far easier to maintain. Elvas thought the plots grew wild and untended; his eyes could not detect, or his mind could not conceive, the design and labor that produced the high yields of the Mississippians' slash-and-burn agriculture, with maize, squash, and beans growing together on hoed hillocks. Food piled up in Anhaica as tribute to the mico. Having found their first stockpile, the Christians decided to erect a camp nearby and winter there.[32]

Two discoveries in Apalachee altered the course of de Soto's entrada. Struggling to understand the Muskogean dialect spoken in the chiefdom, Ortiz gleaned from an informant that the sea was only six leagues from where they camped. A scouting party confirmed the report, and de Soto sent riders to Uzita to tell the ships waiting in the bay to sail north and locate a port closer to Apalachee. Captain Juan de Anasco and thirty men reversed the months-long summer march, backtracking through central Florida to coastal Uzita in ten days. They traveled at night and rested far from Native settlements. Angry Floridians lined the route, eager to ambush the return squadron, but Anasco reached the flotilla. The ships packed up and departed north, eventually discovering a harbor near the chiefdom of Ochuse, sixty leagues from the Mississippian mound center. (The Apalachee complex chiefdom lay in the fertile uplands of northern Florida near where the state capital of Tallahassee now stands.) His communication lines relocated, de Soto hatched a plan for an ambitious march into the interior based on the news Ortiz received from a young Mississippian overflowing with stories about a chiefdom with stockpiles of gold many leagues to the east.

All four of the narratives that chronicled de Soto's invasion mentioned this talkative enslaved youth. Luys Hernandez de Biedma's account, the one source written by a person who took part in the invasion, included the least about him. Nonetheless, Biedma singled him out, which said a lot, for he rarely singled out individuals other than micos. He described the gabby Mississippian as "that Indian," as if his readers already knew him. *That Indian* launched De Soto's search for "the land . . . on another sea." *That Indian* "deceived us." *That Indian* "affirmed the lies he had told us."

*That Indian* precipitated de Soto's Apalachee mistake, his decision to order the ships he just rounded up in Ochuse to Cuba, leaving the Gulf coast in search of the golden city Cofitachequi. *That Indian* needed no introduction because readers could see what the participants could not. In real time, it took months on the road and two weeks in the woods between Cofaqui and Cofitachequi for the Christians to "see the lie of the Indian." In the text, Biedma unmasked him as the culprit immediately. But it was only in retrospect that the Mississippian looked shifty at first glance.[33]

The two next-best accounts, the secondhand report from the Portuguese "Gentleman of Elvas" and historian Gonzalo Fernández de Oviedo y Valdés's narrative based on interviews with an expedition member named Rodrigo Rangel, filled in more details about *that Indian*. They offered a name: Perico. Elvas told where he came from. He was "a youth" captured during a slave raid in a Timucuan town on the borders of the Apalachee chiefdom. The expedition's treasurer, Juan Gaytán, claimed the boy. He drew the attention of Ortiz because he spoke several languages. He was not originally from the place where the Christians caught him. He had traveled there from a very distant chiefdom in the east "in order to visit other lands." He told stories about a place called Yupaha, where a woman mico ruled, collecting gold in tribute from the provinces surrounding her chiefdom. "He," reported Elvas, "told how it was taken from the mines, melted, and refined, just as if he had seen it done." The youth was very convincing: "All when they saw the signs he made believed whatever he said to be true." But, like Biedma, Elvas cast doubt on him from the start. He may have seen the production of gold, "or else the devil taught him."[34]

Elvas recounted Perico's breakdown in Cofaqui. As de Soto and his army prepared to cross the no-man's-land between the chiefdoms, the boy collapsed and "began to foam at the mouth and to throw himself to the ground as if possessed by the devil." The friars prayed over him and he seemed to recover, but in the woods he became disoriented again. Without the guidance the boy promised, the expedition spiraled, all bearings lost. The captive interpreters were no help; the trackless space defeated de Soto and Ortiz; even the several hundred warriors from Cofaqui who came along to bear the Christians' food and supplies and perhaps attack their traditional enemies in Cofitachequi despaired in confusion. De Soto ordered Perico brought before him and "made as if he would throw him to the dogs." Ortiz begged for his life. There was no one else among the captives with whom he could communicate in so many languages. Apparently, the youth knew the coastal dialects along with Timucuan, the language used in the non-Mississippian Florida interior, as well as the Muskogean spoken in Apalachee. He was a spectacular asset, even if he was proving an unreliable narrator.[35]

Oviedo, via Rangel, confirmed many of the details reported by Elvas. Perico led de Soto from Apalachee to Cofaqui and then lost "his bearings." To cover his geographic lapse and forestall a dog attack, he "made himself out to be possessed." Perico recovered and piloted the Christians and their Cofaqui allies into the woods, where they ran out of food after descending into a roadless "labyrinth." Some advised turning back, while others "said that they should go in another direction or another way." De Soto, as was his wont, "said it was better to go forward, without his or their knowing in what they guessed correctly or in what they erred." Perico's confusion abetted de Soto's delusions. To Oviedo, both were liars who specialized in getting people lost.[36]

The author of the fourth and most flamboyant source, the Inca Garcilaso de la Vega, retold Perico's story in his history of La Florida. The son of a conquistador father and an Incan mother, Garcilaso wrote from his home in Spain. He possessed no firsthand knowledge of the Americas. He based his version of events on interviews with Gonzalo Sylvestre, a survivor of the expedition. Garcilaso claimed that the residents of Cofaqui attacked Perico in the night to stop him from leading the Christians to Cofitachequi. Their abuse explained his breakdown and his possession. His demons were fellow Indians.

Except they probably weren't Indians. Garcilaso wrote during a later period when the categories of "Indian" and "Spaniard" carried tremendous weight. A member of both groups, he engaged history to solve the puzzle of his double identity. Masculine honor animated his ruminations on the Spanish conquest in the New World. He hoped to prove that civilized Indians like himself could become gentlemen and enter the highest ranks of a Christian society. Perico may have experienced abuse at the hands of his enemies in Cofaqui, but they could not have punished him for betraying a hemispheric or regional Indian identity. The Mississippian culture spanned the chiefdoms of the Southeast, and the ceremonial complex was a set of beliefs and practices rather than an ethnicity or a race. De Soto and his minions were the ones who thought in universal categories like heathen and Christian, savage and civilized. They abused and tortured the people they so labeled to make them observe these rankings, but try as they might, the invaders never succeeded in turning the Mississippians into Indians. The maize farmers continued to erect mounds, clear plazas, and draw their social identity from a central place in the cosmos, be it in Uzita, Mocoso, Apalachee, Cofaqui, Cofitachequi, Coosa, Tascaluza, Chicaza, Quizquiz, Guachoya, or the dozens of other chiefdoms that claimed an axis mundi.

Perico belonged to no center, marking him as an outsider. Garcilaso took the hazy background provided by Elvas and filled in the gaps with his imagination. Perico, he wrote, had traveled to the Timucuan town where the Christians found him in the service of traders "who were accustomed to enter with their merchandise, selling and buying, many leagues into the interior country." As a servant bound to peddlers, the boy learned many languages as well as the lay of many lands. Commerce broadened his horizons beyond those of most Mississippians at the time of the entrada who stayed within a hundred leagues of the ceremonial centers.[37]

Garcilaso Hispanicized the Mississippians' exchange network. He turned their trade into an activity that resembled Spain's traveling hawkers and peddlers, economic actors he knew. In his vision, Perico grew up in a market-like system where merchants traveled from town to town, buying and selling wares. He wasn't completely wrong. The Mississippians did indeed move "low mass/high volume" prestige goods thousands of miles along pathways that stretched from the Florida coast to mound centers in the middle of the continent. Archeologists have dug up copious amounts of out-of-place materials—shark's teeth in southern Indiana, Great Lakes' copper in Alabama—but they still don't know exactly how the exchange network functioned. Did single individuals bear shell and pearl beads into the interior and bring copper gorgets and clay pipes back? Or were the goods moved in stages, passing through many hands as they made their way to powerful micos and ranking clan members throughout the Southeastern Ceremonial Complex?[38]

While contemplating (and condemning) Perico, Elvas may have let slip a clue as to Perico's place in the network. The youth, he wrote, had the disturbing habit of asserting "to have seen" what "he [only] learned from hearsay." He then proceeded to "enlarge at will what he saw." A skilled linguist, Perico traded information instead of goods. He created pictures of prestige items located in chiefdoms thousands of leagues away. He may have been a Mississippian version of a sales catalog. He absorbed bits of news from across the network and communicated the details of copper production or the splendor of Cofitachequi as if he had seen such things himself. The Christians denounced him for his lies, but perhaps that is how the network survived in a smaller-scale era without major entrepôts like Cahokia. Ceremonial items moved haphazardly across space as micos exchanged gifts or raided enemies. Slaves like Perico held the vision of the whole together through information transactions. They remembered where ceremonial items came from at a time when few people ventured far from their chiefdoms. De Soto's mistake was thinking Perico could locate places he had only heard about. And after witnessing guides being burned alive or attacked by war dogs, Perico had every reason to promote that illusion.[39]

In Cofaqui, the ruse fell apart. While we will never know what really happened to Perico, he seems to have reached the edge of his information network. After recovering from his demonic fit, he told de Soto through Ortiz that a four-day march would bring them to the rich town controlled by the woman mico. De Soto did not believe the rattled boy right away. He directed Ortiz to question the Cofaqui locals about Perico's projected route and travel-time estimate. They "knew of no settlement in that direction," and they could not direct de Soto to Cofitachequi because they did not know the way. Warriors from Cofaqui "sometimes" raided Cofitachequi, but they used "hidden and secret places where they could not be detected." No roads connected the enemies; they did not trade or associate with one another. Only Cofaqui warriors ventured into the woods that separated the chiefdoms, and they would not share their mysteries, especially with a stranger who was only a boy. Perico was struck blind by his inability to exchange stories, and he offered de Soto a best guess to forestall being gutted by voracious hounds.[40]

Perico led de Soto's army and the Cofaqui bearers into a trackless forest. A seldom-visited buffer zone between two chiefdoms, the wilderness puzzled the Iberian horsemen as well as the Mississippian hunters. Both were used to traveling through rough country. But this expanse proved trickier than most. The Mississippian woods contained nonhuman beings with a talent for spreading confusion. In the nineteenth century, U.S. government ethnographer James Mooney interviewed Cherokee religious leaders about their healing rituals and their myths. They told him about the Yûñwĭ Tsunsdi', the Little People. About two feet tall, the Little People danced and drummed in the lonely woods of the Southeast mountains. While not especially mountainous, the forested stretch between Cofaqui and Cofitachequi was certainly lonely. It would not be surprising if the Little People, their long hair sweeping the ground as they danced to the beat of their drums, lived there. The Little People enjoyed mischief, and they hated being disturbed. If human hunters followed the sound of the drums to their homes, the Yûñwï Tsunsdi' cast spells on the intruders, bewildering them. The trauma of getting lost in the forest due to an encounter with the Little People wore off slowly. An afflicted hunter might return to his settlement and continue "like one dazed ever after." The Little People punished trespassers, but they showed kindness to other humans. They rescued children who strayed from their parents in the woods and returned them to their communities. If hunters found misplaced knives or necklaces in the forest, they left them or asked the Little People's permission before taking them. The items might belong to the Yûñwï Tsunsdi' and grabbing them without authorization could bring a shower of rocks thrown from the shadows.[41]

Vengeful, fun-loving, possessive, and kind, the Little People captured the precarious balance that defined the Mississippian belief system. Anthropologist Charles Hudson, the late dean of southeastern Indian studies, saw the Cherokees' Yûñwï Tsunsdi' as holdovers from the Mississippian cult. To him, the forest dwellers revealed the uncertainty of living in the intermediate space between a pure upper vault and a profane lower world. The spirits demanded respect, and while humans learned to approach them with care, controlling them was impossible. The Little People reveled in their unpredictability, mystifying some and befriending others. The Cherokees' stories of disoriented hunters returning home in a daze sounded a lot like nature shock, as did Perico's anxiety attack. "The Little People," wrote Hudson, "could cause a person to become temporarily bewildered, or even to become insane." Perhaps the demonic presence that grabbed him in the woods was not the Christians' devil but rather a band of knee-high drummers with flowing locks and volatile personalities.[42]

Whether or not Little People were residue from the Southeastern Ceremonial Complex, the stories told about them proved one thing: Native American hunters and children got lost in the woods before and after the European conquest of North America. Preadolescence, pedestrianism, and poor visibility flummoxed humans across centuries and cultures.

De Soto's army and its Cofaqui entourage bushwhacked through the forest for thirteen days and forded three rivers, each one wider and more furious than the last. After crossing the third, de Soto escorted Perico to the center of a pine grove and threatened his life. Four days? He fumed. The horses were starving. The men were gaunt. "The youth," reported Elvas, "did not know where he was." After two weeks in the wilderness, one of de Soto's scouts stumbled upon a small village. He returned with some corn and four captives. Ortiz had Perico speak with them. They replenished his spatial imagination and repaired his relationship with de Soto and the army. Biedma remembered their exchange. By speaking with the captives, Perico created a relationship in a space that seemed lacking in human connections. The appearance of mutual intelligibility was enough to restore some faith in Perico, though Biedma still thought the boy a fibber. "He again affirmed the lies that he had told us, and we believed him through seeing the interpreter speak with those Indians." A four-day march, Perico reiterated, would bring them to Cofitachequi. After wandering for thirteen days, convinced their Indian guide had "lost [his] bearings, and did not know where to go or what road to take," the Christians resumed their trek, not on actual intelligence, but on an impression of knowledge emanating from a series of conversations they could not parse. As he did in Apalachee when he described the mining, melting, and refining of gold, Perico produced visible signs of orientation they believed.[43]

The ordeal of getting lost in the "uninhabited region" between Cofaqui and Cofitachequi demonstrated how the Mississippian exchange network fostered misunderstanding and violence. The Christians mistrusted their Indian guides and reacted brutally when they thought they were being deceived. Yet they also recruited them energetically, believed their stories about golden cities, and bet their lives on geographic information that turned out to be wrong quite often. The Christians were gullible, and they were skeptics. Their spatial imagination encouraged cynical naiveté because it was relational and foregrounded people over places. Ortiz and de Soto judged Perico on his relationship with them instead of his connection to Cofitachequi or any other place. Was he a trustworthy servant? Did he know his place? If he truly understood where he belonged in the order of human beings to which de Soto and Ortiz ascribed, he could not steer them too far wrong. In spaces built on relationships, getting lost was a social misstep. Guides confused their loyalties, not their coordinates. Disoriented guides forgot themselves. They were rebels because of it, and as criminals, they deserved to be maimed and mauled.

Movement across Mississippian chiefdoms was difficult without the added worry of a wrong turn bringing a death sentence. Even accomplished networkers like Perico could lose their bearings in a fragmented human landscape held together through imaginative acts as much as material linkages. The Christians punished Indians who led them astray, but they desperately wanted to unearth the pathways they assumed existed in the interior from the stories they heard about powerful lords and stockpiles of gold. This desire for geographic connection rescued Perico. The communication he had with the four captives from the little village was "no little thing because of the great necessity for interpreters that there is in the land." The accidental discovery of a conversation in the wilderness suggested that other linkages existed, hidden from view.[44]

### PROUDLY WOUNDED

De Soto disturbed the isolation of the Mississippian chiefdoms by hauling slaves and agricultural produce across territorial lines. The invaders put on a spectacle of transportation the likes of which the Southeast hadn't seen in many decades. The Natives' trade network moved small items of high ceremonial value. No one in their right mind lugged everyday items in bulk across vast distances. De Soto, with his horses and enslaved laborers, did just that. He seized stockpiles whenever he could and conscripted Mississippians to carry them. In town after town, he ordered micos taken and held for ransom. He demanded food, information, and porters. Requisitioned bearers, or *tamemes,* sometimes numbering four hundred to six hundred, carried dried maize, walnuts, plums, deer hides, and pearl beads from their province into another. At the border, de Soto had their chains unlocked and sent back the ones he did not want to feed or guard. The kidnapping cycle started again with the capture of a new mico.

De Soto and his gentlemen partners amassed labor, food, and treasure. Yet, like all the communities in the lower-density Mississippian era, they struggled to hang onto their stashes. A marching army consumed surpluses, and the Christians sped through calories quickly by feeding maize to their horses. Hunger stalked the expedition. For every "well-provisioned" province there were stretches of "poor" lands with no food, "except a very limited amount for the Indians to eat, and we, with the horses and the people used it up very quickly." News of the invaders traveled faster than they did within regions. The Indians directly ahead of their march buried maize to keep it from them. Torture could pry open hidden reserves. But what violence gathered, it could also destroy. In Mabila, a mico drew de Soto into a palisaded town by promising him porters "for [his] burdens." When the cacique disappeared into a house, de Soto sent a man to retrieve him. The soldier found thousands of Indians "ready for war" waiting in the houses. They streamed out shooting arrows and swinging clubs. De Soto and his men hacked their way out of the town, but in the chaos, the Christians left many of their possessions behind. Once free, de Soto ordered his cavalry to dismount. He assembled four squads of twenty men. Armed with torches, the squads chopped through the palisade and set fire to the town. The flames burned "a quantity of Indians" and "all our supplies," including the two-hundred-pound cache of pearl beads the Christians had taken from Cofitachequi. That night, reported Biedma, they rendered fat from their dead enemies' charred bodies and rubbed the oil on their wounds. The fire had destroyed all their medicine.[45]

To rally his troops after losing the pearls, de Soto misled them. He conspired with Ortiz to prevent his men from leaving for the coast and heading home. The old plan included a reunion with the brigantines on the coast following the plunge into the interior to reach Cofitachequi. The ships, loaded with meat and bread, would provision the men for the winter and carry back the pearls, confirming de Soto's triumph. Now the treasure was gone, and when Ortiz learned from a newly enslaved captive that the ships were waiting in Ochuse, a town on Pensacola Bay forty leagues away, he notified de Soto and was told to keep the information to himself.

Word leaked, however, and some gentlemen in the upper ranks, including Juan Gaytán, the royal treasurer who first enslaved Perico, demanded a meeting with their leader. The circle of honor that had held these men in place from Uzita to Mabila threatened to come apart, with some arguing for a retreat to Ochuse and then to Cuba, and de Soto countering with pleas to stay the course in the interior. De Soto won the point. Biedma reported that "many wished that the Governor would go to the sea . . . but he did not dare, for the month of November was already half over and it was very cold, and he felt it advisable to look for a land where we might find provisions." Garcilaso mentioned that de Soto freed the Indian slave who knew the way to Ochuse soon after the parlay. The dispute fizzled after de Soto turned north and the guide to Ochuse disappeared.[46]

After Mabila, de Soto and his army entered Chicaza, a chiefdom with food enough to keep them alive during a long winter in which "more snows fell than in Castile." In spring, the Indians brought hides for trade and little dogs for dinner. They feigned an encounter—an exchange of gifts, pleasantries, and information—to scout the invaders' defenses. They learned the placement of their sentries, and later that night, dozens of Indians carrying fire in earthen jars stole past the guards and torched the camp, killing "fifty-seven horses and more than three hundred hogs and thirteen or fourteen men." Rain saved the survivors from another attack, leading Biedma to thank God, because "we were so poorly supplied that although we still had some horses, we had neither saddle, nor lance, nor shield, because all had burned." The fire consumed the Christians' clothing, forcing some of the men to weave grass into mats and sandwich their body between them to stay warm. "Many," said Elvas, "laughed at this contrivance." However, after a few more nights spent in the cold, everyone was picking grass and weaving mats.[47]

The Christians lost their shirts, their pants, and their pikes in Chicaza, but they would not lose their way until Guachoya, many leagues and an entire year after the conflagration. De Soto and his gentlemen journeyed to La Florida to accumulate material resources, not to watch their possessions go up in flames again. Coming after the fiasco in Mabila and the decision not to turn south and meet the brigantines, Chicaza would seem a good place for the gentlemen to finally lose their resolve, to call de Soto on his obsessive commitment to moving deeper into the interior and break for the coast. Leaders who cannot secure basic nourishment and warmth for their followers eventually lose them. The presence, even the promise, of food, clothing, and shelter made roaming tolerable. Getting lost was as much about not knowing where to find the necessities for survival as not knowing where to locate yourself in absolute space.

The crisis in goods did not turn into an excuse for giving up because the leaders of the expedition interpreted material ruin as a prod to keep going rather than a sign to give up. The more they forfeited, the less likely they were to go back. Real men marched on without their pearls and stockings.

De Soto and his men desperately wanted to return with more wealth than they had sunk into the conquest, but as early modern men devoted to a code of masculine and martial honor, they chased pain as well as profits. Suffering tested manhood, mimicked the travails of Jesus Christ, and roused the sympathy of the public and the crown. Gentlemen welcomed hardship. Rodrigo Rangel, the expedition member interviewed by historian Gonzalo Fernández de Oviedo y Valdés, witnessed Don Antonio Osorio bear the indignity of wearing a "doublet" made from an Indian blanket after Mabila. His sides were exposed to the weather, and his helmet and boots were gone. Rangel described Osorio in a list of subordinate clauses that combined a dearth of material objects with an abundance of noble bearing: "without hose or shoes, a shield at his back, a sword without a scabbard, the snows and cold very great; and being such a man, and of such illustrious lineage, made him suffer his hardship and not lament." Osorio had given up a yearly income of 2,000 ducats from the church to follow de Soto. An unwise choice, implied Oviedo, who knew "De Soto very well" and thought him a sweet-talking conniver. Yet while he questioned Osorio's judgment, he celebrated how suffering revealed his nature.[48]

De Soto, according to Garcilaso, suffered magnificently too. "He was extremely patient in toil and in need, so much so that seeing the patience and suffering of their Captain General was his soldiers' greatest comfort in the midst of their own afflictions." Physical torment demonstrated the rank of human beings. People at the top of the social order commanded their own bodies like they commanded the bodies of others. Their stoicism in the face of adversity confirmed who they were. De Soto's men could see his greatness when he stayed cool in crushing moments. Pain did not develop his moral fiber; pain divulged it. This marked a crucial difference between the narratives of his trek and the stories of interior journeys Americans would later write. The ordeal of travel, how hitting the road exposed wayfarers to physical discomfort, featured in most tales of movement. Hardship shaped drama, building characters along arcs of personal development and self-discovery. But de Soto and his gentlemen did not see pain and selves interacting like hammers and molten steel. Trauma showed what was already true rather than creating someone new.[49]

### THE LOST

The noblemen in de Soto's expedition displayed forbearance. They acted as if their disasters didn't hurt. Still, not all the members of the expedition endured the pain with equanimity and panache, just as not all of them agreed with de Soto's harsh tactics. Some Christians abandoned their posts and vanished into Mississippian America, and their exits disturbed the routines of noble suffering and opened alternative routes into relational space.

Several expedition members "got lost." A man named Alimamos, "sick with fever," wandered "from the road and was lost." In the forest, he ran into a group of runaway slaves from the expedition, headed toward their homes. According to Elvas, Alimamos urged them "to abandon their evil intentions" and accompany him back to the Christians. Two did as he asked, and they rejoined the column. Elvas took care in his narrative to protect Alimamos. He confirmed that the sick man had indeed lost his way, not his nerve. This backing was crucial because getting lost could be a cover for giving up. Later in his report, Elvas mentioned Manzano, "a Christian of noble parentage," who wandered away "to look for grapes" and "was lost." In his interview with Oviedo, Rodrigo Rangel questioned Manzano's intentions for leaving the expedition: "It was not known if it was from his own will or from losing his bearings." Rumors spread, saying Manzano was unhappy and that he had "requested other soldiers to remain with him." The army had just left Coosa, "the best and most abundant [province] that they found in Florida." De Soto's decision to abandon a perfectly good province for an even richer one broke the ranks. Days before Manzano was lost, a Christian named Feryada abandoned his post. Soon after Feryada went missing, Joan Vizcaino, "a very shrewd black man, belonging to Captain Juan Ruiz Lobillo," deserted. These departures illustrated that not all the members of the expedition welcomed the agony of endless exploration. Some "got lost" and opted to eat grapes with the heathens rather than swallow the daily rations of misery de Soto was serving. Crossing over cultural lines and staying with the Mississippians was an option many of the men considered and some of them tried.[50]

After de Soto died, the suffering continued under Luis de Moscoso. The bane of guides, Moscoso burned, disfigured, and had dogs maul captives who misled him. Two Christians got lost on Moscoso's watch. One, a sick man, wandered away, and Moscoso "suspected that the Indians had killed him." (The man was found and returned unharmed.) Francisco de Guzmán abandoned the expedition at Chuguate, a town in a space that would eventually be considered Arkansas. The "bastard son of a gentleman of Seville," Guzmán came to Florida well provisioned with a bundle of fine clothes, impressive weapons, and three horses. He left his post and abandoned his social rank to be with a Mississippian woman. Furious at the nobleman, Moscoso sent a rider back with a threat: the cacique of Chuguate would return Guzmán or Moscoso would execute the guides the cacique had given him. He received no response. Guzmán was apparently more valuable to the mico than the guides. Tired of waiting, Moscoso gave up and left the Christian behind. The Indian captives survived for a while. Months later, in a dismal province called Nisohone, which was "poorly populated and had little maize," Moscoso had the two guides killed. They kept veering east, instead of west, toward Mexico, where he wanted to go. They also ventured "through dense forests, wandering off the road." Moscoso "ordered them hanged from a tree." Guzmán missed the lynching and the many bouts of suffering and viciousness that followed. In his interview, Elvas denounced the deserter, taking a jab at his illegitimate parentage, but the amorous noble bastard who chose to stay in Chuguate avoided nature shock. De Soto could not claim as much.[51]

Hernando de Soto deserves to be listed among the terribly lost. An illness overtook him, as had happened to Alimamos. Feverish men lost their reason as well as their stamina. Unable to keep up, they fell out of rank, expelled by a triple blow of physical duress, mental incapacitation, and social removal. The sick entered spaces outside human relationships, a frightening void they could not endure for long. Vulnerable and alone, they stumbled around in search of paths, shelter, and sustenance. They experienced the derangement of nature shock. Their lives depended on reconnection. Alimamos happened upon the runaway slaves and persuaded two of them to return to their masters. He reminded the slaves of their social obligations and used those bonds to haul himself back. The Mississippian chiefdoms offered the only alternative to those Christians who chose not to, or physically could not, rejoin the conquest. Society, in whatever form, was the antidote to getting lost. Lone survival—individualism—was not an option.

De Soto's men kept their delirious commander from falling behind or blundering into the woods. Yet, reported Elvas, they did not exactly take good care of him. "Great confusion" bubbled to the surface in de Soto's final days. For the first time, his men felt "the danger of being lost in that land," which brings me back to my opening question: what took them so long? They had been peering into the interior for years, but it was only when de Soto was inhaling his final breaths that the horror of not knowing where they were "stared them all in the face." Instead of gathering around de Soto, they broke apart, each to feel sorry for himself. This was getting lost in a world built on relationships. De Soto's death freed the Christians to look around and let the desperation begin to sink in. With their commander gone, the vastness of the distance separating the men from their goals hit them, and they lost their minds.[52]

De Soto and his followers failed each other. The conquistador broke his promise to lead his men back to the coast. When he turned north after Mabila instead of marching south to Ochuse and the brigantines, de Soto must have believed he could return. He remained confident because he owned beach-reaching technology—horses. The Christians exploited the power of their horses in two ways: the animals gave them an overwhelming advantage in battle (mounted soldiers plowed into pedestrian warriors, skewering them with lances made deadlier with leverage from above), and the animals allowed small parties to retrace inland paths and reach the coast in half the time it took the entire army to move the same distance. De Soto used the horses to reposition the boats from Uzita to a harbor closer to Apalachee. He then sent word for them to sail to Cuba and reunite with him at Ochuse. He broke the horse-coastline connection there and never regained it.

The path to the coast eluded him. Biedma described his predicament and the mounting frustration. De Soto was "determined . . . to find the sea, to make the brigantines in order to send word to Cuba that we were alive, so that they might provide us with some horses and the things we were in need of." However, the massive floodplain of the Mississippi River blocked the way. The scout de Soto sent to find a route to the coast returned, "saying that he did not find a road nor a way to cross the large swamps along the great river." The Indians were no help. Ortiz had fallen ill and perished months before. Perico was also gone. Interpretations had gone downhill. When he tried to ask the locals for directions to a road to the sea, "nothing could be found out about what there might be." Space collapsed on de Soto. The coast retreated from his vision, and instead of an open vista, he perceived limited options: "The Governor, from seeing himself cut off and seeing that not one thing could be done according to his purpose, was afflicted with sickness and died." The imagined geography that oriented him, the assumption that he was navigating an interior with pathways that connected to a coast and to home, slipped from his grasp. When he lost his ability to see the way out, if only in his mind's eye, de Soto lost his courage, his men, and finally his life.[53]

## THE WORDY AFTERMATH

De Soto's journey ended in the murk of the river that drove him to despair. It was a fitting last move for a conquistador who would not rest in peace. (It was also ironic that the Christians dumped their leader into a gateway to the Under World, perhaps feeding his remains to the water cannibals.) When the reports began to filter back to Spain, and the chroniclers replayed the expedition, its brutality sparked controversy. All four narratives of the entrada included descriptions of the repugnant violence committed by the Christians against the Indians. The amputations, hangings, burnings, and dog attacks represented some of the most appalling and miserable scenes in early American history.

Some chroniclers defended de Soto. The Inca Garcilaso de la Vega's revisionist history sought to vindicate civilized Indians like himself. He wanted to prove that they could be honorable Spaniards. He intended to enlarge the circle of men who counted in Iberian society. Chivalry, machismo, Christianity, and an Aristotelian understanding of virtue drove his investigation of the past. Historians like him studied the fleeting moments and personalities of history to catch glimpses of deeper, timeless human attributes.

Garcilaso included a lengthy and florid account of Ortiz's captivity. He used the episode to establish an equivalency between civilized Indians and Spaniards. Honorable gentlemen, he argued, could recognize one another across cultures. Hirrihigua tortured Ortiz and struggled to see the plucky nobleman as an equal after Narváez ruined his face and spoiled his judgment. But Mocoso, the mico of the town where Ortiz found refuge six leagues inland from Uzita, perceived the stranger's worth at first glance. He could see that the captive was an honorable man, and his ability to recognize virtue (and display virtue by keeping his word) proved that Mocoso—and therefore all Indians—could be honorable too. Garcilaso championed a cross-cultural league of gentlemen, which left open the possibility of torturing people—Indians or otherwise—who were not league material.

Garcilaso and the other de Soto chroniclers took part in a transatlantic debate about relationships. Were the Indians God's children? Were they servants of the Catholic Church? Were they vassals of the Spanish king? Torture involved basic questions about the makeup of humanity, kinship, and societies, and because they were being asked during a territorial conquest, these questions were fundamentally about space as well. Could people living far away belong to your religion, your country, your family, and your kind? As Christians, the members of the de Soto expedition answered yes. In theory, all humans belonged to the same God, and all humans living in the Americas outside Brazil were subjects of one ruler, the king of Spain, by papal decree. De Soto believed that torture and slavery brought rebellious Indians into the Christian fold. He felt compelled to punish heathens and criminals to protect the authority that ruled the world through him. Critics, like the historian Gonzalo Fernández de Oviedo y Valdés, who included an account of de Soto's Florida expedition in his *Historia general y natural de las Indias,* charged that de Soto and his henchmen violated their honor when they brutalized and enslaved Indians. De Soto, he argued, had let his greed corrupt him. Rather than bring Indians into lower ranks of the global hierarchy of believers, patiently instructing neophytes and disciplining recalcitrants when necessary, de Soto and his men went wild, lying, stealing, raping, and killing to satisfy their unchecked desires. Instead of instilling discipline in their Indian subordinates, they displayed sinful disobedience to God.

The debaters held nothing back. They questioned the moral foundation of the conquistadors' associations with the Indians. But still they argued within their relational worldview. They could not imagine the possibility of leaving the Natives alone, for that too was a sin. Withholding the word of God and all the interpersonal conflicts that went with evangelizing was a transgression of omission. The Christians' insistence on relationships was not foreign to the Mississippians. They too believed that humans belonged inside families, clans, villages, and hierarchical chiefdoms. The relational worldview produced the horrifying violence that fueled the debates in Spain, and no one sought to topple the hierarchies, only rearrange, excuse, or purify the human connections within them.

Garcilaso would have joined Oviedo's dismantling of de Soto's reputation if he had shared his fellow historian's estimation of the conquistador's dishonor. But he didn't. He portrayed de Soto as a steadfast gentleman, an exemplary counterpart to the many noble Indian micos Garcilaso also celebrated. Conflicts erupted in Garcilaso's Florida when equals conducted just wars across cultures or when gentlemen punished those without honor for crimes such as blasphemy, sodomy, and cannibalism. Garcilaso published his account of the de Soto expedition in 1605, while Oviedo wrote his history in 1546. Their descriptions of torture reflected the shifting political climate in Spain, where the crown and the church heard vigorous arguments for and against the conquistadors' harsh treatment of Native Americans in the years after de Soto's death.

The chroniclers of the de Soto expedition reconfigured groups after the fact to excuse or condemn the Christians' brutality. Garcilaso enlarged the gentlemen class. Indians and Iberians could display honor, write histories, and join the ranks of the *gente de razón*. Oviedo condemned the circle of gentlemen that surrounded de Soto. "Oh marvelous God, what blindness and rapture under such an uncertain greed and such a vain preaching as that which Hernando de Soto was able to tell those deluded soldiers that he led to a land where he had never set foot on it, and where three other Governors, more expert than he, had been lost." De Soto's hunger for wealth and fame disoriented him and his followers. "Oh, lost people," thundered Oviedo, "oh, diabolical greed; oh, bad conscience; oh, unfortunate soldiers, how did you not understand in how much danger you walked, and how wasted your lives and without tranquility your souls!" Sin turned the Christians into lustful berserkers. They lost their way because they betrayed the values—their honor, their reason, and their faith—that defined their social class.[54]

Oviedo thought he knew exactly where to find de Soto: burning in hell. The conquistador's location has proven more of a puzzle to the many investigators who followed. The desire to pinpoint the expedition in absolute space came from many sources. Scholars have tried to link the movements described in the narratives to archeological dig sites. Mapping de Soto's route in relation to field excavations promised to bridge history and anthropology and open a view onto Native America at the moment of contact. Nonacademic Americans also claimed spots along de Soto's trail for pride and profit. All the groups sought to resurrect relationships, to make spatial connections with sets of dead humans lost in time. Where de Soto traveled became a special concern to residents of one Alabama town. In the 1939 de Soto commission report, John R. Swanton declared that Childersburg, Alabama, stood at the site of the ancient Native American settlement of Coosa. Soon after, civic leaders began to tout Childersburg as "the oldest continually occupied city in North America." They were not thinking of the Indians when they boasted of their city's longevity. Rather, they targeted the passages in Oviedo and Elvas that mentioned Manzano, the grape-eating nobleman from Seville who got lost near Coosa (or, rumors said, wandered away on purpose). The leaders of Childersburg drew a line from their ruling class to that one free-ranging Spaniard. When Manzano took up residence in Coosa, history—meaning white history—began.[55]

Señor Manzano made for an unconventional founding father. He was either a gourmand who could not find his way out of the woods or a deserter who traded a noble lineage for a savage existence. For the leaders of Childersburg, however, he was enough. He brought their town closer to an American origin. He was their Plymouth Rock, which explains their perturbed reaction when archeologists moved him. New evidence emerged that suggested the ancient town of Coosa actually lay a hundred miles away. The shifting currents of academia carried Manzano away from the Childersburgers, and the nobleman, whose white blood threaded across epochs to unite the past and the present through place, disappeared once more into spaces defined more by human relationships than lines drawn on maps.

# CHAPTER TWO

# Helpful Woods and Violent Waters

IN THE SUMMER OF 1621 AN ENGLISH YOUTH became disoriented in the countryside beyond the Plymouth Colony. "John Billington," wrote Governor William Bradford, "lost him selfe in the woods and wandered up and downe some five days, living on berries and whatever he could find." Bradford's vertical description of Billington's horizontal predicament captured the panic of getting lost. Up or down meant little in the jumble of paths, brooks, woods, cranberry bogs, and meadows. Spun around, Billington stepped into the ether (or the either). Being robbed of a sense of direction, an awareness akin to the pull of gravity, felt like floating or falling.[1]

The berries hinted at the social turmoil caused by Billington's disappearance. Meals patterned days, signaled communion, and knocked down the recurrent pangs of biological necessity. To run, bodies burned fuel, and their fires needed constant stoking. The time and location of the next feeding was critical human information; cuisine organized societies. The irregular arrival of the meals eaten by southern New England's Algonquians alarmed the English: "it being their fashion to eate all at some times, and sometimes nothing at all in two or three dayes." Their dining confusion betrayed their spiritual haze. "Wise Providence being a stranger to their wilder wayes," wrote William Wood in 1639, "they be right Infidels, neither caring for the morrow, or providing for their own families." The Plymouth colonists starved their first winter in the region, so it was rich for them to pin their superiority to their suppers. Nonetheless, sentiments like Wood's underscored the depth of the English fondness for keeping nature on schedule. Civilization depended on ordering food in its proper time and place. Scattered calories atomized people, turning settled subjects into roaming stomachs. John Billington faced the dislocation of not knowing where his next meal would come from. Food consumed him instead of him consuming food.[2]

The woods upset John Billington inside and out. He walked past the edge of the small territory he knew, a colony hugging the coast of Massachusetts Bay, and discovered nature shock. He also found help. After five days, one of the region's Native inhabitants saved him and passed him east, the length of Cape Cod, to the Nausets, a group seeking justice. The Nausets traded young Billington back to his people for knives, beads, and a pledge of improved conduct. Earlier that winter, the Plymouth colonists had robbed one of the Nausets' maize caches and fired guns at the rightful owners. The attack and theft aggravated a tense diplomatic situation. The Nausets were sick of English fur traders and explorers, coastal-cruising grab-and-run specialists who preceded the Plymouth colonists, stopping on the shores of Cape Cod and kidnapping Native men. To recover their wayward youth, the Plymouth colonists paid for him and for their countrymen's traffic in Indian lives.[3]

John Billington entered what was to him a convoluted space when he lost himself in the woods. Peering at the landscape of southern New England, the most influential men in Plymouth, the ones who wrote the histories, were disturbed by the region's appearance. When they spied the "weather-beaten face" of the coast in the winter of their arrival, they imagined a "whole country, full of woods and thickets" that "represented a wild and savage hue." Actual prospects beyond the shore were no cheerier. "What could they see," asked William Bradford, "but a hideous and desolate wilderness full of wild beasts and wild men[?]" Rather than behold the harshness of the land's "outward objects," the colonists turned their eyes to invisible forces. The radical Protestants looked to their god and constructed a sacrificial narrative from bleak outlooks. Condemned to wander in "desert wilderness out of the way," to go "both hungry and thirsty," to find "no city to dwell," and to "perish in this wilderness," the founding generation suffered so that their children would benefit from their example and see God's "lovingkindness" in their deliverance from their earthly woes.[4]

The English colonists' despairing vision baffled the humans who had been cultivating the desolate wilderness for centuries. The Algonquian-speaking people living near Massachusetts Bay and along Long Island Sound may have numbered as many as ninety thousand before warfare, dislocation, and European diseases began to take their toll in the early decades of the seventeenth century. The Algonquians grew maize in the scattered pockets of fertile soil located near watercourses in the heavily glaciated region. They moved their bark-covered wigwams with the seasons to exploit multiple sources of food. They gathered in large camps near the ocean in the warmer months, where women planted and harvested crops. Expert canoeists, the Natives enjoyed fishing and whaling. They dug for clams, whelks, and quahogs in the mudflats at low tide. Today, archeologists locate their village sites by the buried piles of shells they left behind. During the winter, the Algonquians dispersed into the interior, hunting large mammals like moose and deer and smaller ones such as raccoons and turkeys.[5]

By the time John Billington bumbled into the woods, the Native residents of southern New England had been dealing with European traders and raiders for many years. They had witnessed the devastation of the epidemics the visitors introduced and had developed strategies for acquiring the trade goods they desired while minimizing the violence and affronts they despised. When it came to colonization, they were old hands. The English were the ones who had much to learn.

The Rhode Island minister Roger Williams took it upon himself to educate his fellow colonists. In 1643, he published a "key" to the Algonquian language. He collected phrases from his Narragansett neighbors and commented on their hunting, travel, agriculture, and religious beliefs. In translation, he captured a glimpse of their relational space. The Algonquians of southern New England used several words to describe the forests. *Wèta* meant *the woods. Cuppì-machàug* denoted *thick wood: swamp.* Williams placed the word *wèta* next to the word *wetédg,* separating them with a colon to indicate their shared meaning and frequent pairing in speech. *Wetédg* was Algonquian for *on fire.* In addition to fire, the term *wèta* was related to seeing. Williams listed *wèta* and *wetédg* alongside the phrases *wassaumpatámmin* and *wassaum patámoonck,* which he translated as *to view or looke about* and *a prospect.* In their language, the Algonquians embedded the practice of starting fires in stretches of woods to clear sight lines for travel, hunting, and trapping. They converted verbs into nouns, summoning spaces (the woods) from actions (setting fires). The Algonquians named the landscapes they created through seasonal burning and distinguished *wèta* from the thick woods and swamps untouched by the flames and thus beyond their purview.[6]

The Algonquians managed wèta according to long-held traditions, but these were volatile times and there was nothing static about Native spaces in the seventeenth century. John Billington soloed in the woods for days without human contact because a 1619–20 smallpox epidemic had opened gaps in the political canopy. He could gorge on berries because the bushes had invaded the unplanted and untended maize fields left fallow by the Algonquian agriculturalists who had perished. Plymouth Colony itself squatted in one of these unused clearings. Colonization remade physical and political spaces. In southern New England this led to the rezoning of the human inhabitants. The Plymouth colonists resided adjacent to a string of "so-called monarchies," including the Wampanoags, led by Massasoit; the Narragansetts, ruled by the brothers Miantonomi and Canonicus; the Niantics, headed by Ninigret; and the Pequots, overseen by Tatobem. Colonization helped these leaders consolidate power. They formed tributary alliances and attempted to pass their sachemships to their relatives. The political landscape of southern New England demonstrated the adaptive flair as well as the terrible suffering of its Native residents.[7]

The Algonquians recognized use rights in the woods and in the fields. These rights belonged to families, and they were handed down across generations. The Algonquians did not own agricultural or forest land outright as private property. If a family stopped growing maize, hunting, or setting traps in an area, it was no longer theirs, but the monarchies protected use rights, patrolled borders, and dealt with trespassers. Territorial lines crisscrossed the region. The English did not introduce these lines. They lived inside them. Indigenous power determined the size and placement of their outposts.[8]

The monarchies' foreign policies shaped the colonists' experience of New England's forests. Instead of killing or kidnapping wayward colonists in the wèta, the Algonquians ignored or returned them. Roger Williams underscored the Indians' quickness to come to the aid of the disoriented English. He filled the section of the key devoted to "travell" with questions and phrases intended to solicit navigational help and smooth transportation service: *Tounúckquague yo wuchê. How far from Hence? Yo cuppummescóm min. Crosse over into the way there. Kunníish. I will carry you. Kuckqússuckqun. You are heavy.* By signaling that the Algonquians would rescue them if they strayed, and even carry them if they fell, Williams promoted English coloni-zation. His language guide joined a raft of books and pamphlets crossing the Atlantic to encourage immigrants to come over. The literature reassured would-be transplants that New England's Indians would save them if they got lost in the wilderness.[9]

The Algonquians' hospitality earned them more invaders. In the long run, a fiercer response may have served them better, so why did they help the bewildered strangers who appeared in the wèta?

Rescues had upsides. Rescues created space, brought material rewards, and improved diplomatic relations. Rescues cleared the woods more quickly than violence. Escorting colonists back to their homes removed them from hunting grounds and trapping locations and generated amicable relations instead of retaliatory raids. The Algonquians learned early on how alarmed the English became when one of their number roamed the woods alone. John Billington spent five days outside, a sojourn in the wilderness that not only terrified him but precipitated a region-wide emergency. The thought of young John wandering out there by himself, beholden to no one at all, moved William Bradford to call in a favor from his main Native ally, Massasoit, the Wampanoag sachem, and deploy the colony's limited supply of trade goods to retrieve him. The response proved the lengths to which the English would go to save people from the confounding spaces where they thought no civilized person belonged.

Instead of fighting spatial misconceptions, the Algonquians granted the colonists their wilderness and strategically offered to show them the exit when they got turned around in their hunting territories. The Algonquians' strategy worked for years. The English colonists stayed near the coast and out of the woods. They accepted their Indian neighbors' help and enlisted them as guides and message carriers. The Algonquians and the English fought in other locations. They attacked one another on shore-lines and near riverbanks. They contested the fertile zones where maize grew. Untended livestock entered the wèta and caused steady trouble. However, for a decade or more after they first landed, the English colonists expected and accepted Indian assistance in the spaces they feared to tread by themselves.[10]

Over time more colonists arrived, and as English families grew, epidemics, warfare, and land theft destroyed or weakened the Algonquian monarchies. The woods changed and the chances for nature shock increased on all sides. In 1700, the English population reached around ninety thousand, the old, precolonial human high-tide mark for the region. By then, the Algonquians in New England may have numbered under five thousand. There were fewer Indians crafting fewer wèta. The English never approved of the Algonquians burning the woods, and as their power grew, they discouraged the practice. As a result, cuppì-machàug, those unmanaged spaces of thick woods and swamps, proliferated as colonization advanced.[11]

The story of nature shock in colonial New England ends in a desolate wilderness instead of beginning in one. The colonists avoided the forests and relied on the Algonquians to move them through disorienting spaces. The Algonquians cultivated the colonists' dependence, and they labored to clear their woodland territories of underbrush and interlopers. They decided to reach across cultures and help colonists navigate their woods. They need not have done so. Other options were available to them.

To fully appreciate their choices, the Algonquians' wèta needs to be placed next to other contested spaces. Portages supply a useful contrast. Sites along rivers where rapids or waterfalls forced travelers out of the water, portages turned boaters, canoeists mainly, into supply- and gear-hauling pedestrians. Cast afoot in strange locations, warriors, traders, missionaries, and diplomats from Native and European societies lost their bearings. Some got terribly lost and suffered nature shock. The paths alongside rapids and falls were often zones of political conflict. Social relations churned alongside the whirlpools. War parties attacked rivals, taking captives and enslaving women and children. Violence stalked the riverbanks. The peace the Algonquians cultivated in New England's forests was absent from the portages in the continental interior as groups of Indians and colonists enacted bloodier, but no less relational, foreign policies.

Opportunities to get lost proliferated in North America with the multiplication of colonial powers and Native American nations. By 1621, the year John Billington went missing, France, England, Sweden, and the Netherlands had established their presence on the continent. Spain had lost its monopoly on the Western Hemisphere, just as the Catholic Church, the global institution that granted this singular authority, lost its hold on the universal Christian religion. In the aftermath of the Protestant

Reformation, Europeans splintered along political and religious lines. Many Native peoples experienced similar fragmentations and reformations. The Mississippians in the Southeast, for instance, entered what some historians have labeled a "shatter zone." Groups dispersed and coalesced, creating new nations, such as the Chickasaws, the Choctaws, the Creeks, and the Cherokees, as the old maize chiefdoms collapsed, and the mound-building cult disappeared. The result was a political and territorial hodgepodge with many contested borders. Captives, trade goods, and pathogens crossed frontiers, unsettling Native and colonial communities. Moving through these shifting landscapes challenged the humans' social skills. In print, European men grabbed the limelight as the time period's star navigators. But women and children from all societies covered more ground and passed between cultures more easily. They crossed relational spaces as subjects of surveillance regimes. Native and colonial men misunderstood one another, and they disagreed often, yet they concurred that women and children belonged under their watch. Early moderns navigated the tumult they created together through the relationships they cemented with one another. Individuality was anathema to all of them. No one would be left alone.[12]

The Nausets returned John Billington. They could have tortured and executed him, and had he been full-grown, and had they wanted to escalate their conflict with Plymouth, this might have been a smart decision. The boy's young age opened other possibilities. They could have tried to assimilate him. Native groups throughout North America adopted captive women and children. Colonization fueled the practice as Native nations resisted the decimations of war, slavery, and disease by taking in strangers attained through battle and raiding. The Hurons from the Great Lakes region, for example, "stript" and enslaved the lost people they found in their woods. In relational space, not knowing up from down could land you in an alternative family or a coerced labor situation as well as an unknown place. The Algonquians' catch-and-release calculations existed alongside other political reckonings.[13]

## WILDERNESS REFLECTION

The New England woods represented a confused jumble for some and a managed hunting ground for others. A fractious lot, human beings jammed spaces with multiple perspectives. Riven by class, gender, faith, age, race, occupation, nationality, taste, and ability, humans looked out onto the world through kaleidoscopes of disagreement. One of the first orders of business for any social group was the creation and imposition of shared space. Parents and teachers nurtured common grounds; judges and priests drew lines of authority and morality; bureaucrats and soldiers codified and defended territories. Neither empty nor benign nor singular nor a priori, space was a social and a political project that was never truly settled.[14]

As with the sites they occupied, colonies were never truly settled. The social challenge of colonies announced itself in their declarations of purpose. New England produced two famous mission statements: the Mayflower Compact and John Winthrop's "A Modell of Christian Charity," a sermon given in 1630 to commemorate the founding of the Massachusetts Bay Colony. Without irony, the radical Protestant factions invoked teamwork as their guiding impulse and secret weapon.[15]

The signers of the *Mayflower* agreement pledged to "Covenant and Combine ourselves together in a Civil Body Politic, for our better ordering and preservation." While the Pilgrims sang the tune of cooperation, Winthrop and his Puritans banged it like a gong: "Wee must be knitt together, in this worke, as one man. We must entertain each other in brotherly love. Wee must be willing to abridge ourselves of our superfluities, for the supply of other's necessities. . . . We must delight in eache other; make other's conditions our oune; rejoice and suffer together, allwayes haueving before our eyes our commission and community in worke, as members of the same body. Soe shall wee keepe the unitie of spirit in the bond of peace." If they remained true to one another, God would bless their enterprise. This was the blueprint, the plan for society and space. The Protestants covenanted together to plant foreign lands they considered untended, disordered, and free for the taking. Conquest and community reinforced each other as the wilderness prompted the radical Protestants to stick together and stay militant.[16]

Plymouth's Robert Cushman further summarized how this conception of space and community would impact the people already in those spaces: "This then is a sufficient reason to prove our going thither to live lawful: their [the Indians'] land is spacious and void, and there are few and do but run over the grass, as do also the foxes and wild beasts. They are not industrious, neither have they art, science, skill, or faculty to use either the land or the commodities of it, but all spoils, rots, and is marred for want of manuring, gathering, etc. . . . It is lawful now to take a land which none useth, and make use of it." According to Cushman, the wildness of New England arose from the inability of the Native inhabitants to stay put, bind together, and yoke their labor to the environment. Instead, they flitted over the surface like animals, leaving no signs of permanence, improvement, or ownership. Their lack of community nixed their claims to space.[17]

Cushman wrote to an English audience without fear of Algonquian fact checkers. It would have been easy for them to point out his shamelessness. Cushman and his coauthors wrote to reassure the colony's London investors and potential immigrants that Plymouth's future looked bright. In the 1620s, however, the colony produced more strife than profit. The colonists were the ones struggling to govern themselves and to subdue the land. The fur-trade and cod-fishing ventures were slow to develop, and Plymouth's economic failures stoked religious and social dissension. The English were starving, bickering, and plotting mutinies. Cushman defended the colonists' right to take Indian land by ignoring the ample proof of Algonquian material success and effective resource management. When he described people running amuck, he was painting a portrait of his own tribe.

In January 1621, Plymouth colonists John Goodman and Peter Brown got lost in the woods. The two men spent a terrifying night outside, a stint in the darkness that included an assault, they swore, by roaring lions. Goodman and Brown were out cutting thatch when they decided to take a walk during their lunch break. They strolled by a lake with their dogs, a "great Mastiff bitch" and a spaniel. The dogs caught the scent of a deer and gave chase. Goodman and Brown followed "so far as they lost themselves, and could not find the way back, they wandered all the afternoon being wet, and at night it did freeze and snow." The sun set, and their perplexity grew. They were meatless and friendless. They could find "none of the savages habitations." Forced to "make the earth their bed," the men heard animal sounds in the distance. The roars came closer and closer. Goodman and Brown hauled themselves and the mastiff up a tree, leaving the spaniel to fend for himself. They put the aggressive dog in a headlock to prevent her from running after the beasts out to eat them. As the night wore on, the bellowing stopped, and Goodman and Brown climbed down. They circled the tree for hours trying to keep warm and continued their journey at first light. They passed "many lakes and brookes and woods" until they discovered a five-mile clearing where the "Savages had burnt the space." A high hill afforded them a view. From atop a wassaum patámoonck in the wèta, they spotted the bay and made their way back to Plymouth.[18]

Eight months later, John Billington followed them into the void. The disappearance of wayward colonists epitomized the chaos that traveled with them. Turned around, walking in circles, lost English men, women, and children ran into figments of their own confusion.

That a Billington contributed to Plymouth's turmoil came as no surprise. The family had a reputation for disarray. In an era when households served as microcosms for society, the Billingtons behaved more like a rowdy gang than a little commonwealth. The parents, John Sr. and Elinor, let their children run loose, and they repeatedly exchanged bitter words with their neighbors and the Plymouth authorities. Instead of being happy with the small plot of land the colony assigned him, John Sr. scoured the woods for deerskins and precious stones. The family's rebellion unfolded in a series of social clashes played out in cramped spaces.

The first location to reveal the family's explosive potential was a ship's hold. Francis, the youngest son, fired his father's musket belowdecks on the *Mayflower*. The weapon showered sparks over an open barrel of gunpowder, nearly exploding the boat and its passengers before they made landfall. Transatlantic crossings tested communal sensibilities. Jammed together, swapping germs and verbal barbs, travelers watched sympathies fray in a setting that afforded no escape and little refuge. The *Mayflower* sailed into fiercer civil and digestive storms than most. Scurvy plagued the ship, and the Separatists (radical Protestants who had quit the Anglican Church) fought with the "strangers," a slight majority of the colonists who possessed more conventional Protestant views. Factions divided the colony from the start. The Separatists filled many of the leadership positions, but strangers, like Miles Standish, an experienced soldier put in charge of security by the Plymouth Company, also performed government functions and sided with the radicals. The colony's leaders wrote the Mayflower Compact to end squabbles and stop some of the strangers' more "discontented and mutinous speeches" from withering the colony before its planting. An accomplished spewer of malice, John Billington Sr. signed the document, the poorest individual to do so. For him, the agreement was less a "positive, original, social compact" than a restraining order.[19]

It did not hold him for long. In March 1621, Governor Bradford sentenced Billington to be hogtied in public for loudly criticizing Standish. The accused begged for forgiveness and Bradford relented, it being a first offense. Two months after the elder John's near humiliation, young John went missing. In their accounts of his rescue, neither Bradford nor Edward Winslow, the representative sent to bring him back, explained John's reason for venturing into the woods. He may have been out searching for sassafras or gold or Indian corn, some commodity that might benefit his family. The Billingtons seemed eager to explore their surroundings. Prior to John's disappearance, his little brother Francis, the child with the twitchy trigger finger, discovered the Billington Sea.

In January 1621, Francis went in search of a prospect and found one after clamoring up a tall tree on a high hill outside of Plymouth. From the perch, the fourteen-year-old spotted "a great sea," or so "he thought," a mile or two inland. A week later, Francis and a shipmaster's mate walked to the spot to reconnoiter the intriguing natural body and its possible link to the Pacific Ocean. They explored the shoreline and discovered that while the freshwater pond was substantial, measuring six miles in circumference, it was neither a boggling wonder nor a passage to the Orient. The teens did locate Town Brook, the lake's feeder stream and Plymouth's future water supply.[20]

The "Billington Sea" was a joke and John Jr.'s ramble on Cape Cod triggered a diplomatic crisis, yet the boys' errors in the wilderness ranked among the Billingtons' best days in Plymouth. After John Jr. returned, indignities swamped the household. In 1623, during the first division of the colony's land, the Billingtons received three instead of the four shares owed them. The reason for the shortfall was young John's absence. He had left the family to join Richard Warren's household, perhaps as a servant. He died with the Warrens at the age of twenty-five after an illness, and John Sr. persisted in speaking ill of others in public. In 1624, Bradford accused him of belonging to a rebellious crowd of malcontents who were sending disparaging letters about the Separatist leadership of the colony to the London investors. In 1625, Billington squabbled with Robert Cushman, sent by Bradford to London to placate said investors, prompting the governor to write Cushman and warn him that "Billington still rails against you, and threatens to arrest you, I know not wherefore, he is a knave, and so will live and die." In 1626, the London Company cut its losses and turned the plantation over to the colonists. Again, land and livestock were divided. Although an original planter and a signer of the Mayflower Compact, John Billington was awarded the smallest per capita allotment of all the colonists. He and his family had become marginal participants in a sinking colonial venture. In 1630, the Plymouth authorities sentenced John Billington to death for the murder of John Newcomin. Billington admitted to shooting his neighbor, but he claimed it was an accident. He thought the man was a deer. The jury believed otherwise. Everyone knew Billington hated Newcomin. The two had fought openly. Billington pled for mercy. His fellow colonists searched their hearts and found none. Billington's widow, Elinor, carried on his work. In 1636, she was whipped and placed in the stocks for slandering John Doane, a deacon of Plymouth's congregation.[21]

John Billington Sr. died just as Plymouth Colony discovered a means to secure its economic future. The founding of Massachusetts Bay Colony led to an influx of over twenty thousand English migrants. Plymouth Colony settled into an agricultural groove. The old settlers sold maize and livestock to the newcomers, and the English colonies entered their "Ponzi scheme" decade. Instead of mining gold, trading furs, or hooking and salting cod, established colonists provisioned green recruits. When the English Civil War stopped the flow of Puritans, the New England colonies gradually shifted to trading grain, livestock, and timber with the sugar plantations in the West Indies. Looking back, it is easy to assume that the English colonists were destined to become farmers. Yet few of the men who journeyed to New England plowed the earth back home, and the 1620s were filled with experimental searches for commodities. Agriculture was a colonial improvisation, an adjustment made on the fly rather than a fated outcome.[22]

John Billington Sr., for one, did not seem overly enamored with laboring in the fields. He spent his time in the woods with his gun. The wèta rubbed off on him. Thomas Morton, the leader of Merry Mount, a rival English colony that traded furs for its livelihood and gave the Plymouth authorities fits, called Billington "Old Woodman" and recounted an alternative version of the encounter that stretched his neck: "Billington that was choaked at Plimmouth after hee had played the unhappy Markes man when hee was pursued by a carelesse fellow." According to Morton, Billington was not loathed by all but rather "beloved by many," especially those who, like Morton, combed New England's forests for materials to trade and improve their lots. Morton recalled Billington's interest in the whetstones found on Richmond Island. A sharpshooter with a sharp tongue, it's fitting that Billington was remembered for seeking rocks that honed edges.[23]

The Billingtons left their marks on Plymouth, but a humorous place-name, a missing-person hullabaloo, and a lengthy criminal record were not the monuments to posterity the English came to cherish. They celebrated the towns, the farms, and the churches they planted in New England. They enshrined their agrarian improvisation as the only course they could have followed, and they contrasted their manured fields and settled habitations with the wilderness outside their communities. Their settlements shone like beacons because the "wild and savage hue" of the wilderness provided a contrast. The bleakness of the woods made the radical Protestant's model communities stand out.

The Plymouth government saved one Billington from the wilderness and choked another for orchestrating a murder in the woods. The forest may have opposed their civilization, but it was the English who unsettled the interior. The colonists saw an empty space where there was a wèta. They dropped or floated into a fantasy hellscape, a reflection of their fears and orneriness, and then called upon the Algonquians to retrieve them when they lost their way.

## LOST ON THE BANKS OF RIVERS

In 1615, the French commander Samuel de Champlain became bewildered in the woods north of Lake Ontario. He had traveled to the region in the company of a Huron war party. After laying siege to a fortified Iroquois town, the Hurons decided to retreat for the winter after reinforcements failed to appear. Champlain left Quebec to fight in the war. Spending the cold months with the Hurons did not appeal to him, so he asked the expedition's leaders to help him canoe back home. They tasked four men to escort him back to the French colony. In preparation for the voyage, the men left camp early one morning to hunt for deer. Bored left alone, Champlain decided to follow behind with his gun. A strange bird caught his attention. The fowl was the size of a hen with the beak of a parrot. Its body was yellow, its wings were blue, and its head was red. Hoping to kill it, Champlain chased the bird, which flew in short spurts, like a partridge, from tree to tree. When the bird disappeared, Champlain looked around and realized that he had no clue where he was. He wandered the woods for the next three days, praying to God for a rescue and cursing himself for forgetting his compass. He finally happened upon a waterfall he recognized and followed the stream down to his escorts' camp. The Hurons "begged" Champlain "not to stray off from them any more." Their foremost concern was not the French officer's health or life but rather the political consequences of him not coming back. "If you had not come, and we had not succeeded in finding you," they explained, "we should never have gone again to the French, for fear of their accusing us of having killed you." To protect themselves from accusations, the Hurons assigned a "savage companion" to follow Champlain at all times. The Frenchman marveled at his guide's geographic knowledge. The man "knew how to find again the place from which he started so well that it was something very remarkable." For the Hurons, providing navigational assistance to blundering colonials was good politics.[24]

The colonists' concept of the wilderness presupposed that there were spaces that lay beyond the control of human politics, that there existed sites where nature governed itself. But colonial spaces were never outside politics. Indeed, campsites, portages, and creek-side hunting grounds only appeared lonely and wild. In truth, they were intensely political, attracting multiple powers who clashed over territorial rights, military honors, slaves, and access to European trade goods and alliances. The violence along the water's edge provides a contrast to the amiability found in the wèta of New England. Like the Algonquians' burnt-over woods, portages and camping spots drew competing visions and social practices. Unlike in the wèta, here European evangelists and traders found more hostility than hospitality. In these contested spaces, rival nations stole, enslaved, and executed strays for political ends.

The French sailed the coast of North America and floated into the continent's interior. Watercourses were their forest paths. They sailed and paddled to find and avoid people. Rivers structured their empire by connecting fur traders, military commanders, and Catholic evangelists to Native American customers, allies, and converts. To reach Indian partners, French canoeists had to navigate the political geography of watersheds. This meant confronting the power dynamics of their own crews first. Waterborne travelers ceded autonomy to captains and coxes while afloat. Rivers and streams wandered while sailors and paddlers remained stowed and seated. Navigators took charge and oriented groups, reducing individual choice and self-determination. Shoreline interludes restored independence, which made the portages and campsites dangerous and frightening. Companies broke apart to explore the countryside. Hunters traipsed into the woods and went missing. Priests strolled down the wrong paths and never came back.

Traveling outfits feared the water's edge. The land belonged to unknown people and spirits with uncertain agendas. The difference between camping and trespassing lay in the eye of the beholder; the same rivers that carried traders and missionaries into the interior also transported war parties seeking revenge and captives as well as unpredictable nonhumans alert to offensive behavior. Travelers who wandered away from camps and companies sometimes met ominous fates. Walks in the woods ended in kidnappings or mashed skulls. The uncertainty and threat of violence drove the voyagers back into the currents. The risk was too high for expeditions to rest for days or wait for lost compatriots to return. Traveling parties moved on, praying that wandering persons would catch up at the next anchorage.

For the French, tensions between water transportation and land exploration surfaced early. In 1604, Pierre Dugua, Sieur de Mons, sailed the coast of Nova Scotia, clutching a royal patent that declared him the lord of Acadia. After confronting an illegal trader named Rossignol, seizing his goods, and expelling him from his unauthorized coastal fort, de Mons rounded Cape Sable and ordered the ship anchored in the bay of St. Mary. A priest named Aubry went ashore and "was lost in the woods." The priest's disappearance raised suspicion. In a world governed by providence and malevolence—the devil was an active presence in the early modern era—accidents and bad turns happened for reasons. Aubry had exchanged harsh words with a Protestant shipmate during the voyage across the Atlantic. De Mons had the Protestant arrested. "They waited for [Aubry] for several days, firing guns and sounding trumpets, but in vain; the noise of the sea was so great that no other sound could be heard." After two weeks, they sailed on to explore the peninsula and the Bay of Fundy, down one priest but accompanied by one increasingly nervous Protestant, suspected of having somehow killed Aubry with his wicked speech. In time, the man's outlook improved: "The priest was afterward found alive, but almost starved to death."[25]

Decades later, on a different watercourse, a lost French priest instigated a political crisis. In the spring of 1680, Father Gabriel Ribourde, a French priest in the Recollect Order assigned to the Illinois country, watched months of work torn asunder in seconds. An invading army of Iroquois and Miami mauled the Illinois settlement he was attempting to save. Father Gabriel knew the Iroquois. Years earlier, he had spent time in their villages ministering to them. Following an initial skirmish that bloodied both sides yet left the armies undaunted (the Illinois counted more warriors; the Iroquois and Miami carried more guns), Gabriel and his mission partner, Father Zenobe, tried to broker a cease-fire. The Iroquois and Miami declared that they were starving. The priests asked the Illinois to give the invaders some maize. The sides exchanged food, hostages, "Beaver's Skins, and other Furrs." A promising start, until the Iroquois and Miami, under the cover of peace, approached the Illinois village, knocked down the "mausoleums"— the raised platforms where the Illinois preserved and honored their dead— and destroyed the cornfields. They forced their way into the village and captured eight hundred women and children, tying their hands and collaring their necks with leather thongs in preparation for the long march east to Iroquoia. The surviving Illinois men were burned at the stake or sliced up and eaten.

After observing "the confusion," Fathers Gabriel and Zenobe were brought before the Iroquois leaders, who gave them a set of instructions: Go home and tell what you have seen. Send your "black-gowns" and traders with guns for sale to visit and live with us. But do not pray and trade with the Illinois. To ensure the French got their message, the Iroquois and Miami chiefs gave the priests a letter to present to the authorities in Quebec spelling it out.[26]

Fathers Gabriel and Zenobe joined the French exodus from the Illinois country led by Henri de Tonti, the commander of Fort Crevecoeur, the military and trading outpost in the region. At noon on the first day of the retreat, Father Gabriel's canoe hit a rock in the Illinois River and began taking on water. The oarsmen steered the vessel to shore and worked to repair the leak. While they patched, Father Gabriel went for a stroll. The "fine meadows, the little Hills, and the pleasant Groves" "charm'd" him. He walked for hours, absorbing the beauty of the woods and prairies. The enclosures seemed planned, "dispers'd at such distances, that they look as if they had been planted on purpose to adorn the Country." The delightful pattern induced a reverie. The scenery transported him from the horror of watching the poor savages he intended to bring to God enslaved, tormented, and driven away. A jubilant and distracted Father Gabriel "went so far into those Woods, that he lost his Way."[27]

At least that's how Father Louis Hennipen wanted to remember his mentor's final moments. Father Gabriel did not return from his walk to give his version of the events. As the afternoon passed and Father Gabriel's absence grew worrisome, Father Zenobe jogged into the woods calling out Gabriel's name. After a short while, Tonti put a stop to the shouting. The Iroquois and Miami were still about on this side of the river and the whole region was up in arms; he wanted to put leagues between him and the Illinois country. Tonti commanded Zenobe and the others to return to the boats. They crossed the river and camped for the night. They built a bonfire and fired their guns, hoping Father Gabriel could use the glow and the reports to find his way out of the woods and meet them on the shore the next morning. At dawn, they circled back to resume the search. They found tracks in the glades and prairies, but the elderly feet that had made them were nowhere to be found. Tonti ended the effort at three in the afternoon. Father Zenobe fumed. He cursed Tonti as a coward for retreating across the river the day before when the tracks were still fresh. The French pushed into the Illinois River, having lost a mission, a fort, and a sixty-five-year-old priest, "generally lov'd by all that knew him."[28]

At the pull-out where Father Gabriel lost his way, the concept of the wilderness rolled over like an unevenly packed canoe in a crosscurrent. The Iroquois and Miami invaded to disrupt the budding French and Illinois alliance. A geopolitical struggle capsized Father Gabriel's mission and filled the shorelines of his retreat with portents of violence. Fighting humans made the pull-out chaotic. Hennipen erased the menace. He contrasted the horror of the attack on the village, the burning flesh and the anthropophagy, with the symmetry and the beauty of the woods and meadows. According to him, the garden landscape restored the peace the Illinois' defeat shattered. Hennipen's politics shaped the woods and clearings as much as God's hand or the Iroquois' and Miamis' brutality. He wrote to wound Tonti. He wanted the commander held to account for abandoning the Illinois country and for leaving the priest behind. He blamed both on Tonti's weak spine. Thus, politics of one sort or another surrounded Father Gabriel. The imagined wilderness offered an escape from the turmoil of human violence and incompetence. The wilderness charmed with its orderliness. He got lost in the only interior space that seemed to have a plan.

Months after Tonti and Zenobe returned from the Illinois country, the French authorities learned of Father Gabriel's fate. A Kickapoo raiding party, hidden in the tall grass, had ambushed him and stove in his head, perhaps within an hour of the boat's landing. Father Gabriel was executed in a conflict zone, a space of disputed jurisdiction. Politics not only lurked in the garden, politics created the garden and determined who stayed or crossed over.

Father Aubry launched a tradition of lost French priests on Cape Sable. Father Gabriel counted as a prominent member of this fraternity, but perhaps the most enduring missing French father was Réne Ménard. A member of the Jesuit Order, Ménard traveled from Quebec to serve as a missionary in Huronia in 1641. He went on to minister to the Nipissings and other Algonquian tribes. In 1660, he began a stint with the "Outaouas." The Odawa group Ménard hoped to convert was leaving the Great Lakes for a territory farther down the Mississippi River, near the "Black River." Ménard joined their fleet along with a French fur trader who assisted the priest, mainly by rowing the canoe. After crossing Lake Michigan, the group entered a river moving south. Slow paddlers, Ménard and his countryman lost contact with the Odawas. The pair's progress was slowed further by a set of rapids. The trader pulled over, above the crashing water, and let the priest ashore. He told Ménard to follow the portage, the path worn into the brush canoeists used to haul their goods around the obstacle to keep their property safe and dry. He would take the canoe through alone and meet the priest below the white water. Ménard promptly chose the wrong path, following a deer trail into the woods instead of the human track back to the river. He walked into the interior and was never heard from again. After waiting at the bottom for hours, the trader muscled his way back up the rapids. He searched for Ménard until he ran into a group of Sauks. They told him that they had seen the priest's footprints alongside signs of a Sioux raiding party. They theorized that the Sioux had grabbed him and taken him west into lands that would become Wisconsin. Ménard still haunts the Upper Midwest. He became one of the region's founding fathers. Like Manzano in Alabama, he has served generations of Americans as a retroactive launching point for their history. An adopted Wisconsinite and representative white guy, Ménard initiated history with a wrong turn taken in someone else's territory.[29]

## THE WILDERNESS IN TRANSLATION

In New England, the squabbling Billingtons were the warm-up act for the symphony of discord that followed. The English settlements were thick with intramural conflicts. One of the more spectacular melt-downs occurred in 1635 when the Massachusetts Bay Colony court banished Roger Williams. A fervent Separatist, Williams questioned both Massachusetts Bay and Plymouth's dedication to ridding their churches of the vestiges of Catholicism. He also voiced his concerns about the authority of King James to issue colonial charters without first purchasing the land from the Indians. An antiauthoritarian on conservative grounds, Williams argued that the church and government erred when they mistook their rules for God's commands. He was a prime example of religious sectarianism, factions begetting more factions. Williams and his followers left Massachusetts Bay and settled among the Narragansetts in a village they named Providence and a colony that would become Rhode Island.[30]

True to his beliefs, Williams inhabited land he purchased from the Narragansetts. He was dedicated to fostering amicable relations with his Indian neighbors—to show Winthrop and Bradford how it should be done—and he learned the Algonquian language spoken by the Narragansetts and most of New England's first peoples. In 1643, he published *A Key into the Language of America* to share what he had gleaned. In the section devoted to the vocabulary of geographic movement, Williams attached a poem about the wilderness. The middle stanza dwelt on hardship.

> Lost many a time, I have had no Guide
> No House, but hollow tree!
> In stormy Winter night no Fire
> No Food, no Company.

Williams used the poem to establish his credentials as a wilderness guide of the spiritual persuasion. He was by no means a model woodsman. He froze, starved, and slept in rotting logs. He and his fellow colonists got lost frequently: "I have heard of many *English* lost, and have oft been lost me selfe." But moving through the forest with ease and skill, learning the system of trails, and perfecting survival techniques like starting fires and constructing shelters was beside the point. For all paths and privations led to God: "God makes a Path, provides a Guide, And feeds in Wilderness." In him, Williams "found a House, a Bed, a Table, Company." The wilderness was a negative space where English colonists imagined the inverse of home. In the forest, the walls fell away and the furniture disappeared. This exposure, Williams argued, was a good thing. Stripped of material comforts, wilderness travelers left the ground and rose toward a higher power. "The same sun," Williams wrote, "shines on the Wildenesse that doth on the Garden!" Whether luxuriating in an earthly paradise or lost in "a howling Wildernesse," believers needed to understand that moving closer to God was the point, not finding succor along the way.[31]

The colonists' wilderness moved along two axes in New England. One was horizontal; it lay down in the dirt and stretched away, out there into the woods, swamps, briars, and mountains. The other was vertical, funneling inward and up, toward the realm of spirit where Christians could shed their material infatuations. The wilderness robbed and shocked people. It emptied their bellies and stole their pillows. Divines like Roger Williams perceived opportunity in the abuse. The prospect of being cut loose from the earth excited him. The exclamation points he sprinkled throughout the *Key* betrayed his eagerness to break away. The specter of lost English people rising above the ground recalls William Bradford's description of John Billington Jr.'s nature shock, his drifting up and down. For the colonists, getting lost in the wilderness was a blend of horizontal and vertical movement. It was a ramp. And they aimed to lift off.

Still, while the Christians aspired to rise above the earth, they required Indian help to navigate the woods. Indeed, their need of assistance escalated with the desire to reach a celestial plain. They traveled poorly because their attention lay elsewhere. While Williams and his fellow Christians craved the sensation of floating, in reality they moved on the backs of Indian guides. The colonists imposed their religious wilderness, an imagined space, upon the wèta, a social and biological space overseen by the region's Algonquians.

"It is admirable," Williams wrote, "to see, what paths their naked hardned feet have made in the wildernesse." New England was not a trackless wilderness but rather a worn, intelligible landscape. Trails led everywhere important. The Christians struggled to decipher the landmarks. *Mayuo? Is there a way? Tou nishin meyi? Where lies the way? Kokotemiinnea meyi. Shew me the way.* So they paid escorts to get them around. *Muachase. Be my guide. Kuttaunckquittaunch. I will pay you. Kummuchickonckquatus. I will pay you well.* "The wilderness being so vast," Williams wrote, "it is a mercy that for a hire a man shall never want guides." The English bargained for mobility. They overcame geographic ignorance with trade goods. While their minds drifted heavenward, their hired legs tied them to the earth, albeit haphazardly. Williams hinted at tensions. The Algonquians, for example, moved faster than the colonists. "They are generally quick on foot, brought up from the breasts to running." *Cummattanish. I will follow you. Cuppahimmin. Stay with me. Tawhich quaunqua quean? Why do you run so? Cussasaqus. You are Slow.* Indian guides took clients deep into the interior. Williams recalled journeys of twenty, thirty, and forty miles. He marveled at their woodcraft: "They are so exquisitely skilled in all the body and bowels of the Country." They led him on a "streight course" through forests without paths that he could discern. Their prowess contrasted with Williams's vulnerability. On the trail, he depended on the Indians to keep him alive. *Aquie Kunnickatshash. Doe not Leave me. Mat Kunnickansch. I will not leave you.*[32]

Like Williams, the writer William Wood commended southern New England Indians for assisting English colonists. He included several examples of lost travelers, hunters, and runaways in *New England's Prospect*, a promotional book he published in 1634 based on observations he made while living in Massachusetts Bay Colony from 1630 to 1633. Wood hyped the climate, soils, waters, beasts, and forests of New England. In his hands, the place brimmed, teemed, and afforded. Its prospects glowed. Yet even when placed in the best possible light, New England retained its dark corners. The landscape was too complicated and unfamiliar for the English to navigate on their own. Colonists, Wood admitted, should expect to get lost. And they should expect to lean on Indian hospitality to move out and back from the coast. Thankfully, Wood reassured, the Indians near the settlements were willing hosts. They watched the forests and plucked ramblers from danger.

Wood got lost himself. After surveying the countryside outside Plymouth, he and his associates followed the wrong path back. The day was gloomy, making navigation by the sun impossible, and they had left their compass at home. Night fell with the men having "not gain[ed] an inch . . . for a dayes travel." Flummoxed and hungry, they finally spotted a wigwam. The owner invited them to spend the night and shared a "haunch of a fat Beere." The next morning, Wood paid the son of his "naked" host a plug of tobacco for a "clew." The boy conducted them "through the strange labyrinth of unbeaten bushy wayes in the woody wilderness twenty miles to our desired harbor."[33]

The promotional literature for New England played down fears about getting lost in the wilderness by depicting the Indians as good Samaritans and willing servants. Eager to assist and to do as the colonists bid them, the savages emerged from the confusion of nature to ease colonists into the new landscape. They played host to befuddled guests, and their assistance became a landmark memory, a golden chapter in the stories New Englanders (and later Americans) told themselves about the colonization of the region and the continent. In his 1818 history of early Connecticut, Benjamin Trumbull included an ode to Native cooperation. Instead of fighting them, the Indians took the first settlers under their wing. "They," wrote Trumbull, "instructed them in the manner of planting and dressing the Indian corn. They carried them upon their backs, through rivers and waters. . . . They gave them much useful information respecting the country, and when the English or their children were lost in the woods and were in danger of perishing with hunger or cold, they conducted them to their wigwams, fed them, and restored them to their families and parents." In their promotional literature and their history books, the English and their descendants anticipated and then remembered a moment in time when the Indians helped them stay safe and together in a howling desert.[34]

### RELATIONS OF RESCUE

*Pitchcowawwon. You will lose your way. Meshnowawwon. I lost my way.* Navigating relational spaces could be treacherous. The intricacies of Native American territorial claims and foreign policies sent travelers reeling. Political cluelessness could get you hopelessly lost or perfectly dead. But it could also introduce you to an ally. Cut from their herd, stray humans became targets of calculation, pawns savvier operators moved or sacrificed to pursue domestic and foreign policies. By killing Father Gabriel, for example, the Kickapoos antagonized both the French and the Iroquois, who had granted Tonti's evacuees safe passage to deliver their letter. They could have chosen differently, opening a path that ended with a live priest. Short-term captives were bargaining chips, while permanent adoptees replaced dead family members or were used and traded as slaves. Father Gabriel was probably too old and too male to be adopted. But there was no reason why, had they decided it was in their best interest, the Kickapoos couldn't have held him for a ransom. Or they could have simply shown him the way back to the river to curry favor with the French and the Iroquois. Native Americans helped lost colonists, traders, and missionaries. They murdered some strays and returned others to their folds.[35]

In some colonial settings, Indian helpers entered family lore. The Boydens lived in the Delaware River valley, coming to North America sometime between 1638 and 1655 to farm in New Sweden, a short-lived colony established by Gustavas Aldophus the Great. The Boydens had an "adopted daughter" whose job it was to herd the family's cattle out of the nearby swamps. One rainy day, she went after the cows and got lost in the swamp. She "wandered the wet three days and nights until too weak to go farther," and she collapsed in a weepy pile. A Lenape man heard her crying, took pity on her, and carried her home. According to the family, the incident explained the daughter's lasting tie to her Lenape neighbors: "She always retained a peculiar friendship and esteem for the Natives." In the family's telling, the girl's getting lost brought their ancestors and the Indians together, fostering the cross-cultural amity for which early Pennsylvania was known.[36]

The assistance Indians offered lost people was never as straightforward as it may have seemed to the colonists. For example, the Boydens' adopted daughter bonded with the Lenape in part because she had "learned their language in her infancy." Was she indigenous herself? Might she have been an enslaved "adoptee" running into the wilderness rather than a Swedish girl trying to escape from it? Wilderness rescues reflected many angles and offered many interpretations. What the colonists took for lucky encounters might have been sweeps performed by Indians to rid themselves of unwelcome foreigners. The Natives did not always wait for lost colonists to stumble into them. They actively searched for missing people.

In 1634, two Massachusetts Bay colonists, "one Scott and Eliot of Ipswich," were bewildered on "their way homewards, and wandered up and down six days, and ate nothing. At length they were found by an Indian." William Wood told the story of an "unexperienced wood man" out hunting deer. He traveled far into the forest and could not retrace his course: "The more he fought to direct himselfe out, the more he ranne himself in." It was winter and snow covered the ground. His right foot froze, immobilizing him, and he lay down to die. Six "commiserating Indians," who had heard (from whom Wood does not say) of an English hunter in peril, mounted a rescue mission. They found him in his "snowie bed," wallowing in despair. They bucked him up with strong words and liquor, constructed a stretcher, and carried him twelve miles to his home. Wood shared these details to calm doubts. Prospective settlers needn't worry about their inexperience getting them lost in the wilderness, for the Indians were "well acquainted with the craggy mountains, and the pleasant vales, the stately woods, and swampie groves, the spacious ponds, and swift running rivers." They knew all the paths and all the locales by name. And they "left no place unsearched" as they made their rounds hunting deer, checking traps, and maintaining their sovereignty over territories they considered their own.[37]

Judged by their actions, the Algonquians of southern New England surveilled interlopers and rescued lost colonists when the circumstances proved advantageous to them. William Wood commended the Indians not only for saving lost travelers and hunters but also for retrieving runaway servants and criminals. They assisted in the apprehension of a "certain man" who fled the settlements fearing that a guilty verdict would lead to his execution. He hid in the woods, "betaking himselfe unto the obscure thickets of the wildernesse." The English had no idea where the man had gone, but the "Indians found out his haunt," alerted the governor, and led a posse to his dwelling. Wood labeled the Indians' assistance in capturing the man a form of service to the English. Yet while the retrieval may have curried favor with the powers in Plymouth, it also removed a vagrant from their hunting grounds.[38]

Ridding yourself of an English interloper in the wéta took patience and understanding. They could be offensive and unpredictable. One evening in 1631 a colonist grabbed his gun and went hunting wolves near his farmhouse in Mystic outside Boston. It grew dark, and on the way back he lost the path. He stumbled around in the gloom until he discovered the "little house" of Wonohaquaham, or Sagamore John. The shelter stood empty and secured against trespassers. With no one to let him in, the colonist huddled next to the wigwam. He built a fire and passed the night singing psalms. Near dawn, a rainstorm began. To escape a drenching, the colonist broke into the house, prying it open with a long pole. The sun rose on an awkward situation. The colonist, John Winthrop, governor of Massachusetts Bay Colony, was caught squatting in another's hovel. An Indian woman appeared at the wigwam and tried to enter. Winthrop barred the door and either bade her go away or pretended not to be there (it's unclear from his account how he handled being found out). The woman "stayed a great while essaying to get in." Finally, she gave up and left. Winthrop tumbled out and speed-walked home. His servants welcomed him back with sleepy relief. They had been out in the woods through the night firing guns and hallooing for their master.[39]

John Winthrop knew Sagamore John and his brother James quite well. They headed the Indian village at Mystic. Winthrop carved his farm out of the village's territory. Sagamore John was a host and a neighbor, and he met with Winthrop frequently in his role as a middleman between the English on the coast and the Indian groups living farther in the interior. The colonists leaned on go-betweens like Sagamore John to communicate with other Indians and other colonists. If they sent their own messengers into the woods, they might get lost and require Indian assistance. Having the Natives carry the mail cut down on the rescue missions. In April 1631, Sagamore John delivered a letter from John Endecott to Winthrop that contained a plea from an interior sagamore named Wahginnacut requesting the English to send colonists to live near him and trade for furs. In June that same year, Sagamore John appeared before the Massachusetts Bay court in Boston with another Indian leader, Chickatabot, to "make satisfaction" for "their men" injuring the colonists' cattle and shooting one of their pigs. Later, Sagamore John appealed to Winthrop to help settle a conflict with an English fur trader. Sagamore John and his brother James died in the 1633 smallpox epidemic that swept southern New England. Before his death, he was carried to Boston, where he struck a final bargain. He offered wampum and other gifts to the English to care for him and raise his son among them. If he survived, he promised to live with them as well and "serve their God." Winthrop ushered his neighbor and diplomatic partner into the afterlife by noting that Sagamore John had persuaded himself "that he should go to the Englishmen's God." The governor couldn't hide his skepticism. Winthop's Puritan heaven was more difficult to break into than Sagamore John's hut, and the men's relationship symbolized how even when the colonists and the Indians cooperated in New England, they kept their doors locked and their paradises to themselves.[40]

The humans in southern New England never stood together against the wilderness. Politics filled the emptiest spaces and colored the alliances meant to ease the passage of information and people. The Indians nearest Massachusetts Bay and Cape Cod were experiencing a demographic collapse. They needed friends, and by carrying messages and rescuing lost colonists, they won them. Plus, escorting strays out of the woods served the same purpose as violent confrontations. Most lost colonists had little clue or care that they were trespassing in Indian territories. An ejection from the wilderness may not have taught them to understand or respect Indian sovereignty or use rights, but it did prompt them to graciously thank their hosts and guides for showing them the way out.

## ALONE

The historical records of seventeenth-century New England and the riverine interior where the French and English traded and evangelized are replete with incidents of lost people who wandered alone and were not saved. Instead of seeing these solitary strays as individuals who plunged into an unmediated experience with the wilderness, we should consider how Native territorial strategies and political decisions shaped these forays into spaces that only seemed empty. Absence may not be a reliable indicator of presence, but given the early modern context, I think a reconsideration of wilderness solitude in colonial America is warranted. Withdrawal and evasion condemned lost persons to an early modern hell. If relationships defined spaces, then withholding a connection, watching a lost person stumble around, was an aggressive move. The pull of connection was strong. Forlorn wanderers would much rather switch sides, convert to Christianity or be taken captive, than be left alone. They would rather die in the arms of an enemy than live as autonomous individuals in nature.

One of the prime advantages of knowing a home landscape was the ability to choose when or if to engage interlopers unaware of your presence. Hiding was a skill and a political strategy. In *A Key into the Language of America*, Roger Williams noted that the Algonquians used the unfired and inaccessible woods, the cuppì-machàug, as refuges to protect women and children in wartime. Noncombatants retreated to "thick woods and swamps" while the men joined the fight. Algonquian hunters practiced evading the detection of creatures far more perceptive and jittery than their fellow humans when they stalked animal prey. *Auchaûtauck. Let us hunt. Kemehétteas. Creepe. Pitch nkeméhettteem. I will Creepe.* William Wood described the Algonquians sitting back and observing when they dealt with the Plymouth vagrant who escaped from the colony's magistrate and hid in their woods. After seeing that he was "pistold, and well sworded," they opted to keep their distance and not "grapple with him." They waited until he emerged from his camp and tried to cross a river. They surrounded him at the canoe launch. He ordered them to row him across. The canoes were too tippy for him to operate himself. They acquiesced and grabbed him midstream. They delivered their prisoner to Governor Bradford, accomplishing the dual goals of expelling a bossy, well-armed malcontent and refreshing their alliance with the Pilgrims. Watchful Indians waited for lost colonists to wear themselves down and stumble into vulnerable positions before approaching them. Alternatively, if the trespassers were too dangerous or the political situation too heated, they could just let them meet their fate alone.[41]

In the winter of 1631, a Massachusetts Bay colonist named Christopher Gardiner ran into the woods. Gardiner claimed to be a knight and introduced himself as "sir" to the people in Boston. He built a house seven miles from town and lived there with his young wife, Mary. A letter arrived a month after Gardiner landed, informing Governor Winthrop that Gardiner "was noe knight, but instead thereof, had two wives now living in an house at London." Winthrop sent a group of men to arrest him. Gardiner saw them coming and slipped out the back with his gun. He evaded capture, reported Thomas Dudley, the Puritan leader who served thrice as the colony's governor, but "the way" he chose was worse than prison. Gardiner walked northward, hoping to find "some English their like himself." Dudley thought this unlikely. "Which way so ever hee went," he wrote, "hee will loose himselfe in the woods and be stopped with some rivers in the passing, and notwithstanding his compass in his pocket, and soe with hunger and cold, will perish before hee find the place hee seekes." Without Algonquian help, the fake knight was doomed.[42]

William Wood danced around the nightmare of English colonists dying alone in the wilderness in the 1630s without Indian guides to pull them out. He included several instances of colonists suffering from sudden derangement in the woods, but he approached the subject through another topic: climate. He knew his readers, prospective colonists and investors, worried about New England's weather. They believed that climate determined their health and that their bodies, which were used to the moderate temperatures of the British Isles, might not be able to survive New England's frigid winters and hot summers. Counterintuitively, Wood reassured them with two anecdotes that featured nature-shocked people. In the first story, a mentally "distracted" adult male "broke away from his Keepers" and ran "into the Wood." He "could not bee found with much seeking after." The madman wandered for four days until he "hit home through the unbeaten Woods." To everyone's surprise, he not only withstood the ordeal, tromping around without food, water, or shelter "in the deepe of Winter," he emerged saner than when he went in.[43]

This outcome was wonderfully unexpected, but the resolution of another lost-person incident struck Wood as even more "superlatively strange." A "certain Maide" set out on a short, four-mile journey in a cold snap, thinking she could make it through the woods to a neighbor's warm fire without a problem. Instead, she got turned around and "wandred sixe or seaven dayes in most bitter weather." Her bewilderment demonstrated how English bodies could bear up in the cold. She walked in circles for a week with only a bit of bread and a few sips from a fresh spring until "God by his special providence brought her to the place shee went from." The maid stayed in that place. She grew old in a climate that extended English lives rather than extinguished them.[44]

No matter the brutality of the winter, Wood chirped, pleasant springs followed in New England. The climate froze your toes and burned your skin, but in the end the environment improved you. Even the worst-case scenario, being lost alone in the woods, turned out well. Getting lost proved that English bodies belonged in the wilderness, and that getting lost in the desert invited God's favor. Providence, he reassured his readers, saved English travelers when Indians were absent or unwilling.

Wood exuded optimism in the early years of English settlement. As time passed and agrarian colonization transformed the land, getting terrifyingly lost grew more likely. Winter disorientation was always dangerous. Wayward colonists risked freezing to death, and fewer Algonquians lived near the coast to look out for them. Native villages dispersed and relocated to interior hunting grounds in the colder months. The Algonquian presence grew even smaller as the seasons turned and the years wore on. Epidemics, like the one that killed Sagamore John, reduced Algonquian populations. In 1637, the English planted towns in the Connecticut River valley, increasing their forays into the interior as settlers and messengers marched across the chunk of land that separated the bay from the river. In the fall of 1633, four Massachusetts Bay colonists "endured much misery" after losing themselves on the walk back from Connecticut. They told John Winthrop about their misadventure, and they related the news that "the small pox was gone as far as any Indian plantation was known, to the West; and many people died of it." The next year, the fifty-year-old alderman of Bear Cove lost his way between Dorchester and Wessaguscus. He "wandered in the woods and swamps for three days and two nights, without taking food." "God brought him to Scituate," wrote Winthrop, for the most part intact, "but he had torn his legs much, etc." Disease reduced the chances of colonists finding Indian help in the interior just as the growing English presence on the coast pushed Algonquians out. Fewer Indians in more desperate conditions meant more disorientation—and violence.[45]

In the summer of 1638, Roger Williams wrote to Winthrop seeking his advice regarding a "great hubbub" in Rhode Island. Weeks earlier, an Indian informed Williams that four Englishmen were lost and starving four miles to the northwest of his home in Providence. He sent a guide with provisions and "strong water." Following their rescue, Arthur Peach, his Irish servant John Barnes, and two other Plymouth men told Williams "that they came from Plymouth on the last of the week in the evening, and lay still in the woods the Lord's day, and then lost their way to Weymouth, from whence they lost their way again towards us, and came in again six miles off Pawtucket." The men seemed truly bewildered. They would need help navigating the many forests, clearings, rivers, and swamps between them and their destination—Connecticut. Williams procured them an Indian guide. *Cowéchaw éwo. He will goe with you.* After they had left, an "old Indian" visited Williams and warned him that his Native neighbors had fled their homes to be away from him and the English. They had heard a very different story about the four men, and they interpreted the kindness Williams showed the strangers as a provocation.[46]

Williams came to understand that he had abetted a crime. The four men had assaulted and robbed a currier carrying beaver skins and beads for the son of Canonicus, the Narragansett sachem. Stabbed in the leg and belly, the victim was clinging to "life's thread." Williams traveled to him and heard his version of events: the English had spotted the currier in Plymouth and set an ambush for him "in the side of a swamp a little out of the path." Arthur Peach offered the man tobacco and then knifed him. The man broke free, ran into the swamp, and hid until the robbers gave up their search. The man died soon after giving his testimony to Williams.[47]

Apprehended in Newport, the four were eventually transferred to Plymouth for trial. They confessed to the murder, and Williams and "many of the Natives" witnessed their hanging. Peach died penitent, and Winthrop memorialized him as "a young man of good parentage and fair condition, and who had done very good service against the Pequods." The opening of the English settlements in the Connecticut River valley increased English traffic in the woods and sparked a conflict with the Pequots, who controlled the lower section of the river. Arthur Peach marched to war along the paths he would later use to commit his crime. In the 1630s, the English continued to get lost in the interior, but not all who wandered were lost. War, hunting, and travel enhanced the geographic awareness to an extent that some could perpetrate a fraud and exploit the hospitality the Algonquians showed travelers.[48]

Williams believed Peach's story about getting lost between Plymouth and Providence because English colonists remained capable of earnest displays of spatial incompetence decades into their occupation of New England. In the tail end of the winter of 1641, a three-person committee "of ability and standing" marched from Salem to Dover to settle a dispute with neighboring New Hampshire. The men intended to press Massachusetts Bay Colony's claim over the territory of Piscataqua along the coast, the site of Portsmouth. The arguments about who controlled this land crossed the Atlantic and tangled the rights of multiple proprietors, colonial charters, and local residents in a political rat's nest. In the end, it wasn't the intricacies of property liens and court jurisdictions that confounded Massachusetts Bay's emissaries. On their way back, they literally could not grasp the lay of the land. "Though it be six miles, yet they lost their way," wrote Winthrop, "wandered two days and one night, without food or fire, in snow and wet. But God heard their prayers, and even when they were quite spent, he brought them to the seaside." Even as the English imposed their real estate regime on New England environments clearly in their control, a snowstorm and darkness could plunge them into bewilderment.[49]

In 1642, a man traveling at night between Dorchester and Watertown lost his way. He became "benighted in a swamp" and around ten o'clock a chorus of wolf howls caused him to lose his mind: "Fearing to be devoured by them, he cried out help, help." A colonist living near the swamp heard him yelling and called back. Their shouts raised alarms from Salem to Dorchester. The residents along the Bay thought the Indians "had gotten some English man and were torturing him." The swamps had grown more menacing since William Wood imagined them filled with Indian guides eager to escort colonists out of harm's way. The changes in the land since the 1620s materially benefited the colonists. Their population grew through immigration and natural increase and their towns proliferated. However, even as they grew dominant on the coast, the invaders did not always feel safe. A mix of geography and imagination left spaces for their bodies and their minds to run riot.[50]

In the 1660s, John Josselyn wrote about a neighbor in Maine along the Sacco River who "rashly wander[ed] out after some stray'd cattle, lost his way," and walked "into a Tract of land for God knowes how many miles full of delves and dingles, and dangerous precipices, Rocks and inextricable difficulties which did justly daunt, yea quite detere him from endeavoring to pass any further." Filled with pockets of chaos, the countryside could snatch cows and colonists at any moment. "Many such places," wrote Josselyn, "are to be met with in New-England." As the English settled into the landscape, making their own paths, nodes, and landmarks, perhaps they no longer needed the propaganda about easy climates and helpful Indians Wood and other early promoters sold. As time passed, the wilderness grew in the dark spaces New Englanders seldom visited.[51]

## PORTAGE SHOCK

Colonization opened spaces to be alone, and these voids terrified early modern people. Neither the Indians nor the colonists could abide the gaps, and they interceded to stop isolated persons from lingering in between. This was particularly true for young women, defined by their relationships to men; women's attachments formed their political identities. They were wives, daughters, servants, slaves, maids, or concubines. Men from across cultures banded together to prevent women from escaping relational space.

In 1657, a French trading outfit en route to Iroquoia came across an Indian woman secluded in a gap between indigenous and colonial space. The company had shored its canoes on a large island in the St. Lawrence River. A hunter dove into the woods to "shute for pleasure." He discovered an Indian woman "half starved for hunger, lying on a rock by a water." She was a new Christian, most likely a Huron, though the French narrator of the events does not mention her tribal affiliation. There was no doubt that she was a survivor.

The traveling party, which included French traders, Jesuit priests, and Huron and Algonquian neophytes, had camped at the site of a massacre.

Sixteen days before, another contingent of traders, priests, and converts being escorted by a group of Iroquois came to grief. According to Pierre Esprit Radisson, the Iroquois turned on the other Indians for bringing them bad luck. One of their large canoes had wrecked in the Lachine Rapids, drowning seven of their men. It was a disaster, an ill omen that made the remaining Iroquois rethink the wisdom of bringing the foreigners into their homeland. A peace treaty spared the French, but their Huron and Algonquian partners were fair game. They would bear the cost of the Iroquois' misfortune. Radisson experienced the attack as a spontaneous eruption of blood. With no warning, a war club stove in his canoe-mate's head, showering him with the other man's brains. During the melee, the woman escaped and hid in a rotten tree.[52]

After three days, she emerged to find everyone gone or dead. She looked for food. Days passed and all she could muster was a meager handful of grapes and roots. She curled up on the rocks by the river and waited for death. The French trading outfit found her there and brought her back to camp, where she was examined and given a meal of lukewarm water, flour, and grease. One of the priests recognized her as a convert and "took singular care for her." They put her in a canoe and pushed off. They caught up with Radisson's party within the week. They joined camps, and that night the woman ran away after she saw a man "charging his gunne" and thought he aimed to kill her. Radisson theorized that she may have sought seclusion in the woods to heal herself. The priest brought the Christians together to pray for the woman and observe the miracle of her surviving as long as she did on her own. He also told them to never despair, to thank God for their blessings, and to fear the Lord in heaven more than the Iroquois in their company.[53]

The group traveled on, and the woman, a "poore creature," followed, first in the form of a story, and then in person. Radisson heard that she had entered the woods and had gotten lost: "not that shee knew'd which way to tourne, but did follow owne fancy whersorever it lead her." She wandered for six days, eating "wild garlic, yong buds of trees, & roots." Then, three "hurons renegados" spotted her along the river. They grabbed her and "not considering that she was of their own nation, stript her." It was their policy, Radisson explained, "to strip whomsoever is lost in the woods." The Hurons brought the naked woman to the fort the French had constructed near today's Schenectady, New York. There she met the priest who knew her and had cared for her on the island. Radisson was at the fort as well, and he saw her. To him and the other Christians, she had become a religious object: "a thing incredible." After suffering alone in the wilderness for so long, she solidified into proof of the "mercy of god." Soon, she became another type of possession. The Iroquois escorts who had perpetrated the massacre on the island discovered that the French were holding a survivor. They took her and "makes her [their] slave."[54]

The massacre seemed to trigger an elemental and sudden derangement in the lost woman that brought her into conflict with the rules and assumptions particular to her historical moment. Radisson portrayed her as out of her mind. The violent deaths of the neophyte Hurons and Algonquians—her family?—deeply disturbed her. She seemed overwhelmed by fear and anxiety, and her panic stopped her from trusting relationships, new or old. She was—understandably, I think—evading men who carried guns, knives, and tomahawks. But her isolation was a huge problem for the men who monitored relational space. To them, young women, no matter their cultural affiliation, could not be left alone. In the North American interior, men fought with one another to control space by making or breaking alliances. There was no stepping outside these arrangements. A precondition of being alive was belonging to a family, a clan, a nation, a religion, and a master. Choosing solitude disturbed the power dynamics, and men stepped in to reassert the logic of belonging. They used force to bind women to them.

Relational space entangled all humans, but to stay connected, people sometimes had to break and remake connections. Natives and colonists moved and migrated; hundreds converted and traded sides. Radisson understood these transfers well. When a young man, he was kidnapped by a Mohawk raiding party while hunting ducks with two companions outside the French Canadian town of Trois-Rivières. The Mohawks killed the companions and hauled Radisson back to their village where a family, reeling from the loss of a son in war, adopted him. Radisson took to life among the Mohawks. He learned their language and gained their trust. After six weeks, his hosts gave him the run of the woods. Then he abused his liberty. An Algonquian adoptee convinced him to join a rebellion that grew to include twenty captives. While out hunting, the captives murdered their Iroquois overseers and tried to escape. They didn't get far. A patrol rounded them up, and Radisson and his conspirators stared down the excruciating lead-up to an Iroquois execution, an overture that featured pulled fingernails, the application of hot pokers, and severed appendages. The Algonquian received the full treatment and was put to death. Radisson endured the torture as well, but his adopted family interceded at the moment of execution and pled for his life. Their affection saved him. He lived with his family for several seasons, and after his torture wounds healed, he went on war and hunting expeditions. He witnessed the brutal reshuffling of relationships as the Mohawks captured and then killed or adopted foreigners from other regions, be they French, Dutch, Huron, or Algonquian. In the fall of 1653, Radisson visited the Dutch post of Fort Orange with his Mohawk brethren. The governor offered to ransom him from captivity. After first declining, Radisson accepted and entered the service of a Protestant nation for a year. He sailed to Holland, then eventually returned to Canada to reunite with his French family.[55]

Radisson traveled the globe, bouncing from one affiliation to another. Eventually, he partnered with his influential brother-in-law, a fur trader named Médard Chouart des Groseilliers, and traveled west to the headwaters of the Mississippi River. Des Groseilleirs and Radisson fought with the governor of New France over the profits of the fur trade. After a lengthy battle over permits and taxes, they transferred their loyalty to the English. Based in Boston, Peter Radisson became a founding partner of the Hudson's Bay Company.

A few North Americans could match Radisson's cosmopolitanism, but not many. He tumbled through social worlds. It is telling, then, that his French relatives worried about him getting lost in space rather than to another family or nation. In 1659, prior to one of his trips with des Groseilleirs, they asked him to delay the voyage. "My mother," he wrote, "opposed against it mightily saying I should bee lost in the woods and that I should gett it put off til the next yeare." Oh, Maman, you can almost hear him say. You worry too much. What could go wrong?[56]

The lost woman on the island showed how wrong it could go and why mothers fretted over traveling offspring. Twice she ventured into the woods alone, seeking to escape not only her captors but all human association. This situation was unendurable to the men who happened upon her or heard stories about her. French hunters and Huron renegades dropped their business to put an end to it. The hunter carried her to the priest, while the Hurons stripped her naked in preparation for trading her into slavery. Her solitude affronted men across cultures and regions. When she slipped the French, they sent their God after her. The Christians interpreted the woman's miraculous survival as confirmation of his loving omnipresence. Was she equally enamored with the idea of a deity monitoring her every move?

Radisson's mother needn't have worried. Her son was a social butterfly who darted from one crowd to another, buoyed by his youth, his French birth, his gender, his fighting and hunting prowess, his family connections, and his trading wealth. He used his advantages to navigate a relational world, to always belong, mostly on his terms. The lost woman possessed none of his social or material resources. Different groups of men could claim her because she had been ripped from her family and was therefore vulnerable. She moved between cultures as a slave rather than a cosmopolitan player. The woman could neither choose her associations nor could she choose to be alone. She was made to belong. Enslaved, she was a reminder that while the politics of space empowered some and imprisoned others, everyone ended up bound to someone.

Captivity combined social and geographic disruption. The failure to dislocate captives completely from their former haunts could be dangerous for adopted families. The Senecas, members of the Iroquois League of Peace and Power, or the Haudenosaunee, told the story of two boys kidnapped by the Cherokees. Away from their home territory on the southern shores of Lake Ontario on a hunting trip, the boys were left behind by the adult men to look after a camp. A Cherokee raiding party surprised them and carried the boys south. Adopted by an elderly Cherokee man who had lost his sons in battle with the Iroquois, the boys "grew up with him until they were large enough to go hunting for themselves." The brothers never forgot their former home, though one of them worried that they would not be able to find their way back. When the elder brother suggested they kill the old man and make their escape, the younger protested: "We might get lost if we run away, we are so far from home." They did murder their adopted father and return to the land of their birth. At first, they failed to recognize their own mother. The Senecas returned the strangers' confusion. The brothers looked Cherokee and their appearance frightened the group of women who spotted them on the outskirts of their village. The boys, however, could still speak Iroquoian, and the tenacity of the childhood tongue saved them. Their story was repeated over the years to celebrate how sometimes "the dead come back to life."[57]

Native families that adopted captives had to keep an eye on the new members of their households. Adoptees might stab or strangle them in their sleep; they might also run away on purpose or get lost by accident. Taken from the cultural, social, and environmental spaces they knew, captives were susceptible to nature shock. In 1689, a six-year-old English colonist named John Gyles was taken captive outside Fort Charles near Bristol, Maine, by the Maliseets, a member of the Wabanaki confederacy. Gyles spent six years with a Native master and his family. In the spring of his second year of imprisonment, a group of Wabanaki from Cape Sable entered the Maliseets camp and demanded that English captives be brought to them to be tortured and killed. The Cape Sable group had lost "some friends to English fishermen," and they were out for revenge. Gyle's master and mistress ordered him "run as for my Life in a Swamp and hide." Gyles plunged into the brush. After the Cape Sable Wabanaki left and the threat passed, the family went looking for Gyles, panicking when they could not find him right away. "I heard them say with some concern," wrote Gyles, "that they believ'd that the other Indians had frightened me into the woods, and that I was lost." When Gyles appeared, "they seem'd well pleased." Violent social disruptions bled into space. Captivity induced geographic disorientation, and it fell to Native masters to keep adoptees found and safe.[58]

The catch-and-release proclivities of southern New England Algonquians mimicked the spatial obligations that accompanied cross-cultural kidnappings. They kept watch on wandering English men, women, and children as if they were captives unfamiliar with their surroundings. During King Philip's War, the two practices merged. The Algonquians took prisoners, and they kept their eyes on them to prevent them from getting lost.

### MARY ROWLANDSON

In 1675, rebels kidnapped Mary Rowlandson from her Lancaster home in the Massachusetts Bay Colony. One of over a dozen raids perpetrated by a confederation of disaffected Algonquians from southern New England, the Lancaster attack unfolded to plan. The Nipmucks and Wampanoags struck at night. They killed as many of the town's male defenders as they could, torched their homes, and destroyed their livestock. They rounded up the surviving women and children and marched them into the woods. The rebel army moved east and north, away from the coast, away from their homes.

These captives were not destined for execution or adoption. They were held for ransom, dangled as bait. The rebels wanted the English to chase their women and children into the interior and leave the Indian fields and families alone. The wife of a prominent minister, Rowlandson would fetch a high price. After eleven weeks, the English paid £20 to redeem her.

A typical ghastly evening in a string of dark nights that constituted the regional Indian uprising known among the English as King Philip's War, the Lancaster raid stood out for what Rowlandson came to stand for. After the fighting stopped, when Metacom (King Philip) was killed and the rebel army dispersed or sold into slavery, the English struggled to explain why this calamity had befallen them. They searched for meaning, and Rowlandson led the hunt. In 1682, with the assistance of Boston minister Increase Mather, she published *The Sovereignty and Goodness of God,* a narrative of her ordeal. The book became a transatlantic best seller, the first from the colonies. It's filled with loss. Rowlandson lost friends and family during the raid. Days later, she lost an infant daughter, wounded in the fighting. She lost her dignity and her station. She lost weight (the Indians were marching on short rations and the scraps of bear and horse meat they offered repulsed Rowlandson). She almost lost her faith. Yet in the end, after all the defeats and humiliations, she was redeemed. In loss, Mary Rowlandson found God.[59]

In 1682, Rowlandson stalked for answers in an upside-down wilderness. She reversed Roger Williams's 1643 geography. Instead of a howling negation, a place with "no guide . . . no House . . . no fire . . . no food, no Company," Rowlandson's wilderness overflowed with wonderful things: snug homes, roaring fires, and happy families. Colonization turned the wilderness into home. After decades of hacking and planting, the New Englanders had settled in. Fences lined their fields. Roads connected their farms. Travelers moved easily along paths, reading the blazes locals cut into the trees. New towns popped up to join older ones. Letters arrived from the interior with regularity.[60]

All these pleasant tidings should have raised more alarms. Mary Rowlandson, for one, worried as the wilderness seemed to recede. Wallowing in "prosperity," she sometimes wished for affliction. She felt "jealous" of those "in sickness, weakness, poverty, losses, crosses, and cares of the world," for she believed God loved those he chastened and scourged. After the raid and her captivity, she saw her wish for suffering as yet one more vanity, and that word—*vanity,* as opposed to Williams's earlier *desolation*—defined a new emptiness: "The Lord hath showed me the vanity of these outward things. That they are the vanity of vanities, and vexation of spirit, that they are but a shadow, a blast, a bubble, and things of no continuance." In Rowlandson's mind, the self-absorbed Puritans had strayed from the path. They had grown complacent in their own good fortune, so delusional that some of them wished for hardship to test their faith. (In actuality, all they had to do to find trouble was step into the woods. There were fewer Algonquians looking out for their welfare. The forests were becoming more treacherous for the English.)[61]

Rowlandson and Mather revised the bounteous colonial narrative promulgated by the likes of William Wood. The book of Isaiah gave them their theme: "Thy holy cities are a wilderness, Zion is a wilderness, Jerusalem a desolation." The successful planting of New England brought spiritual ruin even as Zion rose. The rebel Indians were sent to show the English the hollowness of their accomplishments, the error of their ways. The authors of King Philip's War pressed the awful events into a template, and the book of Jeremiah offered a handy metaphor that paired getting lost and enduring hardship with reform and redemption: "My people hath been lost sheep: their shepherds have caused them to go astray and they have turned them away on the mountains: they have gone from mountain to hill, they have forgotten their resting place." The form, the jeremiad, would seem to predict an extended bout of bewilderment for Mary Rowlandson. What better way to find God than to lose oneself in an actual howling wilderness? The New England divines had been building a ramp to God in the interior for years. Mather need only push her out, into the desolation, in order for her to go up.[62]

However, the wilderness had never been empty, and even as the colonists asserted more control over their terrain, building towns and fencing fields, they sought assistance in the gaps, the dark spaces that proliferated as they colonized. Woods and swamps continued to befuddle travelers, and it became harder to find Indian escorts as sickness decimated Native populations and English aggression upset alliances. This did not stop the colonists from seeking Indian navigational assistance, even from their enemies. So, despite the narrative momentum generated by the jeremiad, Mary Rowlandson stayed on the ground and oriented through the help of her captors who plucked her from the spaces she could not navigate. Rowlandson got lost but once during her captivity, and no God rescued her. Her Indian hosts did that, demonstrating a core truth about the early moderns: they would rather spoil a plot device than leave their heroines alone.

Weeks into her ordeal, after watching her infant daughter die and contemplating suicide, Rowlandson heard that her son was being held prisoner in a nearby encampment. She asked her captors if she could go visit him. They granted her permission, and she struck out on her own. She wandered "over hills and through swamps" and quickly got lost. In this bewildered state, her mind wandered to God's mercy: "I cannot but admire at the wonderful power and goodness of God to me, though I was gone from home, and met with all sorts of Indians . . . yet not one of them offered the least imaginable miscarriage to me." She backtracked and found her Indian "master." He guided Rowlandson to her son. Following the visit, when she "was returned" by an unnamed Indian escort, she lost her composure "up and down mourning and lamenting" the state of her family and her inability to protect them. She turned to scripture and Psalm 55:22, "Cast thy burden upon the Lord, and He shall sustain thee," calmed her. That night, the temperature dropped and the family of Rowlandson's master crowded into their wigwam, blocking her from the fire. She roamed the camp, looking for warmth. She went to another wigwam, where a Native woman unfurled a skin and invited her to sit. She fed her groundnuts and "bade me come again; and told me they would buy me." Feeling better, Rowlandson praised God for the strangers' kindness.[63]

Rowlandson excelled at backhanded expressions of gratitude. Her physical bouts of disorientation prompted a thank-you note to God for not letting the Indians harm her. This revelation performed double duty: it robbed the Indians of their self-determination—God spared her, not they—and it told her English readers in certain terms that they did not sexually molest her during her captivity. At issue was Rowlandson's loyalty as much as her purity. She and Mather went out of their way to distance Rowlandson from her Indian captors and thereby deny the long history of cross-cultural neighborliness in southern New England. They didn't want readers to think that she had grown accustomed to Indian ways or had been adopted into a family. They obscured the Algonquians' track record of hospitality, built since the 1620s on many examples of English ramblers plucked out of the woods. The rebels continued to rescue lost people during the war. King Philip's followers looked out for Rowlandson for many reasons. They hoped to ransom her for a goodly sum, and they had grown fond of her wares. An accomplished seamstress, Rowlandson stitched shirts for the Algonquians. Rowlandson and Mather attempted to erase the presence of the Native people who had traveled with the colonists in the lead-up to the war. Still, they depended on them. Without the compassion of Indian strangers, not only would Rowlandson have died, she would have been alone. The authors of Rowlandson's narrative refused to turn her out into wilderness. Even when it suited their political agenda, they could not make New England a trackless void.

The ordeal—and the book dramatizing the ordeal—brought Rowlandson, and through her the entire English Atlantic, closer to God. But the Lord did not embrace his early modern flocks directly. He let the Indians manhandle the English. The rebels broke the peace and brought the self-satisfied Puritans to their knees. They raided towns and outmaneuvered their foes, inflicting damage and extending the war so that the Christians could learn their lesson. They dragged Mary Rowlandson through the wilderness and sustained her on boiled horse hooves and intestines. They tormented and nourished her. They broke her spirit and warmed her bones. They stood by her side and caught her when she strayed. Rowlandson ran a debt of emotional, material, and metaphoric losses. But her Indian adversaries limited her geographic losses to the one. She hated them and despised them for imprisoning her in their devilish flock, yet she found God in their company. Their presence was as necessary to her redemption as the wilderness.

Early modern North Americans sanctified social belonging. Relationships bound humans to one another and suspended them in space. Marriage, family, clan, tribe, nation, and sect determined their location in society and therefore their position in the world. Mary Rowlandson found God after being torn from her family, but the strengths of those bonds defined the stakes of her ordeal. She needed God (and the help of the Algonquians) to survive outside her relations. Rowlandson lamented the disappearance of the wilderness. Without a wild space to test them, the English colonists lost their militant edge. The irony, of course, was that Mary Rowlandson knew an actual wilderness whereas her forerunners wandered through bespoke wèta. As their numbers increased and their power grew, the English cultivated an overgrown forest by suppressing the Algonquians' environmental and political government. War, disease, and slavery destroyed Native communities and the landscapes they built. In 1630, Francis Higginson delighted in the Algonquians' creation: "Though all the Countrey be as it were a thicke Wood for generall, yet in divers places there is much ground cleared by the Indians." "I am told," he continued, "about three miles from us a Man may stand on a little hilly place and see divers thousands of acres of ground as good as needs be, and not a Tree in the same." Higginson adored the open views and the cords of chopped wood New England's abundant, "cheap" timber provided. (An obvious improvement over England's sparse and forbidden forests that belonged to the crown.) He was thinking of his own hearth, but he could have been speaking for both his people and the Algonquians when he declared about his new home: "Here is a good living for those that love good Fires."[64]

Colonization turned the wèta into an imagined space and realized the invaders' dream of a wilderness expanse with a dark and savage hue. The Algonquians survived in New England after King Philip's War, but they stopped rescuing lost people in the woods. The Americans would have to look elsewhere for salvation as they slowly abandoned relational space over the coming centuries in search of a lonelier country for their individualistic children.[65]

CHAPTER THREE

# Children of the Revolution

PAUL GASFORD GOT LOST HUNTING sarsaparilla on the shore of Lake Ontario. Eager to outdo his siblings and collect the sixpence reward his mother was offering the child who picked the most, he scurried through the brush, eyes peeled and legs pumping, giddy to be free of the small boat his family was using to move their belongings from the Bay of Quinté in Ontario to their new home in Niagara, New York. The bigger kids soon made their hauls and sprinted back to the beach to receive their mother's judgment. None of them noticed that Paul was missing, a staggering oversight given that he was "a little over 4 years old."[1]

The adults built a bonfire and fired their guns in the air. They searched the woods for three days but found no sign of Paul. Chances were slim that a four-year-old could survive three nights exposed in a strange place. The little boy must have died, a prospect Paul's mother refused to contemplate. They had to drag her to the boat and pin her to the gunwale to travel on.

Paul's family undertook their journey in 1805 to improve their circumstances. The household's leaders measured the Great Lakes economy and perceived advantage in another location on Lake Ontario. This move triggered other movements. The children were sent to sample the environment in transit, darting out from the shoreline to spot, pluck, and retrieve material the household could consume. The sarsaparilla hunt was also fun, a chance to relieve the monotony of a long voyage in cramped quarters. Paul's mother unleashed her children on the interior to replenish her stockpile of medicinal plants and to teach them to find joy in foraging. That it went horribly wrong showed the episode's human and American nature. Humans evolved to be environmental opportunists. They imagined, sensed, and exploited nature across habitats and food chains. They ate nearly everything, and their ingenuity was as omnivorous as their appetites. But flexibility came with tremendous risk, especially for fledgling scroungers. Humans were not born wily improvisers. They had to be trained to pillage nature, and during the extended tutelage known as childhood, nature sometimes pillaged them.

The American side of Paul's disappearance surfaced later. The first clue was that the authorities did not arrest the parents for negligence upon their arrival in Niagara. No one questioned the wisdom of them sending a four-year-old out into the woods to labor on the household's behalf. That's where American children belonged and what they should be doing. Beginning in the eighteenth century, Americans idealized free-range parenting. Turning from an older, colonial vision of household management, when patriarchs heightened supervision in order to combat their children's innate sinfulness, they blended the revolutionary era's goals of breaking tradition and fomenting independence with the agrarian reality that there were never enough adults around to watch children closely. Kids became the vanguard of the new nation. By going out into the woods and fields on their own, by taking on adult responsibilities at what seems to us absurdly young ages, they modeled the democratic spirit of the age.[2]

Gasford underscored this line of thinking when he ambled into Niagara four days later. Instead of falling apart when he realized that he was lost, he remembered the adults saying that New York lay forty miles away and decided to complete the final leg of the journey on his own. He found the lake and followed the coastline. He dug holes in the beach at night and snuggled deep into the sand to keep warm. A forethoughtful tot, he jammed a stick in the ground before he slept to stay oriented in the right direction in case he woke confused. He nibbled grapes when he grew hungry, but not too many, for he remembered his mother's admonition not to gorge himself and sour his stomach. He spotted three Indians on the beach and hid from them in the woods. He did not want to be taken captive like the white children in the stories told by his parents. He held his breath until their dog, who had sniffed his trail, had passed him by. When he sauntered into town, the place exploded in celebration. The governor heard the astonishing tale and invited Paul to Albany. He declared that "he would have kept [the little boy], if his mother had been willing to give him up." She wasn't.[3]

Paul Gasford's hike was turned into a tiny two-by-three-inch book, a wee tome for little hands. It was counterintuitive children literature: adults gave it to youngsters to end their childhoods. If a four-year-old could stay composed, remember all his parent's instructions, and take command of his environment, what was your excuse? Gasford proved that little Americans were exactly that, smaller versions of independent adults. The final lines about the governor wanting to keep him hinted that despite his precocious independence, the child still inhabited relational space. Family responsibilities prevented a four-year-old from leaving home and setting up his own household. He still belonged to his father and mother. His mother's love warmed his captivity, but over a decade of farm work still lay ahead of Paul before his parents would set him free, and they expected him to labor willingly for the family and apply the same ingenuity and self-direction to his daily labors as he displayed on the road to Niagara.

Getting lost is a touchstone experience of many childhoods. Most of us have endured or stood witness to the scene in the mall, the department store, or the grocery market when the loudspeaker crackles and a voice drones: "Attention, shoppers. Attention, shoppers. Could the parents of a little girl wearing a blue hooded sweatshirt please come retrieve her at the manager's desk?" Children are no match for the caverns of big-box America. They cannot navigate mazes of dress racks or stay on target in row after row of brightly colored packages of granola bars and dishwasher detergents. These are spaces designed to enthrall grown people with credit cards, not short ones with brief attention spans. Unlike sea turtles, master way finders who can traverse a beach in the direction of the ocean minutes after entering the world, children require long periods of guidance until their hippocampi mature and they can conceive and remember routes on their own. Baby turtles hit the ocean quickly because, over centuries, predators have weeded out the lingerers and the makers of wrong turns. Human children have evolved to wander their built and natural environments for years, baffled yet protected by adults who keep track of them—most of the time. Their prolonged geographic naiveté exposes them to harm, but the species puts up with disoriented youngsters to give their brains more time to develop and absorb complex cultural attributes, like political ideologies and child-rearing theories.

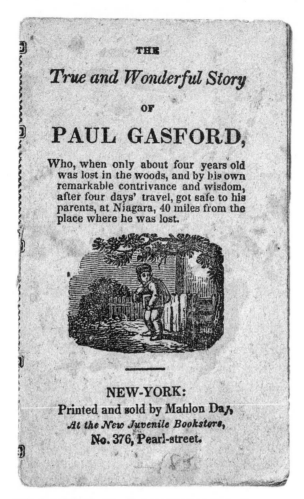

Title page of the small book chronicling Paul Gasford's
remarkable poise and independence. (Courtesy of the American
Antiquarian Society)

Paul Gasford entered the woods to find material resources in a small
body guided by immature navigation software. His short stature limited his
sight lines. Not seeing well is a prerequisite for getting lost. He ventured
into spaces unknown to him, a piece of woods with few personal landmarks. The inability to access landmarks is also a requirement for getting
lost. The final common ingredient may be the most difficult for children to
overcome, and it's the one Gasford handled best and what made his survival
miraculous. Getting lost often involves a lapse in memory. To navigate,

humans must recognize their surroundings, they must be able to locate and to use landmarks, and they must keep track of previous experience.[4]

It also helps if they can astral-project. Using their imaginations to escape first-person perspective, humans can achieve an allocentric vantage point. They can "see" spaces from outside themselves—above often works well for navigators. For all his precociousness, Gasford never hovered above his surroundings. Instead he projected into his parents' heads. He remembered their admonitions. Their lessons directed his movements and his decisions. The hovering presence of his mother and father tempered the horrifying implications of a fully cognizant four-year-old walking away from his family rather than bending every effort to return to them. Revolutionary-era parents may have fantasized about independent tikes, but they remained committed to human attachments. They wanted their kids to stay with them. Indeed, they escalated their feelings along with their freedoms. Love, they theorized, should keep people together. Voluntary bonds of affection united families, communities, and nations.[5]

A society based in love was a sharp departure from anciens régimes founded on authority. Yet for all their disruptive verve, Gasfordian Americans continued to imagine space in social relationships. They simply dreamed of replacing coerced bonds with freely chosen ones. They wanted the freedom to select their partners, their neighbors, and their rulers, not the option to live without them.

The social ideal of independent persons gathering freely in households, communities, and republics clashed with the realities of agrarian economies and spaces. Children, the mentally disabled, and the elderly became confused, got lost, and tripped into nature shock. Paul Gasford might have been able to navigate a coastline on his own, but dependents were supposed to be supervised. Freedom could kill those with underdeveloped, declining, or damaged brains. Parents and caregivers endeavored to keep the spatially challenged close, but the exigencies of rural economies made this difficult. To survive, households put kids to work, having them perform jobs like herding livestock and gathering sarsaparilla. Adults knew preadolescents struggled to remember paths in unfamiliar environments with tangled sight lines. They sent them into the woods nonetheless. They really had no choice.

Frontier households recast bewildered children as precocious republicans. This ploy hid the audacity of the parents' failure. In eighteenth- and nineteenth-century America, people kept eyes on one another. Relational space was still enforced. Local magistrates confronted unknown persons and ordered them to leave if they had no relations or means of subsistence. The scrutiny intensified for humans under the authority of male heads of households. Married women, children, indentured servants, and slaves were trapped underneath overlapping surveillance regimes. The legal system and print media extended the oversight of white male property owners across landscapes and jurisdictions. Gossip networks and informal scrutiny further entangled unfree Americans. Communities noted the physical appearance of apprentices, servants, and slaves. They paid special attention to the clothes they wore. They remembered personal habits, missing teeth and fingers, and the way subordinates spoke. Getting lost in America involved eluding webs of observation and power as well as walking into dark, confusing spaces and forgetting the steps that led you there.[6]

Nature shock exposed the dependencies all humans possessed: their reliance on their senses, on their landmarks, and on their history. Struck blind, lost people forfeited the command of space that came with an actual prospect or an allocentric perspective. Left without landmarks, lost people wandered in circles, undercutting optimistic assumptions about movements yielding advantage and improvement. Cut off from memories, lost people experienced an actual break with the past and found the departure more ruinous than liberating. Nature shock revealed the muddy legacy of the American Revolution on the ground. Autonomy was both a dream and a nightmare. Actual independence felt more like a nervous breakdown than an assertion of personal freedom.

Agrarian communities told stories about individuals who eluded supervision. They told lost-person stories about children, the disabled, and the elderly, but also about confused grown men and women. They told stories about runaway brides, apprentices, and slaves. They recalled the wayward and the waylaid for posterity, suggesting that "settled" towns, homesteads, and plantations had overcome the obstacles to oversight. In order to free themselves from an experience that challenged their aspirations for a social order based on a small group of independent individuals surveilling a multitude of unfree persons, Americans chose to bury nature shock in their past.

**DARKNESS FALLS**

On May 19, 1780, an "uncommon darkness" descended on New England. A "thick, black cloud" rolled from the west and blotted out the sky. Cows wandered home, thinking it was time to be put up for the night. Chickens roosted, and songbirds returned to their nests. In his field, Elias Hemenway steered his oxen toward the barn. The murk had ruined his plowing. He could not see well enough to keep the furrows straight. Householders lit candles on kitchen tables at noon. Miriam Newton noted the day-turned-night in her diary. She remembered the candles and how the cloud made the afternoon and "the night equally dark." Her neighbor in Marlborough, New Hampshire, recalled that it seemed to him as if a judgment had been passed. Egyptian plagues came to mind. The scene left impressions beyond the normal range of senses: this was "a darkness that could be felt." Thaddeus Hastings left his home near Marlborough in the morning. On his return, he walked into the blackout, got lost, "and was obliged to lie in the woods all night." He was not alone shivering in the gloom, for "others met with the same experience."[7]

Miriam Newton kept a diary for sixty years. In it, she collected a handful of natural occurrences that swerved from the norm. The weather events that drew her attention tended to uproot trees, lift houses, and stun people. The Dark Day lived alongside freak whirlwinds, cold snaps, wild thunderstorms, and "dreadful gales." Against these outbursts, Newton banked hundreds of uneventful dates. She paused to write terse descriptions of daily life, marking a pattern in time that absorbed the shock of the occasional disruption. In their diaries, New Englanders summoned the routine: noting the rising and setting of the sun, the changing seasons, the phases of the moon, the life cycles of their farms and their families. The strangeness of the Dark Day stood out against the mundane circuits of cows clopping to pastures, chickens emerging from coops to peck grain in the yard, and neighbors running errands through the woods.[8]

Diarists in preindustrial New England practiced the art of keeping track. They noted debts owed and tasks performed. They recorded endless comings and goings. Most of the diaries lacked self-reflection, the ooze of inner feeling we associate with journaling. The antiques disappoint with their outward focus on what appears to be trivia. Yet historian Laurel Thatcher Ulrich's assessment of a diary a midwife from Maine kept between 1785 and 1812 holds true for other preindustrial tracking devices: "It was in the very dailiness, the exhaustive, repetitious dailiness, that the real power of Martha Ballard's book lies." Ballard's diary wove several movements into the warp of passing time. She documented her own journeys, all the trips she undertook to help her clients give birth; she monitored transactions, the flow of payments she received (or failed to receive) for her services; and she chronicled the rhythms of her household—the chores, the harvests, and the squabbles. The diary threaded movements in space through movements in time, and it reminds us of the inseparability of these concepts. To reflect on the passage of time, to construct the dailiness for which they were famous, the preindustrial diarists expressed time in space, and through the regular practice of taking note of time's passing, they put people, cows, and the darkness in their place.⁹

Ballard mentioned three lost people in her diary. The skies were clear and the weather fine for planting parsnips, carrots, and potatoes in the garden on Saturday, May 22, 1790. Ballard had tea with Mrs. Woodward, and her son Cyrus and a neighbor named David went to the aid of another neighbor, Joseph Prescott, to search the woods for Prescott's daughter, who had been missing since Wednesday. Ballard noted the crisis's end with a brief statement: "It," she wrote, "was found alive." Years later, Peter Clark entered her log. Clark was Hopewell, Maine's recidivist lost person. Suffering from delirium, he would sometimes leave his home and roam the nearby woods. In December 1794, Ballard heard that Clark had walked into the forest in the late evening. A search party located him four days later. He strayed again in May 1797 and this time he did not return. In 1803, a fire consumed the forest's understory, revealing his bones. They identified him by a sleeve button. Ballard concluded her observations of lost people with a clipped description of another incident: on Sunday, May 17, 1795, she wrote, "Mrs. Waid was lost in the woods." Sundays organized time in Christian communities. Diarists landmarked months, years, and lifetimes by noting the passing of the weekly day of rest and reflection. Perhaps the date spoke for Ballard. The regularity of the Sunday counteracted the waywardness of Mrs. Waid. They cancelled each other out, making further comment superfluous.¹⁰

In addition to lost people, Ballard tallied lost possessions. During some of her many journeys to assist in childbirths, she lost her shoes, handkerchiefs, and a mitten. On another day, her daughter Hannah lost a silver buckle. Her sons and neighbors lost cows, oxen, colts, mares, ducks, and swine. Her husband lost a note and a gallon of molasses. The misplaced things resembled the lost people in the diary in that Ballard never betrayed how she felt about their disappearance. She refused to sentimentalize strays in print. Calling Joseph Prescott's daughter an "it" epitomized her dispassion. Still, Ballard cared deeply about her neighbors and family; Ulrich makes this clear. Her diary merely served a different purpose than the ones to which we are used. It was a spatial rather than a psychological document, which made it a social rather than a personal record. Ballard attempted to hold a family and a community together by monitoring their members' locations. The job of the diary was not to integrate material and emotional losses into a story of a personality traveling through a life, but rather to note the time and the place when people and possessions related to the author went missing. Ballard was not the central player in her diary. Instead, she resembled a line judge. She was the official who marked where and when things left the field of play. By flagging lost people and possessions, she mapped the out of bounds for her family and her community.

The darkness and the forest were out-of-bounds, under certain conditions. Neither was disorienting or scary all the time. On the Dark Day, Thaddeus Hastings entered the woods surrounding Marlborough, New Hampshire, confident that he could make his way out. A grown man and practiced errand runner, he had probably trod the paths connecting his farm to the town, the mill, the orchard, or the fishing hole on a thousand occasions. He may even have walked them at night with a torch or with a full moon to light the trail. He was not prepared, however, to travel in the woods during a surprise blackout. The sudden loss of sight turned the local forest and the regular coming of nightfall—sites and time periods well landmarked and memorized—into unmanageable spaces. Unlike a basset hound or a bat, Hastings could neither smell the path nor echolocate landmarks, so he wandered in circles until he tired and lay down, waiting for the sun to come up. With the light, the environment flipped back to the perceptual field in which New England humans maneuvered, and the sleepy farmer struck the path and headed for home.

Thaddeus Hastings's out of bounds differed from Peter Clark's or the Prescott child's out of bounds. A full-grown male in a patriarchal society, Hastings strode wider fairways. Only an unheard-of combination of being in the woods during a midday nightfall could send him reeling into the bushes. Dementia sufferers and children wandered more easily. Their brains were on the move, in the throes of deterioration or development, and they struggled in environments that challenged adults operating at full capacity. Strange spaces with interrupted sight lines, like forests or swamps, or, conversely, spaces with radically open sight lines, like prairies or plains, endangered children and the disabled. If their fellow humans did not police them, they could die lost. Stray children and elders revealed the congruence of physical and social dependence. Sight-dominant animals with prodigious minds, humans leaned on their vision and their memories. But not all humans saw or remembered with equal skill, so those at the crest of mental proficiency looked after those on the rise or the decline. As with getting lost, surveillance tested sight and memory. Since early modern people measured space in relationships, they knotted the two activities: they kept track of themselves by keeping track of others.

## LURKING

Martha Ballard's diary was unexceptional. Most Americans performed daily routines of keeping track. Notes to selves, mental or otherwise, held communities together. The panic and distress of a person getting lost reverberated through webs of relations, prompting those along their strands to mark the occasion when the wandering child or the errant dementia sufferer slipped past the oversight of families, neighbors, and fellow citizens. The effort and resources Americans devoted to maintaining informal and formal spy networks were considerable, and evading them was no easy task. Some of the jolt of nature shock came from the realization that subordinates could disappear when no one was looking.

A devoted caregiver and community organizer, Martha Ballard was the type of person you would want to keep an eye out for you. The same could not be said for most American overseers at the time. The full brunt of community surveillance was on display in places like Virginia and North Carolina. The center of the growth of enslaved labor in North America in the eighteenth century, these colonies split a nine-hundred-square-mile blind spot—the Great Dismal Swamp. The swamp hid people from sight. In the colonial period, thousands of indigenous Algonquians and enslaved Africans found refuge in the wetlands' interior away from English colonists. The swamp hosted Maroon communities that cut themselves off from surrounding hog farms and tobacco plantations. Wealthy planters installed a surveillance regime to keep track of enslaved workers. This regime struggled to see inside the swamp, and the planter society found it difficult to imagine the possibility of Maroon communities existing in the marshlands. Instead, the regime monitored the perimeter of the swamp, keeping tabs

Illustration that accompanied David Hunter Strother's account of Maroons in the Great Dismal Swamp. (*Harper's New Monthly*, 1856. Courtesy of the New York Public Library)

on an assortment of edge dwellers—runaways, hired laborers, and elderly "retired" slaves—who remained in contact with outside communities.[11]

The Maroons and the borderers interacted. When lumber camps began appearing in the late eighteenth century, shingle cutters teamed with Maroons to increase their daily production. Invisible hands split cedar and cypress in the swamp's interior. Hired workers collected the Maroons' bundles and accepted payment for the exaggerated totals from white camp bosses. They split the earnings—which came in the form of provisions— with their silent partners. These relationships were not always cooperative. The hired-out workers from the lumber camps sometimes turned in Maroons for the reward offered by slave owners.[12]

The balance between interior, isolated Maroons and connected edge communities shifted over time. In the nineteenth century canals and railroads pushed into the swamp. The number of Maroons actually increased as edge lands were drained and put into agricultural production. The swamp was the site of complex and shifting material cultures and community dynamics. But you could not tell this from the documents created by the slaveholding community. The English monitored the edge of the swamp, but they could not see the interior spaces that succored the Maroons. They knew individual fugitives entered the swamp, but they assumed that no human community could endure in such a dark and forlorn place.[13]

When slave owners in the counties surrounding the wetlands lost human property, they placed advertisements in the newspapers. The ads extended the reach of slave owners' supervision through a network of readers. Eyes scanned papers and then surveyed rivers, wharfs, plantations, and towns for the persons described in print. Given its proximity and its awesome ability to obstruct human sight, you would think the Great Dismal Swamp would feature prominently in the runaway ads. The place was barely mentioned. The swamp undercut the idea that freedom proceeded in a straight line from agrarian captivity to wilderness isolation. Fugitives used the swamp to evade capture, but they aimed to restore human connections, not break free from them. The swamp helped some disappear and form Maroon settlements, while it allowed others to lurk just out of range of their masters' community in order to stay close to imprisoned wives, children, and extended relations. Either way, the goal was to build and maintain relations in space. Maroon communities wove social networks in the swampy blind spot of the slave regime, while the lurkers used edge habitats to stay connected to friends and relatives. Neither Maroons nor lurkers hoped to get lost. Nature shock was not their goal. They wanted to replace or refurbish personal ties, not escape them.

The Great Dismal Swamp hid runaways from surveillance, but it tested the fugitives' talents for locating themselves in space and finding new communities. The swamp afforded an ideal landscape to get lost in. Flat with occluded sight lines, the massive wetland featured closed tree canopies that blocked light from the sun, the moon, and the stars. Watery surfaces frustrated path making, and the lush vegetation militated against the selection and memorization of landmarks. Native Americans wrung wild protein from the swamp and harvested a cornucopia of plants. The environment burst with catfish, deer, and stands of water-resistant trees perfect for roof shingles. It most definitely was not an idyllic agrarian space, at least for the European transplants, who yearned for orderly fields they could behold from houses on hills. The initial English colonists in Virginia stayed to the north, planting tobacco along the rivers feeding the Chesapeake Bay. The land surrounding the swamp attracted smaller farmers, former indentured servants, and a handful of escaped slaves.[14]

The North Carolina side of the swamp became a haven for semi-feral livestock. Pigs and cows tromped through the muck untended all winter. In spring, their owners collected them, notched the ears of the newborns, and set them loose again. The spirit of the free range rubbed off on the area's proprietors. According to Virginia planter William Byrd, the "borderers" who farmed on the outskirts of the Great Dismal Swamp sank toward savagery alongside their animals: "Both the Cattle and Hogs ramble in the Neighboring Marshes and Swamps, where they maintain themselves the whole Winter long, and are not fetch'd home till the spring. Thus these Indolent Wretches, during half of the Year, lose the Advantage of the Milk of their cattle, as well as their Dung, and many of the poor Creatures perish in the Mire, into the Bargain, by this ill Management." Byrd garbled his syntax, but it's obvious he thought both the hogs, the cattle, and the farmers alike deserved the insult of "Indolent Wretches." To him, the humans left without milk seemed as poor a set of creatures as the pigs and cows munching grass in the swamp. The place undid them all.[15]

Byrd observed the Great Dismal Swamp's social and pastoral scene while serving as Virginia's representative to a 1728 commission tasked with drawing a boundary between the colonies. The commissioners were rich gentlemen. They stayed out of the mosquito-infested marsh while hired line crews entered and mapped the space. Ordering the swamp on paper served the power of the tobacco planters, who were investing their profits in imported enslaved labor and land-speculation schemes. Byrd was the first to promote the draining of the swamp to grow and sell hemp to the rope makers who supplied the rigging for Great Britain's Royal Navy.[16]

The disputed region around the swamp created opportunities for runaways to survive as vulnerable sharecroppers. On the 1728 expedition, Byrd happened upon a "Mullato" family living a half mile inside the edge of the swamp. They claimed to be free, but the "shyness" of the father raised doubts in Byrd's mind. To increase the number of hands on the North

Carolina side of the swamp, free whites "settled" runaways from Virginia "on some out-of-the-way corner of their Land." They vouched for them in exchange for a share of the herds the refugees tended. By surveying the swamp and carving farms from "the filthy Quagmire," the colonial bigwigs hoped to bring government to potentially fertile land being wasted by the lazy, sick, and shady people residing there.[17]

Enslaved persons utilized the Great Dismal Swamp for subsistence, recreation, and refuge. With the formation of the Dismal Swamp Company in 1763, a reclamation venture whose partners included George Washington, enslaved workers from the company's agrarian outpost—the Dismal Plantation—labored in the muck digging canals, chopping trees, and making shingles. The muscle and ingenuity of hired-out enslaved laborers remade the landscape, and the hours they spent in the swamp gave these workers insight into the space. They, for example, knew that some runaways found permanent freedom in the depths of the swamp. A handful of slaves escaped for good and raised families in the quagmire.[18]

The authors of the runaway ads acknowledged that fugitives sometimes used swamps as temporary refuges, but they concentrated their surveillance on the edges of the swamp, where people could see and be seen. Visuality structured the slaveholding regime, and the runaway advertisements privileged its gaze. The masters and their many spies struggled to conceive that which they could not see, opening spaces for maroonage. Many dismissed the notion that families could survive in the morass. So they kept their eyes on the edges of swamps to spot those who emerged.[19]

Observable physical characteristics filled the ads. Runaways were identified by their missing teeth and toes, by their dark or "yellow" (meaning light) complexions, and by their bushy or close-cropped hair. The ads mentioned scars—from smallpox, from whippings, or from the brands some owners seared in their slaves' cheeks. They detailed the clothes runaways wore. An ad placed by Francis Poire in the *State Gazette of North Carolina* in 1793 listed the apparel along with "a NEGRO FELLOW by the name of Sampson" who had absconded. Sampson wore "a blue short coat, a Bath Coating jacket, blue trowsers, and a grey great coat," and he carried "a new brown short coat, two pair of breeches, one of corduroy and the other of brown fearnoughts, and sundry other good cloaths." Sampson stole a black horse to help haul his wardrobe.[20]

Clothing options helped runaways hide in plain sight. The right outfit could fold them into a crowd, allowing them to build new lives as free men and women. The fixation on fashion in the advertisements attested to the social aims of escape artists. Most sought to blend into communities.

While fugitives moved in and out of swamps to remain at large in landscapes organized to keep track of them, the slaveholding power watched populated areas. They worried about boats as well as clothes. The newspapers monitored the transportation system that moved goods and people from plantations to ports. They fought enslaved persons' attempts to use commercial mobility to their advantage. None of the ads suggested that white people enter quagmires to extract runaways.

If an enslaved person's flight path intersected with a swamp, the masters and their network of witnesses would perform some lurking themselves and wait for their reemergence. In 1768, John Mayo alerted the slaveholding community that a "Negro man named Tom," last seen in Nansemond and Norfolk Counties, had gone off without permission. An unnamed informant thought that he might be headed for the outskirts of the Dismal Swamp. He was not in the swamp, but rather "about" it. In 1799, Thomas Fitt posted a notice for Aaron, a twenty-six-year-old man, about five foot ten, with a brand on the side of his face. Fitt thought Aaron might be in the Dismal Swamp, not hiding there but working. He was a skilled "shingle weaver," a trade he acquired while laboring in the Lebanon Swamp. Aaron, Fitt presumed, would seek a "free pass" and employment so that he could "lurk" around Nixonton, where he had a wife.[21]

Just as relationships drew Native Mississippians from their hiding places when Hernando de Soto and his men kidnapped their families in sixteenth-century Florida, connections pulled most fugitives into view in Virginia and North Carolina. The slaveholding power banked on community relationships to reveal the movements of runaways. Mobility buoyed and threatened chattel slavery in the tobacco region. The ability to move human beings, to shift their ownership and relocate their bodies for profit, underwrote the slave economy as much as the labor performed by bound persons. The bipedism of the human species made commodity transfers possible. Like cows, hogs, and sheep, people could be driven from one yard to another. They could also use their feet to fight the system. Running away disrupted the cash flow and foregrounded the human drive to make and maintain affective relationships. In the decades after the American Revolution, many northern states slowly and grudgingly forbade slavery within their bounds. This presented fugitives from southern slave territories within reach of nominally free spaces a difficult choice: their families or their liberty. Before the rebellion, in North Carolina and Virginia, enslaved persons like Tom and Aaron absconded to reunite with their families. Many ran back to the plantations whence they had been sold. They could not take up where they left off, but they could linger in the spaces between private agricultural land and the southern commons— the woods and the wetlands no one owned but everyone used. Swamps abetted the formation of Maroon communities and the practice of "lurking," enslaved persons hanging out along the edges of dark spaces to stay in the proximity of wives, children, relatives, and friends.

Runaways planned routes, selected hiding spaces, gathered clothing, and forged passes to elude a well-funded and highly motivated surveillance regime. They were crafty and driven to reconnect with the people dear to them. Affection brought them out of hiding, but affection prompted many to run in the first place. Community put them in motion. The tug of relationships explains why the runaway advertisements never mentioned nature-shocked individuals. The slaves in the newspapers were lost to their masters, not lost to themselves or their families, and they were seeking to be close to people, not to be alone in a wilderness. The ads portrayed runaways as formidable navigators. Some fugitives, like Larry, an enslaved man who escaped from Benjamin Smith's North Carolina plantation in 1799, had work histories that sharpened their way-finding skills. Before he ran, Larry had been hired out to a waterman named Virgil Dry, who transported hogsheads of tobacco along the Chesapeake's network of rivers, canals, and estuaries. Larry, according to Smith, was either "lurking about some of the plantations on the north-west" of Perquimans County, or "going up and down the river in a boat." Few runaways were regional geographic sophisticates like Larry, but even newcomers to the area moved deftly. In November 1770, three enslaved men fled James Buchanan's Virginia plantation. The men had arrived on a slaving vessel from Africa that summer; they neither spoke nor understood English. Still, they knew enough to head for the edge of a swamp. They were last spotted outside the Chickahominy marshlands, and Buchanan supposed "they are still lurking about the skirts of that swamp."[22]

The runaway advertisements from North Carolina and Virginia contained one lost-person notice. In 1860, a two-year-old enslaved girl named Henrietta went missing. Henrietta had a "round, plump face, small eyes, high forehead, and thin hair." She was "well dressed in blue home-spun." Henrietta may have wandered away or she may have been kidnapped. She was too young to steal herself by running away on purpose, though she was old enough to be someone else's property. If she survived her bewilder-ment or her abduction, she would have to wait until after the looming Civil War to claim the self-possession little Paul Gasford understood as a birth-right. The runaways in and about the Great Dismal Swamp disconnected from one social regime in order to locate another set of relationships. Henrietta was too young to attempt such a leap. And thus she got totally lost, whereas adult fugitives slipped out of sight.[23]

## SLEEP AND DEATH

No bog swallowed Henrietta. She disappeared from a home overlooking Topsail Sound on the Outer Banks of North Carolina. She vanished in broad daylight in the course of a regular day. Her absence infuriated her owner, R. C. Nixon, who posted a $50 reward for her, but he doubled the price for anyone who could "give sufficient evidence to convict any person or persons of having stolen said child." The newspaper advertisement was as much about reasserting his rights as rescuing the two-year-old. After all, she was already being held against her will by the Nixon family. She had been kidnapped at birth. The ad took note of Henrietta to alert the slaveholding community to watch out for scofflaws who did only what all slaveholding communities do—steal people. The villains just did it without the paper-work. The truly missing person, the human being completely erased from history, was Henrietta's caregiver, the mother or the aunt who kept her eyes on the toddler most of the time and, we hope, loved her. Nixon's affront eclipsed their anguish.[24]

Children could vanish in an instant. In 1826, Josiah Fassett, a news-paper correspondent, told of the tragic disappearance of the six-year-old daughter of Alexander Dean Jr. in Luzerne, New York. On a Wednesday in April, the child (Fassett leaves her unnamed) was sent by her mother on an errand to a neighbor's house half a mile away. A patch of woods separated the farms, but a path connected them, and the girl had made the journey several times. She wore "a red woolen frock, a calico sun-bonnet, a cotton shirt and cotton half handkerchief." She was shoeless. A boy in the woods hunting partridges saw her hustling along the path. A young man tapping a sugar maple also spotted her. He remembered her whimpers. Around two in the afternoon, an hour after she departed, the mother started to worry. She jogged to the neighbors, discovered the girl was missing, and raised the alarm. Seventeen adults searched the woods all night. In the morning, thirty more residents from the surrounding towns joined the effort. They found footprints in the mud, but the little girl was gone.[25]

Fassett published his account in the Glenn Falls newspaper. He attached a poem to the bottom. The verse recounted the basic facts of the narrative in rhyme. Midway through, he gave the girl a voice. She announced her name—she was Fanny—and she said good-bye to her parents and all those who searched for her for nineteen days:

> Farewell to all beneath the sun
> My time is past, my work is done;
> Now I am gone you plainly see,
> To dwell in long eternity.

Done wandering the earth, Fanny blazed a trail into the afterlife, and Fassett used her loss to remind his readers that they were destined to follow her:

> Lord, help us now to spend our days,
> That we may live thine holy ways;
> Oh! May we now prepared be
> To meet her in eternity.[26]

Fanny Dean stood at a crossroads in the history of American childhood. Before her lay the sentimental future, when growing numbers of adults would see children as innocents in need of protection. Behind her spread a colonial past, when ministers and parents treated children as unformed creatures, sinful animals in need of strict oversight and discipline. Josiah Fassett looked forward and back, too. He played up sentiment and religion. Fanny's disappearance rent hearts. The "noises that almost sounded like crying" heard by the sugar maker suggested the little girl's distress. The imprints of the "child's bare feet in the mud" evoked the girl's smallness and the speed with which her pudgy toes could return to "mother clay." Fassett lingered in the ashes-to-ashes portent of the scene, but he did not dwell on the decision that launched the tragedy. For all the emotions stirred by Fanny's death, no anger was directed at the mother for sending a six-year-old into the woods alone. Instead, Fassett summoned the network of eyes that tethered American children to the earth. The hunter and the sugar maker saw her, though they failed to recognize the true nature of her peril. The community rallied within hours of Fanny's disappearance. The responsibility for monitoring dependents flowed from families to entire communities. It had to. Rural families needed mobile offspring. Children ventured into unsupervised spaces to forage from nature, communicate with neighbors, and tend livestock, and the ideology of the Revolution transformed the labors they performed in the blind spots into expressions of independence.[27]

Leaving parents' vision to pick mustard greens, deliver messages, and round up cattle, children, be they white agrarians in upstate New York or free young African American hog herders on the skirts of the Dismal Swamp in North Carolina, learned to fend for themselves. Fanny marching alone to her ultimate reward epitomized the optimistic gloss early nineteenth-century Americans applied to lost children. Still, the little girl's death stung. It shattered a family and revealed the tensions of being an American in an agrarian community. The love of liberty may have been so engrained in American farmers that their children displayed the trait as soon as they could toddle out the door, but the impulse to seek freedom could leave children alone in the darkness. American agrarians moved into the continental interior in increasing numbers at the same time as they revolutionized their nation and revised their parenting strategies. Families like the Deans searched for improved circumstances, and they often released their children into strange environments to labor on behalf of their families. Interior movements yielded material benefits and interior movements implied individual freedom, yet interior movements also exposed the limits of the agrarians' own spatial cognition and pointed out the shortcomings of the network of eyes that held them in place.

Josiah Fassett comforted the Deans. Fanny did not lose her mind in the forest and travel into nature shock. She was not a lifeless corpse rotting in a forgotten corner of the woods, but rather a glowing, eternal child. Fassett and the Deans were "respectable members of the Methodist Episcopal Church," and as such they could "plainly see" Fanny's location: she waited in a place beyond perception. Nonetheless, she also waited in a place that was a place and was thus perceivable. The layout of heaven conformed to the expectations of the rural community. Independent Fanny would kill time until the rest her family and her neighbors arrived to look upon her. Heaven operated like a good night's sleep.[28]

Drifting off, sleepers trusted that when they woke, cherished people and possessions would be in their place. For sight animals with active minds, human beings spent long stretches with their eyes closed and their consciousnesses shut down. Getting lost felt nightmarish because it broke faith in that trust. It upset the safeguards that pacified the relinquishment of sensory awareness. Lost people in strange woods entered the night without beds, chambers, or abodes, letting the outside drain heat from their bodies and leaving them exposed to creatures that pounced in the darkness. Lost people entered the night without caretakers and allies. Humans stuck together for many reasons. Groups divided labor; groups helped raise children; groups offered psychological reassurance; groups policed subalterns; and groups supplied eyes to look out while the exhausted closed theirs.

## DARKER

The night unfolded differently over time periods and across cultures. Historians argue that in early modern Europe, for example, people split their sleep, going to bed soon after sunset, then rising a few hours later to talk, grab a snack, have sex, or read the Bible. A second sleep followed the midnight sessions of activity. In electrified societies, people pop up and go down indiscriminately, making humanity a twenty-four-hour species. Getting lost did not return victims to a time period without clocks, lights, or sentries. Rather, it transported them to a frightening place: a social and sensory edge. Children faded from sight and tumbled into nature shock. Some never came back.[29]

In 1823, on the western side of the Appalachian Mountains, the McKenney boys ventured into the dark outside their backcountry farm. Normally, their father retrieved the cows the family let out each morning to graze in the woods. The forest, with its poor sight lines and crisscross of animal and human paths, made the adults uneasy. Sending Robert and William in there was a desperate move.

The McKenneys hailed from Pennsylvania. They migrated over the mountains to what would become Richie County, West Virginia, in 1818. Five years may seem like plenty of time to explore and memorize a new environment, but other tasks preoccupied the young family, and they remained uncertain in the woods outside the clearing the father had spent months hacking into being. He felled trees to build a cabin and to open space for the crops that took up all his time. Mother labored nearer to home. A string of pregnancies limited her mobility; Robert and William were the eldest of the ten children she would bear. She ordered them to go after the cows at the ripe ages of five and two. The animals had to come home. If not, wolves would pick them off in the night, and they needed to be on hand in the morning to milk. She couldn't do it. She was nursing a newborn. Father was gone for the day at a militia muster thirty miles away. Anyway, the job might be good for them. Cow catching would soon be their daily chore. It would teach them to be independent.

The boys stuck to the paths they knew for a while, but their focus drifted as the chase quickened and their desire to impress their mother overtook them. "Unconsciously," recalled the tellers of the family story, "they wandered too far to find their way back." Hours passed, and the mother crossed the line from worry to blind panic. She wrapped up the babe and ran to her in-laws'. All the "able-bodied men" were at the muster, so the neighbor women and elderly men launched the initial search. They sent word to the father, and he returned with others to scour the forest. On the morning of the third day, they found the boys three miles from the McKenney homestead. The five-year-old had given the two-year-old his coat to keep him from freezing. The family's dog had stayed with the boys, and the three of them had curled into a pile to withstand the October nights. The boys reported that the dog had chased another dog, "a big black" one, away from them in the dark. The adults did not believe this. They supposed the dog had actually fought off a black bear, which made the mutt even more heroic. The mention of the bear was the cue for the mother to dab a tear from her eye whenever the family retold the story of the time Robert and William got lost.[30]

Robert and William survived their ordeal and grew up. Their command of the environment increased with their height. Multiple McKenney males felled trees, marked trails, and slaughtered bears and wolves. This outpouring of labor drove nature shock into the past, or so the stories said. The narratives of agrarian settlement succeeded by converting the darkness into a passing moment, a phase in time that resembled childhood instead of a recurring episode that followed every half spin of the globe. The darkness feasted on children, demented old people, and desperate mothers. The darkness arrived at nightfall, but the darkness also existed beyond the boundary of surveillance, where dependents wandered out of sight and ventured outside social ties. The darkness eroded what daily labors and constant supervision built up—the illusion of mastery and control.

In 1821, a brother and a sister, eight and six, got lost bringing in the cattle in Portage County, Ohio. The kids got turned around and tried to herd the animals in the wrong direction. The cows refused to budge, so the children left them and plunged deeper into the forest. When the cows retraced their course and located the farm on their own, the parents roused the community. The men and women of the "thinly settled" county formed a line the next morning and marched through the forest. They agreed to blow their horns twice if the saw signs of the missing kids. Three toots would announce children found. The march lasted for two days, passing "through Lexington Township, Starke County, into Washington of the same, advancing as far as section fourteen, very near where Mr. Tinsman lived." At this spot, an "old hunter" picked up a splinter of spice-wood with peculiar bite marks. The imprints appeared deer-ish to his colleagues, but he knew them to be human. He followed an animal path into a thicket, choked with weeds, used by the deer in the summer to escape the black flies. The little girl rushed into his arms halfway down the path. Frantic, she could not speak and "made an effort to leave and run off into the underbrush." They found the boy asleep under a log. The horns rang thrice, and the company brought the children home. Still, even in the loving embrace of their family, the brother and sister remained out there. They were in shock. "The little boy and girl did not recognize [their parents] but stared wildly round." After a good night's sleep, they snapped back. Indeed, their memories were wiped clean: "They were all right, and strange to say could not remember anything of having been lost."[31]

Nature shock disturbed the memories of bewildered children, and nature shock disturbed the memories of communities that found and lost bewildered children. In New Hampshire, some missing children met dark fates. Two kids, the first in Temple and the second near Moultonborough, wandered away in the 1790s and "no certain discovery of the fate of the lost child[ren] was ever made." "Long before" these cases, at "a plantation on the Suncook River," an eight-year-old boy got lost between his house and a meadow. The boy's mother had sent him to retrieve his grass-mowing father for dinner. The boy ventured out on one path while the father, his stomach telling him it was time to go home, returned on another. Eager to dine, the family waited for what seemed like forever for the boy to come back. Their uneasiness grew as the sun sank. The father "went to find him and had not gone far till he saw with horror a bear start up among the bushes with the

Artist Felix Darley's engraving of a frontier family's chores, including child labor.
(Courtesy of the New York Public Library)

bleeding corpse of the boy between his teeth." The historian John Milton Whiton included the bear attack among his "sketches" of early New Hampshire. The suffering of the dead child and his family represented the horrid baseline to measure the state's "cultivation and improvement."[32]

In 1803, Eleazer Merrill and his son Hiram moved to Litchfield Township, Bradford County, Pennsylvania (northwest of Scranton near the New York state line). They pushed out beyond the "Schoonover place" and "built and moved into a log cabin." (Their neighbors included a single man named William Drown, who secured a spot in local history when he became disoriented and "perished in a snowstorm.") Eleazer and Hiram cleared and cropped, yet despite their labors, the "country" remained "wild" for "a long time." Proof of this wildness came in the form of a stray child: "one of the Merrill children, about three years old, was lost and was not found, though hundreds were hunting, for forty-eight hours." The child's death resonated beyond Litchfield Township. A history of Bradford County recalled the incident and named the child. The Merrills were denied the chance to bury their boy Solomon.[33]

On the opposite side of Pennsylvania, in Mount Pleasant Township outside Pittsburgh, Jabez Stearns, born in 1793, recalled the excitement caused by the disappearance of the Mumford girls during his childhood. Jirah Mumford sent her daughters, six-year-old Deborah and four-year-old Sally, on an errand to the neighbors. Coming back, they selected the wrong path and "wandered into the woods." At nightfall, Jirah raised the alarm and the community mobilized. People searched around the clock, but the girls were still missing three days later. Finally, the father heard the yip of a dog and followed the sound to the girls' hiding place. They had scrunched up in a "clump of bushes," and though they had heard people yelling for them, they were afraid to answer, a symptom of extreme mental disorientation, of nature shock. Jirah fell apart when Deborah and Sally returned. "Delirious with joy," Stearns remembered, "she clasped them in her arms and wept." Even one of the gnarly woodsmen who joined the search for the girls choked up at the sight of the reunion and excused himself to cry in the privacy of the yard. Freed from their mother's clench, the girls told their story. Trip the dog, they said, acted the hero. While they hunkered down in the leaves, the dog fought off wolves, cuddled with them through the night, and spoke for them when they were too afraid to make a peep. "Had it not been for faithful little Trip," concluded Stearns in his recollection, "had he, in his hunger, left them and gone home—they might never have been found."[34]

Some lost children survived; others perished. The themes of exposure and vulnerability in the darkness united the miracles and the tragedies. The daily labor on farms, the endless work of place making, ushered children outside the supervision of families, the social group charged with place keeping. Chores and errands sent immature minds into the woods and into the darkness, where they became disoriented. This could result in nightmarish encounters with wolves and bears in the night. Family pets sometimes rescued children, but the thrilling stories of life-preserving pooches hid ugly truths about parental neglect. In some emergencies, domestic animals became the actors keeping human children alive, an alarming delegation of responsibility. Animals approached space with an alternate set of priorities and a different array of sensory perceptions. Sometimes their agendas and sensitivities lined up with the humans'. Other times their presence led to more suffering. Dogs and horses were unreliable childcare providers.

Animals rescued children, but they also waylaid them. Missing cattle, for example, often resulted in missing children. In Iowa, nine-year-old Reese Evans, "a little fellow," hiked from his house in Newton Township to "watch

some cattle" grazing nearby. He never returned. His father, Ebenezer, organized a search, and "for several days the citizens of that locality scoured the
country surrounding and examined every foot, but found [not] the slightest
trace of the missing child." He must have been eaten by wolves, concluded
some of the more pessimistic observers. Six days later, a neighbor, John H.
Conners, spied the boy's cap and discovered the body, lying facedown and
frozen to the ground in a furrow. The December snow had covered the
corpse and hidden it from the searchers. The child died "forty rods from
the father's house." The cows survived the winter while Reese melted into
the ground.[35]

In Texas, the Moore children, girls eight and ten, set out one evening to
"drive up the cows" and never came back. The community searched "diligently" for days, and Andrew Sowell, a renowned tracker, hunted after them
for over two weeks. He found the shreds of a dress on a thorn bush and the
hoof prints of an old blind horse that had gone missing the same day as
the girls. Sowell came upon the horse at "York's Creek near the Big Thicket."
He returned the animal but could offer the parents only a theory about the
children. The girls had tried to make their job easier by taking the horse to
round up the cows. Partnering with one animal to manage another was the
basic strategy of pastoralism. Horses closed distances between humans and
their herds. They lightened loads and increased speeds. They also helped
humans navigate difficult terrain, especially in the dark. Wanderers relied
on the animals' superior night vision to bring them out of danger. A doctor
in Emmett County, Iowa, for example, explained that he "would drop the
reins on his horse's neck and trust the animal's instinct to guide him home"
on cloudy, moonless nights. Animal partners, however, traveled through
lives of their own. Steeds grew old and their eyesight weakened. Blind horses
did little to improve dark situations. In Delaware County, Ohio, a blind horse
traveling at night toppled over the ridge separating Alum and Big Walnut
Creeks. The rider, Ira Bennett, grabbed a bush on the way down to save
himself, while "the horse was found dead at the bottom of the cliff the next
morning." The Moore children were never located, and the neighbors split
their opinions over whether they thought the Indians had stolen them or
they had simply perished "in the woods." In their effort to find the family's
cows, the girls located oblivion instead.[36]

By noting lost children in the dark, agrarians across the United States
attempted to domesticate nature shock. They marked the times family

members and neighbors got horribly lost in diaries, newspapers, and local histories. These narrative cairns oriented communities alongside geographic landmarks. The two often overlapped, as memory, storytelling, and physical signposts combined to anchor points in space. In telling stories about lost people, families sometimes created ironic memorials to forgetting. The brother and sister from Portage County, Ohio, for example, were so traumatized by spending two nights by themselves in the woods that they could not recall the details of their ordeal. The community remembered for them, noting their derangement in local lore. Through storytelling, the residents of Portage County associated getting lost with childhood. Communities narrated their own life cycles, claiming that they had matured out of their bewildering past. Nature shock began to live in another kind of darkness—the mists of time.

In doing this cultural labor, local historians obscured the reality of agrarian settlement. People kept getting lost. Families continued to send children out-of-bounds on chores and errands, and the young and the vulnerable continued to slip from view. Communities still rallied to save the ones who got away, if not in person, in the stories they contrived to hold their place.

Frontier derangement could strike anyone. Nature shocked individuals of all ages when their vision failed, their landmarks disappeared, and their memories crumbled. The farming communities in Portage County, Ohio, remembered the brother and sister who got lost and forgot the trauma in self-defense. They also recalled a story about a grown man, a property-owning agrarian, who boggled his mind in a confusing environment. One day, Mr. Johnson became disoriented in the woods. After hours of roaming, he happened upon a farmstead, to his great relief. The place was squalid. An old horse nibbled tired blades of grass in the front yard. A log house slumped in the shadows. Mr. Johnson felt embarrassed for the farmer who lived there and rode the nag, who looked "poorer than Job's turkey." Then Mrs. Johnson opened the cabin door and asked him where he had gone off to.[37]

## CONSIGNED TO HISTORY

The passage of time illuminated dark spaces. Farmers cleared forests and cut paths. Sight lines opened. The work of place making shifted from physical exertion to narrative revision. As the nineteenth century wore on, children, sentimentalized as innocents rather than valorized as budding republicans, stayed closer to home. Longtime residents of rural communities searched their memories rather than the woods to find lost people. To measure the progress, local historians interviewed old-timers and recorded their testimony. A market developed for this lore, and publishing outfits in Chicago and Boston produced county almanacs and pioneer memorials.

A writer from New Haven, Connecticut, Henry Howe was one such collector of lost histories. In 1846, he traveled through Ohio, visiting with old-timers and corralling their memories into a book. The *Historical Collections of Ohio* sold eighteen thousand copies, making it one of the best-selling nineteenth-century books about the state. Howe went on to produce similar compendiums for other states and counties. He even produced a local history of the United States. These books sold unevenly. Howe began to raise subscriptions for his publications. People paid $10 to see their families appear in history.[38]

In early editions of the *Historical Collections*, Howe concentrated on the missteps of American soldiers and regiments who got lost in the woods while fighting the Shawnees or Miamis. In later ones, he shifted his focus to the pioneers and their children. He dug into the material from his interviews in the 1840s and rehashed stories from the numerous Ohio county histories that appeared between the first printing of his best seller (1847) and later editions (1890). He included the story of the missing kids from Portage County and the humorous confusion of Mr. Johnson as well as the tales of Mrs. Tillotson (lost while gathering water in the woods), David Beebe (Mrs. Tillotson's neighbor, lost in the woods for "4 days and 3 nights"), a child found dead (lost in a forest while trailing her mother, who was visiting the neighbors), and William Brayton (lost going after some stray cattle). He preserved the narrative of the Irish mother who burst into her neighbors' cabin and screamed that her boy was missing. "Wringing her hands and crying out," she declared that her "poor son John" had walked into the forest earlier in the day and had not come back. "What shall I do?" She wailed. "The opossums will kill him and the deer eat him. . . . It will be such a disgrace to the family." The neighbors rallied. They fired their guns into the air and built a bonfire." The "strapping" sixteen-year-old John Widney, unmolested by opossums, stumbled into the gathering half an hour after the beacon was lit. In the mirror Howe and others provided, Ohioans could remember incidents of getting lost as jokes or tragedies. Either way, they enjoyed the perspective

Howe offered. They belonged to a new age, for the era of nature shock lay behind them.[39]

Nature shock, the published materials suggested, was a long-ago predicament. Townships, counties, and states eventually grew out of it, and Howe and his local-history colleagues helped readers imagine what it felt like. In the "early days," wrote Howe, "it was the easiest thing in the world even for grown people to get lost." "The sensations on such are described as terrifying. The mind's senses become wild with bewilderment." The confusion traveled from the woods into the clearings. "Lost Old Settlers have been known to pass within a few yards of their own doors without recognizing a familiar object." The saddest outcomes in the lost-pioneer story vault were the ones about the Old Settler who died from exposure yards from his own doorstep.[40]

The memorials theorized a time solution for a recurrent space problem. The lost histories posited that the American frontier retained special conditions for bewilderment: thick forests, lots of outdoor chores, and many young, isolated, and fertile families with severely limited capacities for adult supervision. The frontier was scary, but it yielded Americans of admirable orneriness. Pioneers raised children with the bark on. Sure, some wandered away, but those who survived captured the essence of republican independence. Moderns knew they were modern because they did not get lost.

They, of course, were fooling themselves. Humans got lost throughout American history. Darkness occluded mid-latitude sight lines every single day. People wandered into landscapes unfamiliar to them, and they daydreamed and misremembered, losing track of travel times and landmarks. The selective memories of the frontier closed the epoch of bewilderment prematurely, and lost individuals appeared rough-hewn and independent only in retrospect. Read outside the framework Howe and others constructed for them, the lost stories highlighted the dependence of children, women, and the elderly. They showed grown men panicking in spaces they supposedly commanded. The idea of the frontier suggested that the history of agrarian communities progressed toward legibility and contentment. Old settlers read home landscapes like they read local histories. Both planted people firmly in place. Yet those same stories contained evidence that nature shock was a lingering condition rather than a passing phase.

On March 9, 1876, the Honorable Dexter Horton stood before the village of Fenton, Michigan, to dedicate its "new engine house and firemen's hall." Instead of cracking a bottle over the building's prow, Horton launched the firehouse with a lost-child story. He rolled back the years to 1834 and asked his audience to imagine Clark Dibble "threading his way through the trackless wilderness from Shiawassee to Grumlaw (now Grand Blane), [when] . . . by some mistake he got on the White Lake trail." When he came to "Hillman's, he started to make farther north, and first discovered this beautiful place which is now our village." Founded by a wrong turn, Fenton in 1876 connected to Fenton in 1843 through its landmarks—Grand Blane, White Lake Trail, Hillman's place—invisible to the founder, but present to Horton and his audience, who knew them and could picture them gone to recover Dibble's discovery moment. In Horton's story, families followed the trailblazer to the village site, and weeks had not passed "before the cry came from the little band in the wilderness, Lost! Lost!" Louisa Cheney, a "sweet cherub of seven years," had wandered away from her mother and some older children while on an expedition to find a place to plant the family's corn. They last saw the girl "around a little swale," Horton explained, "where Chandler's house now stands." Residents from Fenton, Grand Blane, Groveland, Holly, and White Lake gathered to search for Louisa. For three days they hunted. R. Winchell, a mill hand, wore himself out looking. He collapsed in bed and dreamed of Louisa in her hiding place. Jerking awake, he proceeded to the spot. That site, said Horton, "was just over the hill where the Baptist seminary now stands." The rescued child "afterwards became the first wife of Galen Johnson."[41]

Judge Horton combined a rite of passage, Louisa's nuptials, with prominent landmarks to scroll time forward and back. Louisa would grow up to initiate the sequence of people who would wed Galen Johnson. The marriage pulled the child forward in time, but it also cut her off. She would die, and Johnson would take another wife. Louisa was not present in 1876, but her connection to Johnson, who was, kept her around. Places existed in similar strings of memory. The raising of a house, like Chandler's, or a public building, like the Baptist seminary, brought "the swale" and "just over the hill" into the community. The structures' appearance, both their initial construction and all the changes from paint, weather, remodeling, or dilapidation, registered the passage of time. The inhabitants of Fenton made history with their barns, their homesteads, their firehouses, and their seminaries. Landmarks helped them remember the stories connected to structures just as the stories helped them remember the landmarks. The double function of place creating history and history creating place underpinned identity and orientation. The Fentonites knew who they were by knowing where they were. And their rootedness enhanced their independence. On the frontier, people kept their attentions tethered to the moment at hand lest someone get lost. After the frontier, later generations could let their imaginations roam because their location was settled.

Still, the import of Dibble's Mill (where R. Winchell labored) or Chandler's house dropped precipitously outside the earshot of Judge Horton's oration. These details suggested the deep connection the residents of Fenton felt to their landscape, but their sensations of permanence belonged to them in that locale. They were communicable only through analogy. To free the stories from their spots, the compendium makers folded neighborhood landmarks into grander narratives of the frontier and the wilderness. Thousands of Fentons were founded, built up, and memorialized. People raised in rural communities across North America might recognize Hillman's or the White Lake Trail in the farmsteads and the paths by which they oriented. And they all belonged to the drama of agrarian settlement, a movement composed of a blizzard of anecdotes about locals turning ordinary hills, swales, bends, fields, prairies, and pastures into landmarks festooned with memories.

Nature shock spurred memorials because getting lost threatened projects of settler colonialism. The bewildered could not see or recognize landmarks, and they garbled the memories of their own paths as well as the histories of the places that might have reoriented them. Their mistakes or misfortunes cast them out, and communities organized to recover them with a vigor that suggested existential threat. Finding the lost resembled going to war. Regiments mustered; commanders issued orders; triggers got pulled. Lost people haunted rescuers' dreams.

To calm the emotions nature shock stirred up, community leaders like Judge Horton resurrected memories of children gone missing. Getting lost became a historical phenomenon associated with an early, long-ago wilderness or a passing frontier. As communities settled, installed landmarks, and infused them with memories, they told stories about the passage of time. Nature shock became a memory, and in some instances, the memory became a spatial landmark that demarcated the end of an era.

Lost place-names dotted the American landscape. Usually, they referred to a natural feature that got lost. The many Lost Creeks and Lost Rivers, for example, indicated watercourses that disappeared underground and could no longer be followed. The creeks themselves "got lost," though it was also true that someone trying to stay on them to reach a larger stream would get lost too. Several places were named after lost people—and their dogs. In Kilkenny, New Hampshire, in the southern division of Coos County, two mountains, "two giants of nature," usurped "a greater part of the territory." They were the most prominent landmarks in the area. One of the peaks commemorated a human known as Willard, who "lost his way and wandered for three days on these mountains." Willard could not locate his camp, which was on the east side of the mountain. Each day, his dog Pilot would leave his side and venture on "an exploring expedition." The dog returned in the evening. Willard presumed the hungry animal was out searching for food. On the third morning, Willard, "being nearly exhausted," followed his dog who, true to his name, "piloted him through the tortuous windings of the mountains to his camp." The residents of Kilkenny called the second peak Pilot in honor of Willard's "disinterested friend." A town and two lakes in Massachusetts were named after Mr. Chauncy. In 1767 the Reverend Ebenezer Parkman explained their origin: "In the early times one Mr. Chauncy was lost in one of the swamps here; and . . . from thence this of the town had his name. Two ponds, a greater and a less, are also called Chauncy; most probably from the same cause." Chauncy's misadventure stuck in three places, revising other local histories. The greater pond was named Naggawoomcom before it memorialized a missing person.[42]

The early memories of frontier settlers were not the earliest memories in these landscapes. The Chippewas and Odawas, for example, lived in the Saginaw valley before Clark Dibble founded Fenton and Louisa Cheney got lost. Louisa wandered away during her mother's expedition to find an opening in the forest to plant an emergency crop of corn during their first year in the valley. She was looking for an abandoned Indian field. The Treaties of Flint River (1837) and Saginaw (1838) opened the way for Dibble's 1843 dispersion from Grand Blane to the site that became Fenton. No "trackless wilderness," the Saginaw valley was a neighborhood in transition. With the government's assistance, the new inhabitants pretended that they had happened upon an empty scene, but the arrowheads the farmers plowed up each spring recalled the presence of the former residents. The Fentonites erected landmarks upon landmarks. Aggressive forgetfulness accompanied the making of memories. The erasure of Native spaces added yet another tint to the agrarian darkness. The colonists refused to see the evidence of human habitation that surrounded them. Instead, they perceived a wilderness and then proceeded to get lost in their own blindness.

Lost children supposedly represented the peculiar hardships of frontier settlement. Once Americans pinned a place down, marked and memorized it according to their own specifications, conditions improved and parents were able to supervise their children with more care. In theory, they could rest easy knowing that little ones would no longer toddle off into the woods and die. But children remained short and scatterbrained after firehouses rose and forests fell. They continued to struggle to peer over things, to astral-project into eye-in-the-sky allocentric perspectives, and to integrate paths. Children still went missing, though it became harder to see them in the records of communities that had convinced themselves that getting lost was a historical condition.

### DISAPPEARED TRACKERS

Children were not alone in the dark. The list of nature-shocked agrarians included old men, women traveling with babies, inexperienced teenagers, and an assortment of injured, sick, and starving people. Elisha Keyes recalled an incident from his childhood in Jefferson County, Wisconsin, in the 1830s. A neighbor roused Keyes's father on a frigid winter night to join a search for "old Uncle John Atwood," who was "the oldest man in the neighborhood." He had gone out during the day, "wandered too far and could not retrace his steps." He would most certainly freeze to death. He "must be found and cared for." The searchers located him a mile from his cabin. He had burrowed into a haystack to escape the cold.[43]

In 1795 Revolutionary War veteran Joseph Barnett erected a lumber mill on the site that would become known as Port Barnett in a place that would become known as Jefferson County, Pennsylvania. Getting back to the founding moment of Port Barnett required some travel through subsequent places. According to the *History of Jefferson County*, published in 1888, Barnett and his brother, also a millwright, entered the country on Meade's Path, an old packhorse trail "leading westward." They followed the path "to the present site of Brookville, crossing Sandy Lick four times, first below where Garrison's mill now stands, again at the bottom at Port

Barnett, then near where the Brookville depot now is, and again where the covered bridge now stands." Oriented by standing structures, readers could imagine the Barnetts and their brother-in-law gathering at the curl in the river where the mill would go up and trigger a chain of transformations that would culminate with them. (Like Fenton, Michigan, Port Barnett was a built and inhabited environment prior to Joseph's appearance. "Nine Senecas of Cornplanter's tribe," who were "in the neighborhood," helped raise the mill. They welcomed Barnett and sponsored the new business.)[44]

In 1797, Joseph Barnett brought his family to live in a cabin next to the mill. His eldest daughter, Sarah, who had a twin brother named Thomas, was seven at the time of the move. At fourteen, Sarah got lost.

One evening, she caught the chore of bringing home the cows. The "animals had strayed farther than she anticipated, and before she found them, the night set in, and with a thunder storm coming on, she became bewildered and frightened, and lost her way." Fear grabbed Sarah and she imagined that wolves were chasing her. She wanted out of the woods immediately so that she could see her pursuers. When she popped out of the canopy at Mill Creek, the power source for her father's mill, she waded into it and huddled on a boulder midstream to wait out the night. Meanwhile, the family and the neighbors had started the search. They yelled for Sarah, and their dogs bayed. When the noise of salvation reached Sarah, her nature shock warped the sounds into wolf howls. The rescuers found Sarah at daylight and brought her ashore just in time to watch the rock disappear in the "raging torrent" of Mill Creek in full flood due to the thunderstorm. No one asked Sarah to hunt cows after that but, she reported later, "had her father bade her go, she would have gone despite her fear." Joseph Barnett, it seems, was a stern disciplinarian and "none of his children ever thought of disobeying him." Even when they got married and left home, the children bowed to his authority.[45]

Sarah lived into her nineties. "A remarkable woman, as vigorous in intellect as she was in body," she served as the caretaker of "the early settlement and building up of this country." In 1877, a reporter for the *Jefferson County Graphic* interviewed her about "the early days." Like Martha Ballard in Maine, Sarah monitored the comings and goings in her community: "She took a deep interest in all public matters . . . so that she kept herself posted in all that occurred." Still, though a revered elder, Sarah was not an action figure like her father. Joseph Barnett fought wars and built mills.

He commanded environments and people, earning a reputation as "the patriarch of Jefferson County." Sarah became "Mrs. Graham" when she married Elisha Graham, a millwright himself, in 1807. Her brilliance shone in relation to him. She was "in all respects a very helpmeet." Neighbors considered Sarah "a woman of strong principles." But she did not acquire her moral fiber by fighting wolves or by enduring the frightful night on a cold rock. Instead of being forged on the frontier, her strength of character came from her father. She inherited it "from her worthy sire." Sarah Graham tangled with the wilderness, yet she stayed as confined as before in the relationships that held her in a subservient place. The men in her life tasted freedom—and bled for it. Her father participated in the Revolution, her son fought for the Union during the Civil War—and she remembered, keeping track to prevent them from getting lost.[46]

Wives and daughters ventured into the darkness. They trekked into forests, swamps, prairies, and deserts, environments with sight lines shut tight or blown wide open. They struggled to see and remember landmarks. Their work, chasing cows or picking mulberries, consumed their attention. They forgot their paths. Females got lost just like their male counterparts; glitches in seeing and remembering knocked them off track. The many incidents of women and girls getting lost make one thing clear: their gender did not pin them at home. In agrarian environments, women and girls traveled to labor, worship, and socialize. Their mobility was essential to the survival of households and communities. Martha Ballard's errands as a midwife did more to propagate her society than any man walking to a haymow or going off to a militia muster. Women reproduced the next generation. Without children, frontier settlements were flat and futureless. Villages moved through time on the backs of their kids. Women were the ones who remembered, who took notice of the hill by the creek where the old barn stood next to Gardner's place before the seminary went up there. They recalled lost landscapes and lost people. The job of tending history fell to both genders, yet women shouldered more responsibility for place making. In the post-revolutionary world where four-year-old boys trained to live independently, women generated the sentiments that lured free agents back.

Lost boys and men wrestled with their gender. Going astray tested independent manhood. Freedom could be gained or lost in the woods, the prairies, or the deserts. Boys could fail to reach independence and old men could feel it pass through their fingers, but lost girls and women confronted an even more tangled set of expectations. They too experienced unfettered individualism and frightening isolation in bewildering spots. Yet, while they confronted the same dislocation as those gendered male, females could not claim the freedom men projected into wilderness. Subsumed under fathers and husbands, girls and women lost their way, their names, and their independence.

In 1796, a New Hampshire woman left her four daughters at home while she went to bring in the cows just before dark. In the woods, she "became bewildered, and had no idea which way pointed home." After wandering the forest paths for hours, she spied the "dim light" of Benjamin Badger's house. Mr. Badger was a neighbor who lived two miles by a crow's path from her own. By the time Mr. Badger grabbed a lantern and escorted the woman home, it was near midnight. They found three children asleep on the floor, but the fourth, Nancy, age eight, had left hours before to find her mother. The already adrenalized situation boiled over. The mother and Mr. Badger ran into the dark shouting for the child. They found her asleep, curled next to a log on the wood path half a mile from the house. Nancy, as the mother "always expressed it" when she told the story, " 'had cried herself to sleep.' "[47]

The sentimental ending brought the story back from the brink of the horror of two females being cut off from the men who defined them in one evening. The rollback continued after the story. In the published account, Nancy was not afforded her own name until the concluding paragraph of the vignette. The curtain closed with the author casting her into the future, when she would get married and serve as the adjunct of a husband and her male offspring. Little Nancy would become "the wife of Captain Thomas Stewart, and among her children now living are Col. Thomas W. and John H. Stewart, merchant tailors of Concord." Marriage likewise subsumed Nancy's mother. The central player in the lost episode, she was identified only as "the widow of Asa Harriman." The community and history knew her in relation to a dead man. He was her landmark.[48]

The widow Harriman operated a household. Her job description mirrored Benjamin Badger's. She ran a farm like him, without a Mrs. Badger to lighten the load and sit with the children while she fetched the livestock. Alone, the widow Harriman shouldered more responsibility than her male colleagues. Yet in her misadventure, she lost her name while Mr. Badger received full billing. Widow Harriman rescued herself and her child, with an assist from a neighbor with a lantern. Being human, she lost her way in the woods; being a woman, her tracks as an independent house-holder were covered up by the men who perceived her not as an equal but rather as a deceased man's helpmeet.[49]

The responsibility for maintaining households fell equally to men, women, and children. The shared project cast all family members into the woods and into danger. Yet adult males were the only ones to emerge from getting lost as independent persons. In Orangeville, New York, a sprinkling of families planted farms at the turn of the nineteenth century. The Duncans, Dotys, Sayers, and Chases clustered around a spring on "lot 12." In the summer, the farmers, who owned but a few cows each, sent their "small amount of stock" to browse in the woods. They sent their wives in after to find and drive the cattle home in the evenings. The farmers relied on the cows' determination to seek the grass, water, shade, and salt. The animals converted the wilderness into muscle and milk, enriching their owners on nature's account. The agrarians profited from their bovines' mobility, but they also suffered from the trouble the animals caused. Stray cows could be claimed by another human. Or they could leave the agrarian economy completely and own themselves by going feral. They could be eaten by wolves, ingest poisonous plants, or break their legs in the holes of woodchucks. To channel the benefits of the free range back to them, agrarian families teamed up to locate their animals. Men, women, and chil-dren chased cows. Mrs. Duncan performed the chore for her family, and she fully understood the risk involved. One summer evening, while searching for the cows, she "lost her way, and had to pass a restless and perilous night in the forest." The husband who maintained his animal property through the labor of his wife had a name. He was John Duncan. The anonymous missing person and the cows were recognizable only in their relationship to him. The family cooperated to navigate and exploit inte-rior spaces. The John Duncans of the world took the credit and the profit.[50]

Cows wandered landscapes and ate plant cellulose that humans could convert to milk and meat. Agrarian households accepted this energy, and they searched for their own sources of stored sunshine. Foraging humans went around domestic livestock intermediaries and sampled sugary nature straight from the vine. In 1828, three girls "ranging from ten to seventeen years of age" left home "in a quest for wintergreen-berries." They entered the woods outside Machias Corners in Cattaraugus County, New York, where they "lost their way, and began wandering." They could not gain a prospect, for "go whichever direction they would, it was all, all wilderness; no opening could be found." Dinnertime came, and the family spread the news that the girls were missing. People hallooed for them into the night and after a rainstorm forced most of the searchers to retire, two men stayed out to listen for "any unusual sound or cry of distress." The next day had been set aside for the militia to gather at Machias Corners. Instead of marching around the green, the company plunged into the woods after the children. Two men found the girls later in the day "away up on a high bluff, near the creek." They were identified as cold, hungry, and scared, which may as well have been their names, for the girls remained anonymous outside their relationship with men. They started the berry hunt the "three daughters of George Arnold," and they ended up in the anecdote's post-script known by their husbands: "Although this happened fifty years ago, the girls (now quite elderly ladies) are all here to-day, viz., Mrs. Chester Ashcraft and Mrs. Nathan Ashcraft, of Machias, and Mrs. Mercy Read, of Arcade."[51]

## BELLS

Agrarian households spit out members like frogs flicking tongues into a bug hatch. They tested and tasted their surroundings, stretching the relationships that bound them into a family. Getting lost threatened to sever the connection between spouses, parents and children, brothers and sisters, masters and servants. The agrarians risked amputation to gain material advantage. They were dependent on their environments, and they were dependent on one another. To survive, if not thrive, households cast their lesser appendages into the wind to see what they might reel in.

No practice better exemplified the precarious balance between hanging onto dependents and letting them fly than the belling of children. E. J. Dye entered the world and the history of Brookfield Township, Ohio, on November 19, 1812. He would mature into a community pillar. A farmer and stock raiser, a member of the Methodist Episcopal Church, he served as the justice of the peace for eighteen years. His childhood was less secure. He remembered "when the whole township was sparsely settled." He took on the job of finding the family's cows at a young age. Before he slipped into the woods after them, his father would tie "a bell upon him so that he might be found in case he lost his way." The clanks were the soundtrack of

Dye's youth; they brought him back to his and the community's early days when fathers risked their children's lives in the backwoods.[52]

One night in 1844, Wilson Satchell, a ten-year-old from Union County, Iowa, was settling into the darkness with his family. The rituals of turning in clicked off: dinner passed, plates were put up, furniture was moved to prepare for sleep. Then a noise roused the cabin. The bell on their lead sheep came "tinkling" through the walls. "They must be brought home," said Father. Wilson was sent to put the animals to bed. He did not return. His family searched for him all night. Days passed without sign of him. Dark thoughts filled their heads: " 'Indians have taken him or wolves have eaten him.' " On the third day, he was found alive and intact in neighboring Mahaska County. Wilson "was not the only child lost" in those "early days." To hang onto their metaphoric as well as actual lambs, the local historian who remembered Wilson Satchell's ordeal reported, adults " 'belled' " their children "to keep them within hearing." The tinkling registered parents' care but also the reality of their situation. Both children and livestock had to wander out of sight to harvest the bounty of the woods and prairies. To exploit free grass, to grow their herds and their families and leave the hardscrabble "early days," the agrarians gambled on creatures that, once sent off, might not find their way back.[53]

Did the revolutionaries who dangled cowbells around their children's necks continue to believe in the possibility of toddler liberation? How could the same generation that venerated Paul Gasford's independence bell its progeny along with its goats? The bells recalled the premodern era, when children were seen as little animals, sinful creatures to be broken, to be observed closely and guided firmly. Yet the bells also echoed the frontier, a place short on shepherds yet thick with stock and spawn. Did the bells announce the dawning of a new age of individual freedom and self-determination, or did they ring in the old days, signaling a retreat back to the reality of humans' dependence on their senses, their environments, and one another?

On April 23, 1791, a woman gave birth to a son in "a rude hut" alongside "a packer's path in Cove Grove, distant three miles and a half" from what would become Mercersburg, Pennsylvania. The hut's owners would eventually sell the structure and leave for town. Their progeny would reside in a fancy house on Main Street. In 1830 or 1832, the hut followed the family. The new owners dismantled the log home and reassembled it on Fayette Street in Mercersburg. In 1886, two "very aged people," "John Rodgers and his wife," resided there. Their creaky bones gave the place an antique feel, which suited its new purpose: the hut had become a landmark when the child born there in 1791 ascended to the presidency of the United States. The Rodgers moldered in James Buchanan's natal cabin.[54]

In 1885, following the Civil War that Buchanan's inept leadership did so much to bring about, local historians dug up the Cove Grove site, unearthing revolutionary-era pennies along with other metal objects. Though it's unclear whether they actually found a cowbell, the detritus at least brought cowbells to the excavators' minds. If only "the hut and these coins [could] tell their simple story," wrote one, "they could give many incidents connected with the early life of the boy who, with a bell about his neck to prevent his being lost among the rocks and bushes, was securing that training which subsequently qualified him for a life of distinction and public trust."[55]

Frontier origins had been a trendy qualification for higher office since Andrew Jackson's "common man" campaign in 1828. Buchanan's successor in the White House, Abraham Lincoln, famously exploited his frontier upbringing. But Jackson's Indian fighting and Lincoln's rail splitting seemed more manly, vigorous, and proto-presidential than a boy with a bell strung around his neck clanging from the rocks and bushes every time he moved. Cowbells empowered parents, not children. They increased the adults' supervisory range, bringing more senses to bear on the problem of keeping track of moving offspring in woodlands, swamps, and prairies. The bells suggested that, Gasfordian spectacles of precocious wayfaring aside, American children were not mentally equipped to traverse environments on their own. Instead of sounding the triumph of frontier liberation, the bells tolled the humiliation of frontier childhood. To be young was to be treated like a cow. The dirt in Cove Grove told many Buchanan stories. The one about the great man springing from common soil rested alongside the one about the overworked mother who belled her children to keep them safely tucked in the herd.

The bells tolled an even more somber knell of American surveillance. In Buchanan's time, blacksmiths attached bells to the iron collars slave owners requisitioned to clamp around the necks of incorrigible freedom seekers. Like the cowbells agrarian parents hung around their children's necks, the belled collars increased the sensory ability of supervisors, adding to the slave regime's reach and depravity. The bell collars were designed to stymie mobility. Their ringing not only betrayed their wearers' movements, they destroyed the possibility of them surviving independently in the southern commons. In a narrative of his life in slavery and his eventual escape, Charles Ball reported meeting a belled fugitive in the swamps of South Carolina. Ball was in the woods scrounging for protein to supplement the punishing diet of greens and bread he received on his plantation. The collared man's name was Paul. He had been born in the Congo and had run away from his American master several times. During his last attempt, he had survived for six months in the swamp until an enslaved woman he often visited on the edge of the mire betrayed him.

Paul received a severe whipping and a collar with an "iron rod extending from one shoulder over his head to the other, with the bells fastened at the top of the arch." He escaped again, but the collar changed life in the swamp. The noise of the bells frightened all the animals with meat on their bones, so he slurped raw turtle eggs for sustenance. He moved only at dusk and dawn, "lest the sound of his bells should be heard by some one, who would make his master acquainted with the place of his concealment." The bells drove Paul to despair. He climbed a tree with a rope around his neck and jumped. The smell of his decomposing body wafted through the swamp. Ball followed it to the scene. The crows would not touch the corpse, for every time they landed for a peck, the bells would ring and chase them away.[56]

Unable to reach the liberty he so desired, Paul from the Congo hanged himself from a sarsaparilla tree, the same species that launched Paul Gasford's miraculous hike. In the mental spaces crafted by nineteenth-century Americans, grown men could be belled like children or animals, and four-year-old boys could master their environments like grown men. Neither scenario reflected the truth on the ground. Children got lost often and found nature shock while fugitives from slavery navigated outlands as expert survivalists and master orienteers. The histories of agrarian communities dealt with these spatial and social realities by denying them. They pretended that, when left to their own devices, very young boys could locate independence in the woods. Communities hid and ignored the Native landscapes they invaded. They highlighted the fields they cleared, the cabins they built, and the firehouses they consecrated. To prove their independence and mastery, they admitted to getting lost in order to mark their progress. These same agrarian communities dismissed fugitive slaves' persistence for decades in so-called wildernesses like the Great Dismal Swamp. Enslaved persons' miraculous self-rescues and community-building efforts somehow proved their inferiority. By making homes out of mires, runaways demonstrated their natural compatibility with "astonishing and horrible place[s]" rather than their determination to find liberty in disorienting environments. Maroon settlements stayed invisible in part because whites could not imagine them. The darkness of the swamp hid the fugitives while exposing the limits of the slave regime's perception.[57]

# CHAPTER FOUR

# Homing

A MULE CARRIED JACK INTO A SUMMER CAMP bustling with Oglala Lakotas, fur traders, and overland travelers. He swayed in the saddle, gripping the pommel as if it were the rail of a storm-tossed ship. Oglala women and children "poured out of their lodges" and encircled the animal and its rider. Their screams and cries drew more onlookers. Even at rest, Jack rocked and rolled, and his "vacant stare" sent shivers through the crowd. Three Oglala hunters had rescued the man after discovering him lying facedown alone on the plains. He had gone missing thirty-three days before in early June while out chasing wayward oxen and horses for his employer, John Baptiste Richard, the bourgeois, or proprietor, of Fort Bernard, a trading post on the North Platte River.[1]

According to Francis Parkman, a Harvard historian traveling with a company of fur trappers in 1846 to recover his health and collect literary "sketches" for a book about the Oregon Trail, Jack looked a fright. His "cheeks were shrunken in the hollows of his jaws" and "his eyes were unnaturally dilated." His shriveled lips pulled back from his teeth, giving him the smile of a corpse. He wore only a jacket and a pair of ripped trousers. After being separated from his fellow wranglers during a storm, he had wandered "bewildered in the boundless, hopeless desert that stretched around him." He tromped through the brush for weeks, eating crickets, lizards, and three raw prairie dove eggs. When his strength finally gave out, he crawled on all fours until the bones of his kneecaps were "laid bare."[2]

Jack's appearance dismayed the Oglalas, who found his "haggard face and glazed eye . . . disgusting to look upon." One of the French-speaking voyageurs heated up a bowl of gruel to feed the emaciated man. When the liquid touched Jack's lips, he "seemed suddenly inflamed into madness." He begged for more. The trappers refused his entreaties, worried that a gorging after weeks spent fasting would kill him. They set a watch on him that night to monitor his intake, but he slipped into the Oglalas' portion of the camp and ate every morsel he could find. He survived the "effects of his greediness" and later left the region for a job back east. Jack enjoyed "tolerable health," though he remained "slightly deranged" long after he got lost on the plains.[3]

Jack suffered nature shock. Parkman attempted to capture the experience with his descriptions of Jack's worn body and haunted eyes. He communicated the insanity of extreme bewilderment by noting Jack's crazed behavior in camp. He also included a sequence of dreams to conjure the man's delirium. While lost, Parkman reported, Jack walked at night to avoid the heat of the day. Noon found him curled up in the open, his subconscious feeding him glimmers of a former life. When he lay "down by day to sleep in the glaring sun," Jack informed Parkman, he dreamed of "the broth and corn-cakes he used to eat under his old master's shed in Missouri."[4]

Before Jack ran into trouble on the grasslands surrounding the North Platte River, he ran away from slavery on a border-state farm. As a fugitive, Jack's employment options were limited, and the multicultural workforce of the western fur trade offered a haven. He signed on with Richard, who oversaw a "motley crew" of Canadian Métis, Spaniards from Taos, "Mexican Indians," French-speaking *éngagés* (contract workers), and American whiskey traders. An "inexperience[d] and helpless" hunter and horseman, Jack's western reinvention was clumsy. When he got lost in the thunderstorm, Richard's men gave him up for dead because he was so clearly out of his depth in his new environment. When confronted with an expanse without landmarks, his mind returned to the shade of an agrarian outbuilding and the taste of soup and johnnycakes. He "homed" along a pathway familiar to nature-shocked nineteenth-century Americans.[5]

Human beings can visit places in memories and dreams, and while this talent helps them to hover above geographies, to gain allocentric perspectives and picture vast and complex landscapes no two eyes could possibly see, their homing abilities pale next to flocks of scavengers who peck discarded bread crusts and French fries on city sidewalks. Common rock doves or pigeons can detect magnetic fields, read sun positions, and recall mental maps. The birds' way-finding skills are so impressive that researchers must treat them like black-op prisoners, hooding their tiny heads and placing them in sensory-deprivation containers to ensure they will not ruin experiments by tracking their position in the van (or plane) on the way to a release site. Theories abound to explain their prowess. One rests on the iron particles that have been found in the cells of pigeons' beaks and chest muscles. The magnetite crystals line up with the earth's magnetic fields, and they may create smells or pulling sensations that reel the birds back to natal lofts.[6]

Blinded, spun-around, and confounded humans had fewer built-in modifications to point them toward their nests. Instead, they imagined homes as a palliative, recalling the sensations of being in place to calm the desperation of feeling unmoored. Unable to find their way back, they traveled home in dreams, and if they survived, they recalled their mental return trips in letters, interviews, histories, and memoirs. Their homing filtered into print and was preserved to illustrate the psychological disaster of getting lost. Sometimes, in the wide open, the bewildered involuntarily revisited humid climes. Their minds sought shade and refuge while their skin burned and their bones bleached.

In the early to middle decades of the nineteenth century, nature-shocked Americans on the plains and prairies fantasized about woodland agrarian homes. They teleported eastern farms onto semiarid grasslands in moments of sheer panic. The locales they imagined emerged from real social and material spaces, making their memories ambivalent at best. Jack's dream home, after all, also served as his prison. Agrarian homes were shot through with inequities and animated by endless routines of coerced work. The power of the state backed the authority of male heads of households. Property laws, marriage contracts, and voting restrictions ensured their sway. Wives, children, servants, apprentices, and slaves labored to create and sustain households, but free men, nearly all of them white, were supposed to own and govern them.[7]

The records of the lost included members from all ranks in agrarian households. Women, children, servants, and slaves became disoriented while laboring on behalf of homesteads. They got lost herding livestock, picking berries, gathering herbs, and traveling rural roads in storms or at night. Some of them got lost while attempting to break free from homes. Jack proved that nature shock could tempt even the fiercest self-emancipators to wax nostalgic for past meals. The dreams of home differed for those considered dependent or "covered" by the legal identities and personal authority of adult male patriarchs. For them, getting extremely lost and longing for sheds and corncakes signaled the depth of the hold households had on them. The tendrils of agrarian authority reached into fugitives' subconscious. For many dependents, then, homing was a nightmare.[8]

Jack's dream had the opposite effect on Francis Parkman, who felt at sea in the motley collection of races, genders, and nationalities he encountered in the camps and trading posts along the North Platte River. Parkman tossed around slurs like "squaw," "mongrel," and "negro blood" without embarrassment. He believed in his innate supremacy, and he recounted Jack's hallucination to reassure his white audience that the tethers of American households clung to runaways in distant lands. Stretching the bonds of home into contested edge territories appealed to white male American authors. They repeatedly cast their chases, searches, expeditions, and quests as extensions of agrarian households. Adult male hunters of various sorts left home to fortify home, not to escape it. They expressed their freedom, their individuality, by expanding the boundaries of relational space to the outskirts of their nation's territory.[9]

In the Declaration of Independence, Thomas Jefferson enshrined the pursuit of happiness alongside life and liberty as the three most obvious reasons for breaking and remaking a government. For him, the pursuit was not some vague longing for comfort or an abstract desire for fulfillment. The chase was a physical compulsion, more analogous to a natural law than a private aspiration. Free persons scattered along predictable lines because objectives pulled them with magnetic force. You could read their progress with a compass, and according to him, governments would do well to harness this drive rather than stifle it.[10]

Unlike Hernando de Soto, Jeffersonian hunters, explorers, mappers, and wranglers (many of whom, in the de Soto tradition, also plunged into the continental interior after treasure, land, and pigs) moved through spaces believing that individuals formed their relationships instead of their relationships forming them. Free men lived with choices the way early moderns endured hierarchies. Both conditions were foundational views of the world.

The choice to leave an agrarian home to pursue wild game or wayward animals could result in bewilderment. Hunting was, and still is, a good way to get lost. Hunters forgot themselves when they plunged into environments, focused on an objective rather than their bearings. They abandoned remembering, the laborious keeping track of steps, hours, sun positions, compass readings, bends, switchbacks, and forks. They paid no attention to blazes on trees or storied landmarks. The goal overpowered the route. Fully invested in the chase, they refused to pause and reflect to achieve allocentric perspectives. They might catch their quarry, look around, and realize that the pursuit had taken them to an alien place. Unaware of their environments, they could be ambushed by a storm, an accident, or nightfall. In the heat of the chase, they could violate property laws and political boundaries, enraging other humans with their unwelcome intrusions. The chase could get you shot as well as shocked.[11]

The hunt isolated individuals with the object of their desire. The object of the pursuit subsumed other relationships. Thus, running after an animal—or a gold mine or a literary reputation—expressed the pursuers' freedom, but it also fastened them, sometimes intimately, to that thing. Obsessed hunters surrendered the power of choice to their objective. The thing being chased often decided the course of events, and the target's agency combined with the intimacy of the predator and prey relationship led to confusion over roles. Sometimes, as in the case of Jack, pursuers became the pursued. They turned into the misplaced objects in need of going after.

Jack's situation showed how complicated nineteenth-century chases could become. On the ground, pursuits tangled liberty and subjection. A man hunting fugitive livestock for his employer, Jack got lost while pursuing the freedom to build a life outside slavery. His disorientation turned him into a multifaceted missing person. He was lost to himself, to John Baptiste Richard's crew, and to the Missouri slaver who claimed to own him. Nature shock robbed him of his limited choices. On the plains, Jack had nowhere to turn, and his subconscious mind transported him to the last place he wanted to go.

The Oglala hunters rescued him in more ways than one. They happened upon Jack in the pursuit of their own objectives: they were provisioning their households and patrolling their territory. Jack could find a refuge outside the American slave regime in part because in 1846 the Lakotas exercised sovereignty over the region of the North Platte River. The fur-trade companies and overland travelers journeyed through this space with their permission. The spectacle of Lakota power drew Francis Parkman to the Oregon Trail. He hoped to witness an "Indian war," and rumors of an impending fight between the Oglalas and the Crows had him ready to scribble when Jack swayed into the camp.[12]

By reporting to Americans back home, Parkman integrated the West into their imagined national space. He worked to familiarize them with Lakota camps and multicultural fur-trading posts—fixing other people's homes and territories in his readers' minds so that they might begin to think of these spaces as contiguous with their own. Traveling into foreign territories in pursuit of "sketches," the writer prepared the region for the American conquest. When his readers entered the Great Plains, they would encounter the scenes Parkman planted in their heads rather than the emptiness Jack perceived.

At least they would until something unforeseen happened. Literary oversight was not an accurate guide for navigating geographic space. Americans continued to get lost on the plains long after treaties, wars, and massacres convinced them that the North Platte River valley was their country. By discovering bewilderment in pursuit of horses and freedom, Jack caught Parkman's eye. He became an anecdote at the leading edge of an expanding American nation Jack wanted to avoid.[13]

Nature shock exposed the confusion of American white male pursuits. Running after an object of desire was an individualistic move undertaken for relational ends. Free men pursued game, land, profit, and celebrity in the name of agrarian domesticity. Yet chasing was an activity as likely to carry a man away from a hearth as bring him back home. Getting terribly lost laid bare the conceit that the pursuit of happiness brought about spatial coherence and social harmony.

In the nineteenth century, the heads of agrarian households pushed the edges of relational and national space into the continent's midsection. They invaded grassland environments—the prairies and the plains—to consolidate patriarchal authority, which they conceived of in relational terms. They drew their power from wives, children, servants, and slaves. By leaving home, these men extended the lines of domestic authority through leaps of imagination. They dreamed of being in control, of being the head of a home, while traveling abroad. The tension between their mental maps and their actual locations jump-started individual space. The chasers shirked the duties of personal surveillance and tried to oversee households from afar. To do this, they leaned on the mail, the telegraph, and the newspapers. Their long-distance power grew as these impersonal networks strengthened over the latter half of the nineteenth century. Jack and Parkman met at the turn toward individual space. They weren't there yet. Modernity merely beckoned in 1846.

The Americans' arrival on the prairies and plains dislodged Native farmers. The Indians claimed the grasslands and made homes by moving frequently to escape winter storms, locate migrating game, and exploit the region's diverse habitats. The invaders misjudged the space and misunder-stood the Natives' peregrinations. In ignorance, they cut new edges and discovered new perplexities. On the plains, the lines demarcating safe spaces from danger zones shifted at night and during storms. Blizzards swallowed hunters, sometimes costing them frostbitten toes and fingers. The grass-lands drew American men seeking the political independence and material prosperity a farm and a family guaranteed them. But they built their domains in the middle of volatile open spaces they neither comprehended nor controlled. Their conquest of the grasslands would go on for decades as generations pursued agrarian households in environments that punished stationary targets.

## HUNTING FOR A HOME

David Crockett chased bears, squirrels, raccoons, votes, women, laughs, celebrity, and money. In 1834, he crafted a political biography with the assis-tance of a friend and fellow congressional representative, Kentuckian Thomas Chilton. In the book, the two spun woodsy frontier tales to bolster Crockett's reputation as a good-natured, authentic child of the forest. The story of Crockett's wooing of his first wife adhered to this formula by combining romance, humor, and titillation with the backcountry predica-ment of getting lost.[14]

In 1809, Crockett agreed to take part in a communal predator hunt that promised "the best sort of sport." Not yet a skilled hunter, he soon became separated from his wolf-exterminator colleagues. He found himself in a "strange woods, and in a part of the country which was very thinly inhabited." The clouds rolled in and he "began to get scared." Turned around, unable to gauge his position by the sun, he "didn't know which way home was, nor any thing about it." Crockett switched objectives; instead of wolves, he aimed for a way out. But his sense of direction failed him: "I set out the way I thought it was, but it turned out with me, as it always does with a lost man, I was wrong, and took exactly the contrary direction from the right one." Crockett and Chilton paused here, at the height of discombobulation, to offer some advice to "young hunters." Do not trust your first instincts: "Whenever a fellow gets bad lost, the way home is just the way he don't think it is." Crockett stumbled through the brush for "six or seven miles." When he was about to give up and go to sleep in the spreading gloom, his salvation appeared in a flash. He spotted "a little woman streaking it along through the woods like a wrath [wraith]."[15]

The woman turned out to be the true object of Crockett's desire—Polly Finley. The two had been involved in a tumultuous courtship. They met the previous fall at a harvest festival, and Crockett's prospects looked bright until Polly's mother flipped her initial support from him to a rival suitor. The wolf hunt commenced at a low point in his pursuit of Polly Finley. It was a chase within a chase. Within a chase. Polly was out hunting too. In the woods searching for her father's horses, she ran into Crockett, but she "had missed her way, and had no knowledge where she was, or how far it was to any house, or what way would take us there." Though frazzled and exhausted, Polly "looked sweeter than sugar" to Crockett, who professed to love her "almost well enough to eat her." The two happened upon a path that led them to an abandoned house. They "set up all night courting." Six weeks later, they wed over the objections of Polly's mother. At the age of twenty, Crockett had reached adulthood. He had found a mate and thus a home.[16]

When David carried Polly across the threshold of their first abode, the couple entered a physical structure built to cultural specifications. Crockett sought a home to become a free man. And he needed Polly to accomplish this transformation. Her labor would turn the cabin in a clearing they rented into a home. She went to work spinning thread and weaving cloth and proved herself industrious "at almost any thing else a woman could do." David took pride in her homemaking, for it reflected well on his husbandry. Her sweat built his equity. His independence resulted from his control of a household—a structure on land brought into production by a workforce bound by blood or contract to him. Polly entered her first home under contract, and she brought two cows with her to sweeten the deal. She labored for the household and bore several children, fulfilling Crockett's ambition to step into the agrarian republic as a full-fledged citizen. Households operated like small-scale republics. They trained adult males for leadership and provided material support for their political rights. Crockett became eligible for office in his home.[17]

Which he struggled to hang onto. Polly and David rented their first homestead and no matter how hard they spun and plowed, they could not get ahead. In his biography, Crockett admitted that "I was better at increasing my family than my fortune." They moved once and then again. David took up hunting as his primary vocation, pulling the family farther west into spaces where wildlife flourished but permanent residences did not. Polly died in 1815. David remarried. He chose a new mate whom he did not love at first. He sought a household manager, not a sweetheart. He kept uprooting his family. Crockett, of course, met his fate in Texas at the Alamo, finding in death what eluded him in life—a personal association with a fixed place.[18]

At their wedding, Crockett and Finley freed themselves from households controlled by other people, but the two struggled to establish their own home. They were poor, and the frontier economy kept them moving. Their restless devotion to a home just over the horizon captured the impulse of the

Idealized engraving of a frontier home, 1867. (Courtesy of the Library of Congress Prints & Photographs Division, LC-USZ62-69024)

age. In the nineteenth century, self-made Americans idealized the home and the chase simultaneously. They inherited notions of republican independence and subscribed to a nation founded by free men who sprang from microcosmic authority generators—working households. Then they watched millions of men use their place-bound freedoms to, in Crockett's words, "hunt some place better to get along."[19]

The countervailing forces of movement and domesticity played out differently across classes and genders. In 1849, George Nichols wrote letters to his mother and father as he prepared to join the rush to the California gold fields. To his lawyer father, George wrote detailed accounts of his preparations for lighting out. He chronicled the price of feed, saddles, and harnesses. He took pains to explain where the reliable wagon makers in Pittsburgh acquired their spokes (machined in Manchester) and to pass along the advice he'd been given about weaning the mules from their grain diet before they arrived on the plains. The animals "will wilt right down" if not accustomed to grass. To his father, George communicated his enthusiasm for the chase, including reassurances about his fitness: "I am perfectly well and think I can stand the journey."[20]

He switched genres in the letters he sent his mother. Instead of livestock tips and equipment lists, he filled these missives with longing for his home in Buffalo, New York: "I think everything at home must be in order by this time. The flowers blooming at the windows, the trees in the yard beginning to bud & blossom; the carpets on the floors, chairs around the room. I almost see you showing Margaret the secret mystery of roasting meat. Charley running in with a letter from father." Buds and blossoms, carpets and chairs, mother and sister in the kitchen, little brother hustling in with the mail—these were the ingredients of a fondly remembered upper-middle-class home in 1849. When George conjured the domestic ideal he summoned pruned nature, material possessions, femininity, and the U.S. postal service.[21]

In his letters, George paired material concerns with sentimental pronouncements. The emotions may seem antithetical to the things, yet they combined to announce the family's commitment to the ideal of the American home as well as to the best transportation their money could buy. Instead of filling his wagon with goods and using them to form relationships with other humans, to turn strangers into friends and family, as fur traders and imperial diplomats had been doing in the North American interior for centuries, he intended to keep his property and maintain his emotional attachments to his home. The food and equipment, the mules and the Pittsburgh wagon—and all those handwritten letters—signified order, happiness, and self-reliance. George Nichols took his leave of home, but it's unclear if he ever truly stepped away from it. George carried his mother and siblings in his memories. He would cook his beans and bacon over smoldering dry buffalo chips on the high plains, but the fire that burned brightest for him, that oriented him on the road, flickered in a hearth in upstate New York.

The Nichols family fumbled their passage across the continent. George died on a steamboat on his way to the Overland Trail. For all the care he took in gathering equipment and news, in documenting his choices and his emotions, he could not synchronize his pursuit of gold with his desire to stay home. The well-heeled Nichols shared little with the rough-hewn Crocketts. But they shared this.

## SINGLE HUNTERS

George Nichols never married. The home of his daydreams belonged to his parents. Had he survived, his trip to California may have matured him and given him the financial and emotional independence to launch his own household. Getting lost in the transition from one home to another tossed bachelor hunters into quizzical spaces. When father-hunters became bewildered provisioning agrarian households, their disorientation looked like a sacrifice. It confirmed their status as protectors and providers. When bachelors got turned around and descended into mania, whom did their discombobulation serve? Was their suffering evidence of stoic nobility or rash stupidity? When single men dashed into strange woodlands and onto uncharted plains, were they making wise choices worthy of virtuous free persons or demonstrating an inability to govern themselves? When bachelors descended into nature shock, what locations entered their dreams, a past home ruled by a father or a future home they might never see?

Baltimorean John Fowler immigrated to Pike Township, Ohio, as a single man in 1811. The bachelor traveled to his neighbors' homes to observe the Sabbath. He rose early one Sunday at James Thrall's place in southern Clayton Township and spotted a deer passing the cabin. He chased after the animal without bothering to put on his hat, slip on his shoes, or grab his coat. The pursuit lasted much longer than he expected. The demands of the hunt—"watching, laying in wait, and following up"—drew all his attention and stole his sense of time. "Toward evening," Fowler broke concentration and "discovered that he had lost his bearings, and was sadly bewildered." He gave up on the deer and hunted for home. He walked for hours; darkness seeped between the trees. But he "could make no progress in getting out . . . for he could tell by a very large tree that was blown up by the roots, and other land-marks, that he was traveling in a circle." The uprooted oak haunted him. He circled back to it "more than twenty times." The fallen tree stood for his inability to walk in a straight line. Fowler passed into nature shock: "He did not know how many miles he had wandered from home, could not form an idea where he was, and was sure his was a very bad case of 'lost,' and he began to weaken." He climbed a tree in an attempt to gain some perspective and cried his throat raw screaming for help.[22]

The brothers Robert and John Colborn, out in the woods on Monday morning to scavenge resources for their household, heard Fowler's ragged moans and followed them to his location. They helped him down and soothed him until he regained his composure. Knocked wobbly, Fowler struggled to integrate the experience of his lost Sunday into the stories he told himself and others told about him. Fowler stood out among his peers for his independence and prowess over nature. A flinty woodsman, the man his neighbors called "the first white" person to settle in Pike Township, Fowler was "not a man to scare at trifles." In 1816, he wed Sarah Brown, a transplant from Virginia, and the two started a family. In 1817, Fowler cemented his local fame by rescuing fourteen-year-old Hannah Coddington when she got lost in the woods. Travelers called the path he blazed between his cabin and the Thralls' place "Fowler's path." The denizens of Pike Township followed the trail to visit the inhabitants of Clayton Township for "more than twenty years." They recognized the orienting skill of the path maker each time they walked it. In his dotage, Fowler was the picture of environmental mastery: "His gun and fishing rod were the companions of his old age. . . . It was a common occurrence to see him in the dusk of the evening wending his way homeward with a bunch of squirrels or a string of fish." Yet that night lost in the woods rendered him "pale, anxious and well nigh exhausted." He shivered when he recalled his nature shock, the "sickening, despairing 'turn around' that overcame him."[23]

For John Fowler, getting lost was an odd turn of events, a detour in a life that otherwise proceeded according to a predictable and respectable pattern for a rural American man. The incident in the woods haunted him, but both he and his frontier community got over it. Other single men followed more treacherous paths. One of the first American farmers to invade Warren Township, Poweshiek County, Iowa, a man only known as Mr. Bivens lived alone as a bachelor, making him an oddity in the agrarian incursion led by families. Bivens, according to local history, "stayed in the community with no permanent occupation." One day, out hunting, he got lost and "remained out over night." He died from exposure after reaching the home of Jacob Yeager. The year was 1848. The community buried him in its "newly laid out cemetery," but it did not mark his grave. The story of his getting lost and dying offered the only proof that Mr. Bivens ever existed.[24]

Abraham Weast cut a faint trace through the history of Bradford County, Pennsylvania. He arrived there in 1804 and squatted on land that would become "William Moshier's farm." It's unclear if a wife or children helped him with the improvements he made to the land before he sold it to a man named Sprague in 1807. Weast was remembered neither as a family man nor a householder; rather, he "was a noted chopper and hunter." The locals described him as a "smart woodsman" with impressive wilderness skills.

And they enjoyed telling the story of the time those talents failed him. One day, Weast decided to walk to Mill Creek. It was a trifling expedition. He didn't even bother to bring his gun. Not too far along, he "became lost and wandered in the woods for three days." As darkness closed on the third day, he spotted a farm with a turnip patch. The owner found Weast on his knees in the dirt, devouring the roots as quickly as he could pick them. He took the deranged hunter into his cabin and fed him "venison soup" until he "came around." The taste of the broth restored Weast: temporarily rendered a turnip gobbler by his missteps, he became a predator again, a woodsman. The community remembered him as the man who cut Moshier's farm from the woods, as the man who swung an ax and fired a gun better than most. People remembered him by himself. For all his impressive masculine accomplishments, he was missing a household to oversee. Politically, he was homeless. Being nature shocked by himself on the edge of the community defined his marginal social position.[25]

Unlike Mr. Bevins and Abraham Weast, John H. Semer entered the annals of Van Wert County, Ohio, as a founder and a father. Semer moved to the western Ohio region in 1852. At that time, writes local historian Thaddeus Stephens Gilliland, Semer was "one of the few white settlers in that wild region." There was only a small crowd of people around to boss, but Semer took charge nonetheless. He convinced his neighbors to name their township in honor of Andrew Jackson and served as the township's treasurer. He and his wife Catherine populated Jackson Township with ten children. Unlike Weart, who squatted on frontier lands, improved them, and moved on, the Semers were stickers. The family originated in Pennsylvania. After several moves, they chose Van Wert County as the spot to make their stand and start broadcasting a farm and a family across time instead of hauling them across a continent. Some of their children moved away, but John Jr. stayed in Jackson Township all his life. In 1870, he operated a farm known as "one of the best cultivated in the county." Twice married, he fathered twelve children. Held in "confidence and esteem" by his community, John Jr. was elevated by his farmer brethren to the township's board of trustees and the school board. He served as justice of the peace for more than twenty-five years.

Yet even a deeply rooted and highly visible family like the Semers had ghost limbs. In the early days of the family's stretch in Van Wert, two of John Jr.'s brothers, ages ten and fifteen, went hunting in winter to replenish the household's larder and break the monotony of being cooped up. They became lost "and wandered around until dark when they crawled into a hollow log." When the moon rose, their mood brightened. They believed they could find their way home navigating by its glow. They tumbled out of the log only to discover that their frozen, benumbed feet would not carry them. Desperate and drifting into shock, they returned to the hollow log. The elder wrapped his little brother in his coat. The neighbors, searching through the night with torches, found the pair in the morning. The children's "feet were so badly frozen that they had to be amputated above the ankles." The residents of Jackson Township buried the boys' blackened appendages in the past. The incident illustrated the sacrifices "pioneers" made so that later generations might enjoy the fruits of going nowhere. But in the county history, the brothers stayed missing. John Jr. inherited the Semer mantle of community leadership. His brothers remained frozen in time: underage hunters, footless and nameless.[26]

Single males sometimes encountered nature shock on the road to adulthood. Young men ventured to the edge of agrarian settlements on missions of subsistence and self-discovery. They sought to prove their mettle as independent men, but when they stepped over an edge into territories unknown to them, territories sometimes patrolled by men from other nations on their own missions, they risked the personal sovereignty they hoped to capture. Such was the case in southwest Texas in 1865, when four boys set out for a place known as "the sink of the water" outside Seco to hunt renegade cattle.

A day into their search, they rounded up a lost soul along with the cattle: Ludwig Mummie, an "old man" who "had been lost part of two days and a night" coming through the mountains from "Bandera to D'Hanis." One of the boys, August Rothe, escorted the "very hungry, and almost delirious" man to camp. They fed and caffeinated him, and Mummie rode on. The next day, Indians attacked the cattle hunters. Rothe and a boy named Jacob Sauter escaped, but their two friends, George Miller and Herbert Weynand, were killed.

Ludwig Mummie was the nature-shocked individual in the Seco incident. His discombobulation survived in local Texas history because it dovetailed with an even more memorable incident of frontier violence. Had he stayed, the story went, the well-armed old man may have been able to prevent the loss of Miller and Weynand.[27]

The lost cattle drew the young men into a disputed and confusing landscape. The cattle stepped away from the bonds of ownership and domestication when they sauntered out of town. Chasing them, the boys entered a space where their connections to family, community, and nation fell away. The teens were the definition of "cowboys." Weynard was only twelve years old. Adulthood remained well ahead of him. The other three were approaching an age when they could assume the roles of husband, father, voter, property owner, and Indian fighter, the stations that defined political maturity among white Texas settlers, but they weren't there yet, and they were no match against Native American fighters who had either reached adulthood or were on the raid to acquire the military experience and livestock to do so. The local historian who described the episode denied the Natives human specificity. They stayed generic and villainous "Indians" throughout, but given Seco's location, the group most likely belonged to the loose confederacy of nomadic bands that made up the Comanche Nation. The Comanches measured manhood in livestock ownership, horses especially. Young men participated in raids to acquire herds that signaled their ability to marry. Without animals, they could not find mates; without mates, they could not enter adulthood. The Seco cowboys and their Native adversaries may have been working toward the same goal when they met and tried to kill one another.[28]

American parents sent their children into the woods, onto the plains, and across the deserts to induce early-onset independence. Kids as young as four or five could start cultivating the habits of self-reliance rounding up livestock on the family's behalf. The Seco incident fit the agrarian pattern, to a degree. Wrangling cattle in a contested space overseen by Native Americans demonstrated courage. The risk turned the experience from a chore to a rite of passage. But the teens did not enter the proving ground boys and come back men. After they met with violence, they were still boys, just dead or traumatized ones. Rothe and Sauter emerged from the ordeal more damaged than triumphant. And they weren't the only husks of masculinity in the desert. Ludwig Mummie turned the rangeland coming-of-age story into a weird sideshow before disaster struck the boys. Mummie was an autonomous white adult male with "a good gun, pistol, and plenty of cartridges." Yet there he was, completely lost, his mental acuity scrambled, begging four children for directions, beans, and coffee. The "unsettled" grazing lands around Seco did not reveal male character in this episode. The frontier brought grown men and dependent teenagers to their knees, exposing an undertow of dependence that pulled stories bristling with totems of nineteenth-century American expansion in more vulnerable directions. Crossing over an agrarian edge into nature shock or violence robbed men of their personal sovereignty.[29]

Before the ambush, the Seco boys may have foreseen a bright, independent future for themselves. They sought to become a version of Ludwig Mummie on his better days by successfully completing a roundup that would bring them closer to liberation. But manly self-reliance was not their destination nor the destination of most agrarian males who wandered too far afield and encountered nature shock.

## A WALDEN INTERLUDE

Before turning to a pair of lost newlyweds, I want to single out a final lost bachelor, an idiosyncratic one from the woodlands of New England. Henry David Thoreau wrote glowingly about getting lost in *Walden*, his account of living alone for over a year in the woods outside Concord, Massachusetts. He recommended bewilderment. "It is a surprising and memorable, as well as valuable experience," he wrote, "to be lost in the woods any time." Getting lost broke wanderers free from their routines ("we are constantly, though unconsciously, steering like pilots by certain well-known beacons and head-lands") and brought about a new appreciation of "the vastness and strange-ness of Nature."[30]

Thoreau urged his audience not only to rethink the woods but also to reconsider the settled spaces they inhabited. For him, wildness was a perspective rather than a location, and the universe opened to everyday philosophers who imagined forests, chipmunks, beans, and barns anew. Getting lost profited wanderers by awakening perceptions: "Not till we are lost, in other words, not till we have lost the world, do we begin to find ourselves, and realize where we are and the infinite extent of our relations." People truly saw their place in the world when they lost their bearings.[31]

Thoreau was an alternative agrarian. He grew his own food and carved a homestead out of a tangle of trees, yet he denounced the commercial agriculture practiced around him. He settled land, yet he protested the Mexican-American War and rejected the call to establish farms in foreign territories. He brought fresh insights to an old woodlot, yet for all his rambunctious reimagining, Thoreau presented a rural terrain conven-tional bachelors could recognize. In *Walden,* he inverted expectations, yet those expectations belonged to a generation of Americans transitioning from a relational space to an individualistic one. Thoreau wrote about living alone, yet getting lost brought him back to the "infinite extent of our relations." When he ventured into the woods, he hoped to merge with a universal oversoul, not discover his personal freedom. He was not hoping to get lost and drop out; he was looking to get lost and find connection.[32]

Thoreau played with elements of disorientation familiar to his agrarian audience. He started the getting-lost passage in *Walden* in the dark. Leaving a "bright village parlor or lecture room," he stepped into the night to walk back to his cabin. The darkness intensified as the woods enveloped him. Thoreau navigated by the stars, which appeared every so often in the gaps in the forest canopy. On cloudy nights, he felt for the path with his toes. He moved at ease and did not worry about getting lost, but he met people in the forest who were afraid of the dark. He encountered two men so intent on pulling fish from Walden Pond that they forgot to proceed home before sundown. Thoreau pointed out the path that would take them to their abode, which was only "a mile off through the woods." They missed the path and wandered all night, slipping past their house several times, and finally arriving at their door at daybreak, exhausted and drenched from a rainstorm. Thoreau heard stories of people "going astray even in the village streets, when the darkness was so thick you could cut it with a knife, as the saying is." He knew other people who got lost in snowstorms. The blanketed landscape confused them on roads they had "travelled a thousand times." For Thoreau, not seeing well was a first step toward geographic confusion and spiritual insight.[33]

Thoreau observed his neighbors' bewilderment. He watched the darkness enfold them and collected anecdotes about bad-weather ambushes. Though enamored with the idea of getting lost, he lingered outside the phenomenon for the most part in his writing, preferring to study the reactions of others. He stepped down from his observational perch for a few paragraphs in an article he wrote about an 1846 expedition to Maine's Mount Katahdin. After traveling to Bangor by rail, Thoreau entered the backwoods at the end of August in the company of two boatmen-guides and three Maine businessmen. They wound their way up the river branches and lakes of the Penobscot watershed and reached the base of the mountain on September 7. Eager to witness the geology above the timberline, Thoreau twice left his associates to be alone in the vast grayness of naked rock and low-lying clouds.[34]

The stubborn mists played tricks with Thoreau's vision. Winds cleared pockets of light that closed as quickly as they opened. During his final ascent, Thoreau first lost sight of his companions in the "cloud-factory" and then lost his view of the rocks. "Occasionally, when the windy columns broke in to me," he wrote, "I caught sight of the dark, damp crag to the right or left; the mist driving ceaselessly between it and me." It was the sensory depravation as much as Katahdin's altitude or immensity that induced Thoreau's awestruck reaction to the summit. Next to Walden Pond, Thoreau nestled into nature, domesticating it. On Katahdin, Nature rejected him and suggested, in a booming voice, that the little man return whence he came, "where I *am* kind." Unable to see, Thoreau felt an uneasy isolation. "Why came ye here before your time?" asked the mountain. "This ground is not prepared for you." More alone than he could imagine, Thoreau contemplated falling into shock, not being able to form "substantial thought and fair understanding," his reason "dispersed and shadowy, more thin and subtle, like the air." He scurried down to meet his companions, who were picking mountain cranberries and blueberries in the lower elevations, where the clouds dispersed, and nature revealed itself to be the nurturer of humanity. Thoreau provided an agrarian ending to his Katahdin adventure. Instead of planting a flag and reveling in their conquest, the campers went scrounging.[35]

Back in Concord, Thoreau and his neighbors floundered in the woods; they took wrong turns at night, and they became confused when storms rolled in. They kept tabs on their livestock, their children, and their demented relatives to prevent infrequent but inevitable spatial confusion from escalating into town emergencies. Thoreau communicated with his American audience through a shared conception of agrarian space. He singled himself out from his countrymen, contrasting his comfort with being lost with others' trepidation. He pleaded with his readers to drop their defenses. Once they pushed through the shock of disorientation, they would awaken as if from "sleep or any abstraction," and instead of going through the motions of neighborliness out of fear, they would recognize their deeper connections to nature and to one another. These transcendental bonds superseded ties to a town, a state, a party, or a nation. In the paragraph following his ruminations on getting lost, Thoreau mentions his arrest for nonpayment of taxes in protest of the Mexican-American War. Going astray was a prelude to him going to jail.[36]

Episodes like his tax protest signaled that Thoreau was not a run-of-the-mill frontier bachelor. Most of the single male agrarians who got lost in the North American woods were dedicated expansionists seeking to cut farms out of recently conquered territories. Yet Thoreau's radicalism sprang from a similar vision of the land. For all his rebelliousness, Thoreau relished the privilege of oversight. He was a consummate (and a professionally trained) surveyor. He knew where the boundaries lay, and he preferred to stay within them. By blocking the view, the cloudy summit of Katahdin offered him a glimpse at the edge where geographic, social, and cultural space fell away. He sensed nature shock and retreated. Thoreau climbed down, went in search of a berry patch, and savored the taste of home.

## LOST NEWLYWEDS

John Little traversed a bewildering landscape with his new wife, Maria, when they escaped the United States for Canada in 1841. Born in North Carolina, John tended his white owner's mules and hogs on Sundays throughout his youth. This job carried him into the woods, where he learned to hunt rabbits and to fish. At ease in the commons, the edge spaces outside the agrarian settlements where southerners ranged livestock and harvested wild plants and animals, Little fled to the forests and swamps on more than one occasion to evade his masters. He was an accomplished lurker. When his second owner threatened to sell him to a trader bound for Georgia, he lived in the edge-lands uncaptured for two years to stay near the farm that housed his mother.[37]

His masters knew he would run and that he could fend for himself, so they factored his autonomy into their management of him. Some took it upon themselves to break his spirit. They beat him with paddles and whips and welded chains around his ankles to inhibit his dexterity and to torment him. Others bargained with him, trading better treatment for him sticking around. Finally, a North Carolina master sold him to a farmer in Tennessee. He transferred the headache known as John Little, at a reduced price, to another state, hoping that distance would mute the affectionate relationships that provoked his flights in the first place.

In Tennessee, Little could not return to his birth family, but he found someone else to run for. He married Maria, an enslaved woman on a neighboring farm. Nine months into their partnership, he was "jerked right up" and taken to a plantation near Memphis. He was to be sold and taken into the Deep South. Little escaped but was caught by a patrol on the road back to his wife. Held in jail, he broke through the roof and hobbled into the woods, his legs shackled in irons. After finding a blacksmith shop and filing through his chains, he planned his final getaway. He gathered food and clothing and waited in the woods outside Maria's farm. Through intermediaries, he alerted her to be ready to head north on the appointed night. A confidante betrayed the couple, and the two were forced to leave in haste without most of their provisions. They walked the 140 miles to the Ohio River with the clothes on their backs and an uncured ham, which they ate raw, "like a dog."[38]

John Little was a navigational savant. Filled with removals, flights, solitary interludes on the edges of white agrarian spaces, and recaptures, his enslavement was so action packed that it was hard to keep track of all his movements, much less corral them into a narrative. In the whirlwind of comings and goings, he was the one person who knew where he was the whole time. Little passed between farms and outlands. He moved across county and state lines. He ran enchained, and he lived at large. He could travel unseen at night in the woods, and he could travel in broad daylight on horseback along the main roads. He was as spatially nimble as they came. Nevertheless, the free states of the Midwest confounded him. He and Maria entered Illinois at Cairo and promptly got lost.

John and Maria Little crossed into an unstable space when they breeched the border of slavery and freedom. They entered a puzzling interior where intentions became as hard to read as landscapes. To regain clarity, the couple sought the Canadian line. For them, Illinois, Iowa, Indiana, and Michigan were as unfathomable and difficult to navigate as a prairie in a blizzard in the dead of night.

The couple aimed for Chicago, but they "wandered out of the way" and met the Mississippi River instead of Lake Michigan. In Iowa, they entered the Black Hawk Territory and Little became "so lost and bewildered" that he had to risk going "up to a house to inquire the way." He and Maria lucked into a man "with true abolition principles." He turned them around and told them to be careful, another couple had been nabbed in the neighborhood recently and taken back to slavery. Principled as he was, he declined to help them recross the river. Back in Illinois, Maria reached the end of her stamina. She was "completely worn out" and the couple reeled in indecipherable space: "It was three months from the time we left home. . . . We were in the woods, ignorant of the roads and losing our way."[39]

One Sunday night, John stumbled upon a road sign. He could "spell out print a little" and deciphered "5 miles to Park's Landing." The pair set off in that direction, but since the two could not be seen on the road and had to travel at night in the woods, they could only guess the location of the town. On Wednesday, they came to a crossroads and found the same signpost—"5 miles to Park's Landing." They were circling, wearing out, getting no closer to freedom. Little described the experience as being in a wilderness. It was a well-populated desolation. They could glimpse homes through the trees, see and smell the smoke rising from the chimneys. But they "had suffered so much from white men, that [they] had no confidence in them, and determined to push through without their help." Finally, in desperation, John approached an Illinois man, not knowing if he would find "a friend instead of an enemy." The stranger proved sympathetic and helped them to Chicago, where abolitionists funded their passage to Detroit, where they crossed to Windsor, Canada, and reached free soil.[40]

Little retold the story to an American interviewer years later from his home in Ontario. He looked back on the United States and slavery from the perspective of a successful Canadian farmer. He and Maria had established an agrarian household. They cut a farm from "Queen Victoria's dominions," chopping trees "day and night" to clear 110 acres to grow wheat. Maria worked by his side in the fields. They accumulated "two span of horses, a yoke of oxen, ten milch cows and young cattle, twenty head of hogs, forty head of sheep." "I have two wagons," John Little reported, "two ploughs, and two drags." The thriving farm proved his independence: "If there is a man in the free States who says the colored people cannot take care of themselves, I want him to come here and see John Little." Although Maria labored as long and as diligently as John to create their prosperous farm, John pushed her into the background when he claimed political freedom at the end of their shared dangers.[41]

Little first tasted freedom chasing hogs and mules on Sundays in the woods of North Carolina. Like his adolescent colleagues throughout rural North America, Little assumed the responsibilities of a full-grown worker at a young age. Early-onset adulthood made him self-reliant. Little's autonomy was a boon for his master, to a point. The slave's wood-craftiness enforced the slave owner's dominion over the roaming animals set loose to grow fat on the southern commons. Spatial expertise, however, gave the child leverage. When his master threatened to sell him, Little could escape and lurk. Here's where the enslaved child and merely dependent white children parted company. Little used his autonomy to defy his owner and remain near his mother and then his wife. He fled to the woods and lived alone to escape a household out to destroy his family. White agrarians believed they reared miniature individualists in the name of propagating relational space. The kids would grow up to found nuclear families. Young men and women eventually peeled off and established their own households filled with subordinates whose labor buttressed the independence of the male head. Male freedom rested on the control of others. In the case of slaves, that control was supposed to be total. Slave owners established their independence by denying households and families to equally adamant seekers of agrarian homes like Maria and John Little.

## ON THE PRAIRIES

The Littles muscled a Canadian forest into an agrarian homestead. They cleared fields and killed wolves, opening spaces for crops and livestock. Their log cabin served as a beacon of John Little's authority. He ruled an independent household, and the occupants under his supervision worked together to banish the wilderness and establish a pastoral enclave. From John Little's perspective, the landscape told a story of exertion and progress. The dead trees and skinned predators marked history, showing the arc of male freedom.

Nineteenth-century agrarians borrowed the spatial grammar of expansion—the log cabin in a clearing of stumps surrounded by a dense forest—from an earlier period of colonial cross-pollination. In the seventeenth century, Finns in New Sweden merged their building, hunting, and agriculture practices with those of the Native Lenape. Together, they created a mobile bundle of technologies and practices that featured notched logs, burnt fields, tree girding, men's hunting, and women's farming. The movement started in the Delaware and Susquehanna valleys and spread across the Appalachians when land-hungry colonists with traditions of religious dissent adopted the frontier culture and used it to carve and claim independent households.[42]

Treeless prairies and plains jumbled the signposts of settlement. Invaders reproduced symbols of progress from woodland memories. They shipped in wood to build permanent homesteads and bounded their fields with fences. They enclosed home spaces while they ventured into "wild" commons to hunt wolves, turkeys, deer, and pheasants. They pointed to visible fruits of their families' labor and cited the outbuildings and plowed furrows as evidence of their self-sufficiency and dominion over the earth. The grasslands, however, punished stationary targets. In winter, when the snows fell and the winds howled, blizzards trapped people who indulged in permanent homes. The Native residents of the grasslands moved their villages seasonally to exploit a variety of resources and escape the whiteouts. They used mobility to meet the challenges of the grasslands. Instead of acknowledging their savvy, the settlers argued that the Indians' transience proved their incompetence and justified their removal.[43]

American farmers ventured onto the Iowa grasslands under the protection of the federal government. Government agents negotiated treaties with the Sioux, Iowas, Sauks, Foxes, Winnebagos, and Potawatomis, and armies enforced those treaties' removal provisions at gunpoint. Portions of the territory that became the state of Iowa had been promised to the Sauks and Foxes following the Black Hawk War and to the Potawatomis after they ceded their lands surrounding Chicago in an earlier treaty. The government renegotiated these land cessions within a few decades. When news reached white farmers in the surrounding states that the government had voided the Black Hawk Purchase (1833) or signed removal agreements with the Sauks and Foxes (1842) and then the Potawatomis (1846), they rushed into Iowa. The farmers often portrayed themselves as a geologic force; they were an unstoppable wave, a "restless tide." But political transactions opened spaces for them, not the ineffable motion of nature or history.[44]

Once on the prairies, the farmers noted the paths and landmarks the Natives left behind. An Indian trail ran through Carroll County, traversing the length of the "eastern tier of townships." The path "was as straight as the flight of an arrow and was worn deep into the prairie sod like a furrow." Sodbusters turned up flint arrowheads, stone hatchets, and human remains. An army expedition discovered a lookout platform forty feet up in a grove of trees, proof that the previous occupants knew how to manufacture visual prospects in flat terrain. Native Americans constructed paths, built dwellings, and set fires to regenerate grasslands. Perhaps their most extensive environmental management strategy was movement. Unlike the white settlers, who were property owners obsessed with hanging tight to quarter sections on township maps, the Indians migrated with the seasons. They moved camps to hunt, farm, and harvest sugar, and they sheltered their families and their horses in the river valleys during the winter.[45]

The white settlers beheld the Indians' adaptive meandering and denounced them for it. The savages, they argued, let the buffaloes cut trails for them, and their vagrancy indicated their shiftlessness. They showed desire "to make no improvements," so they "were finally driven from the track by those who would." The "uncivilized aborigines roamed over the prairies wild and free unfettered by the restraints of statutory law and uncircumscribed by township boundaries and county lines." Still, by paying more attention to grid outlines than weather patterns, the industrious civilizers found themselves in climatological pickles, such as the winter of 1856–57, when "people in the villages were lost within two blocks of their houses." The snow fell for months and "there were not fences and nothing in some directions but a trackless prairie." Winter claimed the lives and the limbs of shut-ins who refused to budge in the face of the blizzards that descended on the grasslands like clockwork.[46]

In 1911, Chicago's Pioneer Publishing Company unveiled the first volume of Luther Brewer and Barthinius Wick's history of Linn County, Iowa. Linn squatted in the middle of the state, two counties over from the Illinois border. It included the town of Cedar Rapids. The early settlers interviewed by Brewer and Wick remembered living with bands of Winnebagos, Sauks, and Foxes in the 1830s and 1840s. Susan Shields learned to speak Ho-Chunk, the Siouan language of the Winnebagos, to help her father run a trading post in Cedar Rapids. Robert Ellis communicated to both Algonquian-speaking and Siouan-speaking Native groups in a trading pidgin. On a winter journey from Cedar Rapids to Fort Atkinson, he stopped at an Indian camp near Quasqueton to inquire if he could hire someone to help guide him across the prairies. No one accepted the offer; it was too dangerous. When Ellis announced that he would proceed alone, an "Indian shrugged his shoulders and replied, 'wolf eaty you.' " Ellis trudged through the snow to prove the naysayers wrong. He reached a cabin after dark after nearly perishing from the cold.[47]

The Indians' white neighbors remembered their tastes and movements. The Natives relished sugar and flour, and they traded game for both. "The localities much frequented by the Indians were along the Red Cedar and Wapsie rivers, Cedar lake, Indian creek, and Palisades Linn Grove, Scotch Grove, and Prairie Creek." Brewer and Wick reported that "in these places they would remain for weeks at a time, when they would all pull up and leave on some hunting trip, not returning till in the fall or spring the next year." Even after they signed treaties of removal, some groups continued their migratory circuits: "Many of the tribes kept coming back to their old hunting ground and finally were permitted to remain on the Iowa river." The memories Brewer and Wick collected revealed a mental landscape constructed from seasonal movement and strategic camping that lived beneath the rigid township boundaries and county lines. The Indians exploited the prairies differently than the Americans, yet both found common ground, for a while. The settlers and the Native Americans, for example, both loved sweets, and maple syrup crossed ethnic and racial frontiers to bring their communities together. The "pioneers of Linn county found them friendly, hospitable, devoted and loyal friends." They remembered their Indian neighbors warmly—until they forgot them. The creators of county histories noted prairie paths, winter migrations, and trading relationships even as they spun theories that denied the former inhabitants the ability to create and linger in prairie landscapes.[48]

## LOST FATHERS

Inclement conditions on the prairies distorted perceptions and dimmed memories. Snowstorms tested the bonds of agrarian space. Leonard Fletcher Parker, historian of Poweshiek County, Iowa, described the sensations of a radical climatic shift on "practically an unobstructed plain." In summer, breezes crossed the wide-open landscape and softened the heat, but in winter during a blizzard "every blast seems death laden, and the music of the storm is funereal." To capture the terror for his readers, Parker imagined a "prairie resident" caught in the open during a storm. The character "lashes his team into a run. The track is filled. His landmarks are becoming invisible. . . . A moment ago he could tell where he was. Now he is utterly uncertain of his location or of the direction he should take and hold." Parker gave voice to the storm. It whispered in the ears of the lost man's kin, huddled and worried in their leaky frontier cabin. The wind shot through gaps in the chinking and whistled: "Gone, gone, gone, forever." Lucky, Poweshiekians trusted their animals. If they possessed last ounces of strength to give, "worn-out horses found [their owners] shelter" in the form of the home of a hospitable stranger. Not all the imaginary people made it through Parker's fictional blizzard. "Here and there," he reported, "an unreturning neighbor made that blizzard the saddest of memories." Nature shock on the prairies and plains animated mental landscapes. Houses moaned and neighbors mourned as traveling agrarians wandered off the grid.[49]

Forced to venture out into the landscape to provision their households and maintain their communities—visiting was one of the few ways to keep in touch with neighbors—the agrarians codified their anxieties into boilerplate narratives of wanderers taken by surprise in the wide-open spaces. All that remained for a historian such as Leonard Fletcher Parker to do was fill in the names of those who went astray, those who got rescued, and those unlucky souls who drifted blind into eternity.[50]

Fathers decided whether families stayed in a home or strayed into the open. On January 6, 1856, the Bonwell family traveled from their farm in Butler County, Iowa, to attend the funeral of Eliza J. Newhard in Clarksville.

The gravediggers chipped at the frozen turf for hours to lay Newhard to rest. The services concluded near dark and Shadrach Bonwell directed the horses pulling the sled with him, his wife, and children for home. By the time the family stopped at Lenhart's place, a "storm was raging." Lenhart begged the Bonwells to stay the night. Shadrach, however, refused the offer. He was worried about his stock. The family would push through. Wife and children tucked into the sled, Shadrach snapped the reins and promptly lost the road. He missed the house and drove out onto the prairie. The horses drifted with the storm, coursing northwest. The Bonwells reached a patch of timber and rested in the windbreak. With enough strength for one last pull, the horses reached the safety of Daniel Kinsley's cabin.[51]

Meanwhile, the Bonwells' disappearance kicked the community into emergency action. Soon after leaving Lenhart's homestead and becoming bewildered, Shadrach had fired his gun to summon help. The wind whipped the sound around, catching the ears of several neighbors but giving them little idea as to where the report came from. At sunrise, searchers followed the tracks "over the entire circuit" until they reached Kinsley's and found everyone safe.[52]

Irving H. Hart, historian of Butler County, concluded the Bonwell anecdote with a joke. He quoted one of the crustier and more downbeat members of the search-and-rescue party who, after surveying the tracks of the Bonwells' sled, theorized that "they have evidently struck one of the sinkholes on the prairies and all went to hell together." Hart included the line to relieve the tension of the near tragedy and illustrate the rough humor frontier types preferred in olden days. Sentiments did indeed often shade toward noir. Shadrach may have deserved to go to hell for his stubborn insistence on proceeding home in the storm. Was his stock worth more than his brood? The family met the storm coming from a funeral. Counting blessings and appreciating neighborly comforts should have been at the forefront of their minds. Instead, the father tempted fate and played loose with his family's lives. Moreover, the joke's landscape hinted at a darkness that could be found on the treeless prairie. The quip hit home because everyone within hearing distance understood that the most likely location for a hell mouth to open and swallow a family was on the unobstructed plain. The wide open let in plenty of light, yet with so few landmarks to steer by, the grasslands could produce a gloom as deep as any forest.[53]

Blizzards exposed the peril involved in provisioning immobile house-holds. In the winter of 1836–37, the snows began in November in Cedar County, Iowa, and continued into March without the usual midwinter thaw to clear the roads on the prairies. "Great billowy drifts" formed over the roads, making horses and oxen useless. As provisions grew low, men set out on foot to reach towns thirty or forty miles away. Andrew Crawford walked thirty miles to Rockingham to purchase food for his family. He was packing the goods home on his back when a storm hit. He "lost his way, or rather, the points of the compass, and guided his course by the wind." He reached Sugar Creek, two miles above his farm, but he "was so bewildered or blinded that he could not distinguish his whereabouts." Darkness seeped around him as he shuffled along the ice of the creek, hoping it would lead him somewhere. Just as he was about to give up, to "lie down in despair," he happened upon the path James Burnside had dug from his farm to the creek to bring his cows to water. Crawford staggered to Burnside's cabin, but his walk on the ice had exacted a toll. "The flesh peeled from his face, his hands were badly frozen, and the ends of his feet fell off, leaving only the stumps or upper part [of] the ankle joint." The mission Crawford undertook to rescue a frozen household diminished his range. He walked with a cane for the rest of his life, though he remained nimble enough to run for office; he served as the constable of Cedar County until his death in 1856.[54]

Dr. Samuel Ballard told a story of getting lost in a snowstorm while out hunting with "Uncle John" Jenkins in December 1852. The two men were on the prairie, camping with a company of surveyors tasked with subdividing township 80, range 35, in Audubon County, Iowa. Ballard and Jenkins started westward from Blue Grass Cove. A heavy snowstorm caught them later in the day. The blowing snow cut visibility and scrambled their sense of direction: "We got bewildered, lost all idea of direction and wandered around long into the night, completely lost." Dr. Ballard kept his wits about him, but Jenkins, his feet frozen and hurting, became despondent. He awoke from the stormy night "much discouraged, still complaining of his feet, and expressed doubt we should ever reach home again." Jenkins also abandoned his confidence in Ballard, who declared that he had seen the North Star in a break in the clouds the night before. Feeling adrift, not knowing which direction to turn, Jenkins barked at the doctor: "And who in the hell, sir, told you what was north?" He reluctantly agreed to follow Ballard for the rest of the day, but still he "rebelled and became more obstinate than before." He moaned about his aching feet, said they were going in the wrong direction, and threatened to lie down to die, for there was no hope. Dr. Ballard finally smacked Uncle John in the face to snap him out of his delirium. The hunters reached a stretch of prairie Ballard thought he recognized. The doctor hallooed for Zach, the white hound he had left behind at Blue Grass Cove. The dog heard the call and ran to the pair. The camp cook followed the dog's tracks to the lost men.[55]

Samuel Ballard recounted the tale of his bewilderment and John Jenkins's nature shock often. The narrative bounced along the familiar ruts of agrarian homing. Ballard and Jenkins were out on the prairies in the middle of winter to map the region for settlement and to harvest the grasslands' plentiful wild game. When they got lost, Jenkins's frostbitten feet undermined his courage and he voiced his longing for home. That Jenkins's mind drifted to shelter and his family should not come as a surprise given the pain he felt. Dr. Ballard emerges in the story as the sensible survivor. He spotted the North Star and stayed present in the moment while Jenkins plunged into fanciful daydreams and unreasonable gloom. Yet agrarian households were material and social realities as well as abstract constructs. Dr. Ballard persevered in survival mode because his actual domestic situation was as frigid as a prairie blizzard. Uncle Jenkins may have been the luckier hunter; he had a convivial home where his thoughts could return.

A self-taught physician, Samuel Ballard grew rich practicing medicine in the environs of Iowa City. He visited patients on a circuit that stretched into the rural hinterlands. He kept a relay of horses saddled and slept as he rode to reach his clientele. The historian of Audubon County reported that Ballard took in fees that "sometimes exceeded two hundred dollars a day." He invested the proceeds in frontier land and livestock further west. Ballard "owned thousands of acres of the best timber and prairie lands in what is now Exira and Oakfield townships, and adjoining, in Cass county." He built a modest house among his fields and forests in Oakfield Township. Strangers would never guess that the "richest man in the county" lived in the "one story building, boarded up and down with rough, undressed oak boards, battened, unpainted and unplastered." The unwelcoming exterior reflected its owner's personality. Ballard "was disagreeable and a hard man to deal with." He "constantly quarreled with his tenants, hired help, and others who dealt with him." He had a reputation as a "hard master to his sons."[56]

Ballard's fields "were filled with herds of fine cattle, and droves of hogs," but he could not protect them from neighbors who stole his animals. Eventually, he sold his livestock because he could not trust his fellow agrarians, who judged him unworthy of his wealth. Ballard, wrote the historian, "did nothing for the upbuilding of his neighbors, or of the community in which he dwelt, consequently he had no friends, even among his kindred." Mrs. Ballard resided in Council Bluffs. The doctor paid for her to live there in "good style." The arrangement puzzled Ballard's rural neighbors: "The relation which existed between the Doctor and Mrs. Ballard was never understood by outsiders, but probably was not congenial." Samuel Ballard owned thousands of acres in Audubon County, and his exploits earned him a central place in the county's history, yet he never made a home there. His neighbors punished him for not living up to their expectations for community and household leaders.[57]

Rural fathers looked more like Uncle John Jenkins with his complaints and frostbitten toes. Missing male body parts littered agrarian communities. Farmers lost hands to threshers, fingers to bucksaws, and legs to militia cannons. In his history of Decatur County, Indiana, Lewis Albert Harding listed the amputations county residents endured after the Civil War battles of the Wilderness, Manassas, and Winchester. He also included the arm Marine Tackett lost when a cannon misfired during the celebration of the election of Governor Morton as well as the lower-left leg that teamster Nicholas Longworth lost when he "met with an accident" in Cincinnati. Historian Henry Kiner marked the arrival of mechanized farming in Henry County, Illinois, on November 5, 1891, with the removal of Hazlett South's arm by a shredder. Since that day, the dawn of the age of whirring gears and blades, he joked, "one-armed farmers are more frequent than lone hands in a euchrefest."[58]

The reference to the card game euchre signals that we are in the deep weeds of midwestern history. In the continent's center, rural Americans identified community members by the quality of their farms, by the size of their families, by the number of years they had inhabited one place, and by their record of sliced, torn, and blasted limbs and appendages. These injuries altered the course of lives, carving personal histories into watersheds, pre- and post-disaster. The agrarians and their big-city publishers shared the losses and memorialized the pain in their local compendiums of frontier life and family lore. When individuals forfeited bits of themselves, households and townships suffered a loss as well. Everyone went down a hand. All the stories of toes frozen, fingers chopped, and arms pulled from sockets fortified community relationships. True founding fathers gave of themselves rather than "accumulate lands and property for [their] own selfish aggrandizement" like Dr. Ballard.[59]

Not all fathers were equal. The histories of rural settlements reveal tensions between large landowners and those squatters and scroungers who scrambled for subsistence. Poverty drove some farmers to hunt more often, more widely, and more aggressively than others. They entered blizzards to go after prey; they messed with deadfall trees that kicked back when they chopped them; and they trespassed on the property of wealthy neighbors, sometimes pilfering a hog. Few hungry and desperate agrarians entered the annals of local history because the compendiums celebrated farmers and families who stayed and prospered. Movement was the frontier remedy to impoverishment. Squatters and scroungers picked up and left when proprietors filled the grid and cut their access to timberlands and hunting grounds. They moved, that is, if they still could walk.

Henry Nolf immigrated to Jefferson County, Pennsylvania, sometime in 1818 or 1819. Besides erecting one of the earliest sawmills in the county, Nolf's major accomplishments included both dying and almost dying. One time Nolf and Lewis Doverspike were out hunting in the northern section of Ringgold Township. They were walking a few hundred yards apart when Nolf spied and shot a bear. The wounded animal charged him, knocked him to the ground, and clawed and bit him. The screams drew Doverspike. After his gun misfired, Doverspike drove the bear off his partner by clubbing the animal in the ribs with the rifle. After being chased around and up a tree, Doverspike loaded another round and killed the bear. Nolf, writhing in a puddle of blood, begged Doverspike to end his suffering. Instead, the burly hunter lifted him on his shoulders and carried him "three miles to a house" where they patched up Nolf so that he could die another day.[60]

That hour arrived a few years later when Nolf was out hunting in the winter with his son George. The two built a rude shanty and set up camp. Henry journeyed into the woods to find a tree to chop for firewood. The one he chose split apart at the trunk, turned unexpectedly, and killed him. George found his dead father and traveled three miles to the nearest farm to "get help and a team." The locals from "the Dutch Settlement" formed "an inquest." They gathered later that night, passed around a jug of whiskey, and proceeded to enact more of a spree than an inquiry. They approached Nolf, unpinned his corpse, and placed it on a sled. They headed for Milliron's, the nearest house. On a turn somewhere between the accident scene and Milliron's, Nolf's remains "rolled out of the sled into the snow." When a member of the well-lubricated crew pointed out that the subject of their inquest had gone missing, another mused that the old hunter must be out running after prey "on a deer's track." They slid back, reclaimed the corpse, and "took him home." Henry Nolf fought a bear and was smashed by a tree, yet the most indelible mark he left was as an object of humor. His inability to stay still, his propensity to pursue deer even in death, showed both the absurdity and the desperation of the chase. Nolf was not a poor farmer; his investment in the sawmill testified to his stature. Yet, like the impoverished squatters who poured through the woods of Pennsylvania and out onto the prairies of Iowa, he would not be still. Provisioning an agrarian household required constant and risky maneuvers. The payoff for stalking dangerous animals and chopping into widow-making trees was a home, a place to remember and, more important, be remembered. The irony was that you could roll off the sled, a forgotten corpse, in pursuit of memorialization.[61]

The wide-open spaces of the Midwest played tricks on memory. In August 1900, journalist and congregational minister Rollin Lynde Hartt wrote an article for the *Atlantic Monthly* chronicling a disappointing visit to Iowa. He quoted his travel companion, a woman named Helen, who observed the state's expanses and found them disorienting and depressing. "You wake up morning after morning," she said, "to find yourself in nowhere in particular." She went on to describe the effect of living nowhere on Iowans' collective memory: "Happy that people who have no history." Hartt naturalized the Iowa farmers the same way the farmers naturalized their Native American predecessors. "From prairie grass to wheat," he wrote, "from wheat to clover, from clover to corn,—such are the short and simple annals of Iowans."[62]

Members of local-history societies bristled at the suggestion that the unyielding sameness of the prairies robbed them of their past. They quoted Hartt quoting Helen in the prefaces and introductions to their county histories. These two East Coast snobs were the kind of effete intellectuals they wanted to disprove. Yet even the most industrious of Iowa's local chroniclers had to admit that coming to naught was a possible outcome to all their work. The publishers of *The History of Jasper County, Iowa,* an 1878 compendium sold by Chicago's Western Historical Company printing house, included a plea to future generations to take up the pen and write their recollections down. "May we be permitted," the publishers wrote, "to express the earnest hope that before another generation shall have passed some other and able pen will have gathered and recorded the historic events that are to follow the close of this offering to the people of Jasper County." In order to keep history from "going to grass," as Hartt put it in 1900, the Iowans would have to feed their anecdotes to the nation's publishing industry and work as hard at preserving their lore as they did at growing corn, cows, and hogs. Memories must be defended "from generation to generation; and to this end public records, private journals and newspaper files should be carefully preserved." Historical societies were as integral to the American conquest of the grass-lands as plows or guns.[63]

### FROM HOMING TO HAULING

Henry Nolf got lost in the afterlife due to the amateurism of nineteenth-century mortuary practices. Accidents occurred, corners were cut, and bodies went missing when neighbors processed and buried neighbors. Nolf's community could laugh at him being misplaced because they believed his battered corpse rotted in the past, on a frontier they recalled but that no longer touched them. Ferocious bears, widow-making trees, and merry bands of German undertakers belonged to another, wilder age. Life in western Pennsylvania had settled by 1888, the year the Syracuse, New York, publishing firm of D. Mason unveiled the *History of Jefferson County.* The editor of the compendium, Kate M. Scott, praised Nolf and his generation of "prominent men and pioneers." She was also out to bury them.[64]

Nolf's remoteness was a literary invention. Mass mailings and mass printings signaled how much the United States had changed. The output of news, books, and correspondence went from a stream to a torrent in the years between the American Revolution and the Civil War, prompting some scholars to declare that an information revolution had taken place. Yet, while the advents of the penny press, a steam-powered national mail service, and a truly homegrown publishing industry were real and impressive, the grip of industrial information could still slip at dramatic moments. Blizzards on the Great Plains, for example, collapsed sight lines and spun travelers around long after trains and Sears catalogs arrived in the Far West. In January 1888, the same year the residents of Jefferson County memorialized Henry Nolf, a wicked storm swept the interior of the continent. A "seething mass of snow" "blinded" hunters, errand runners, cow chasers, and schoolchildren. Dozens of Americans "lost their way and perished." A human rather than a historical condition, getting lost changed with the times, but it never disappeared. Americans' expectations changed, however. Their information networks emboldened their movements, and they grew frustrated when gaps appeared and loved ones fell through them.[65]

In fact, the installation and operation of communication networks got people lost. During the winter of 1856–57, snowstorms blanketed western Iowa, halting the mail service between Council Bluffs and Boone. The mail rode in stagecoaches, and the drivers suffered to fill the company's government contracts and keep rural Iowans informed. One driver "got caught in a snowstorm and became so bewildered that he drove around in a small circle all night." He thought he was following a straight course: "He said he was confident of getting into the road every moment, and never dreamed of going over the same ground the entire night." They found him in the morning and carried him to the nearest house. They pondered whether "one or both" of his frostbitten feet would have to be removed. The snow drifted higher than the stagecoaches, yet the mail moved even when the teams and coaches could not. The companies transferred the job to men on horseback, and when the mounts foundered, the mail was "delivered on foot by strong men." Rural Americans pursued information as they did salt, deer, grindstones, and wayward cows. News provisioned households alongside food, water, and fuel, and the hunt for words could bewilder and hurt as much as any other.[66]

The same snowstorm that crippled the stage driver on the Boone to Council Bluffs circuit killed William Rice, "who drove the mail on the trail from St. Ansgar." Lost in the storm at night, Rice was found the next morning "near Rock Falls." He was whisked to the cabin of "Mr. Olson," where his rescuers tried to revive him, but "the effort was useless as he had been frozen to such an extent that death soon resulted."[67]

Short haulers brought the mail from transportation centers and handed the packages and letters to local mail carriers. The bigger circuits ran through interior cities such as Denver, Laramie, Virginia City, and Salt Lake City to prairie depots like Omaha, Nebraska, Atchison, Kansas, and Council Bluffs, Iowa, creating a new coast and interior in the grasslands. Iowans ventured out from the tall grass to the scrubby plains to transport goods. Some of them got lost. J. D. Allison was born in Gentry County, Missouri, in 1846. When he was six, his parents moved the family to Mills County, Iowa. He grew up there, studied at the common school, and married Maggie Kerlin on May 27, 1875. Allison launched a household with Maggie and entered the hauling business. He "made ten trips across the plains." On one trip, "he was lost and was for six days without food." At home in Iowa, he spun tales of fighting with Indians and recounted the "wonderful hardships" he endured out west, including the time he walked "from Virginia City, Nevada to this county which he accomplished in fifty six days." His cross-country travels turned Allison into an exotic male creature in late nineteenth-century Mills County, a place local historians were trying to paint in as soothing colors as possible by contrasting its present yawn-inducing state with the untamed expanses farther west and the dead frontier that lay in the past.[68]

T. K. Tyson traveled the plains five times between 1864 and 1867. He never got lost, providing a counterexample to the wanderers who missed their turnoffs and forgot their landmarks. His travels showed the routine boredom, punctuated by infrequent moments of terror and weirdness, that went into creating the regularity of transportation and information networks. Tyson's road through the interior was hard to miss. Teams of mules and oxen had beaten a "wide track" along the Platte River route connecting Denver to the jumping-off cities of Omaha, Atchison, and Nebraska City. In some places, the road widened to "a hundred yards or more," especially when the teamsters' path crossed the trails to California and Oregon. Farms and gold drew people across the interior, and their movements ruined the ground over which they passed: "It is next to impossible to raise a good crop on any of these old trails." The roads, the cities, and the gold and silver rushes that bankrolled both, intruded upon the territories of Native Americans, threatening their sovereignty and trashing their hunting grounds. Tyson witnessed the response. "The sight of the demolished ranches and remnants of burnt wagons," he wrote, "grew to be a common experience with us." He did not romanticize the violence. When rural communities in Ohio or Michigan wrote about their frontier pasts, they erased Natives from settled landscapes by consigning them to history. Tyson watched the conquest unfold in real time, and it scared him. He was not sure the conflict would be resolved in his favor. He was equally uncertain about his future as a teamster. Death by ambush belonged to a list of "common experiences" that aggravated him. His troubles included balky animals, awkward loads, evenings spent downstream from rival teams (oxen and horses muddied and fouled streams when freed to drink after a long day in the traces), and the early miles of every trip before drivers and beasts discovered their rhythm. Tyson, however, directed his biggest gripe at his employer, the Nebraska City–based Russell, Majors, and Waddell. He did not like its rules of professional comportment. The company forbade its employees from using profane language, a directive Tyson found intrusive and goddamned impossible to follow.[69]

T. K. Tyson spent long hours on the plains muttering curses under his breath. For extended stretches, his western work proved to be as dull as post-frontier life in Mills County, Iowa. Indeed, at one point Tyson's monotonous job and Mills County's modern tranquility converged. One of his caravans launched from there, and he remembered the Mills County to Denver trip long after its completion. It proved to be among the strangest of his teamster career. He rolled west from Iowa with a wagonload of cats. Tyson noted the cargo, but he did not answer the many questions raised by it. Who ordered the cats and why did they want them? Was Denver lacking cats? Were these parlor cats or back-alley mousers? What sounds and smells did a wagonload of cats emit after seventeen to forty-five days spent on the road? History will never know, for Tyson skipped past the cats to describe the load of onions he brought to Denver in the winter of 1865 and sold at a loss for 15 cents per pound, underscoring his impersonal connection to his freight. Deep down it did not matter to him what he carried. The stuff in the back paid him when he completed its journey from one market to another. He pursued transaction, not possession. He aimed to hold and transport things across the spaces between markets, the gaps where goods had less or no value. He hauled commodities and facilitated commerce for a wage rather than to chase a profit or a homestead for himself. Tyson provided households with cats and onions, yet this provisioning was becoming ever more abstract and distant as go-betweens like him brought items to buyers, removing the consumers from the chase as well.

The future did not belong to agrarian households. Back east, in places like Thoreau's New England, economic production escaped the confines of the home. Most of the sons and daughters of nineteenth-century farmers would labor for wages like T. K. Tyson, enduring the surveillance of uptight bosses instead of the critical gaze of patriarchal kinsmen. Like work, travel became impersonal. Opting against the old rules of mobility, transcontinental voyagers cut ties with Native inhabitants. They relied on the federal government, the steamboat and stagecoach companies, and the postal service to move them, their goods, and their information without the early modern colonial encumbrances of gift exchanges, intermarriages, and political alliances. The nineteenth century witnessed the erosion of relational space and the rise of individual space. In individual space people and property moved from points A to B unchanged by the geographies or the societies between them and their destinations This change did not happen at once. Indeed, it is still happening. Transcontinental travelers continued to encounter ragged edges in the rush to seamless transportation. Relational ideas lingered as individual space emerged.

# CHAPTER FIVE

# Dead-Certain Mental Compass

THE SUN CROSSED THE CALIFORNIA SKY. A patch of turf absorbed the passing rays. A herd of cows spied the grass, now tucked in the shade of a stand of trees, and moseyed over for a meal. The blades moved through the cows and exited in piles under the trees, so ending Samuel Nichols's journey to the West.

Or maybe his trip started that way. It's hard to tell where Samuel Nichols ceased or began. A lawyer, husband, and father from Buffalo, New York, Nichols had no intention of rushing to California until his son George, the would-be gold rush adventurer, connoisseur of wagon-wheel spokes, and daydreamer of roasted meats and delivered mail, convinced him to bankroll a family expedition. George traveled to Pittsburgh and arranged for the purchase of vehicles and supplies. Samuel met George in May, and they loaded their wagons, groceries, and equipment on a paddlewheel bound for Independence, Missouri, the jumping-off point for the Overland Trail. George never left the boat. On May 6, 1849, Samuel wrote his wife Sarah Ann informing her that their son had died from cholera on the river west of St. Louis: "Our lovely George is no more but is numbered with the dead."[1]

Instead of preparing for a transcontinental journey, Samuel hired mechanics to build a large wooden casket that held a smaller tin coffin. The workers stuffed charcoal between the wood and the tin and submerged George's body in alcohol to prevent him from traveling into putrefaction.

Samuel accompanied George to Buffalo, stayed there that winter, and then booked passage to California through Panama. He arrived in San Francisco in the summer of 1850 and caught a steamboat to Sacramento to prospect mining claims. He fulfilled his son's dreams of seeing the excitement and died from the same killer.

Before cholera took him, Samuel dictated a letter to a man he had met in Sacramento named Luther Cleaves, instructing Sarah to drop a lawsuit he had pending in New Jersey, to put all their property in her name, and to keep their sons "under her control until they were old enough to manage business for themselves." Cleaves oversaw Nichols's burial in the state cemetery in Sacramento.[2]

Months later Sarah wrote a family acquaintance in California seeking a fuller account of her husband's whereabouts. He visited the cemetery and spoke with the sexton. Nichols was gone. The body hadn't been moved, but the reference points that held it down had. With so many people out hunting treasure, the cemetery grounds lay open to wandering cows, and they "knocked down all the head boards that ever put up." Sarah kept trying to find Samuel, but unlike her son's flesh, her husband's body was taken from her.[3]

Samuel Nichols got terribly lost, which was no small accomplishment in an event as well mapped and thoroughly documented as the gold rush. By 1849, migrants to California could follow instructions offered in letters, guidebooks, newspapers, and government reports to find their way to the diggings. If they went overland, they traversed a landscape of ruts, signposts, monuments, and military forts. Print guides located campsites, river crossings, and desert passages, and individuals could retrace the guides exactly by attaching odometers to their wagon wheels. Ocean travelers depended on ship crews and steamboat companies to keep them oriented, but they also posted and received mail. The passengers on some ships published their own newspapers, a reassuring echo of the information networks they left behind. Just as wildfires sometimes create their own weather patterns, transcontinental movements in the 1840s generated storms of written material that lifted passengers to destinations thousands of miles away.[4]

With loads of information came raised expectations. Sarah Nichols anticipated Samuel's return, breathing or boxed. His journey to California strained the bonds of family affection, yet the rush of news promised to keep him tethered and available for recall. No matter the calamity, arrangements could be made to bring wanderers home. When Samuel fell through the net of communications nineteenth-century Americans strung across the continent to keep track of one another, he pioneered a new form of getting lost. He died, and his body fell apart, decaying into molecules that fertilized the grass and fed the cows, but the wretchedness of his biological dissolution paled next to the horror of the disruption in his data trail. Sarah expected illness and death. What she could not abide was silence.

Americans' devotion to transcontinental news could be extreme. In 1850, the *Boston Daily Atlas* printed two letters from ships headed to California through the Straits of Magellan. Captain Morton reported that his schooner was forced to retreat from the Straits and put into an Argentinean port after encountering "a severe gale, in which she sprung her foremast and jib-boom." The repaired ship completed its passage through the Straits in October. The second schooner, the *Roanoke,* had an easier time. It sailed through on October 19 and reached San Francisco in time to celebrate the New Year.

The captains kept Boston readers informed of their progress, or lack thereof, by writing reports, sealing them in bottles, and tossing them overboard. The bottles washed ashore, where they were picked up by Tierra del Fuegians. The Natives exchanged the notes for supplies at fur posts. The fur traders handed them to ship captains sailing back to Boston. Eventually, the letters reached John Tirrell Smith, Esquire, who knew the editor at the *Atlas.* The hottest shipping news passed through a most improbable network crossing several cultures and covering the length of the Western Hemisphere. As a communications strategy, throwing bottles into oceans would seem as wise as paying your mortgage by scratching lottery tickets. And yet the ship captains hurled them, confident that their reports would not only reach living beings who could read but also ones with literary connections. Before they flung their missives to the waves, they scribbled, "Please publish" on them.[5]

"Information appears to stew out of me naturally," wrote Mark Twain in the prefatory note to his 1872 travel account of the overhyped, get-rich-quick American West. "I regret this very much."[6]

In *Roughing It,* Twain satirized Americans' demand for western news. Samuel Clemens journeyed west with his brother Orion in 1862. Orion had been appointed by Abraham Lincoln to serve as the secretary to the Nevada

Territory. Twenty-six at the time, Samuel worked as his brother's aide and then tried his hand at prospecting, mining, and horse trading. He failed at all these ventures and gave up actively seeking his fortune in the West. He turned from doing to describing. A reporter for newspapers in Virginia City, Sacramento, and San Francisco, Twain contributed to the industrial production of information. *Roughing It* was the topper on the mountain of reading material rushing from the West. In the opening pages, Twain recounts boarding a stagecoach in St. Joseph, Missouri, and finding it stuffed with mail: "A perpendicular wall of mail matter rose up to the roof. There was a great pile of it strapped to the top of the stage, and fore and aft boots were full. We had twenty-seven hundred pounds of it aboard."[7]

Twain wrote about getting lost. One winter, a blizzard caught him and two companions on the road to Carson City, Nevada. The snow hid the trail, but one of the men, a veteran Prussian tracker named Ollendorff, "said his instinct was as sensitive as any compass, and that he could 'strike a bee-line' for Carson City and never diverge from it." Ollendorff led the party and soon shouted: "I knew I was dead certain as a compass, boys! Here we are, right in somebody's tracks." The men spurred their horses to catch up with the party ahead of them. They trotted for an hour, the tracks looked "new and fresher," and the contingent ahead appeared to grow more numerous. It was a company of soldiers. No, it was a regiment of five hundred cavalry! At last, someone reined in his horse to deliver the punch line: "Boys, these are our own tracks, we've been circussing round and round." Ollendorff and his "mental compass" were "in disgrace from that moment."[8]

Information stewed out of Americans, and the federal government partnered with transportation firms to haul their output across oceans, deserts, and mountains. Highly publicized events like mineral rushes attracted drifters from across the globe. An international and an intranational space, the West gathered opportunists from France, Hawaii, Sonoran Mexico, Chile, and China while sustaining hundreds of independent indigenous nations. Many eastern Americans squelched this plurality in the letters they wrote home. They held onto their prejudices and their possessions, expecting the multicultural space to bend to them rather than them to it.[9]

The federal government of the United States assisted by deploying its navy and army to conquer Alta California and New Mexico during the Mexican-American War. The government maintained military posts in the continent's interior and sent agents to negotiate with Indian nations for overland passage. The government financed regional information mines: scientific explorations, map-making ventures, and resource surveys. Newspaper reporters accompanied military-style fact-finding missions. Information connected the United States to the West and began the uneven and violent process of incorporating it into the nation.[10]

The federal government also supported Nichols's fallback mode of transportation—the steamboats. Steam propelled Nichols around the continent, against currents and up rivers, into the California interior. Treasure hunters filled the boats' decks, sharing gossip and pathogens, and the most profitable transportation companies moved information along with passengers. A lucky few steamboat companies contracted with the federal government to carry the mail. These arrangements allowed them to operate "packet" routes. These scheduled circuits meant that boats did not have to wait in ports to fill their holds on return voyages to turn a profit. The bags of mail chugged back and forth while the human cargo and all their supplies mainly shipped west. Information kept the engines at full boil.[11]

Amateur letter writers and professional authors papered the East with western reading material. All this news gave the impression that the region was being absorbed into the United States much like the frontiers that preceded it. Soon, local authorities would build stronger fences to keep cows out of graveyards. The place would settle, become contiguous with the rest of the country, and the chaos of the gold rush and the spectacle of the overland trail would recede into the past. Local histories would bury nature shock. Getting dreadfully lost would fade into the western past as it did in the stories Americans told about the eastern woodlands and the midwestern prairies. Correspondents won the region for the nation through grandiloquent and petty acts of surveillance. By spreading words across spaces to demarcate territory and survey resources, to tell stories of derring-do and righteous violence, or merely to keep tabs on neighbors and loved ones, countless authors extended the reach of Americans' social and imagined spaces while violating the sovereignty of others' homelands.

Mark Twain, however, perceived a flaw in the American conquest. Instead of a modern nation overtaking a wild frontier, he saw the coming information storm. Much of the verbiage emanating from the West could not be trusted. Hundreds of thousands of Ollendorffs sold visions of promised lands and inevitable progress. But their dead-certain mental compasses were screwy. Rather than achieving clarity through firsthand observations and industrialized communications, the stewers of information circussed around, lost in their own tracks.

Amateur and professional writers expanded the actual and conceptual geography of the United States. They ventured into foreign landscapes and surveyed them for audiences back home. The West yielded material for authors with grand ambitions and pedestrian goals, and their narratives, both scribbled and printed, cast a net of imagined social connections across the North American continent. Many wrote to suppress difference and claim spaces as part of a unified nation. They sought to obliterate regional spaces and introduce seamless transportation and communication to support the movement of individuals. Yet new edges formed as old connections faded. Individual space overtook relational space, but pockets of interpersonal territory remained, and nature shock revealed them. Samuel Nichols was not the only soul to disappear into a transition between spaces.

### AMATEUR INVASIONS

Travel in the interior of the continent appeared retrograde in comparison to the eastern United States, where canals and railroads were beginning to move people and commodities in higher volumes and at higher speeds. In the West, humans and animals continued to lumber at a pedestrian clip. Yet the roaming hid a hotbed of innovation. The Great Plains were a site of disruption long before coal-fired engines arrived. In the eighteenth century, Native Americans captured horses originating in Spanish New Mexico and used them to pursue the grasslands' massive bison herds. Nomadic nations like the Comanche, Sioux, and Cheyenne formed fluid and extensive territorial spheres of influence defined by strategic mobility.[12]

Starting in the 1830s, seasonal pulses of trekkers from the United States ventured onto the Great Plains, not to trade, to farm, or to fight, but to reach the other side. They started when the vegetation greened in the spring and passed through the Rockies at midsummer. Some stopped at the Great Salt Lake, while others hustled over the Sierra Nevadas or the Cascades before winter snowed in their trails. They pursued Zions or farmsteads or gold and silver bonanzas, and while animal muscle powered their movements, as it had their predecessors' in the fur trade, many of the overland riders perceived racial incompatibility where earlier traders and diplomats had spied potential allies and perhaps family relations. The newcomers observed and wrote about people and places, creating records of surveillance they shared with families and communities back home. Their communication network grew in strength as amateur and professional authors pounded the same topics repeatedly like road crews swinging sledgehammers to drive in mileposts.[13]

In May 1849, a gold rush caravan from western Tennessee met a contingent of Comanches on the trail from El Paso to California. The party's diarist, F. A. Percy, wrote to the editor of the *Clarksville Jeffersonian* to keep the hometown crowd apprised of the Clarksville Company's progress toward the gold fields. The Comanches, he sneered, "were the ugliest set of beings I ever saw or ever wish to see, all were nearly naked, riding horses, the women riding the same style as the men." Both sexes straddled "fine horses." The Americans stole one of their ponies, a perfectly justified theft, Percy wrote, for "no doubt they stole it." The next day, several mules went missing from the immigrants' caravan. The next night, the Tennesseans ambushed the Comanche families asleep in their camp. Percy bragged that he killed "his man." His only regret was that he could not see well enough in the dawn light to retrieve the scalp.[14]

Percy's racism presupposed an unbridgeable distance between him and the "Red Skins." The animals at the center of the dispute between the Comanches and the Tennesseans suggested otherwise. Both groups relied on mules and horses to move. The animals saved the humans the trouble of firing their own muscles and increased the weight of the loads the travelers could bear. Whereas canoes facilitated exchange in the glaciated and well-watered portions of North America, large herbivores carried the consumer economy into arid regions packed on their backs. The Tennesseans and Comanches robbed and raided at the tail end of the grasslands' cellulose boom, a story, over one hundred years old, of continual adaptation that pivoted on Native Americans' deployment of equine power to secure bison robes, enemy captives, and more horses to trade for Euro-American manufactured goods like pots, blankets, and guns. Horses and mules moved an economy that created wealth by cementing relationships.

The argonauts and the Comanches bowed to the rituals of exchange when they initially greeted one another. One of the Americans, a member of a crew from New York traveling in the same wagon train with the Clarksville Company, spoke Spanish and dickered with the Comanches' leader, who also knew the language. The leader asked for a "passport," a written declaration from these gold rushers that informed other gold rushers farther down the line that his band of Comanche families was friendly. The New Yorker drew up a letter and "gave them some biscuits and tobacco." Like the many cultural exchanges involving material goods and information that preceded it, this presentation of gifts created peace, which the Tennesseans later nixed when they rustled the horse. The fact that the Comanches asked for written assurances and the Tennesseans felt unbound by the transaction executed by a New Yorker hints at the larger problems travelers and Indians were experiencing in the interior in the mid-nineteenth century. American aggression was eating away at older ways of doing business. The Tennesseans were using equine power to hang onto their possessions rather than trade them. They were not interested in fostering relationships with Native people.[15]

The Comanches tried to address the threat posed by the American travelers. That's why they requested the "passport" from them. They did not need the piece of paper to facilitate their own movements. Through their raiding and trading, the Comanches impressed observers with their military strength. Americans who chose the southern route to California read about the Comanches' power in personal letters and in the newspapers and they worried about attacks, but when the Tennesseans confronted Comanche authority, they misinterpreted the warnings given them. Instead of seeing gift exchanges and nighttime horse raids as exercises in Comanche sovereignty, as police actions, they perceived them as random acts of kindness or as criminal offenses.

The interlopers paid more attention to the families and communities they left behind than to the relationships in front of them. They wrote reports, letters, and journals to keep distant relations informed of their movements. The Natives they encountered on the road were props in a drama being played out for others. The travelers overacted, shouting and gesticulating as if crowds from home were always watching them. After the morning ambush, the forty-niners cheered the retrieval of their mules. The violence fed their belligerence. They "vowed vengeance from that time on all 'Red Skins,' of whatever tribe, friendly or not." Given the interlopers' unpredictability, the Comanches thought it best to have them declare their intentions in writing. The "passport" helped the Comanches navigate the wild swings in behavior, mental capacities, and attention spans displayed by the different gold rush companies.[16]

Artist Solomon Eytinge's 1872 depiction of emigrant travel. Note the focus on self-contained domesticity and transportation—being at home away from home. (Courtesy of the New York Public Library)

In 1849, another company of gold rushers from Tennessee pushed onto the plains. The East Tennessee and California Gold Mining Company numbered fifty men armed with "Colt's repeating pistols and bowie knives and tomahawks" organized into military ranks under the command of "General" Anderson, a "gentleman in every sense of the word." The outfit included "ninety-six horses and eighteen wagons." Anderson and his men voted to chart a southerly course through Santa Fe after hearing reports that there was not enough grass along the more popular route tracing the North Platte River to Fort Laramie and through South Pass.[17]

They left Jamestown, Tennessee, on May 15 and reached Fort Leavenworth, Kansas, in August. From there, they jumped off onto the grasslands. The scribe tasked with documenting the company's progress in letters sent back to the editor of the *Knoxville Register* described the move: it felt like entering a "vast ocean-like plain" where "as far as the eye can reach, there is nothing visible but grass, grass."[18]

When travelers looked out at the unbroken miles of the North American interior, they saw a navigation challenge so immense it recalled other coasts and expanses. The wielders of ocean metaphors vacated landscapes of their occupants. Native American nations and their territorial rights disappeared as the fictive waters rose. A retired British naval officer, Frederick Marryat, toured the United States in 1836–37. He published his diary, in which he struggled to communicate his feelings about the landscape west of the Mississippi River: "To describe these prairies would be difficult; that is, to describe the effect of them upon a stranger." He reverted to his nautical background. "There you are," he wrote, "as if on the ocean—not a landmark, not a vestige of any thing human but yourself." The grass stretched to the horizon, and when the wind whipped through the long stems, "the surface gently undulat[ed] like the waves of the ocean. . . . It gives you the idea of a running swell." Marryat watched the grass roll from the back of a horse. With neither a boat crew nor a train of teamsters to keep him oriented, he experienced being cast away on land. "I have found myself lost," he wrote, "as it were; and indeed sometimes, although on horseback, have lost myself, having only the sun for my guide." The grasslands induced the queasy sensation of being adrift alone, which was why traveling companies enforced military discipline to keep all hands on deck.[19]

To cope with this daunting landscape, the Tennesseans spent most of the summer in Missouri and Kansas trading their corn-fed stock for "grass-fed mules and horses." The animals tested skill and patience; they gobbled thousands of hours of work. Their needs drove the daily routine on the trail. After grazing and resting at night, the animals pulled throughout the morning, but at midday the wagon trains had to stop for a few hours for the stock to recover and refuel. An afternoon haul brought the wagons to another camp where the animals were cut loose for another night of munching and sleeping. The quality and quantity of feed varied. The wagon trains waited for the grass on the plains to ripen each spring, and they raced across them before the summer heat and the grazing pressure along the well-traveled roads killed it. Some nights, drovers had to lead animals far from camp to find good grass. Other nights, the animals took it upon themselves to find a patch worth eating. Strays and runaways were constant. Each day, horses bucked and bolted; mules ate reins, halters, and pieces of wagons; oxen drank too much water and grew balky with upset stomachs. Humans cursed and lashed out. The grind of muscle-powered transportation turned many travelers against the very idea of going west. "I will say this much to friends who want to go to California," wrote James Riggin to his wife Rebecca in Missouri: "stay at home." The journey put Riggin in mind of a human and animal hybrid: "No man should start unless he has the constitution of a mule."[20]

The enchanting and "wondrous" plains quickly grew wearisome: "The sameness is so great that one soon becomes tired of gazing on it." The bored reporter from Captain Anderson's Tennessee outfit scanned the horizon for news. It rolled up in the form of wagoners leading ragged teams back to the United States. They complained of lost horses and mules and "scanty provisions." The reporter inquired about signs of buffalo. The animals, the returnees said, were numerous 120 miles into the interior, but take care, "chasing them is dangerous." Soon rumor became flesh. "We saw the first buffalo," the scribe wrote, "and J.S. and R.D. killed a very large one." Within weeks, however, the bison joined the grasslands in the category of wondrous turned mundane through constant repetition. "We have had buffalo in abundance," he wrote, "and some are become somewhat tired of it." Part of the dissatisfaction came from Captain Anderson's order forbidding the company's rank and file from hunting the animals with their horses. The herds were off limits to everyone except a team of designated meat hunters and the officers, who chased them with pistols drawn for sport. The rest watched, chewed, and swallowed their resentment. The reporter put the best face on the situation he could: "One of the great recommendations to buffalo meat is, that we can eat till really fatigued with the labor of eating, and yet we can relish the next meal just as well." But the all-bison menu paled next to the thrill of pursuit. "It must be great sport to chase buffalo with horses," he speculated. "We are not allowed to chase the buffalo on our horses, and only kill those we cannot well avoid killing." The risks of a charging horse snapping a foreleg in a prairie dog hole or a thrown hunter being separated from his mates and getting lost in the open grass were too great to let the grunts have a turn. Instead, they were free to shoot animals that wandered too close to the train, their high adventure reduced to an execution on the side of the road.[21]

The Americans defended against the flatness and immensity of the Great Plains by herding together in the middle of a road. Those who peeled off to run down the bison sacrificed their grip on the extensive lateral landscape. Plunging into the grasslands after the bison herds proved a momentous distraction, which is precisely why bored travelers did it, but in their rush to find relief, they risked disorientation. The Americans could not have designed a sport more likely to get them lost. During bison hunts, they ventured into environments unknown to them; they abandoned their land-marks and struggled to acquire their bearings; and in the heat of the chase they disheveled their short-term memories. The flat expanse afforded few prospects; it was impossible to imagine, much less see, the space from above. Add an excited horse into the mix and you have the ingredients for an unforeseen (but all too predictable) accident and the dislocation of mental, social, and geographic space.[22]

Charles Reimer got lost hunting buffalo on the plains near the place where the Santa Fe Trail crossed the Arkansas River. Reimer was a partner in Major Steingrandt's wagon company. Reimer and Steingrandt led a group of German-speaking migrants tucked into a train of loosely affiliated gold rush companies, mainly from Illinois. On the morning of June 15, 1849, Reimer went out hunting and failed to return. The men in the train expected Reimer to "come in every minute," but when the shadows grew long and he still hadn't appeared, they sent word to their neighbors, a contingent of Arapaho hunters camping nearby with their families, and offered them a reward "to bring him in." The Indians declined the invitation.[23]

The night passed, and still no Reimer appeared. The next day, a party of nine Americans saddled up to look for him and the bison. They brought in a heap of buffalo meat, but saw no evidence of the lost man, which sent H. M. T. Powell, a diarist in an Illinois company, into full Hamlet mode: "Alas! Poor Reimer, your fate is a hard one." He was "doubtless lost." "God help the poor fellow, for man seems to care but little for him." The specter of Reimer "made a prisoner or scalped by the Indians" sobered the campers: "The Angel of Death still hovers over our party. Who will be next?"[24]

The Arapahoes were more levelheaded in their assessment of the situa-tion. Bison hunting was dangerous, they explained: "It is likely he has been killed by a Buffalo bull, as such things do happen sometimes." They took care to distance themselves from the lost man. When asked, they said they had neither seen him nor heard of his location. They had their own missing-person problems. On the morning the wagons pulled out, an Arapaho man visited the gold rush camp. The Americans hurled questions about Reimer at him, and he returned fire: "Have you seen my wife?" She had been "missing since yesterday."[25]

In August, the news reached Powell that "little Charles Reimer" (the diminutive was used to distinguish him from another, taller Charles Reimer in the train) had been saved by the same Arapahoes the Illinois diarist and others had suspected of killing him. Reimer was "found by the Indians after wandering for four days and taken to their camp, where he was treated, provided with moccasins and passed on [to] the Emigrant Train with which he came to Santa Fe." Reimer's happy ending was short lived. In October, Powell and his crew overnighted next to the Gila River, in what would become Arizona. A man from Peoria pointed to a hole dug in the bank of the river, "half scraped out by wolves." That's where they buried "poor little Reimer." After arriving in Santa Fe, Reimer had sprinted ahead of the Illinois companies while they lingered in town. He was keen to reach Steingrandt, miles to the west on the trail toward California, and "regain his property." Powell did not reveal what killed the man other than fate: "Poor fellow; it was destined that he should not get through." The mystery of it all struck him. Why did some people survive while others fell and had their bones scattered along the road? Powell shrugged at the thought and scribbled on, leaving unsaid the obvious cause of death. Little Reimer was a modern paradox: a well-informed and well-provisioned individual led astray by the news and the equipment he thought would deliver him to his destination. He almost died running after bison for sport, and he met his final reward rushing after his possessions. He navigated an unfamiliar territory by the guidance provided him in print. His reckless hunting signaled his familiarity with American print culture. He reenacted the cliché of chasing bison on horse-back the books and papers sold as the apex of western adventure. Riemer dug his grave in individual space, but for all his modernity, his body moldered just outside relational space. It was the Arapahos, after all, who rescued him from nature shock on the plains. They fed and clothed him even though they were reluctant to associate with the trespassers from the United States. The overland travelers pestered their bison herds and accused them of murder and kidnapping, yet they extended Reimer a helping hand in the spirit of cross-cultural generosity.[26]

A previous generation of invaders may have paused at the edge of the plains and traded the objects in their possession to the residents living there to access their geographic knowledge. Traders forged human relationships through objects, while modern travelers, like Reimer, held onto their property. Trade cemented alliances, whereas transportation stiffened animosities. The Arapahoes took pity on Reimer when they escorted him back to the trail, but the two camps feasting on bison next to the Arkansas in June 1849 suspected the worst of each other. Powell accused the Indians of killing the wandering German, while the husband with the missing spouse searched for her in the interlopers' wagons. The Arapahoes refused to go after Reimer the first night he failed to return despite the offer of a reward. The two parties were not friends.

Print oriented travelers inward. Hunters chased bison to join an event being played out in distant letters, books, and newspapers. Readers got their fill of bison before they ever met the herds in person. A trip across the plains was incomplete without seeing one and shooting one and writing about seeing one and shooting one. Writers showered the bison with anecdotes. Words drifted around the animals and other celebrated western beings and features. Travelers who stopped in Salt Lake City composed nearly identical paragraphs about the Mormons' marriage and religious practices, while wagon riders who crossed the Rocky Mountains in midsummer described scenes of freezing ice cream with glacier snow. Notices and mentions festooned highly visible rock formations along the trail, instructing audiences to see castles or chimneys in granite and sandstone. Repeated mentions accreted landmarks, and the bounty of reading material tricked Americans into believing that they knew the place and could find their way through it without incident.[27]

In 1846, a teenage girl traveling overland wrote letters to her cousin in Illinois. The letters told a story of runaway animals, a bum shortcut, and a trail lost in the snow: "The farther we went up the deeper the snow got so the wagons could not go. . . . The mule kept falling in the snow head foremost and the Indian [hired by the party to guide them over the Sierra Nevada] said he could not find the road." The final letter ended with the line "What we had to eat I can hardly tell you." The piles of discarded supplies and equipment, the stench of rotting animal corpses, and the nightmare of family members frozen in the snow and eaten for survival were not hopeful endings. Yet bad news was still news. The horror of the Donner Party inspired countless newspaper articles, published memoirs, and historical retrospectives. The meadow where they died and dined became a landmark.[28]

Overland travelers wandered off track to locate runaway animals, to rescue possessions, or to rest, nurse, and bury human bodies. The migrants knew their positions, thanks to their maps, their books, and their correspondence; it was their connections to moveable property that steered them wrong. Groups betrayed by information, like the Donner Party, tumbled into danger when their animals wandered away and their supplies gave out. The possessions the travelers brought with them bound them into relationships they could neither predict nor control. The lines of wagon trails and mapped routes offered impressions of controlled and managed space, but when animals ventured off the road, or when snowstorms obscured the path, confusion found the trekkers and carried some of them into nature shock.

The oxen, mules, and horses that drove their movements relied on the grass, and the travelers drew wood and water from local sources. Still, they sizzled bacon and flapped jacks over the borrowed flames, weighting down their animals with imported comestibles, preferring their own grub to the nutrients cycling through strange environments. In 1849, Joseph Goldsborough Bruff kept a journal of his journey to California at the head of a company of gold seekers from Washington, DC. He counted hundreds of dead animals and wrecked equipment along the trail. On a day in September, he listed "14 dead oxen, 2 dead horses, 2 dead mules, 6 discarded oxen, 1 cart, several fragments of wagons, &c." His company staked out their mules and cattle at night and stationed pickets to guard them. Despite the precautions, livestock strayed: "We missed 11 mules this morning, owing to the carelessness of the sentinels. They had strayed and 2 hours delay to find them." "The emigrants," Bruff noted, "have such reluctance to guard-duty, or neglect so, that they are constantly losing their animals." Those who lost animals left notes blaming the Indians. One read: "The dead horse & mules in the [valley] bottom, had been shot by the Indians and belonged to Mr. ——." Americans butchered lame animals and burned possessions rather than let the Natives have them. Before he reached the diggings in October, Bruff passed the "vestiges" of a recent emigrant camp that was "accompanied by the usual garnish of wheels, hubs, tires, chains, yokes, clothes, old boots, and lastly—an empty liquor case."[29]

James Riggin, the Missourian who counseled his wife to tell their friends to stay home, traversed the interior in 1850 over the same trails Bruff had followed the year before. In his letters to Rebecca, he tallied the damage done to his livestock: "We lost our pride cow at green river while I was sick. We found an ox there & worked him on to the desert of Humboldt river. There some of Hayes' and Crows oxen gave out & they threw away their wagon & put their things in ours & doubled teams. We got safely through losing another ox & when we got to Carson River we had one ox stolen and our mare also which left us with two yoke & one cow & we lost the last cow 16 miles from Hangtown." The catalog of losses confused avoidable death, theft, and vagrancy. He lost animals to overexertion, sore feet, alkali poisoning, and malnutrition. Riggin and his partners facilitated these casualties through their role as lead animals. They drove teams too hard, slacked on guard duty and let them wander into trouble, and compromised their animals' safety at river crossings, on steep downhills, and along stretches of desert. The herds followed their unreliable human leaders, or acted according to inclinations of their own, which led to more trouble. They refused to move, stampeded, or simply walked away when the mood to be elsewhere struck them. Finally, rustlers stole animals. Riggin believed that Indians pilfered one of his oxen and a mare. Many overland animals were rustled twice. Animals ran away, stealing themselves, and then other herders, Indians or other Euro-American migrants, gathered them up.[30]

Riggin included among the lost drowned animals, exhausted animals, footsore animals, back- and leg-broken animals, stolen animals, and stray animals. *Lost* contained a multitude of situations and actors. At the end of the trail, it was Riggin who felt misplaced. "If I was back & knew what I know," he wrote Rebecca, "I would not cross those plains for a pile of money. It is the hardest trip man ever took." The stretch of desert between Humboldt Sink and the Sierra Nevada was particularly dispiriting: "I think in 45 miles there was 2 thousand dead animals & the worst smell I ever smelt." The corpses weighed on him. A typical nineteenth-century agrarian-capitalist, Riggin conceived of domestic livestock primarily as labor providers and as property. He pushed them hard, bought and sold them, even ate an old, gnarly ox or two in a pinch. Still, he could muster sentimental attachments to livestock. In his letters home, he often asked about the health of the family's horses, which he called by name. He connected to the animals he remembered fondly from home even as he detached from the rotting piles of animals he saw on the road.[31]

Riggin struggled in California. The West let him down, stripped him of his illusions. He responded by extending his stay. He would come home, he wrote Rebecca, as soon as he made enough money to prove their separation hadn't been "lost time." The Riggin family spiraled into a gold rush cliché. Rebecca raised their child alone and reassessed her marriage choice while James "saw the elephant." James understood that he was pushing the limits of Rebecca's patience, and he included a cartoon of an elephant in his correspondence to admit his folly. Published by Cooke & Le Count, a San Francisco printer, the image featured a bull pachyderm surrounded by stereotypical gold rush activities: men camping out, men washing gravel, men cooking dinner, men digging graves, and men beating mules. The elephant symbolized the hard-won insight that came from seeing California for yourself. Riggin knew the truth behind the hype: the promised spectacle, the enormous prize that climaxed the show, turned out to be a load of work, death, and animal abuse. The circus beast symbolized the diminished visibility caused by all those personal letters floating back east across Americans' information network. The news from California obscured the truth. Riggin saw the reality, but he still could not give up on his dream of riches. As a result, he circled around, preferring to go nowhere over going home.

## WRITERS AGAINST REGIONS

Jermain "Jarm" Loguen, a pistol tucked into his belt, spurred his trusty steed onto the road. The man and animal cast a formidable silhouette. The rider wore a long overcoat and a fashionable hat. He carried a silk umbrella to block the elements. The man's gear and his bearing declared his independence. He was posing as a free individual on a journey through Tennessee and Kentucky.

Loguen and his partner John Farney rode in broad daylight and approached houses and inns at dusk to request pallets for their bedding and corn for their horses. They acted as if they belonged on the thoroughfares, and they carried false papers to back their play. Only lower-class whites troubled them. Roving in packs on foot, the patrols hunted runaway slaves for the cash reward. Loguen and Farney fended off these squads with gentlemanly violence. They stood up for themselves, threatened physical retribution to the first person who dared molest them, and watched the rest scatter. And then they quickly moved on before reinforcements gathered. Loguen and Farney were courageous, but they knew not to push their luck.

The riders crossed the Ohio River on the winter ice. They celebrated their escape from slavery on the Indiana shore by firing their guns into the air. The display shocked a group of whites who had gathered on the bank to watch the pair come across. The onlookers scattered into the woods. A free black man approached the pair and told them to run. Black fugitives, he explained, were not free in Indiana. Gangs like the one they had just dispersed would hunt them down and send them back to their owners.

Go to Canada, he advised; follow the North Star. There were some abolitionists around who might help, but the bravado that had carried them this far would not keep them safe in the free states. Whites in Indiana eyed all blacks with suspicion. They should "walk softly away, so as not to awake the people." Keep to the woods. Indiana was not "the promised land," but rather a wilderness "full of enemies, dangers, and trials."[32]

The fugitive Jarm Loguen and the argonaut James Riggin were contemporaries who grew up within riding distance of North American borderlands. The Missourian Riggin crossed an ocean of grass to reach the diggings in northern California, while Loguen navigated the precarious roads of Tennessee and Kentucky to reach Indiana. Both had their illusions stripped from them. California flopped as a golden paradise, and Indiana bombed as a land of freedom. Neither Riggin nor Loguen surrendered to their disappointments. Riggin sent letters home to tell his wife to inform the neighbors that the rush was a hoax and that she should not expect him back anytime soon, while Loguen published an abolitionist tract in 1859 chronicling his journey from slavery to freedom in the 1830s. Jarm Loguen and James Riggin traversed American regions based on faulty information. The words that put them in motion—letters from the trail or rumors about the North— proved false, and they used their personal experiences to set their readers straight. They revised the narratives of two popular movements, journeys to wealth and escapes to freedom. In the process, they redrew the boundaries of spatial imagination to mark actual geographies as terrains of bewilderment and frustration instead of dreamed-of promised lands. Neither California nor Indiana ended their movements or their stories.

Riggin's audience was local and intimate. His letters connected him to Rebecca, their farm, and their rural Missouri community. His correspondence domesticated a sensational international event. Riggin used his freedom as a white male head of a household to leave his responsibilities. Rebecca could not stop him from going to California. Riggin reported what he saw and declared the animal abuse on the overland trail and the hype of the gold rush in violation of his moral standards. But when Riggin debunked the region, he debunked himself. His letters never resolved the tensions in this contorted posture. He was a hypocrite for promoting rural values while he undermined them by fleeing his home.

Jarm Loguen also wrote to settle an ethical dispute. He wanted his readers to understand how the toleration of slavery in the South bewildered people in the North. Slavery was insidious, penetrating the spaces declared off limits to it and infiltrating the moral character of Christians who believed themselves safely distant from its sins. Unlike Riggin, who traded on the notion that farmers anchored an upstanding nation, Loguen preached the instability of white homes. When he and John Farney ventured into Indiana they discovered that free white agrarian households could not be trusted. The inhabitants of some lived up to the commitments to republican independence and Christian charity they espoused, while others hid moral rot. Knock on one door, and you might discover a sympathetic ally. Pound another, and a gapped-toothed degenerate would try to wrestle you to the ground and slap chains on your ankles. Loguen asked his audience, most of whom were white northern abolitionists sympathetic to his cause, how long will you stand for your country to be part free, part slave, and all distorted?

Jarm Loguen mapped the true contours of American liberty in his narrative. White supremacy flattened the geography of the United States. Instead of a south-to-north gradient, with freedom increasing with the rising degrees of latitude, one racist society blended into another. Following the American Revolution, state governments and the U.S. Congress tried to draw boundaries around slavery. Between 1777 and 1804 a string of northern states gradually passed abolition laws. The 1787 Northwest Ordinance barred slavery in the Northwest Territory, including the chunks of space that would become Ohio and Indiana. The Missouri Compromise of 1820 etched a line across the territories acquired at the Louisiana Purchase at the north latitude of thirty-six degrees, thirty minutes, banning slavery north of the boundary. These geographic measures collapsed after the Compromise of 1850 and the 1854 Kansas-Nebraska Act. Some northern states like Indiana tried to prohibit free blacks from immigrating, and southern slave owners recruited the federal government to intervene in the northern states to help them retrieve their property. The Compromise of 1850, which brought California into the union as a free state, featured an aggressive federal fugitive slave provision. The northern states and territories were free from slavery, but they were never free to the enslaved. Upon his arrival in Indiana in the 1830s, Jarm Loguen learned that boundaries internal to the United States meant little to his personal freedom. He adopted the trappings of a free individual to pass through Kentucky, but the Hoosiers' loyalties bewildered him. He found himself in a relational space of concealed sympathies. By

1851, it was even more clear that only an international border could block the slave power. That year, Loguen and his colleagues in the Rochester and Syracuse antislavery movement stormed the hall where William "Jerry" McHenry was being arraigned under the Fugitive Slave Law and rescued him. Abolitionists spirited him to Canada. Having passed through the wilderness of the United States decades before, the emancipated Loguen came back to reform the relational space of the North. He helped construct an abolitionist network dedicated to moving the enslaved out of the slave-holding South and guiding them through the treacherous North.[33]

Fugitive humans upset white Americans' attempts to resolve their political and philosophical differences through regionalism. Slavery would not stay within spaces they demarcated for it because slave owners tested the limits and enslaved people refused to honor the lines. Slave owners transported human property across regional borders, triggering legal confrontations that culminated with the Supreme Court's 1857 *Dred Scott* decision, the ruling that erased the free-state/slave-state distinction. A small number of enslaved runaways, most of them men without families, transgressed regional boundaries on their own. Proximity to a free state offered the best chance for escape. In the decades leading up to the Civil War, the slave population of the United States shifted toward the cotton-growing regions of the Deep South. Slave owners in Virginia and Kentucky sold millions of people and transported them south, away from the border. Among the 4 million enslaved people, perhaps one hundred thousand successfully escaped. Among these, a handful published accounts of their journeys.[34]

Some of the printed stories of self-emancipated enslaved persons traveled back south, if the postmasters let them through. The steam-powered presses of the communications revolution dropped the cost of print materials, and the post office became a weapon in the slave controversy. Abolitionists mass-mailed southern religious and civic leaders. Proslavery agitators protested the mail. In 1835, a mob ransacked the post office in Charleston, South Carolina, and destroyed pamphlets and newspapers sent by the New York–based American Anti-slavery Society, justifying their actions by saying that the literature was intended to provoke a slave revolt. President Andrew Jackson sided with his fellow slave owners and urged postmasters to block the mailings. Congress came within one vote of forcing the national postal service to enforce local censorship codes. At the same time as the U.S. postal service stretched west to ease the crossing of the continent, nervous politicians attempted to sever the lines of communications running north and south to prevent the spread of abolitionism.[35]

Abolitionists and southern politicians fought over what information passed across sectional lines. The slave regime wanted to spread its news north and block the abolitionists' propaganda from coming south. The politics of regional information created stretches filled with unknown dangers for runaways. Outside their home landscapes, fugitive slaves passed through regional spaces designed to trick, trap, and misinform them. Slave owners purchased advertisements in newspapers offering rewards for the return of their property. Runaways had to dodge patrols who quizzed them about their movements and requested to see their passes, and they had to slip through populations filled with eyes trained to spot them through printed descriptions of their bodies, their clothing, their habits, and their speech patterns. Farther north, they confronted a human geography as difficult to read as any physical terrain. In a strange place, without landmarks, memories, or maps to orient them, runaways were forced to gamble on sympathies impossible to discern and foolish to trust.

In 1830, Jarm Loguen and John Farney left the Ohio River and got lost within a few miles. They wandered for three days and nights in an "immense forest." The snow-covered path was "circuitous and angular"; instead of leading them north, toward Indianapolis, it turned back toward Kentucky. On the third day, "hungry beyond endurance," they risked capture by requesting a meal from the white squatters whose hovels dotted the forest's undergrowth like fungi. The owners, "a set of broken down slave-holder's sons," refused to feed them. Delirious and bewildered, Loguen and Farney became even more discouraged. They "began to talk of returning to Kentucky."[36]

They stumbled into a white abolitionist household. The "lady" of the cabin cooked them breakfast while the "landlord" revealed the geography. "You are going right back to slavery again," he warned them. "The nearer the river you be, the more liable you are to be taken and returned into Egypt." Steer north. Go to Canada. The ordeal, however, had shaken the men. Out of the woods, they remained confused and in shock. They were ready to give up and turn back when they saw the kindness leaking from their hostess's eyes. Her tears along with the mountain of bacon she fried for them convinced them to soldier on. They reached Canada, and Loguen later returned to the United States to preach and agitate as an abolitionist.[37]

Loguen and Farney traversed a regional wilderness with the help of a timely intervention and an international border. In 1860, the year after the appearance of his autobiography, Loguen received a letter from the daughter of his former master in Tennessee. She demanded that he pay her $1,000 for stealing himself and Old Rock, the mare he rode away on, and blamed him for forcing her family to sell Loguen's brother and sister and "12 acres of land" to cover the loss. Loguen sent her letter and his reply to the *Liberator,* a northern abolitionist newspaper, for publication. He denounced her cruelty and castigated her for selling his family members. "Wretched woman!" he wrote. "Had you a woman's heart you could never have insulted a brother by telling him you sold his only remaining brother and sister, because he put himself beyond your power to convert him into money." Slaveholders punished runaways by dismantling their families. They broke relationships by taking advantage of regions. Capitalism and geography created southern subspaces. The prices for slaves rose the closer you came to the cotton-growing regions of the lower Mississippi valley. Southern slaveholders manipulated regional space to profit and to punish fugitives like Jarm Loguen. Then they denied the regional boundaries drawn up by their political adversaries. They claimed the right to buy and sell humans everywhere in the United States, and they expected Americans in other regions to respect this right.[38]

The contention that slavery transcended space led to confusion when enslaved persons' interior experience of getting lost came into conflict with their owners' conceptions of profit and loss. John "Fed" Brown, for example, fled slavery many times. He eventually reached Great Britain, a free space definitively beyond the reach of his masters in the United States. From London in 1855, he published an antislavery narrative of his life. He recounted one of his early attempts at self-emancipation. He escaped from his Georgia master, De Cator Stevens, and traveled into Tennessee with a forged pass. Brown kept off the roads, but one day he stumbled across a white man in the forest. The woodcutter, named Posey, interrogated him. "Are you free?" asked Posey. "Yes, sir," Brown answered, and showed him his papers. Posey spotted the forgery and smelled a reward. He lured Brown to his cabin, promising to furnish him with a more convincing fake pass. Once there, Posey excused himself and returned with a two-man posse. They held Brown at gunpoint, bound his hands and feet, and questioned him further. "Who do you belong to, sir?" De Cator Stevens, Brown replied.

"Where does he live?" Georgia. "Then what are you doing here?" "I got lost, sir." "Oh, You got lost, did you? And pray, sir, did you come here on purpose to get lost?" Posey asked. "No, sir," Brown responded, "I got lost before I got here." The order of Posey's queries indicated how ownership transcended space. *Who do you belong to?* came before *What are you doing here?* Brown answered the first truthfully, suggesting that he knew the "to whom" but not the "why here." The economic relationship that defined his legal status was still intact; he simply did not know where he was on a map.[39]

Slave owners like Sarah Logue, the daughter of Jarm Loguen's former master, tried to collapse space into the lines connecting them and their property. Fed Brown took this orientation to its logical conclusion. If slavery was boundless, how could he wander out-of-bounds? When you did not belong to yourself, losing yourself was not a crime.

Runaway slaves battled the twisted logic of the property regime. They fought a legal system, a police state, and an information network intended to stifle their independence and stymie their movement. In addition to these formidable obstacles, runaways contended with the innate navigational glitches that bedeviled all human travelers. They bumbled into landscapes with radically obstructed sight lines. They struggled in spaces without landmarks. They reeled in territories with too many twists and turns to remember. Their nature shock held to the human pattern, and it belonged to the antebellum moment. Being the object of pursuit as well as the pathfinder made the situation substantially more confusing. Unless they were pretending to be free, runaways adopted stealth. They hoped to move undetected, so they chose to travel through forests; they turned into swamps; and they walked at night. Not being seen came with the disadvantage of not being able to see. Fugitives entered edge spaces defined by poor visibility, where past experience and mental maps proved useless, and getting lost rivaled getting caught for the worst-case scenario.

Henry Bibb recalled the dangers of fleeing into a swampy forest: "We made our way down to the Red river swamps among the buzzing insects and wild beasts of the forests. We wandered about the wilderness for eight or ten days." His willingness to plunge with his family into the "swamps of Louisiana among the snakes and alligators" demonstrated his desperation. "Nothing I say, but the strongest love of liberty, humanity, and justice to myself and family, would induce me to run such a risk again." In Bibb's telling, nature savaged the family. A pack of wolves surrounded them, and

Henry scared them off, yelling and brandishing a bowie knife. After a lengthy search, they found a driftwood bridge to cross the Red River. On the other side, they entered a jumble of "canes, bushes, and briers" and ran out of room to maneuver. A trailing cadre of bloodhounds found them. Bred to rely on senses other than sight, the animals tracked by smell, and they used noise—their infernal baying tormented Bibb—to coordinate their chase and flush their quarry. Even their floppy skin helped them slip through the landscape. Instead of being cut by the thorns that rent the runaways' skin, the hounds' elastic folds slid past the barbs. Unable to avoid the spikes of the vegetation or defend against the dogs, Bibb surrendered to prevent his children being savaged by the bloodhounds. The swamps, forests, and canebreaks proved insurmountable: "We did at one time chance to find a sweet potato patch where we got a few potatoes; but most of the time, while we were out, we were lost."[40]

Like the Bibbs, Charles Ball got turned around in a swamp. Following the North Star to reach Maryland from South Carolina, he traveled cross-country in the dark, "without regard to roads, forests, or streams of water." One night, he "became entangled in a thick and deep swamp." The trees were so tall and dense that "the interlocking of their boughs, and the deep foliage in which they were clad, prevented me from seeing the stars." Not knowing which direction to head, he wandered for "several hours, most of the time with the mud and water over my knees, and frequently wading in stagnant pools, with deep slimy bottoms." He "became totally lost, and was incapable of seeing the least appearance of fast land." He pulled himself out of the water at the first tussock he found and waited for the sun. Dawn arrived murky and overcast, and visibility remained low: "I found myself as much perplexed as I was at midnight." He could not tell east from west. He was running low on food. He sloshed into a deep pool and noticed a long tail swish in the water. He scrambled up the trunk of a fallen cypress tree and watched an alligator swim past. He determined to wait right there until the clouds cleared. On the morning of his third day in the swamp, the sun finally shone through. He used the orb to steer back to where he had entered the swamp. Famished and suffering, especially from "the loss of a very valuable part of my clothes, which were torn off by briars and snags," Ball lay down on the dry land and waited for night to come "lest some one should see me moving through the forest in the daylight." The darkness, the bane of his existence for seventy-two miserable hours, was still his best friend.[41]

To reach freedom, runaways moved at times and into spaces best avoided if you wanted to stay oriented. Instead of resting when the sun set, they moved at night. Instead of avoiding swamps, they charged into the muck. Instead of seeking help from other people to stay safe and within bounds, they skirted communities and kept to themselves. Runaways could get even more lost when they were found. During one of his escape attempts out of Georgia, Fed Brown was directed by a fellow slave to a stop on the Underground Railroad in Tennessee. The house was a night's travel away, and the friend told Brown to hurry: "He impressed upon me the necessity of making up my mind to accomplish the distance before day-break, or I should certainly be lost; that is, captured." Slavery turned American regions and the pursuit of freedom inside out. Finding a way through Tennessee, Louisiana, or Indiana was a challenge far greater than making it out to California.[42]

The stories of fugitives from slavery who got lost survived in abolitionist literature. Their disorientation and nature shock communicated the terror of being alone, separated from families and communities, unable to discern friend from foe. Through their narratives, the authors presented readers with a corrective overview of the United States. Black abolitionists endeavored to rewrite mental maps, passing furious judgment on a deluded and divided nation. Corrupt parts, they preached, could never make a virtuous whole. Authors like Jarm Loguen, Fed Brown, Charles Ball, and Henry Bibb used the grammar of space and the nightmare of getting lost to convince readers to end slavery, fight racism, and unite the regions of the United States.

## BEWILDERED IN THE COPPER REGION

Charles Whittlesey answered the call to unify the country. He had been fighting against regional divisions his entire adult life. Before drawing his sword for the Union—he served as Ohio's assistant quartermaster general and as a colonel in the Twentieth Ohio Volunteer Infantry—Whittlesey drew lines on paper as a surveyor, geologist, and historian. After graduating from West Point with a degree in geology, he worked in the field, mapping land and material resources for the government and private mining companies. Unlike the gold rush reporters and the black abolitionists, Whittlesey was a professional informant. He collected material through his numerous expeditions and spent hours in archives and doing fieldwork, which he composed into articles and books on geography, archeology, geology, meteorology, local history, antiquities, and limnology. He wrote about the water levels of the Great Lakes and the history of the city of Cleveland. He published articles about the ancient mounds of the Cuyahoga valley and the early French fur trade. Other professional authors stole from his stash of midwestern curiosities and arcana. The knowledge he gathered made Whittlesey rich—mining companies paid him to locate coal seams and copper belts—but the theft of his information embittered him. He never forgot the accolades he lost to others.

A publishing machine, Charles Whittlesey facilitated the arrival of American hegemony in the remoter bastions of the Upper Midwest. He charted, mapped, and narrated space, giving readers, miners, investors, farmers, lawyers, and clerks information they needed to enter the region and connect it to the markets and culture of a contiguous United States. Whittlesey aimed to minimize local eccentricities and relationships. Armed with his articles and maps, travelers could move in and out of areas without befriending the people living there. Whittlesey described the copper region as a transitional space. It was moving away from a Native American homeland and a motley fur-trade zone toward an American industrial site. The place was neither wild nor empty. Its time was merely over. As the modern engulfed the ancient and the early modern, Whittlesey surveyed and wrote to facilitate the absorption.

Whittlesey's copper expedition launched above the rapids on the St. Mary's River, the waterway connecting Lake Huron and Lake Superior, on August 14, 1845. The exploration party, sent out on behalf of the Detroit-based Algonquian Mining Company, split along two tiers: the gentlemen and the hired hands. Josiah R. Dorr, a Detroit merchant and iron manufacturer, led the group. Whittlesey, a company trustee, acted as the surveyor and geologist. Daniel P. Bushnell lent his ethnographic and diplomatic chops. He had served many years as the federal agent at Wisconsin's La Pointe Sub-agency. A fourth, unnamed gentleman entertained the others with his witty complaints about the food and sleeping arrangements. Whittlesey introduced the workers by their first names: Mike, a sailor from "the whaling grounds of the Northwest Coast," was the cook; Charley, a "giant from the Low Countries," hauled provisions and gear; Patrick, an Irishman, performed odd jobs and acted as Whittlesey's chainman; and Martin, a "sprightly young man" and novice backcountry traveler who nonetheless took to camp life "like a veteran" and "slept like an opium-eater," performed the duties of company clerk. Whittlesey reckoned the group's exact global position by measuring its progress from the first principle meridian, a true meridian run with "great care from the base line" by U.S. government surveyors twelve miles north of Detroit. The first principle meridian passed through Sault St. Marie at the shipyard and was the primary reason the expedition proceeded from that spot.[43]

Whittlesey tried to plot the expedition's movements with government maps. This was a tough job, given that travel on the Great Lake and the surveys' Euclidian grid existed in contrary realms. The maps spoke in the language of right angles—meridians, baselines, townships, quarter sections, and section corners. This was not how voyagers normally conceived of the Great Lakes. Instead of worrying about abstract coordinates, they paddled canoes within sight of the jagged shore. They went ashore when the sun dipped and their vision dimmed. They measured space in distances from put-ins to pull-outs, by hours rowed and inlets passed. Whittlesey's company sailed yawls rather than canoes, but otherwise they proceeded in the same fashion, eyeballing the shore and anchoring their craft each sundown. Whittlesey's goal was to integrate this sensory- and-history-based method of navigation, which generated its own language, landmarks, and traditions, with the government survey maps, which were haphazard and unfinished. The government's grid fell off the farther inland you marched. Like everyone else, the surveyors hired to map the region had followed the routes of least resistance. They paddled and stuck to the shore, pocketing their fees while leaving big swaths of the copper region unmapped. Whittlesey hiked in from the coast with his instruments and his chainman, Patrick the Irishman, to locate key geographic features—waterfalls, river forks, river sources, and mountain ranges—and place them on the grid correctly. The company brought Indian agent Bushnell along to converse with the Ojibwes. Whittlesey translated as well. He converted local terrain into ranges and sections.

The ghosts of previous half-done jobs haunted Whittlesey. The company arrived in Copper Harbor and began exploring the interior in September. Whittlesey discovered that the government maps, "instead of assisting the explorer, were for the interior so erroneous, that mistakes equal[ed] a day's travel." In a country impregnated with iron, compasses proved as unreliable as the maps. Whittlesey, Patrick, and the hands packing in food and supplies navigated by their observations of the sun and by their "woodsman's instinct." Both sun navigation and wilderness savvy proved fair-weather strategies. When the clouds rolled in, they all got lost.[44]

This happened to Whittlesey twice, and he described it as a "species of delirium." Without a compass, a map, or the sun, he explained, the copper region traveler fell back on judgment. But judgment eroded as the problems escalated. "With the mind in a state of perplexity," wrote Whittlesey, "the fatigue of travelling is greater than usual, and excessive fatigue, in turn weakens, not only the power of exertion, but resolution also." Ill-equipped wanderers could not hole up and wait for the weather to clear. Soaked, cold, and hungry, they sought immediate relief and scrambled for an exit. The strongest woodsmen panicked: "The wanderer is finally overtaken with an indescribable sensation—one that must be experienced to be understood—that of *lostness*." Deranged in body and mind, a lost person fell out of step with his environment. "He stumbles onto a trail he has passed before, or even passed within a few hours, he does not recognize it; or if he should at last, and conclude to follow it, a fatal lunacy impels him to take the wrong end." His own tracks become the tracks of other men, and should the sun break through the "fogs and clouds," he continues to struggle to comprehend, for in his "addled brains" "the world seems for a time to be turned end for end." No one was safe when lostness overcame them. "Even Indians and Indian guides become bewildered," Whittlesey wrote. They "miscalculate their position, make false reckonings of distances, lose courage, and abandon themselves to despair and tears." Gray skies melted humans along the Great Lakes into puddles of emotional goo.[45]

Whittlesey fought the insanity of nature shock with the grid's cool precision. A correct reckoning would bring the "singularly wild and disordered" copper region to heel. But he struggled to achieve uniformity with the information at hand. One day in late September, for example, his "office map" told him that if he and Patrick followed the "correction line" at the "southwest corner of town[ship] 51N, range 40 W," they would strike Lake Ontonagon after a ten-mile march. Instead, they found themselves hip-deep in a marsh. The lake was in truth fifteen, not ten, miles away. The company sent one of the hands to the forks of the Ontonagon River with a supply of pork and beans for the surveyors. Rain and miscalculations delayed Whittlesey and Patrick from reaching the rendezvous, and the packer left with most of the supplies after spending two cold nights waiting for them. Whittlesey and Patrick used the food they had left to backtrack to the coast rather than pushing further inland as they had previously planned. "This is an instance," Whittlesey reflected, "of hazard and disappointment, and it is difficult to see how it could have been avoided." Even with the "greatest sagacity and forethought, small parties, who do not survey and mark their courses and distances"—in other words, parties that did not correct the grid even as they followed it—"cannot avoid occasional perils."[46]

When the men weren't imperiled themselves, they told stories about the imperilment of others. Whittlesey heard that the summer before two prospectors left their camp to reach a copper vein only two hundred rods away (a rod is five and a half yards). They carried neither compass nor food, for only an imbecile could miss a spot so close by and known to both men. Instead of finding the copper vein, Whittlesey reported, they took a wrong turn and "got entangled among swamps and hills, and wandered forty-eight hours in the woods, bewildered and lost." No journey, Whittlesey lectured, was too short to go unprepared. Even the locals could get lost in the woods. One day, "a half-breed" was "sent out to bring in a deer that had been killed some miles from the post." The man "lost his way, and slept in the woods one night." He sauntered in the next afternoon, and his boss asked him where he left the deer. The man rubbed his belly and delivered the punch line: "Ugh! Got him—do you s'pose a man is to starve?" Unlike the surveyors, the local guides and hunters could feed themselves in the wilderness even though they too toed their edges of spatial cognition when they circled in the swamps and hills.[47]

Whittlesey concluded "Two Months in the Copper Region," the essay he published in 1846 to prepare Americans for the interior along the southern shore of Lake Superior, with a series of tips and recommendations. Those who reached Copper Harbor, where six hundred "labourers, agents, clerks, superintendents, and mining engineers" had planted a town, could expect semimonthly mail service. Letters and packages were hauled in on the backs of packers from Green Bay. Surveyors should plan to bring a "solar compass"; a pocket compass was good enough for regular travelers, though they should check their readings against the sun. Hunters could expect to find pheasants, red squirrels, rabbits, and mice. In June and July, everyone could enjoy the "myriads of moschetoes and sand-flies."[48]

The pleasure of travel "depended on the outfit." Each man should purchase and transport two pounds of solid food per day. Tea, coffee, salt, pepper, and sugar were luxuries but well worth bringing for their convivial and civilizing effects. The same was true of spoons, knives, and forks. Flannel shirts and "heavy cotton ticking" trousers wore well and protected their occupants from the weather and the stickers in the swamps. Likewise, a "heavy Mackinaw blanket" was "the most necessary article to the voyageur and woodsman." No man should arrive in the copper region without a knapsack, a hatchet, and a map case with a government survey curled inside, preferably a recently revised one. If he bought and transported the necessary items, he "may count upon as much enjoyment, on a trip through the Lake Superior country, as he will find at home." Loaded with food, clothes, and information, he could leave home and feel at home. Whittlesey's article prepared the traveler for infiltrating a remote region by making its tangled geography navigable and its complicated history ignorable.[49]

Whittlesey wrote to ease transportation and plug the copper region into the industrial economy of the United States. He advised readers to haul their own "outfit"—weapons, provisions, and maps—which inflated their sense of autonomy: they moved without local connections or social ties. Whittlesey observed the Indian and "half-breed" residents of the copper region in order to bypass them. He hired some of them to pack his stuff or to show him where to find astonishing hunks of copper ore—a sample boulder from 1763 weighed sixty pounds—but he carried enough food and information to move without their help. His outfit freed him from paying them mind. In the end, he advised travelers to trust their compasses, their maps, and him rather than the region's Native inhabitants. Indian guides, he warned, duped their clients. Since whites started their "wild goose chase" for the mineral rights in the region, Indian guides had "sprung up on all sides." They promised "monster" boulders, but after a "seven, ten, or twelve days' journey," they professed that they could not take prospectors to the exact place because the "Great Spirit and the tribe will destroy or otherwise injure him who shows it to the white man." This, Whittlesey explained, was a ruse, performed to conserve the guiding racket: "If such a rock were actually visible, no Indian would show it, so long as he can get one-half of his yearly support from it as a guide." Plus, the "proceeds" from any copper discoveries were divided by the tribe, "a large portion" carved off for the local chief.[50]

Whittlesey intended this last quip to disabuse contemporary white Americans of the wisdom of hiring Indian guides, yet he also framed his modern racism around his perceptions of ancient history. Americans, and especially Charles Whittlesey, associated mining, smelting, and metal work with human progress. Advanced cultures, they theorized, manipulated their environments to produce tools, religious icons, and weapons. Whittlesey saw evidence of historic mining when he toured the copper region in 1846, and he looked for—and found—signs of old mining activity elsewhere in the Upper Midwest. These discoveries challenged his racism. He believed that the current inhabitants of the region were feckless and duplicitous; they could not have exploited natural resources with any skill. Therefore, he hypothesized, another group must have preceded them and mined the area's pure copper. These ancients produced the copper artifacts antiquarians dug from the mounds of the Ohio and Mississippi valleys. Technology and progress skipped the Ojibwes and the multicultural offspring of the fur trade. Americans inherited the mantle of civilization from a distant "ancient race."[51]

Whittlesey pried the copper region from the Ojibwes, printing tall tales about race, progress, and ancient history. He aimed to erase regional lines and regional populations, but he disappeared into a region despite his national aims. If Charles Whittlesey is remembered at all, he is remembered as a midwestern scholar and writer. His body lies in Cleveland's Lake View Cemetery and his papers rest in the Western Reserve Historical Society. Like most things midwestern, Whittlesey ended up stuck between more scintillating locations—the East Coast with its bustling cities, the South with its gothic rot, and the West with its optimistic summits. The flyover zone, the most "nowhere part of America," according to essayist John Jeremiah Sullivan, the Midwest is one of the nation's most forgettable landscapes. In the nineteenth century, the region lost people to the gold rush. It exuded the dullness from which clerks and letter carriers hoped to escape. It was the moral emptiness, "the wilderness," through which Jarm Loguen and John Farney struggled to pass. It is fitting that Whittlesey got stuck there, too. He rejected the interpersonal world of trade and "half-breeds," and he could not bring the copper region into the modern age because the government maps had been poorly made. In the gap between the two, he discovered nature shock, a state where delirium turned one's own tracks into someone else's.[52]

Whittlesey got lost in history, but his mapping and publishing helped bring the copper region into the nation and thus into individual space. He belonged to the army of surveyors, agents, reporters, and correspondents who fanned out into the interior and altered space through the production of industrial information. News blanketed the continent, closed distances, and ironed out difference and diversity. The government and the publishing market equipped individuals to slip into homelands, regions, and sections without bothering to befriend, contact, or contract the people living in those spaces. The United States tightened its control over the map, ushering in a modern era of transportation in which goods and individuals moved quickly across vast spaces without encumbrance. Still, relational space never disappeared completely, and lost individuals searched for locals to relate to during emergencies when their maps failed them and they experienced the "fatal lunacy" of nature shock.

## LOST PATHFINDERS

Like the black abolitionists who battled slavery in print, John C. Frémont acquired a national audience writing about his passage through a region inscrutable to him. Like Charles Whittlesey, Frémont was a professional surveyor and an enthusiastic author. In contrast to Whittlesey, however, Frémont knew how to keep his name before the public and how to protect his "discoveries." The "Great Pathfinder" popularized the American West and published maps and descriptions of the routes eastern migrants took to reach the Pacific Coast. He documented pathways cut by others as well as the discoveries he made himself. He was an accomplished self-promoter who plowed a thoroughfare through nineteenth-century American print culture with help from two key partners, a frontier guide named Kit Carson and a well-placed spouse, Jessie Benton Frémont. Carson played the man-who-knew-Indians foil to Frémont's dashing officer/explorer/scientist act, while Benton Frémont juiced up his reports with adventuresome flair and helped him secure the captaincy of four western expeditions through her father, Missouri senator Thomas Hart Benton. Frémont worked for the Corps of Topographical Engineers. The federal government sponsored his adventures, and he worked to stitch a transcontinental nation together through published information. His reports combined scientific observations and gripping tales; he collected data and observations. He journaled and he mapped. With the aid of Carson and Benton Frémont, he prepped travelers for navigating the West by giving them specific directions and wild fantasies. Geologic notations, longitude and latitude readings, and weather reports introduced epic buffalo hunts, hairbreadth escapes, and Indian fights. The Frémont team created a mental map of an America West. Travelers from the East could reach California with a map, an odometer, and Frémont's printed guide. And they could reach the summit of their dreams—get rich, witness savagery, and hunt a buffalo. They could also write about their experiences, stew information out of themselves.[53]

Animals were the prime culprits of human bewilderment on Frémont's expeditions. Men peeled off from the main group to retrieve missing oxen, horses, and mules, and hunters plunged into unfamiliar territory to find and kill prey. Both circumstances worried Frémont. "I have always been careful of my men," he wrote, "and my journeyings lost but few." "A man lost from camp was likely to lose his life." Frémont mentioned one man getting lost on his first expedition. It was a mundane yet instructional bout of confusion. Early in the trip, a barn-sick horse bolted for home after the company stopped for the night on the banks of the Mishmagwi River in Kansas. Frémont ordered a party of three to retrieve the animal. All except one returned. The holdout "lost his way in the darkness of the night, and slept on the prairie." He walked into camp the next morning, soggy from a heavy rain but otherwise intact.[54]

Frémont himself got lost chasing bison early in his western career while serving as an assistant to the geographer Joseph Nicollet, the leader of a Corps of Topographical Engineer expedition to the Missouri and Mississippi Rivers in 1838. Intent on killing a bison cow from horseback with a pistol, he galloped out of sight of his hunting mates and spurred his horse onto the plains. The cow escaped, and Frémont paused to rest his horse. He looked around and realized that he was all alone and that he "had no idea where to look for camp." A bison track took him to water, where a rescue party sent by Nicollet found him the next morning. "To be lost on the prairie in an Indian country," he wrote, "is a serious accident, involving many chances and no one was disposed to treat it lightly."[55]

When not chasing ungulates on the open prairies, Frémont was eating them out of desperation above the timberline. In 1844, Frémont diverted his second expedition to California after reaching the Oregon Country. His decision to turn south and cross the Sierra Nevada in the depth of winter defied explanation. Frémont said he did it to save his stock: having just reached the Pacific, they were in no condition to walk back to the United States. Yet the California detour killed more animals than it refreshed. The expedition plowed into forty-foot snowdrifts, and the animals weakened without grass to eat. Frémont left Oregon with sixty-seven horses and mules and one dog. He arrived at John Sutter's fort in the Sacramento valley with thirty-three mounts and without the dog, which the men ate. Despite the havoc the trip wrought on his animals and his men, their well-being seemed the hindmost in Frémont's consideration. He crossed the Sierra Nevada to reconnoiter Mexican California, look for the Northwest Passage across the continent, and collect scientific discoveries for himself and his nation. Crossing the mountains drove the expedition over a political and a cognitive edge. Several men got terribly lost in the mountains, and their derangement upset the overweening confidence Frémont and his coauthors communicated in their reports, maps, and adventure tales. Frémont's men descended into nature shock, and their extreme spatial turmoil contrasted sharply with their mission to write the West into a coherent United States. Frémont experienced and then Jessie Benton Frémont balanced the drama of horrifying bewilderment with the spectacle of geographic discovery. On the ground, Frémont and his men struggled to move and to feed themselves, but in print the narrative cast their lostness as a necessary precursor to California being swallowed by the United States.

The sorry condition of the animals divided the expedition. Frémont ordered a contingent forward while a second group under Thomas "Broken Hand" Fitzpatrick trailed behind to bring up the slower horses and mules. Every night, a gunshot called the campers to dinner. They were slaughtering their fattest horses to fuel their own bodies. They left the emaciated ponies and jack mules to nibble bridles, saddles, and one another's tails for nourishment.

On February 25, Frémont ordered a small party down the Sierra's Pacific slope to reach the grass in the American River valley. The eight-man squad comprised Frémont; cartographer Charles Preuss; Theodore Talbot, a protégé of J. J. Albert, who was the chief in the Corps of Topographical Engineers; and lead guide Kit Carson. The rank and file of the party was made up of French Canadian laborers Baptiste Derosier and Raphael Proue, a hunter from St. Louis named Charles Towns, and free African American Jacob Dodson, who served as Frémont's valet.

The eight escaped the snow, yet they struggled to find pasture for their livestock on the steep hillsides, which afforded "but a few stray bunches of grass." The strain broke the animals and the men. Frémont's favorite horse, Proveau, stopped in his tracks and refused to clamber up the rocky slopes. Frémont assigned Dodson to stay with Proveau and nurse him along. That night, Towns grew "light-headed" and wandered "off into the woods without knowing where he was going." Frémont ordered Dodson, who had just arrived in camp with Proveau, to venture after the increasingly loony hunter and bring him back, a task he completed successfully. The next day, Proveau and Towns's prized horse, Columbia, wandered away. Derosier volunteered to find them. He failed to return that night, and the expedition traveled on, camping next to a runoff-gorged river. While Frémont worried that the missing Derosier may have become "bewildered in the woods," Towns, "who had yet to recover his mind," stripped down to his skivvies and dove into the "cold mountain torrent" as if "it were summer and the stream placid." After fishing Towns out of the freshet, the camp watched a nature-shocked Derosier stumble in. There in body, his mind, like Towns's, appeared to be lost. The ordeal had pretzeled Derosier's sense of time and location. He imagined that he had been gone for several days instead of the one and that he had returned to the campsite he had left from. His confusion rattled the men: "It appeared that he had been lost in the mountain, and hunger and fatigue, joined by weakness of body, and fear of perishing in the mountains, had crazed him." You knew "times were severe" when "stout men lost their minds" along with their horses.[56]

Then the cartographer went off the map. The party stopped early on March 2, following an arduous "march of only a few miles." Charles Preuss, walking ahead of the column, was unaware that the main group had called a premature halt. Alone and exhausted, he decided to stay put that night rather than retrace his steps back upriver. The next day, Frémont grew ever more anxious and puzzled at the group's inability to run across him on the "broad plain-beaten" trail. He sent Derosier to hunt for him. On the evening of March 4, Preuss wandered in on his own. The mapmaker related his ordeal. There were too many "Indian trails" to guess which one Frémont would choose, so Preuss charted his own course down the river, crossing from side to side, and every so often climbing up a hill to gain a perspective and "obtain good views of the country." Time passed and his energy flagged. He scrounged, digging wild onions out of rock crags and munching the owners of an anthill. He caught small frogs in a pool, yanked off their hind legs, and ate the meat.

Everywhere he found evidence of the valley's Natives. He spotted their footprints and their old campfires. As he grew more desperate, Preuess longed to run across one of their huts. Unlike Carson, he was not afraid of Indians and "didn't see a murderer in every miserable human being." He appreciated relational space, and in his state of bewilderment hoped to locate some of it. He came upon six Natives roasting acorns outside their home. He "gave them to understand that I was hungry." They "immediately served me acorns" and "filled both my pockets to capacity." Preuss offered them his pocketknife in return. His energy revived, he finally lit upon the path that reunited him with his comrades.[57]

There was irony in Preuss's acorns. In 1846, the German would publish one of the most influential maps in American history. Preuss's map of the continent detailed the route to Oregon, freeing overland travelers to cut ties with Native partners and rely on industrial information to direct them. The combined report of Frémont's first and second expeditions and Preuss's map helped usher in the idea of transcontinental transportation. Instead of a cross-cultural and personal endeavor driven by relationships, western movement became an inward-looking literary affair. Congress authorized the printing of ten thousand copies of the combined report in 1845. A year later, a ten-foot-long version of Preuss's map hit the market. It was designed to be wound on a roller and hung from a wagon.

When he got lost in 1844, Preuss could not foresee his role in liberating interior travelers from making alliances and asking for directions. In his diary, he straddled individual and relational space. In his panic, for example, he engaged in long-distance homing. He kept his wits about him until the last night. With no wood to start a fire and storm clouds promising rain, he ate raw frogs and moaned to a person on another continent: "Oh, my old sweetheart! If you knew how badly off I am at the moment!" At his breaking point, Preuss traveled to Germany. He recalled his wife as well as the butter from his "childhood days," hallucinating the slabs of milkfat spread across the thick crusts of bread his aunt gave him. His diary nestled memories of domesticity next to snowbanks and butchered mules. Unlike Towns and Derosier, however, the mapmaker found his way back from nature shock rather quickly. "Everything will be all right," he wrote, "if I only keep a stiff upper lip." To stay sane, he redirected his attention away from his distant home to the ground under his feet. He focused on contacting actual people and asking them for help. "I wish I would come across a hut. I can see plenty of tracks." Trade and the kindness of strangers brought him back from the edge. Relationships saved him, and his rescue demonstrated how relational space could endure on the margins of national cartographies. Preuss's maps helped modernize and depersonalize the American interior, but he survived into that future on the acorns given him by Native Californians.[58]

## LOST IN YELLOWSTONE

In the late summer of 1870, Truman Everts joined a scouting expedition across the Yellowstone Plateau sponsored by the federal government. Nearsighted and encumbered by neither wilderness experience nor savvy, Everts won his spot on the team through his connections. An expert navigator of modern organizations, he prowled bureaucracies, political parties, and patronage networks. During the Civil War, he served as a sanitary commission agent for the Union, and afterward he secured an appointment as the assessor of internal revenue for the Montana Territory. Prominent men from the Montana Territory filled the ranks of the 1870 Washburn-Langford-Doane expedition, and he was lucky to be asked to join. Between jobs that summer, Everts was hunting a new sinecure. The 1870 Yellowstone venture was one of three federal expeditions intended to finally and properly "discover" the wondrous hot springs, geysers, and volcanoes that Americans had known about since fur trappers entered the region in the early 1800s. The members of the Washburn-Langford-Doane party would add detail to the backlog of too-weird-to-be-true information about the landscape surrounding Yellowstone Lake. The men's credentials would turn rumors into maps and reports with government authority. Their exploration felt historic to them because they were the ones doing the exploring.[59]

Truman Everts went missing on September 9. He separated from the column in the morning while the men and horses threaded through a dense pine forest filled with deadfall obstructions. This fragmentation was normal. Riders peeled off alone or in pairs to climb hills or investigate natural curiosities, and they returned to the campfire in the evening to relate their adventures. The expedition leaders grew worried only when Everts had been gone for two days. The men built a bonfire and fired their guns to signal their location. When that failed, a search party backtracked and left notes for Everts on trees near the shore of Yellowstone Lake. The expedition moved on, blazing trees and leaving placards in the hopes that the unemployed assessor would find his way back to them.[60]

Everts took getting lost in stride, initially. He welcomed the thought of spending the night in the woods alone. He was a romantic. The sites of Yellowstone enthralled him. He appreciated the "grandeur, beauty, and novelty" of the place and reveled in the "grandest landscapes I ever beheld." His mood dipped after his horse ran away with all his gear and supplies except for a pair of opera glasses. Panic gurgled up to join the sparkling jets of the nearby geysers. The darkness scared him. Indians worried him. A contingent of Crows had observed the Washburn-Langford-Doane party as it moved across the Yellowstone Plateau. Like the colonial wildernesses that preceded it, the Upper Yellowstone region was tangled in human politics. The federal government ignored Native territorial use rights and expelled Indian "trespassers" to cordon off the natural and national wonder. In 1872, the cavalry of the U.S. Army would begin to patrol the area to keep it pristine. Cut off from his group, his gun missing with his horse, Everts feared "meeting with Indians." The thought gave him "considerable anxiety." But as time passed and his hunger grew, his thoughts re-formed. Falling in with a "lodge of Bannocks or Crows" began to seem preferable to escalating the "terrible consciousness of the horrors of my condition."[61]

Everts wandered for days and then weeks. He survived by eating the roots of thistles. He dismantled the opera glasses and used one of the lenses to focus the sunlight and start a fire. He weathered rain- and snow-storms. For a while, he lived in a bower he placed over one of the plateau's steam vents. He kept warm as a foot of snow fell around him, but on the third night, he broke through the crust of earth covering the natural caldron and burned his thigh. The leg injury joined his frostbitten feet to put Everts in mortal danger. His weight plummeted; the flesh on his feet pealed off, revealing the bones of his littlest toes. Everts hallucinated forest monsters and "an old clerical friend" who consoled him and offered navigational advice. One night, Everts passed out and fell into his fire, adding a singed hand to the growing list of maladies that also included a "compact mass" of undigested thistle fibers that sat in his gut like a cinder block and "suspended the digestive power of my stomach."[62]

His backcountry vacation was ruined. "A gradual mental introversion grew upon me as physical weakness increased," he wrote in an article for *Scribner's Monthly.* "The massive scenery which, on the upward journey, had aroused every enthusiastic impulse of my nature, was not tame and spirit-less." Everts's thought turned to death, heaven, and home. He longed to see his daughter again.[63]

Jack Baronett, a market hunter and gun for hire, and George A. Pritchett, a prospector, discovered Everts on October 16. From a distance, they thought he was a bear, but the closer they got, the more confused they became. "When I got near it," recalled Baronett, "I found it was not a bear, and for my life I could not tell what it was." He "went up close to the object; it was making a low groaning noise, crawling along upon its knees and elbows, and trying to drag itself up the mountain." When Baronett realized it was the lost man from the Washburn expedition—he and Pritchett were out hunting both bears and the $600 reward being offered by Everts's associates in Helena—he spoke to "the object of my search" and received no reply. Everts had joined the wonders of Yellowstone. He was a site to behold: "His flesh was all gone; the bones protruded through the skin on the balls of his feet and thighs. His fingers looked like bird claws."[64]

In his article for *Scribner's*, Everts brushed off his nature shock. He remembered snapping back when Baronett and Pritchett appeared and asked, "Are you Mr. Everts?" "Yes, All that is left of him." And he rebutted later accounts that portrayed him as deranged for days after his rescue. Baronett, Pritchett, and others insisted that "his mind wandered most of the time," that he "was constantly delirious," and that he was "temporarily insane." Everts did admit, however, that alone, in the throes of bewilderment, he'd experienced disconcerting out-of-body spells. "By some process," he wrote, "which I was too weak to solve, my arms, legs, and stomach were transformed into so many traveling companions. Often for hours I would plod along conversing with these imaginary friends." He re-created his deteriorating mental state in print for a national audience, but he tried to isolate the craziness within the confines of an unexplored wild region. In Yellowstone, his painful ordeal and mind-boggling suffering joined Old Faithful and the hot springs as curiosities. Evert made a spectacle of himself, and his story of getting lost became a national park monument. But the instant he reentered civilized society, he wanted his sound mind back.[65]

Everts was an ambitious man with a reputation to preserve. When the traumatic events of his thirty-seven lost days were behind him, he fought to reclaim his sanity and display his self-mastery. He ended the *Scribner's Monthly* article with a plea to his readers. When they traveled to Yellowstone, he encouraged "all lovers of sublimity, grandeur, and novelty" to remember him stumbling around in the wilderness and to enjoy the "happy contrast with my trials." Instead of driving them insane, the landscape would "delight, elevate, and overwhelm" their "minds with wondrous and majestic beauty." Everts's nature shock paved the way for tourists to discover mental health in sublime nature. The Washburn-Langford-Doane expedition and Evert's disappearance from it helped establish the Yellowstone valley as recreational wilderness. The horror of Evert's ordeal underscored the valley's wildness while the information provided by the expedition's reports and the *Scribner's Monthly* coverage reassured visitors that Yellowstone's natural excitement would heal their minds rather than push them over the edge.[66]

After getting terribly lost, Truman Everts left Montana and moved back east. He was not a young man when he frostbit his feet, burned his extremities, and watched his body weight plummet to a reported fifty pounds. The oldest member of the Washburn-Langford-Doane expedition, the fifty-four-year old seemed destined for a lifetime of illness and debilitation. But he advanced into his dotage with his mental, if not his moral, compass intact. Everts, whose first marriage gave him a daughter before it ended prior to his western career, fathered two more children, one at the age of seventy-five and another at the age of eighty-five. He managed these time-defying acts of sexual reproduction by marrying a much younger person. Sometime in 1880 or 1881, at the age of sixty-four or sixty-five, Everts wed a fourteen-year-old girl. The couple established a household in Hyattsville, Maryland, where Everts secured one last government job. He worked for the U.S. postal service. The elderly patriarch labored to maintain the "gossamer network" that brought the West into the American nation.[67]

# CHAPTER SIX

# Keep Your Head

G. NELSON ALLEN RUMMAGED THROUGH THE interior of North America in search of a comfortable location for his head and a lively market for his business. The storekeeper traveled west sometime in his youth, camping for several days along the Gila River, where Indians stole two of his horses. Years later, in 1858 and back home in New Philadelphia, Ohio, he read a newspaper account of a gold strike along the Gila. The story prompted him to wax nostalgic in a letter to his married daughter Emma. She knew his western backstory, which freed Nelson to splatter his memories all over the page instead of organizing them into a sequential pattern. He wished he'd known about the gold back then, he wrote. A stray nugget or two would have paid for the lost horses. It was hot out west, "the hottest place I was ever at." The sun broiled his hide, so he slept during the day and traveled in the moonlight. In Tucson, a Mexican woman "opened my shirt bosom to see that I had not been browned by the sun." Everyone was afraid of the Apaches and the Navajos. At night, "all living things of any value" were herded behind the town walls and the gates were closed. "I am feeling my head," he quipped, "to see if my scalp is there."[1]

The subject of G. Nelson Allen's head rolled through the family's correspondence. He suffered from debilitating migraines, and in 1860 he moved his family from New Philadelphia to Prairie du Chien, Wisconsin, which he thought would be more conducive to his health. Emma, who lived in

Burlington, New Jersey, stayed in touch with her parents and her younger sister Lizzie through the mail. Many letters featured Lizzie's frolics with Beppie, the family dog. Emma owned a mutt named Captain, and the sisters bonded through their pets.

"Nobody dies here," Nelson wrote Emma from Wisconsin, "unless they bring some disease with them." Emma's mother, Elizabeth, concurred: "Thy father is like another man in this climate so much better." Nelson's spells came "once or twice a fortnight" instead of the "2 or 3 attacks of headache in a week" he had experienced in his former home. Still, Wisconsin had its ups and downs. "The country round about here is very hilly and I don't like to climb large hills." Nelson and Elizabeth began to contemplate additional moves. First, they would try Hancock County, Iowa, and if that place did not suit them, they would lug Beppie and Lizzie to the Pike's Peak gold rush. Colorado being famously void of large hills.[2]

Iowa struck Nelson as promising but primitive. He was too old to build a farm and a store from the ground up, and he and Elizabeth preferred "more life and excitement." They aimed for the Rockies. Nelson contracted James Albee, a young man whom he had met in Prairie du Chien, to drive a second wagon. In exchange for his labor, Albee received free transportation and meals. In April 1860, the Allens and Albee set out for Council Bluffs and the Platte River Road. They did not make it out of Iowa before they got lost. They missed the trail and cast off into the flat nothingness of a twenty-mile stretch of prairie. Nelson and James set out in opposite directions in search of wagon ruts. Hours later, James returned, but Nelson was gone. Elizabeth tied a "big white towel" to a whip stalk, stood on the wagon's driver seat, and waved it for hours. The emergency upended the daily schedule. Lizzie went to bed without her supper. Nelson eventually wandered in while the child slept. A few weeks later Beppie went missing and was never heard from again.[3]

The blank prairie lingered in Elizabeth's mind. She brought up the incident in an 1887 letter to Emma. She remembered being frightened and swinging the white flag. She noted Nelson's relief and exhaustion when he reached the wagons: "He was so tired and yet so glad." The powerlessness of getting lost triggered other sorrowful memories. Elizabeth described their return from Pike's Peak. Albee stayed in Colorado, and Nelson's headaches worsened to the point that Elizabeth took on his jobs as well as her own. She drove the oxen—and "did the cooking as usual & attended to everything the best I could always caring for the child also and mending up our rough dried shabby clothes, washed in the cold river Platte." The exertion nearly killed them both. The couple returned to Ohio, where a doctor "did not know which of us would die first." When Nelson did succumb to his illness, Elizabeth blamed his "sad ending" on their wanderlust: "Nelson was not able to stand such a journey, so often ailing & not as young as he had been." She concluded: "I was not young either."[4]

The ground shifted under Americans' spatial cognition between 1860 and 1887, and Elizabeth Allen's memories tracked the ambiguous movement from relational to individual space. Transportation and communication networks knit the United States and the rest of the continent together, opening paradoxical spaces for individuals to free themselves while being supported by impersonal businesses, governments, and organizations. The paradoxes of individual space overturned some of the older assumptions about travel. Instead of bringing households with them, either physically or mentally, travelers sought to leave their homes behind. They pursued vacations, brief and joyful disconnections from the everyday grind of domesticity. Vacations altered the definitions of labor and play. On the road to Colorado and back, Elizabeth Allen performed all the chores that turned a campsite into a home away from home. She "was the cook, dishwasher &c. all through the five months and I was glad to get anything good to serve up." She rose out of bed before everyone else, built a fire, and cooked breakfast and lunch so that the men could enjoy their noon repast on the moving wagons. She hustled and planned, and when Nelson fell ill, she carried the entire weight of her family. Exertion defined Elizabeth's experience of space: "The West was more of a wilderness when we were on our travels." The region felt wild to her because she endured profound isolation as the sole caretaker of a sick mobile household. She felt out of sorts on the plains because poor health and distance had unraveled the relationships that defined her place in the world. The definition of the wilderness had changed by 1887. Recreationists entered scenic locations to enjoy respites from modernity. Male recreationists with means had options other than wives to shoulder camp labor. Elizabeth Allen's recollections of the trail were prompted by Emma mentioning in a letter that James Albee, their old Peak's Peak driving partner, was reportedly in California, camping in the mountains, and that his meals were being prepared, not by him or his wife, but by a Chinese cook. Instead of a rolling home, Albee dined in a pop-up restaurant, which struck Elizabeth as absurd.[5]

After the American Civil War, the meaning of outdoor activities like camping, hiking, canoeing, and skiing crossed the line from work to leisure. Elizabeth Allen camped so that her family could cover the distance between Iowa and Colorado. James Albee covered a distance so that he could camp. Americans traveled into spaces that challenged their navigational skills—deep forests, puzzling mountains, and ragged and shifting shorelines—to enjoy themselves. Fraught environments attracted recreationists seeking an escape from grimy cities and noxious factories. Like G. Nelson Allen, these travelers chased relief of one sort or another. Unlike him, they did not uproot their households to achieve it. They vacated their homes for a brief disconnection and then returned, hoping a sojourn in nature as a free individual would reinvigorate their bodies and calm their nerves.[6]

The onslaught of modernity pushed Americans toward scenic oases; romanticism pulled them there. Launched in Europe in the eighteenth century, the romantic movement envisioned nature as a retreat brimming with complex and intense feelings. Romantic nature exuded the sublime, an aura at once beautiful and awful, thrilling and otherworldly. Romantic getaways possessed vistas, waterfalls, jagged cliffs, and maybe a few ruins. In the ideal, only a handful of people, perhaps a hotelier, a cook, and a few guides, lived in romantic nature. Governments sometimes emptied landscapes when the inhabitants spoiled the sensations, the grandeur, and the emptiness. Work needed to blend into the scenery. Sport hunters visited thinly populated areas in season, but for the most part romantics chased soul-rattling emotions rather than material advantage.[7]

Moderns traveled into romantic nature first on railroads and then in automobiles. Industrialized transportation made mass movement into the wilderness possible. Indeed, industrial capitalism created the modern wilderness through its opposition. Nature became tranquil, salubrious, and invigorating when home became synonymous with rapid transit, clogged urbanization, and unceasing stimulus. Nature cured when cities grew sick and maddening. The antidote and the disease imagined one another in the outpouring of words from publishing houses. Industrial information underpinned the sublime. Outdoor authors told nature seekers where to hike and where to pitch their tents. They instructed them in canoeing and walking. They told them what to do if they got lost and nature shock descended upon them.[8]

Industrial capitalism defined the modern wilderness as a romantic space where individuals might heal themselves and lose themselves. These propositions, however, remained separate for most of the twentieth century. Getting lost was not a form of recreation but rather a derangement at odds with the wilderness goals of self-reliance and mental stability. Advice columnists, guidebook writers, and government officials produced reading material for the masses to prevent them from getting lost on vacation. And when tourists did get bewildered, the advisers gave instructions on how to calm their minds and stave off nature shock. Authors provided recreationists with basic orienteering skills to keep them in bounds and intact. Park officials and concessionaires offered warnings, maps, and guiding services. When visitors did wander into trouble, volunteer and government-backed search-and-rescue teams looked for them. Getting lost ruined vacations, and it wrecked the wilderness solitude by unleashing impersonal organizations into sublimity. Mass communication, transportation, and consumption supported the modern fantasy of individuals being alone in nature. However, when federal bureaucrats, soldiers, park concessionaires, and lumber company employees swept wilderness playgrounds in search of a wayward hiker, primeval pretensions and illusions of isolation suffered alongside the missing person. In an emergency, nature parks and reserves revealed themselves as modern creations, and lost consumers exposed the vast and invasive infrastructure that delivered sensations of disconnection and orchestrated individual communes with nature.

## THE MANUAL

Elizabeth Allen wove Nelson's getting lost into the warp of family relationships. The incident nearly wrecked her traveling household. It upended the daily schedule and foreshadowed more sinister interruptions. The experience settled into Elizabeth's memory bank adjacent to Beppie's disappearance and Nelson's death. She paired his getting lost on the earth with his departure from it.

Contrast Elizabeth's longing for Nelson with Elon Jessup's essay on not wandering away in the July 5, 1922, edition of *Outlook* magazine. In "Getting Lost in the Woods," Jessup offered a modern vision of getting lost unstrung from the emotional ties and filial bonds that had defined the experience for centuries in relational space.9

For Jessup, getting lost was a psychological condition rather than a social predicament. "Almost everyone gets lost sooner or later," he explained, "at least for a few minutes." Even "woodsmen," nature boys with an instinctive sense of direction, misread their inner gyroscopes once in awhile. The reaction to a navigational error spelled the difference between a child of the forest and a "city-bred person." Old hands hunkered down, knowing that they could survive for days in the woods, eating roots and berries, until a person stumbled upon them or they happened upon a landmark they recognized. The uninitiated depended on compasses and maps, and when the going turned strange, they had less confidence and knowledge to fall back on. Disorientation, however, did not necessarily lead them to becoming lost. If a banker remained calm—and remembered the advice from all the outdoor periodicals he'd consumed—he could pass through the fog and find his way back to the trail. The trouble started when "evil spirits" entered disordered minds and overturned common sense. The "most important of all rules for a person lost in the woods?" "Keep your head."10

Born in New York, Elon Jessup began his journalism career as a foreign correspondent. In 1915, he represented *Harper's* magazine in automaker Henry Ford's "Peace Ship," a publicity campaign intended to end World War I. Later in the war, he accompanied a humanitarian mission to bring an anti-typhus vaccine to the Serbian Army, reporting on the effort for the *New York World*. He lived oversees until the outbreak of World War II, when he returned to the United States and moved with his family to Woods Hole, Massachusetts. Jessup supplemented his reporter's salary by authoring outdoor recreation how-to articles and books. An avid hiker, skier, canoeist, climber, photographer, snowshoer, and yachtsman, he specialized in sports and pastimes appropriate to the New England coast, the White Mountains of New Hampshire and Maine, and the Adirondacks. He was a regional coach and giver of advice, but the how-to genre and the push to broaden his readership coaxed Jessup toward generalities. He enforced a law of averages to universalize his northeastern expertise, which often produced sentences like "The average man or woman of today participates in some form of outdoor recreation" or "Strange as it may seem, the average city-bred person doesn't know how to walk." Everyone, he implied, could follow his instructions to motor camp, ski, or "not drown" successfully wherever they drove, schussed, or swam.[11]

Jessup's dedication to generality and abstraction was impressive. If mountain climbers, he argued, adhered to his rules, they need not worry overmuch about rock beneath their boots: "It does not make a vast amount of difference where one learns, for the fundamental principles of mountaineering hold good the world over." The same was true of getting lost in the woods. Indeed, getting lost in the woods laid bare a mental precipice over which everyone teetered all the time. "I do wish to emphasize," he wrote, "that [going out of one's head] is always a possibility and sometimes becomes more than a possibility." Spatial insanity could strike in town or in the timber. "Just as cool reasoning serves as a curb upon crazy, unwise impulses which come to one in every-day life, so may it down the impulses of panic and terror which assail one who is lost in the woods." The din of modern life inured average citizens to the "rumbling" presence of the "the little blue devils of terror" waiting to escort them to a freak-out. Visitors did not find trouble in the wilderness; they brought their troubles with them.[12]

Jessup's devils and spirits echoed the nature shock Charles Whittlesey and Truman Everts suffered on their expeditions. Jessup may have read Whittlesey's article or run across one of the many regurgitations of the surveyor's "fatal lunacy" comments in publications like Henry Howe's *Historical Collections of Ohio*. The mental crack-up theory of bewilderment had been coursing through American print culture for decades before Jessup theorized about irrational impulses shocking the brains of confused recreationists. The compendiums of industrial information gathered local stories about lost children who hid from their rescuers and wayward hunters who failed to recognize their wives or their cabins upon their return.[13]

Jessup's definition of getting lost held to the traditions of nineteenth-century delirium even as it broke toward twentieth-century psychoses. "That which happens when a person is lost," Jessup wrote, "is a gap has occurred between known surroundings, a thread has snapped." Gaps and threads seem familiar enough, but Jessup's surroundings were not Whittlesey's poorly mapped copper region nor the lost children's agrarian patchworks of forests and fields, and the thread being snapped was not the line tethering a lost person to a household or a settlement. It was the individual's grip on his or her own head. By 1922, getting lost was an eternal internal struggle rather than a temporary communal affair.[14]

By preaching universals, Jessup and his how-to colleagues liberated getting lost from the past. They released the experience from local frontier histories and sweeping narratives of transcontinental overland journeys, just as these nineteenth-century visions of getting lost had plucked the experience from early modern hierarchies, trade alliances, and religious epiphanies. Eighteenth- and nineteenth-century agrarian communities associated getting lost with the chaos they perceived in Native landscapes. Once they applied their families' labor to forests, swamps, and thickets, they no longer got lost, supposedly. The experience became a memory, a historical epoch. At the same time, government mail service and mapping expeditions encouraged individuals to invade the interior en masse. Printed trail guides and personal letters convinced treasure hunters like Samuel Nichols that they could retain their household connections despite thousands of miles separating them from their businesses and loved ones. The mapping performed by Charles Whittlesey and John C. Frémont, and the activism of black abolitionist writers, aimed to unify the territorial United States. The survey grid allowed prospectors and farmers to shortcut relational spaces where trade and family ties kept members in bounds, while the Civil War ended what had become intolerable regional discrepancies. Whether they fought to make the country all free or all slave, the dedication to "all" reflected a turn in how Americans perceived space. The Union won the battle on many fronts, including spatial imagination. After the war, the federal government sent troops south and west to bind rogue confederates and rebel Indians to it instead of to their nations within nations.

State and national governments, recreation-industry entrepreneurs, and private clubs carved pocket gardens out of the seamless United States where harried individuals could relax, exercise, and confront their neurology. Niagara Falls, summer resorts in the Poconos, the Adirondack forest preserves, fishing camps in Michigan, California's Yosemite, dude ranches across the West, and geyser-popping Yellowstone were staged as temporal anomalies. They drew clients back to relational space: the agrarian frontier or the multicultural fur trade. In a world of rapid flux, these places stood still. They were the geographic equivalent of the sound of crickets. The urge to preserve altered the strategies visitors used to stay found and sane. On the agrarian frontier, communities banded together to keep track of one another and wrestled nature into compliance as households. Families cleared forests, drained marshes, and erected landmarks.

They braided stories into landscapes that turned confusion into clarity. Decades earlier, in many of these same wilderness spaces, fur traders navigated unfamiliar terrain with relationships formed through exchange. But tourists visited these echoes of the long ago as individuals. They went to re-creations of relational space to be left alone.

Tourists sought leisure, not labor, and they paid private and public workforces to transform landscapes to accommodate them, to clear their ski trails and to collect their campground garbage. Customers and service providers conspired in the illusion of restful timelessness, and the impersonal cash nexus encouraged tourists to believe that they were indeed by themselves in sublime nature. The feeling of detachment was an amenity, and clients and managers pushed the limits of safety to conjure sensations of being out-there, on the edge of the known world. These impulses made going on vacation truly dangerous. A hidden crevasse, a flooded stream, or an irate grizzly bear could mangle a holiday. Visitors accepted risks because they expected nature to blow their minds—in a healthy, sublime way. The inconceivable was a romantic objective, and predictably, tourists struggled to navigate what they could not conceive.

## BRAINS ON VACATION

The movement back to nature registered in sore muscles, blistered feet, and sunburned cheeks. Lungs huffed fresh air while nostrils filled with the scent of pine needles and sagebrush. Thunderstorms raised the hairs on necks and forearms. Rain pelted tents and torsos. Being in nature drew attention to baseline bodily functions. Outdoor recreationists were forced to strategize their eliminations. Where to seek relief, how to execute the movement, and what to do with output became a puzzle that could not be settled with a flush. Having to confront your feces epitomized the physicality of camping, hiking, or canoeing. You knew you were in nature when you remembered how your body felt and worked.

Given the centrality of sweat and sensuality to wilderness appreciation, it's easy to forget that hauling oneself back to nature was supposed to be primarily a cerebral maneuver. The brain was the organ that most needed to go outside. In his 1918 *A Guide to the National Parks of America,* Edward Frank Allen imagined a traveler to Glacier National Park stepping off the train "at Belton" and joining a clutch of men and women gathered around a campfire at dusk. The group tittered back and forth, bouncing the day's adventures off one another: a snowstorm broke out "up near Gunsight Pass," a grizzly bear shuffled "across the trail," a "ten-pound trout" was hauled from Red Eagle Lake. The ricochet of voices stirred the "cobwebs of the indoors" in the observer's "brains." With the dust of the city still on his shoes, he yearned for tomorrow and his chance to plunge into "the freedom here in the wilderness, and the simplicity and beauty of unspoiled woodlands." Like Jessup, Allen stressed the mental aspects of returning to nature by trapping readers in the grammatical second person, a projection akin to the view in a first-person shooter video game. Readers saw the "stupendous views" of Glacier Park through the eyes of an authorial "you." Spurring a horse along the trail to Sperry Glacier Camp, wrote Allen, it strikes you that "this is real traveling, and the thought that this is the only way you can go—the way the pioneers went—appeals to you." Guidebooks instructed readers not only where to go and what to see but what to think and how to feel.[15]

The mental focus of the literature reached back to the initial stirrings of the modern wilderness when the stresses of industrialization first started driving Americans mad. In 1849, Joel Tyler Headley published *The Adirondack; or, Life in the Woods.* A Presbyterian clergyman, Headley left his post in Stockbridge, Massachusetts, in 1842 when his "overwrought brain" chased him from the profession. He toured Europe and then tried to make an escape closer to home. He spent two summers in "the pathless and unknown wilderness of central New York." There, with "rest and quiet" his "only companions," he "cast aside" the "mask society compels one to wear" and threw off "the restraint which the thousand eyes and reckless tongues about him fasten on the heart." His free soul "rejoiced in its liberty and again becomes a child in action." Flooded with "excitement and rapture" after viewing "wondrous and glorious spectacle[s]," Headley discovered in nature the harmony of spirit, body, and mind he could not orchestrate in Stockbridge.[16]

Sick minds remained central to outdoor recreation as the movement proliferated. In 1872, Henry Perry Smith declared camping in the Adirondacks the best remedy for readers seeking to flee "the treadmill of labor, the anxieties of politics, the perplexities of traffic, and [to escape] from the chain-like task of a weary and overtaxed brain." In 1883, Charles Hallock told hunters that "the bodily powers are not the only ones which should be well developed for the brain should be active and energetic as the body itself." In 1890, George O. Shields connected brains, guts, and vacationing in the outdoors: "We live, in reality, only when digestion is good, when circulation is free, and when the blood, in healthful pulsations, goes bounding into the brain." "It is good," he wrote, "to abandon care for at least two months every year. Let us go into camp, live nature, and grow healthy." In 1923 O. E. Meinzer, in his preface to John Stafford Brown's *The Salton Sea Region, California,* alerted readers to the glories of the southern California desert and its settling effects on the nerves: "It is a country of distant views and grand panoramas, visible only from the mountain tops but also from alluvial slopes. These great distances and magnificent land-scapes tend to enlarge and ennoble the human mind." Paid for by the federal government's Department of the Interior, Brown's report was not a tourist brochure but rather a survey of regional water use and resources. It was a planning document intended to inform hydrologists and irrigation experts and convince politicians to green-light desert reclamation projects. Even in the dry habitat of a bureaucratic white paper, authors soothed readers' troubled minds by offering them scenic views of nature.[17]

Outdoor authors borrowed techniques from novelists to construct subjectivities for their readers to consume. They used the tools of novelists to generate intimacy, to collapse multiple perspectives into one average head. Guidebooks and how-to articles cloaked their fictional mechanisms in no-nonsense pragmatism. They were instruction manuals, after all. But publishers would have killed the genre long ago if only travelers read travel literature. For every reader who trailed Joel Tyler Headley to the Adirondacks or Edward Frank Allen to Glacier National Park, thousands more journeyed no farther than a comfortable chair in their living rooms. Vicarious vacations prepared tourists for mental epiphanies, and outdoor authors wielded literary devices to release imaginations into the wild.[18]

Advocates of outdoor recreation spliced mind alteration into sensual experience. Bodies crossed the territory from cities to remote nature, while minds tripped from overstimulation to peace. Vacationers teleported to saner versions of themselves. An evangelist for walking, sleeping, and glorying in the woods outside the northeastern Boston to New York City urban corridor, William Henry Harrison Murray instigated meetings of minds in his writing to demonstrate how brains might improve through brief exposures to nature. Connecticut-born, Murray graduated from Yale University in 1862. He labored as a pastor in Boston and spent his summers in the Adirondacks. In the late 1860s, he started a second career. He lectured and wrote newspaper articles and books that championed outdoor recreation. In 1870, he published *Adventures in the Wilderness; or, Camp-Life in the Adirondacks.* The Reverend William Murray became "Adirondack" Murray, "father of the Outdoor Movement." Murray taught overtaxed information workers like himself how to escape "the sights and sounds and duties" that gripped them in "an intense, unnatural, and often fatal tension." Snared in worry, wrestling with concerns no less weighty than damnation, clergymen benefited most from a sojourn in nature. There, in the woods, "they would find that perfect relaxation which all jaded minds require." The wilderness transported "the clergyman's brain" to a place where "all pure things passed by or forgotten come back to us, and the past, in reference to whatever of goodness and truth it had in it, will be, to the holy, an eternal present." For Murray, minds cut loose in nature broke the shackles of chronology to remember what had been forgotten.[19]

Murray built the outdoor movement on the contrast between cities and woodlands. To reach the eternal present in sublime nature, however, he traveled beyond town and country dichotomies to the grid cells of the hippocampus, where memories created space. To remember, tourists had to forget. Unconsciousness prepared campers to receive the woods' full medicine. In a novelist mind-meld, Murray carried readers to a whispering brook, where on a "bed of balsam," they could lay down their heads and curl up with a dog named Rover. The stream sang, "the ripples were playing coyly with the sand," and the pines "lulled" with their "low monotones." Dew gathered on the trees' limbs "like gems upon their spear-like stems." The sleeper "sank, as a falling star fades from sight, into forgetfulness." "Ah me," wrote Murray, "the nights I have passed in the woods! How they haunt me with their sweet, suggestive memories of silence and repose." Outdoor recreationists returned home with fond recollections of forgetting.[20]

Murray's recipe for mental health sounded a lot like getting lost. He ventured into a strange environment alone at night and misremembered. The drip and gurgle of the woods counteracted the clatter of Boston, which assaulted the nerves like "steel-shod hoofs" smiting "flinty pavement." To embrace the wild, campers had to forget the city. The shock of waking in a peaceful glade, the split second of not knowing where you were, captured the essence of both a good vacation and a bout of disorientation.

Murray hired guides to reel him and his family back if they wandered too far into unspoiled nature. "A good guide, like a good wife," he wrote, "is indispensable to one's success, pleasure, and peace." But not all guides were good. Some talked too much. Some were lazy, ignorant, or untrustworthy. In time, evangelists like Murray spread the outdoor movement to middle-class families who traveled to nature on their own in automobiles and who could not afford to hire personal woodland servants. They replaced expensive guides with cheap print. Magazines and books told the masses how to lose their worries but not their way.[21]

"This book," declared George Shields in the opening paragraph of *Camping and Camp Outfits: A Manual of Instruction for Young and Old Sportsmen*, "contains practical points on how to dress for hunting, fishing, or other camping trips; what to provide in the way of bedding, tents, eatables, cooking, utensils, and all kinds of camp equipage; how to select camping grounds; how to build camps, or shelters of various kinds; how to build camp fires; what to do in case of getting lost." Urban-born recreationists who did not read or follow instructions courted misfortune. "Whoever takes to the woods and water recreation," wrote Horace Kephart in *Camping and Woodcraft: A Handbook for Vacation Campers and Travelers in the Wilderness*, "should learn how to shift for himself in an emergency." The rich "may employ guides and a cook," but "the day of disaster may come, the outfit may be destroyed, or the city man may find himself some day alone, lost in the forest, and compelled to meet the forces of Nature in a struggle for his life." When that day arrived, the prepared remembered the instructions from the manuals: the true danger of getting lost was in their heads.[22]

Lost Americans congregated in predictable locations at unsurprising moments: landscapes with blocked or radically uninterrupted sight lines made more perplexing by an unexpected storm or nightfall. Weather and topography contributed mightily to disorientation, but you would not know this from the outdoor recreational literature. After cursory mentions of compasses, maps, and remaining mindful about distances, turns taken, and landmarks, the advice providers returned, like a herd of peckish zombies, to the brain. "All men," wrote Dr. Eugene L. Swan in *Harper's Camping and Scouting*, edited by George Bird Grinnell, "who have experience in the woods agree that the first thing to do when lost is stop at once, sit down, and calmly think it over." All men also universally agreed that "*any one* may become lost." "There is hardly ever any real danger," continued Swan, "unless the boy gets frightened and loses his 'nerve' completely." Edward Breck, author of *The Way of the Woods: A Manual for Sportsmen in the Northeastern United States and Canada,* concurred with the conventional wisdom: "Don't get flurried." "Most of us have gotten lost; the situation is not so tragic as it often appears to the tenderfoot." When lost at dusk, pause, sit down, "put on a pipe," and meditate on the situation. "Before making up your mind . . . do a lot of thinking, and, once again, don't allow panicky feelings to enter your heart." Far worse calamities could befall a person than spending a few days in the woods. "The chances are that you will soon get out; but, if you don't, what of it?" "Many a man has got lost and staid lost a week or a month, and come out smiling in the end." Don't "make a condemned fool of yourself" and get "scared and excited" and start running. "Show yourself a philosopher" rather than a nitwit. Don't be the guy who "has run himself down, and died of starvation and exhaustion, or, when found by his friends, has been a raving maniac." The choice was yours: "Which will you do?" The experts agreed that nature shock was an individual choice rather than an accidental outcome.[23]

### AVATARS

Once again, the psychology of outdoor recreation tempted writers to lecture directly to "you." The novelistic mind-meld stripped away the specificity of people and places. Admonishments like "Keep your head level and your course straight" applied across geographies and demographics. Any head could be leveled along any course to prevent *any one* from getting lost. The literature promoted autonomous individualism by obliterating personal and environmental contexts.

Many authors used the old Enlightenment trick of speaking in universals but meaning a specific gender, race, and class affiliation. The subject receiving the instruction to "keep your head" was more likely than not assumed to be a white, middle-class man. For example, the author of a 1905 article in *Forest and Stream* entitled "On Not Getting Lost in the Woods" began by addressing "people," "any one," and "those who are lost" and then switched, mid-opening-paragraph, to "When a man is really lost he is practically insane and incapable of reason." If any question remained about the sex of "you" by the end of the piece, the pseudonym the author chose to sign off with confirmed his perspective. He was "Manly Hardy."[24]

If the gender of Manly Hardy's assumed audience was hard to miss, so too was its race. Manly Hardy told the story of a Penobscot Indian guide named Sebattis Dana. The guide became disoriented and wandered in circles in the Maine woods. His missteps, according to Hardy, truly proved that "any one" could lose his way. Hardy knew that his readers would believe that Indians rarely if ever got lost in the woods because Indians were supposed to be wild and premodern. The story illustrated the universal law of getting lost by asserting and then subverting a racial stereotype. At least Hardy named Dana and acknowledged his presence in contemporary Maine. Most authors ignored the Native people who worked or resided in scenic vacation spots, and Indians were conspicuous by their absence in the modern wilderness. When the topic of getting lost came up in the literature, outdoor enthusiasts summoned Indians and then dismissed them with a joke. The American nature writer and outdoor advocate Ernest Thompson Seton rewarmed an oft-told quip in "Woodcraft," a 1905 article he wrote for London's *Windsor* magazine: "When you do miss your way, the first thing to remember is, like the Indian: 'You are not lost; it is the *teepee* that is lost.' It isn't serious. It cannot be unless you do something foolish." The founder of the Woodcraft Indians, a forerunner of the Boy Scouts, of which he was an early promoter, Seton used the advice givers' "you" to appropriate Native wisdom. The lost person he was instructing to lighten up was a white boy in the woods pretending to be an Indian.[25]

Outdoor authors segregated the races in time. Native Americans belonged on the opposite side of the modern divide. Recreationists made it their mission to walk Indian paths, learn Indian place-names, and retell Indian stories. They liked to think that they shared Native peoples' space as well as their love of the wilderness, even if history had split the appreciators of nature into separate epochs. Modern outdoor enthusiasts could only dream of being in the presence of Indians in nature.[26]

Whereas time explained why it was safe to assume that an autonomous individual on vacation in a remote park was probably white, space foretold that the generic camper was most likely rich, or at least middling to well off. A class gradient, starting high and ending low, followed routes out of town. Slickers clashed with hicks in the backwoods. Getting lost signaled that you might be urban, and therefore a fool. Yet the ability to avoid getting lost, or at least to face inevitable disorientation with a calm and reasonable mind, showed that you belonged in the woods, or the mountains, or the desert, as much as any local. Knowledge obscured class. A well-read and properly equipped tourist was indistinguishable from a native-born local.

In 1928, Vance Randolph published an article in *Forest and Stream* magazine with a title that announced his theme: "Lost in the Ozarks: 'A Feller Caint Git Lost in Three Mile o' Timber.' " He intended to spelunk the cultural chasm between the city and the country. Before plunging into specifics, Randolph laid out the universals of bewilderment. "Some fellows," he wrote, "lose their heads entirely the instant they realize that they are lost, and gallop off through the woods in a near-hysterical condition." Driven berserk, the lost "run right through clearings and past lighted cabins without seeming to see them at all." Jimmy Hale was one such fellow, and his squirrely behavior under pressure showed how a poor attitude could expose the literary assumption that reading about navigating a wilderness was as good as navigating a wilderness. Being informed was not the same as being crafty.[27]

A tall "New Englander" in his twenties, Hale fancied himself an expert archeologist because he had "read some books." He traveled to the Ozarks to search the region's caverns for prehistoric artifacts, carrying letters of introduction from friends of Randolph's back east. Randolph took Hale a hundred miles into the Missouri woods. The pair slept with "tie-whackers," independent lumber workers who camped in shanties, felled trees, trimmed them into railroad-standard dimensions, and slathered them with creosote for a few cents per tie. Hale quickly wore out his welcome. The young doctor, wrote Randolph, "knew too much, and his good-natured contempt for my poor knowledge and attainments irritated me." He lectured his host on woodcraft, critiquing his fire-building skills and correcting his identification of woodpecker species. Two weeks into their trip, Hale left camp to hike "about three miles" through the woods to reach a nearby village and call his girlfriend. Relishing a morning free of Hale's "putrid hokum," Randolph urged him on his way, calling out as he entered the trees: " 'Well, don't get lost!' "[28]

Which, of course, he immediately did. Hale failed to come back that night. Thinking the lad had decided to bed down in the village, Randolph held off searching for him until noon the next day, when he enlisted a tie-whacker named Lem to help find Hale. The two nosed their way "over the frozen hills like a couple bird dogs." A light snow had fallen, and Hale's tracks were plain to see once the pair ran across them. Lem observed the footprints and tried to understand the man who had left them. "He couldn't of got lost noway," Lem exclaimed, "a feller caint git lost in three mile o' timber." Alas, Hale was no ordinary specimen, explained Randolph. He was a "city man" who might not "know enough to get his bearings."[29]

Lem followed the tracks, around and around, and arrived at a diagnosis: "He must of went plain loony." The searchers found where Hale had slept, a small cavern under a bluff, and in the next hollow, they spotted their man. He was marching along "shaking his head and tossing his arms wildly about." Randolph called to him. Hale turned, glared at his host without comprehension, and charged him, "frothing and spitting like a wounded wildcat." Randolph ducked behind a bush, and the two "played hide-and-seek around a hazel thicket" until Hale spun off alone into the woods. Lem and Randolph discovered him facedown in a snowbank a hundred yards away. After pouring corn whiskey down his throat to deaden his nerves, they carried him back to Lem's cabin. The next morning, he remembered only a few details, like crossing his own trail and becoming frightened and running blindly through the forest. Lem went out to hunt down the missing pistol Randolph had loaned Hale. He collected the money, the box of matches, and the uneaten sandwiches the city man had tossed in his panic, but there was no sign of the gun. Randolph and Lem packed his bags and sent him home to Massachusetts.[30]

At first blush, Randolph's public humiliation of Jimmy Hale would seem a refreshing reassertion of local knowledge and social bonds. Hale could navigate the "North Woods," where urbanites flocked to managed resorts and manicured parks to restore their sanity, but the Ozarks were filled with knottier pines. You could not "read a few books" and conquer them. Knowing *the* place required knowing *your* place, honoring the expertise locals had gathered through years of work and occupation. Newcomers might start by befriending someone like Lem, asking him to tell them a few stories, and writing down his garbled wisdom. That's the route Randolph followed to become a published expert on the Ozark environment and its people. Born in Kansas, Randolph was a child of the information class. His father was a lawyer and his mother a teacher. Randolph graduated college and went on to receive a master's degree in psychology. G. Stanley Hall, the first president of the American Psychological Association and proponent of evolutionary theories of childhood development (as well as eugenics), mentored him. After moving to Missouri in 1919, Randolph devoted himself to the study of Ozark folklore. He also collected Native American artifacts, writing an article for the *New York Times* about unearthing flints, arrowheads, and baskets in Ozark caves. Randolph was a more respectful version of Jimmy Hale, not an alternative one.[31]

"It would take some doing," wrote Brooks Blevins in the preface to the reprint edition of Randolph's *The Ozarks: An American Survival of a Primitive Society*, "to convince me that anyone has ever been more connected to a region than Vance Randolph was (and is) connected to the Ozarks." Through collecting and publishing, Randolph "defined the Ozarks." He occupied a space that used to be owned by primitive peoples, both Native Americans and white working-class tie-whackers. Dissecting and preserving folk culture in print, he pushed Indians and rural whites back in time. Lem became a "survivor" who transmitted lore from a premodern epoch. His "caints" and "aints" were dying words. Transformed into a historical subject, the Natives and working-class denizens of the Ozarks lost their place, which Randolph inhabited and then defended from relic hunters like Hale. The smarmy New Englander played the interloper to Randolph's embedded scribe, yet both used other peoples' information to claim the wilderness as their own.[32]

Randolph offered etiquette advice, too. If urban readers behaved less like Jimmy Hale and more like him, they could pass for country. A dose of humility would mute the class differences between outdoorsmen and backwoodsmen. The fact that Randolph, Hale, Lem, and presumably most of the subscribers to *Forest and Stream* were men helped soften their antagonisms, moving the discussion away from zip codes, tax brackets, and educational degrees. Instead of Brahmins or rubes, the respectful individuals who gathered in the woods and sometimes lost their way could reach a common ground as "fellows."

Men skewed the outdoor literature to claim universal human autonomy for themselves, but this did not mean that women were absent from the modern wilderness. Physiological theories of anxiety purported that women were especially vulnerable to nervous attacks, and the male-dominated medical establishment used diagnoses of mental illnesses like neurasthenia and hysteria to shut women indoors, arguing that their fragile constitutions were best kept away from the ravages of modernity. But not all doctors, and certainly not all women patients, accepted this advice. If the outdoors cured men's jaded heads, it could likewise sooth women's brains. Outdoor guidebooks appeared for women and girls seeking to expose their minds to nature and improve their psychological well-being.[33]

Camping reproduced urban households in the woods, and many camping guidebooks assumed women and children would accompany men into the interior. "Seriously," thundered Horace Kephart in *Camping and Woodcraft*, "is it good for men and women and children to swarm together in cities and stay there, keep staying there, till their instincts are so far perverted that they lose all taste for their natural element, the wide world out-of-doors?" To prevent children from becoming lost on family excursions, he advocated hanging cowbells around their necks "before you let them go into strange woods." A breather in nature promised to reinvigorate all genders and ages, proving the universal benefits of outdoor recreation. If you had a mind, you could ease it in a remote scenic location.[34]

Theoretically, at least. Invitations, it turned out, could be rescinded as quickly as they were tendered. Kephart sent families camping in one paragraph, only to make women and children disappear in the next: "The best vacation an over-civilized man can have is to go where he can hunt, capture, and cook his own meat, erect his own shelter, do his own chores, and pick up again those lost arts of wildcraft that were our heritage through ages past, but of which not one modern man in a hundred knows anything at all." Such displays of vigorous honey-doing may have cheered wives and children who performed these mundane tasks on a regular basis without applause from outside experts, but Kephart meant to exclude them. Men would act, reaping the mental and physical rewards of wildcraft, as women and children watched. Going camping strengthened a man's grip on his body, his mind, and his family.[35]

The outdoor advice aimed at girls was similarly double-edged. No matter their gender, the writers agreed that developing minds needed to be let outdoors. Girls' freedom, however, came with a string of orders and restrictions boys escaped. Dan Carter Beard, the founder of the American Boy Scouts and author of many of that organization's guidebooks, never outlawed giggling, but Jeanette Augustus Marks, the author of *Vacation Camping for Girls*, did: "Nothing is more wearying, more lacking in self-control than such a manner, nothing so exhausts people." "Such giggling or laughing or silly talking," she wrote, "is to the mind what St. Vitus's dance is to the body—an affliction to be endured perhaps but certainly not an attraction and not to be cultivated." She recommended silence in the wilderness and concluded her camp manual with a list of do's and don'ts that spanned the helpful (*Don't cut your foot with an ax*) to the absurd (*Don't be dowdy in the woods*) to the obscure (*Do be independent. Camp is no place for necklaces, however beautiful*). Camping freed young women from "fussiness or display of any sort," but cutting loose turned out to be a command itself. For girls, the outdoors sprouted as many rules as trees.[36]

Adolescence was the ideal time to send modern brains into the wilderness. Not yet burdened by adult responsibilities, young people could enter nature and strengthen their minds before civilization addled them. Getting lost in the woods challenged girls to remain sane. "If by some miscalculation," wrote Marks, "a girl should get lost let her realize then that the great demand is that she keep her head on her shoulders where it has been placed." Marks advised girls to sit down and mull the situation over to avoid panic. As time passed, so did gender. Night closed in, and Marks switched to the second person. "If darkness is coming, settle down where

Unknown group of women enjoying the recreational outdoors sometime between 1915 and 1920. (Courtesy of the Library of Congress Prints & Photographs Division, LC-DIG-ggbain-26032)

you are." "Keep your body warm and dry and your head cool." "You have nothing of which to be afraid except your own lack of common sense." Getting lost tested the discipline of disembodied minds: "Here is a chance for your 'nerve' to show itself." The payoff for keeping your head was individual autonomy. In the wilderness, stoic girls, those who ditched their necklaces, rejected dowdiness, kept their toes safe from axes, and adhered to the long list of rules and guidelines laid out for them, might join the universal "you."[37]

The psychological panic of getting lost camouflaged difference. In 1913, the Boy Scouts' *Official Handbook* revisited the landmarks of bewilderment. The manual's passage on getting lost in the woods opens with a wise scout, a Manly Hardy type, fielding questions from a pack of adolescent boys. "Did you ever get lost in the woods?" they ask. The elder rubs his beard and ponders the topic; then, clearing his throat, he launches into a monolog delivered to "you." Everyone gets lost, he says. "Hunters, Indians, yes, birds and beast, get lost at times." Then he tells his joke. "The first thing to remember is, like the Indian, 'You are not lost, it is the *teepee* that is lost.'" Stay lighthearted to keep fear at bay. "The worst thing you can do is get frightened"; "It is fear that turns a passing experience into a final tragedy"; "Only keep cool and all will be well." The old-timer rattles off a chain of instructions, advising "you" to seek higher ground, search for a landmark, build a fire, look for the Big Dipper, lick a finger and feel for the wind, and mark a trail with charcoal. Here he rounds the corner and heads back to himself and the original question. "I have been lost a number of times," he says, "but always got out without serious trouble, because I kept cool."[38]

The composers of the *Official Handbook for Boys* declared their organization's gender bias with the subtlety of a cannon barrage: "The BOY SCOUTS OF AMERICA is a corporation formed by a group of men who are anxious that the boys of America should come under the influence of this movement and be built up in all that goes to make character and good citizenship." The members of the board of editors who prepared the handbook gathered their material from "men eminently fitted for such work." The getting lost section of the handbook was authored by Ernest Thompson Seton. It was not a new piece of writing but rather a reprint of an article that first appeared in 1902 in the *Ladies' Home Journal*. Seton's initial audience was grown women projecting their imaginations into the perspective of young boys listening to an adult man lecture about how everyone got lost. Though dedicated to boys, the scouting guide contained a hidden history of diversely gendered minds communing with one another.[39]

The Boy Scouts preached the wilderness gospel. To cure their troubled insides, modern Americans were instructed to proceed outdoors. Guidebook authors carried readers there by jumping into their heads, serving up disembodied minds that many genders, classes, and races could inhabit through the universal "you." The default recreationist was white, middle-class, and male, but the genre's mental focus opened the window just a crack for others to go outside, in print and in person. As the mass media developed in the 1930s, with radio and photojournalism coming together with guidebooks and magazines to promote outdoor adventure, nature stories teleported readers, viewers, and listeners, a collective "you" sometimes numbering in the thousands, into the minds of a few lost individuals.

### DONN FENDLER

On July 17, 1938, a twelve-year-old Boy Scout named Donn Fendler summited Baxter Peak on Maine's Mount Katahdin with his friend Henry Condon. The boys had scrambled to the top ahead of their main hiking party, which included their fathers and Donn's two brothers, Tom and Ryan. Clouds rolled in, and droplets of mist collected on Fendler's sweatshirt and thin summer jacket. His teeth chattered, and he grew scared. He decided to backtrack to find his father. The child of an outdoor guide, Condon refused to go along. He hunkered down and waited. Fendler missed the trail and became lost. Nine days later, he stumbled out of the woods, sixteen pounds lighter, missing his coat, his pants, his sneakers, and the tip of one of his big toes, but clinging to a story of excruciating loneliness that would resonate with millions of people.

Fendler's ordeal played out in a split screen of radical individualism and mass media interconnection. While he stumbled through days and shivered through nights, collecting insect bites, bruises, and hallucinations, the press broadcast the search for him. Reporters explored the space between the recreational wilderness and the information infrastructure that, by 1938, included print, telephones, telegraphs, radio, and motion pictures. "Thousands of mothers in America," wrote the editors of the *Boston Transcript,* held their breath while reading "the papers daily for word." News consumption built a physical link to the lost boy: "There was a stout trail of hope being blazed for the boy." The twists and turns of Fendler's actual wanderings mimicked the switchbacks experienced by those following the story. Audiences despaired, gave him up for dead, and rejoiced in his unbelievable comeback. That Fendler spotted a telephone line and used it to guide himself to a cabin and safety epitomized the contradiction at the heart of his accident. Cut off from his family, he traveled inward, down the rabbit hole of his preadolescent mind. And millions of people traveled with him. Fendler reached national celebrity by burrowing into his interior self and coming back out again.[40]

As the outdoor guidebooks predicted, he encountered a substratum of insanity the farther he delved. On the first day, the clouds played tricks on his mind: "It's an awful thing to get lost in the clouds. You see things that aren't there at all. Rocks look like people and shaggy animals." On the morning of the second day, Fendler woke up and swore that he saw Henry Condon standing behind a stump. "You may think this was a dream, but it wasn't. My eyes were wide open and I saw everything. I know it wasn't a dream, even though it sounds crazy now." A Boy Scout, he remembered the instructions to "keep his head," yet his brain kept slipping. "It's queer what funny things go through a fellow's head in a fix like that." He dreamed of ham sandwiches and bears the size of houses. By day 6, he was so battered, hungry, and exhausted that his waking mind and his unconscious rolled over one another like eels in a barrel. He disappeared from himself for chunks of time. He blinked and sunrise turned to noon, noon to night. On the last day, he "seemed like somebody else. I was just watching myself do something." Nearly gone—"I was on a merry go-round, going 'round and 'round and up and down, and I tried to hang on for fear I'd fall off"—he reached the bank of a river and the owner of a cabin across the water, Nelson McMoarn, a guide who summered with his wife at their camp on the Penobscot, spotted and saved him. Fendler spoke to his mother on the telephone that night. As with many lost people before him, his delirium lingered into his rescue. He strained to remember her voice.[41]

The media rejoiced. Fendler's story started as an ember, a paragraph or two in the regional papers, and rose in prominence as the days passed and the search mounted. Begun by two forest rangers stationed at the bottom of the trail to assist summer tourists, the emergency response spread to the Maine State Police, the timber crews from the Great Northern Paper Company, the area's professional outdoor guides, and recreational mountain climbers with rappelling skills. The governor of Maine called out

Millinocket's National Guard. The unit set up a field tent to feed hundreds of rescuers. Two bloodhounds were flown in from New York State to spell worn-out local dogs. Reporters from Bangor and Boston picked up the story in its early days. Soon, journalists from the *New York Times* and the Associated Press nationalized the coverage. Readers of the *Atlanta Constitution* and the *Los Angeles Times* knew who Donn Fendler was before anyone knew where he was.

Reporters highlighted the size of the search. An adult "army" stormed the wilderness to find one child. They interviewed "expert woodsmen," including district forest supervisor Harry Tingley, who said: "If it were my boy, I would have bidden him a sorrowful good-by by this time." The discovery of footprints two days after his father reported Donn missing lifted hopes for a while until bloodhounds tracked the sneakers' scent to the edge of a four-hundred-foot precipice. "I'm still trying," despaired Donn's father, "to make myself believe there's still some faint thread of hope." "Veteran mountaineer" Roy Dudley told a reporter that it was only " 'faintly possible' that the boy could have survived such a fall." "Trained woodsmen" marveled that Donn had survived one night of exposure at "near-freezing tempera-tures" on Baxter Peak. The authorities reduced the search battalions to a skeleton crew after the second weekend. Instead of a boy, they expected to find a body, if they were lucky.[42]

When Fendler appeared thirty-five miles away from the primary search area, he set off an autonomous bomb. The newspapers credited his survival to his Boy Scout training and his faith in God. With a bit of "nature lore" and a lot of prayer, Fendler accomplished what the employees of the United States Forest Service, the experts from the lumber industry, the brotherhood of outdoor guides, the mountaineering community, and the soldiers belonging to Company I, 103rd Infantry could not. Donn, according to the AP reporter, "literally found himself after being lost for eight days in the tangled underbrush of Maine's northern wilderness." He modeled courage and self-determination in a world dominated by gigantic impersonal forces. He showed the professionals that a solitary individual, though immature, naked, injured, emaciated, and lightly connected to reality, could pull through on the strength of his character.[43]

Ralph T. Jones wrote an editorial for the *Atlanta Constitution* two weeks after Fendler's return. He linked the twelve-year-old's "manhood," his deter-mination "to push away despair, to disregard apparent hopelessness of the task, to keep plugging, plugging, trying," to the Great Depression. Donn's father owned a clothing manufacturing business in Rye, New York. He specialized in religious vestments and earned enough to take his family on vacations to Maine every summer. Still, according to Jones, the child of a financially stable middle-class family represented the downtrodden, "who have struggled unendingly against debt, those who have grimly clung to the effort to provide food and clothes for wives and babies, when it seemed there were no jobs, no hope." By going on a hike and getting lost, Donn Fendler rescued the dignity of adult men who "scorned to accept relief when they could, by any device, make an honest dollar themselves." The media turned Fendler's recreational accident into productive labor and his suffering into a rebellion against experts and skeptics who doubted the character of average Americans going through hard times in their "daily lives."[44]

The celebration of Donn's survival began hours after McMoarn spotted him shivering on the opposite shore and continued until Fendler died at age ninety in 2016. After his release from the hospital, the citizens of Rye, New York, threw him a parade, as did the residents of Millinocket, the Maine town nearest Katahdin. Theodore Roosevelt Jr. inducted Donn into New York's "Order of Adventurers" over the radio, and the Maine Guides Association made him an honorary member of its organization. The Maine Boy Scouts presented him with an "Indian war club," and Maine's governor, Lewis O. Barrows, made Donn "governor for a minute" on Wednesday, July 30, 1939. In 1941, Fendler visited the White House, met President Franklin Roosevelt, and received a gold medal of valor. Chief Needahbeh of the Penobscot Indian tribe ceremonially adopted Donn at the New England Sportmen's and Boat Show, and the membership and guests at the eighth annual roundup of the Massachusetts Fish and Game Association gave him a standing ovation. Fendler appeared at Boston's Cathedral of the Holy Cross to be honored by five thousand Catholic Boy Scouts.[45]

Fendler's celebrity increased with the publication of *Lost on a Mountain in Maine*, the young-adult novel speed-written by Joseph Egan in the months after the rescue. While Fendler convalesced at Egan's Cape Cod home, the author and the survivor chatted for a few hours each day, laying down the track for a story that would run for decades. In November, the *Boston Globe* serialized Fendler's as-told-to account. The Wells Publishing Company brought out the book after its run in the *Globe*. It sold (and continues to sell), going through four reprints, the latest in 2011.

Maine's public elementary school teachers adopted the text for its fourth-grade "Maine Studies" curriculum. Irvin "Buzz" Caverly, the director of Baxter State Park between 1981 and 2005, remembered the book from his childhood education: "I think every classroom in the state of Maine, from the time I was in first grade, the teacher was reading that story. It was one of the things that attracted me to the park." Fendler stoked the connection between his accident and childhood education by traveling to Maine as an adult to speak at schools, libraries, and Boy Scout gatherings. Donn eventually joined the army and made his career as a soldier. After being posted in West Germany and commanding a battalion at Fort Campbell, Kentucky, he retired from the service in 1978 and settled in Clarksville, Tennessee. He asked that his ashes be spread over Mount Katahdin.[46]

Joseph Egan erased himself from *Lost on a Mountain in Maine*. He limited the book's view to Donn's, melding the boy's and the readers' minds, in a move that would make Stephen King, Maine's most famous novelist, proud. The intensity of the first-person perspective was the novel's defining feature. Unlike the second-person outdoor advice articles that lectured boys and girls to calm down, be reasonable, and think through their bewilderment, Egan let Donn emote, panic, and go a little insane. There were no flashbacks or cutaways. Egan did not introduce other characters, like a know-it-all woodsman to track the wayward adolescent and explain to young readers how not to get lost, or sympathetic figures like Donn's mother, father, or siblings. The domestic ideal remained unspoken. Egan offered young readers little assurance that, in the end, all would be well. As generations rose to Maine's fourth grade, they experienced Donn's getting lost in the novel as their parents and grandparents experienced Donn's getting lost in the newspapers. They knew a boy was lost alone in the woods and that he might die. The book re-created the twelve-year-old's peril and declared his independence by cutting him loose from every human relationship except for the one roping him to an audience.

As an act of pedagogy, Donn Fendler's bewilderment proved more accessible than instructional. His wilderness skills were thin and his judgment poor. He could neither start a fire nor orient by the stars or the sun. Nature de-pantsed him and stole his sneakers. He remembered to follow streams down toward larger rivers and perhaps habitations, and he looked out for blueberries, but compared to Paul Gasford, the revolutionary-era wilderness savant who recalled precise directions and distances, who placed a stick at the head of the holes he dug for beds to stay on course in case he woke confused, and who kept his wits about him at all times, Fendler was a mess. Egan called him a "slight, highly nervous, city-bred child—inexperienced in either mountain-climbing or woodcraft." Fendler violated many of the rules set down in the outdoor advice literature. Foremost, he lost his head.[47]

But then he found himself, signaling a shift in the history of North Americans venturing over cognitive edges into nature shock. Previous generations of outdoor recreationists sought to avoid psychological break-downs. They entered the woods to heal their anxious minds, not confuse them further. Donn wandered into insanity and stepped through it into celebrity. His derangement became a gateway instead of a disability. Like the Protestant divines in New England's colonial past, he found God in the interior: "I said my prayers. . . . I felt that God wanted me to get out." Fendler, however, genuflected in an altered media environment. Radio and print photography broadcast his voice and image into millions of American homes. He went up Katahdin an anonymous boy and came back an auton-omous hero. He was an intimate stranger, every mother's lost son, America's Boy Scout.[48]

Journalists wrapped the Fendler story around other lost children. In 1941, five-year-old Pamela Hollingsworth wandered away from her family while vacationing on New Hampshire's Chocorua Mountain. Lost for eight days, she survived a week of September nights with the temperature drop-ping to twenty-two degrees Fahrenheit. Police officers, forest rangers, game wardens, National Guardsmen, and units from the Civilian Conservation Corps joined the search for Hollingsworth. A plane circled the forest canopy while bloodhounds padded through the underbrush. A reporter from the *Boston Globe* flashed back to Fendler on Katahdin. The episodes bore "a striking resemblance." Both children "were dressed in light summer clothing, both "were given up for dead," and both "were found on a moun-tain trail." In 1970, a twelve-year-old boy named Daniel Crowley became lost hiking to the summit of Mount Passaconaway, New Hampshire. He spent a week in the woods. After his rescue, the *Boston Globe* sent a reporter to interview Pamela Hollingsworth, all grown up and working as a "public relations director of a New York-based national retailer." The journalist folded Hollingsworth's miracle into Crowley's remarkable story, tucking Fendler's sensational escape in as well. All three children fit the human-interest pattern. Cast into the wilderness alone, they tested the faith of the audiences that followed their trail in the papers and on the radio. Their survival proved that mere children could summon the courage to pass through physical torment and mental anguish and come out, not only okay, but stronger for the experience. Just as Fendler felt bold enough to joke with his father, tell his old man that he needed to toughen up, Crowley boasted to reporters that he "could have lasted a while longer" and that he couldn't "wait to climb the other four mountains (surrounding his summer camp) to earn my five merit badges." The lost babes of New England taught the adults who staffed state governments, timber corporations, sheriff departments, militias, and federal bureaucracies that professionalism and managerial oversight were no match for prayer, heart, and pluck. In the woods, on vacation, the little people rose up against the faceless powers of modernity and showed that individuals could save themselves.[49]

Of course, not all lost children returned from the wilderness. Unexpected rescues felt miraculous because they rescued stories from the horrible endings readers feared. Lost children appeared frequently in American newspapers. Instead of intrepid individualism, most stories revealed the children's vulnerability and powerlessness. Urban children went missing, and searchers found their bodies suffocated in abandoned refrigerators or chopped up and hidden in ice coolers. In rural areas, tikes as young as three wandered into the woods and died. In 1952, three small children, two five-year-olds and a four-year-old, ventured from their family home in Wisconsin on a cool, clear March afternoon to go play in the section of Nicolet National Forest that abutted their backyard. A blizzard caught them. Authorities and family members searched for two days and found one of the children alive. The other two had frozen to death huddled in an outbuilding of a hunting camp. Mary Ann, the four-year-old, survived with "no serious effect from the 10 degree temperatures." An inexplicable divergence in core body temperature saved her and killed her playmates. Hers was not a story of a will's triumph over nature; rather, it was a puzzle "doctors were at a loss to explain."[50]

Children also got lost and died on vacation in scenic nature. In 1951, searchers discovered the frozen body of twelve-year-old Robert Kaboos in a rugged section of the Sierra Nevada north of Huntington Lake. Robert had gone fishing with his father, William. The two set out from Fresno in the final days of April when a snowstorm caught them unprepared. Volunteer mountaineers and the local sheriff's department located the father's body first. He had left his son to try to find help. The boy was found when a searcher spotted his shoe protruding from eighteen inches of snow. In 1965, Robert Rossetter strayed from his summer camp group during a hike in Colorado. Two helicopters and over one hundred people, "including teams of mountaineers from Aspen," searched for "the youngster in the rugged snow-capped mountains." They found Rossetter's body drowned at the confluence of two rivers. He had tried to ford the streams, slipped on a rock, and fell and hit his head. His parents collected his remains and buried him near their home in Geneva, Illinois. In 1984, Laura Bradbury disappeared from her family's campsite in Joshua Tree National Monument. The National Park Service and members of Sierra Madre Mountain Search and Rescue Association coordinated a search that lasted for five days and included aerial surveys of the desert by helicopter. Laura's parents and several police departments continued to look for her when the effort in Joshua Tree was called off. They distributed 2.5 million flyers bearing the picture of the blond three-year-old with her "Little Dutch Girl haircut," offered rewards, and collected hundreds of thousands of tips and sightings. They theorized that drug dealers, or maybe a satanic cult, had kidnapped her and spirited her out of the park and California. Years passed, and the parents and the police turned on one another, trading accusations in the press. In 1990, a DNA test applied to skull fragments found near the campsite indicated that Bradbury most likely died there. She probably never left the wilderness. The authorities closed the case. The unconvinced parents searched on.[51]

Instead of calming minds and soothing brains, children lost in national parks and recreational wildernesses stoked mass anxiety. The Bradbury case was especially troubling—and media friendly. The little girl from Huntington Beach came to be one of the "best known missing children in the United States." Her fame rivaled Adam Walsh's renown. Walsh was the Florida child who went missing in 1981, was later found murdered, and whose father, Bill, went on to advocate for vigilante crime stopping as host of *America's Most Wanted*, a weekly television program. News coverage of the Bradbury disappearance featured her dogged parents using cutting-edge technology like personal computers to gather information and transmit the child's angelic picture. The stories also emphasized the parents' refusal to quit looking, which in an information age meant their endless pursuit of publicity. Patty and Michael Bradbury met with business leaders and elected officials to keep their daughter's image posted and circulating. They enlisted the help of Ricky Schroeder, the child actor and Patty's distant cousin, to film a commercial featuring Laura's story. The televangelist Robert Schuller responded to the family's entreaties and broadcast a dramatic re-creation of Laura's disappearance on his syndicated Sunday morning *Hour of Power* TV show.[52]

Media coverage kept Laura alive by keeping the child abduction issue hot and positive. "The point is reached," noted Jay Howell, director of the National Center for Missing and Exploited Children, "where the issue is no longer newsworthy as a positive, consciousness-raising story. At that point the media begins to pick it apart and look for potential weaknesses." Questioning journalists sowed doubt, killing speculation, which was the lifeblood of a press campaign. If the audience stopped believing that the victim was still out there, the story would sputter and the child would die.[53]

When Donn Fendler passed away, Ryan Cook posted a video of himself speaking about the lost boy's legacy. A movie producer and director, Cook had been working on the financing for a *Lost on a Mountain in Maine* feature film for many years. While the movie remained an uncompleted project, Cook believed in the story's relevance in the digital age. "Donn Fendler's legacy," he said, "will live on forever." In 2014, two years before his death, Fendler contemplated the durability of his celebrity, especially in Maine: "Maine people are rugged people. They're resourceful. They're resilient. They're outdoors people. People in Maine could relate to exactly what I was going through. They knew. They knew the woods. They knew the bugs. They knew the whole thing." Carved in the outdoors, their individualism rivaled his. Mainers appreciated Fendler's generosity and support. Nearly perishing on vacation did not turn him against the recreational wilderness. "What a great advocate he has been for our state, especially the Katahdin region," noted Lucas St. Clair. "He never blamed the woods, despite what he went through." Fendler knew his part. He, for instance, aww-geed the governor of Maine in 2007 when the politician honored Fendler with a lifetime state fishing license on the capitol steps. "I really don't deserve this," Fendler said. "I was kind of a dumb kid who got lost and wandered around the woods. They made a big deal about it."[54]

His false modesty rang true. He had withstood a rather normal human predicament to become "an American legend." Short and hindered by underdeveloped hippocampi, children often struggle to stay oriented. Add fog, inexperience, and a rugged landscape, and Donn Fendler's bewilderment and descent into nature shock seems more ordinary than otherworldly. The difference between his getting lost and the thousands of other human children who wandered around in the woods, the mall, or the grocery store was how adults treated the incident. Americans interpreted Fendler's getting lost as an act of radical individualism. The editorial staff of the *Boston Globe* drove home Fendler's unprecedented autonomy in an "Uncle Dudley" column that appeared on July 27, 1939. Uncle Dudley was the folksy voice of common wisdom editors of the *Globe* had been adopting since the 1890s. Following Fendler's rescue, the Uncle Dudley column ran with the headline: "He Found Himself." "Because this lad found himself," the editors opined, parents would allow "young boys [to] enjoy the adventure of the New England mountains and the woods trail, to camp and climb in Summer fun and to grow hard and self-reliant in the joy of testing their mettle and learning the ways of natural man." "Donn Fendler's contribution to American civilization may be greater than he will ever know. America needs to raise the kind of boys who want to venture and grow strong in such exercise and needs the confidence that they can safely venture: that if lost they will find themselves." Because Fendler "did not lose his head in the awful aloneness of an ordeal," because "Donn Fendler was lost and found himself, very many other boys are less likely to be lost, but if lost are less apt to become panicky, far more likely to come safely through." Uncle Dudley charged right up to the edge of proclaiming that individuals could find themselves by losing themselves in recreational nature.[55]

# CHAPTER SEVEN

# Male Pattern Trail Loss

IN 1968, EDWARD ABBEY PUBLISHED A NATURE memoir from observations he collected while working as a summer park ranger in Arches
National Monument outside Moab, Utah, in the 1950s. Abbey gloried in the
beauty of the desert environment. In quiet moments, before the crowds
gathered, the arid landscape rattled his psyche. It was big and bleak, with
plenty of room to imagine himself apart from civilization. The desert
inspired sublime revelations with its stark grandeur, but the desert was
under assault from a sinister force Abbey deemed "Industrial Tourism."[1]

A federally protected site with public servants hired to patrol its campgrounds and assist its clientele, Arches had fallen prey to the illnesses of
modernity that had infected urban spaces decades before and necessitated
the creation of nature preserves. In season, the monument was overrun
with gangs of Bermuda-shorted slobs towing families in sedans and
campers. They drove into the wilderness, drove around the wilderness, and
drove out of the wilderness. According to Abbey, the internal combustion
engine was robbing American males of their love of freedom as well as their
connection to "Mother Earth." He advocated banning cars in national parks
and forcing tourists to walk, even if this led to them getting lost and
perishing. For him, dying bewildered was preferable to living in the sterile
confines of an automobile interior.[2]

The federal government coddled visitors. "The trails are well marked," wrote Abbey, "easy to follow; you'd have to make an effort to get lost." In person, Ranger Abbey played the part of the helpful assistant. He joked with tourists, telling audiences in the campgrounds and picnic areas to "be sure to let him know if you get lost." Later, in print, Abbey challenged his male readers' masculinity. He advised them to "leave the old lady and those squawling brats behind for a while, turn your back on them and take a long quiet walk straight into canyons, get lost for a while, come back when you damn well feel like it, it'll do you and her and them a world of good."[3]

Being subservient to pampered men upset Abbey. Helping those who would not help themselves, suckers who willingly sacrificed their independence to roll with brats and old ladies, triggered some of his most spectacular rants. One morning, the radio summoned Abbey to a manhunt, "not for some suspected criminal or escaped convict but for a lost tourist whose car was abandoned two days ago in the vicinity of Grandview Point." The search yielded the body of a sixty-year-old amateur photographer with heart trouble. Abbey and his partner retraced the man's footsteps. He had entered a dead-end ravine, lost his bearings, and exhausted himself in a scramble to climb out.[4]

Abbey's ruminations on the dead man measured the depth of the writer's alienation and the lengths to which he thought American men would need to go in 1968 to reconnect with virile nature. Abbey cheered the old man's demise. In his mind, the man had the "good luck" to "die alone, on a rock under the sun at the brink of the unknown, like a wolf, like a great bird." Abbey imagined the man's final moments: "Except for those minutes of panic in the ravine when he realized he was lost, it seems possible that in the end he yielded with good grace." "His departure" cleared the way for the living, who, according to Abbey, needed to confront the limits of nature and human life. The desert was the site to perform this reckoning. Abbey concluded the chapter with himself "sinking into the landscape" and then soaring "on the wings of imagination" until he became smaller and smaller, an insignificant speck in a magnificent setting.[5]

Edward Abbey turned going on vacation into a blood sport. To recover their dignity, "simple-minded" male tourists needed to burst their shackles and "set off on their own, and no obstacles should be placed in their path; let them take risks, for godsake, let them get lost, sunburnt, stranded, drowned, eaten by bears, buried under avalanches—that is the right and privilege of any free American." Calm and solace were antique wilderness values. Abbey's sublime wasteland cracked skulls and scrambled brains, all for male tourists' own good. Anything that took vacationers away from their cars improved society. Abbey preferred carrying bloated corpses to being stuck in traffic. Years after his Arches sojourn, Abbey wrote about being "trapped in a millrace of streaming traffic" while driving to San Francisco. He made "a momentary mistake" and exited the highway only to find himself "lost in the true horror of Santa Clara and San Jose." Like the old man in the ravine, Abbey groped for a way out. "How can humans," he barked "endure this mad mechanical circus?" Feeling like a speck on a California freeway brought Abbey none of the perspective he found in the immensities of Arches. Freeway disorientation induced road rage, not what-is-my-place-in-the-universe noodling. Perceptions of immensity and insignificance depended on the scenery. Both the national parks and interstate highways belittled people, yet one restored what the other disturbed. By the late 1960s, Americans sought off-ramps to imagined spaces that lent grandeur and meaning to shrunken lives.[6]

Edward Abbey was no thought pioneer. He restated bromides about masculinity, nature, and freedom introduced a century before by writers like Ernest Thompson Seton, Theodore Roosevelt, and Daniel Carter Beard. The vigor school of American manhood sent males into the wilderness to counteract the withering effects of industrial capitalism. Boy Scout expeditions and adult vacations spent hunting, fishing, and hiking repackaged the labors of frontier agrarianism as leisure pursuits. Clerks hauled packs and tracked game; bosses cast flies and rode horses, and schoolboys earned badges in plowing, beekeeping, and blacksmithing. The sweat, skill, and risks involved in these exercises were real, but the products were ideological—and spatial. The labors of manly outdoor leisure reenacted the physical routines of conquest and settlement to reassure boys and men that their power transcended the sites and temporalities of the nation's mythic frontier creation. If American individualism began and ended on the frontier, then overcivilized desk jockeys had to locate pockets of throwback nature to reach into the past and recover the coordinates that underpinned their authority.[7]

Abbey sensed a threat to the back-to-nature rituals. Automotive tourism encouraged men to bring their families on wilderness vacations. The station wagons cluttered the social, mental, and geographic austerity of free male

individuals confronting nature alone. To escape the crowded and domesticated wilderness, real men followed Abbey's advice and upped the danger.
They struck out on their own. They wandered off the trail. They got mind-
blowingly lost, and they liked it.

Sort of.

While the memoirist advocated nature shock, the public servant
worked to rescue lost hikers. Both the seekers of adventure and the
searchers for lost adventurers reset the edge of cognitive geographies,
altering the ways Americans saw public lands and public service. The
quest for authentically virile and potentially deadly wilderness experiences
rose in tandem with the organization and proliferation of rescue services
after World War II. Finding lost people professionalized at the same time
as getting lost became more attractive to white male–led subcultures
yearning to escape modern disorders such as professionalism. Men grew
more optimistic about getting lost as their rescuers grew more proficient.
Together, the enthusiasts for breaking free and the experts in retrieval
created overlapping mental spaces of reckless, and sometimes imbecilic,
male convenience. Nature shocked beyond the edges of perception where
social, imaginative, and geographic common grounds fell away. Those
who aimed to get lost in the macho wilderness, therefore, were not truly
after nature shock. They hoped to find a space that harmonized gender,
power, and nationality. A space where individual American men were free
to enjoy deep woods and high deserts and the services of community-
based volunteer organizations. They wanted the rush of feeling like a
speck in an awe-inspiring wilderness and the solace of knowing that no
matter where they roamed, someone was looking out for them.

Technology encouraged the paradox of cutting loose while staying
connected. Those station wagons Abbey loathed expressed consumers'
desire to mobilize their family units—to take their relations into nature.
Abbey's hyper-masculinity blinded him to the real emancipatory possibilities this represented. He portrayed wives as a ball and chain, but women
sought freedom in the wilderness alongside men. The backcountry and
the rock face may have been gendered male, but that did not mean that
women could not enter wild spaces and claim the promise of escape and
liberation. For some women, the machismo added to the challenge. It
raised the stakes and testified to the exceptionalism of their backcountry
achievements. For many women, man-made individual space offered the

chance to break free from male-dominated relationships and redefine personal freedom.

## GET LOST IN MONTANA

The Federal Highway Act (1956) financed the construction of thousands of miles of restricted-access speedways. The roadwork took decades to finish. Dignitaries celebrated the completion of I-80, spanning Teaneck, New Jersey, to San Francisco, California, in 1986. The final links making I-90 a continuous path from Seattle to Boston were hammered in place by 1991. The next year, the construction of I-70 ended with the opening of a section through Colorado's Glenwood Canyon. Like the railroads before them, the highways remade the interior as they crossed it. The federal highways sped movement, rerouted traffic, and altered perceptions of time and distance. Visions of cars ripping across the continent in parallel lanes stoked imaginations, but two words that did not appear in the official title of the federal legislation bent minds at crazy angles. When people talked about the new federal highways, they called the concrete lines an "interstate system." Being plugged into a system that bypassed older anchor points stirred paranoia and sparked revolt. Freedom seekers cut across traffic and searched for spaces outside the system to get lost in.[8]

Boosters lauded the convenience and modernity of the federal highways. Commuters rode the interstates out of the cities that drove them insane. By cutting time, the highways shortened distance. Definitions of faraway depended on traffic patterns. The intensity of the rush hours to and from work and the proximity of one's driveway to an interstate on-ramp determined the acceptability of commutes rather than absolute miles on maps. Americans spread out, creating new places like strip malls, mega truck stops, and Disneyland.

Droves of people took to the highways even as people worried about the idea of being associated with droves. Interstates freed automobilists from the local. Commuters motored past business districts infested with stoplights and speed bumps intended to steer them into parking spaces outside independently owned retail and dining establishments. The interstates killed small businesses and main streets and accelerated strangeness. Travelers moved from government-sponsored rest stops to corporate-franchised gas plazas in anonymity. Consumer identities replaced human affiliations. Instead of interacting as personalities with unique backstories connected to a region, a state, or a town, the denizens of the interstate system related through cash. They were units in a system of commerce: buyers or sellers, valued guests or service providers.

The bypassed townspeople lamented their inability to reach into the diverted stream of wallets and purses, but they also eyeballed outsiders with suspicion and locked their doors to protect against the killers on the road. The flow of traffic included customers and suspects. Americans feared the likes of Charles Starkweather, a prototypical midcentury juvenile delinquent who went on an eleven-person killing spree in 1958. Starkweather hopped on I-80 outside Lincoln, Nebraska, after murdering his girlfriend's family. He and the girlfriend, Carol Ann Fugate, sped across the interior, exploiting the interstate system's convenience and anonymity to maim and move on, until they were caught in Wyoming. They lent menace to a road network that both liberated motorists and freed demons.[9]

Starkweather, Fugate, and millions of tourists staged getaways on the interstates. They drove into the Badlands to evade capture or they pulled into Yellowstone or Arches to enjoy the scenery. The popularity of auto vacations soared, and a family jammed into a station wagon, hurtling down an interstate to Disneyland or the Grand Canyon, symbolized the American good life to some and soul-crushing normality to others. Nonconformists bucked the system by attacking the highways. They staged getaways in print, advocating for the discovery of the real America off the interstates. They argued for unsystematic wandering, for getting lost.

No one confused Arnold Bolle for a hippie or a serial killer. A University of Montana forestry professor, Bolle was an expert conservationist with a background in western tourism. In 1970, Montana senator Lee Metcalf asked Bolle, then serving as dean of the Forestry School, to lead a commission investigating clear-cutting in the Bitterroot National Forest. The "Bolle Report" criticized the U.S. Forest Service for violating its "multiple-use" directive. The trees were not merely board feet to be mined by timber corporations, but a public resource to be managed for aesthetic, environmental, and recreational values. A life-long outdoorsperson, Bolle operated a dude ranch in Wyoming before joining the University of Montana's faculty. In his spare time, he enjoyed hunting for geodes and looking for discarded antique bottles in abandoned mining towns. He practiced the multiple-use ethos he preached, and he saw the West's national forests as sites of recreation as well as extraction. Indeed, in 1967, the Montana Outfitters and Guides Association asked him to come speak about profiting more from wilderness recreation. The prospects for outfitting dollars looked bright, he reported, if the guides could wrangle another out-of-control federal entity—the interstate highway system.

"When interstate highways are completed," Bolle predicted, "more people than ever will cross Montana—and spend less time here than before." The state's outdoor recreation industry would have to work harder to lure customers and organize politically to "fight for high quality recreation without honky-tonk development." To achieve these goals, Bolle suggested rebranding bewilderment: "A good way to get [auto tourists] interested in Montana would be to sell them on the idea of 'getting lost' by leaving the highway and visiting less travelled areas." The slogan "Get Lost—in Montana," he declared, "might well be adopted by those who want to promote wilderness travel." Bolle anticipated that the interstates would transform tourists' spatial cognition. Once they experienced highway travel, the cruise-controlled ease of moving fast without thinking much, they would consider exiting the system for a jumble of back roads a form of getting lost. Tell them, exhorted Bolle, that leaving the interstate is good for them.[10]

Getting lost for fun slipped into travel magazines and newspaper lifestyle columns beginning in the 1960s. The shift in outlook can be seen in two articles separated by fifty-one years that shared the same title: "The Art of Getting Lost." In 1913, a writer for the *Washington Post* contemplated the slim possibility of wealthy tourists or wanted criminals disappearing without a trace. "All over the world," the columnist wrote, "there are wandering alone tourists and sightseers, restless for adventure and excitement, who will all turn up in their own time and be accounted for." The "machinery of protection" had reduced the number of people who vanished for good to a "negligible number." Even "the defaulting bank cashier trying to hide his identity in a sun-scorched port of call" knew the difficulty of staying incognito: "The facts are that in spite of the vastness of the earth, the millions of its population, and the complexities of life in both civilized and uncivilized countries, getting lost is an art." Modern communication had forced embezzlers and trust-funders to plan it out. Even undeveloped backwaters had officials with connections ready to notice and report missing persons in 1913. A dragnet of rescuers had developed to scoop up lost persons.[11]

By the 1960s, when the world had shrunk further, and tourist bureaus and police forces tracked people with enhanced vigor, getting lost took a comedic turn. It was something that happened to clueless white men. A retired member of the *New York Times* editorial board, Robert L. Duffus, wrote about his lifelong habit of getting lost in a travel book excerpted in a 1964 issue of the *Times* under the headline "An Old Innocent Abroad: The Art of Getting Lost." Duffus admitted that he found navigating foreign cities impossible. In Rome, he "got lost almost every time I left the hotel." Duffus endorsed disorientation. Unlike tourists who clutched guidebooks and maps, he found spatial confusion a "wild thrill," even though his frequent disappearances strained his marriage. In his travel memoir, Duffus slipped into the role of perpetual naïf: "But, for me, the tendency to get lost is not an evidence of senility. It is more like a habit. I used to get lost when I was as young as 5, whether or not I was told to do so." His parents, his wife, Roman police officers, and London cabbies righted his course whenever he strayed, giving him the freedom to not think about space. This made him appear stupid, but ignorance also yielded wonder. He was never sure what he would find along paths made obscure by his inattention.[12]

The befuddled grown man on holiday was a recurrent character in post–World War II getting-lost lifestyle pieces. Persons of stature in work habitats and home settings, these men grew baffled in spaces outside the office or the regular commute. They circled parks and playgrounds, adamantly refusing to heed the calls of loved ones to please stop the car and ask for directions. Breadwinners turned dolts, the vacationing white males of middle America became objects of jokes and derision. They were the sock-and-sandal-wearing weaklings Edward Abbey railed against and the ugly Americans who stormed tourist Paris or Venice, only to become turned around and, sheepish, require to be escorted back to their hotels by bistro workers and gondoliers. Their bewilderment embarrassed onlookers, but some of the men, like Robert Duffus, wore their lostness proudly. They diminished their mental capacities on purpose to observe the world from an alternative angle.

In 1963, freelance travel writer William Stockdale praised getting lost on vacation in the *New York Times* travel section. "There are few delights," he wrote, "to match being lost." The panic of bewilderment roused emotions and sharpened minds: "A lost person is an observant person." Stockdale branched out from stupefied men to include baffled women in the ranks of the happily lost. He welcomed them with an insult. "Less experienced women drivers," he reported, "may find it easier to get lost and stay lost." Later in the article, he showed women the exit, switching to the universal male. All humans should "assault the unknown" and accept getting lost as "one of the few adventures left to man." Recreation could get people lost at the beach, in a forest, or on the streets of San Francisco. They could get lost on back roads, parkways, and "superhighways." Yellowstone or the Poconos offered "splendid places to get lost." "No doubt there are many parks and wilderness sites where, if you ask the superintendent, he will direct you to an area where you may get lost." A twist of perception that could be equally applied to a city or a wilderness, getting lost broke free from confusing places like forests and prairies or conditions like snowstorms and darkness. Instead, getting lost became a filter or a dial one clicked to change the view.[13]

Stockdale embraced lostness with cheeky verve, but he hinted at a real tourist predicament. People invested in vacations to collect memories, but by 1963 many travel destinations had grown forgettable. Landmarks drew crowds—that's what made them landmarks—yet overexposure could tip them into decline. Preferred vacations spots rose and fell. Niagara Falls, Times Square, the Strip in Las Vegas, and Atlantic City's Boardwalk all famously crashed until rehabilitated and rediscovered. Fatigue could strike a place, a mode of transportation, or a method of recreation. In a topsy-turvy leisure environment where tourists never knew if a destination would tickle their fancy or deaden their minds, playing dumb increased the chances of encountering a surprise, of locating a moment worthy of recollection. Getting lost, according to Stockdale, opened tourist sites up to "a rebirth of all creation with everything becoming new and fresh." Once a fear that kept travelers at home, getting lost prompted vacations in the information age, and perhaps the delight many took in befuddlement explained why, in a period of history overstuffed with brochures, guidebooks, maps, newspaper travel sections, webpages, and Yelp reviews, so many people on vacation behaved as if their brains were damaged.[14]

In a 2017 interview with the *Missoula Independent,* Jack Welch, the CEO of Bozeman's MercuryCSC advertising agency, could not recall the "aha moment" when the slogan "Get Lost—in Montana" broke out from the "the process of pushing and changing words and changing images until you get to a place and you're like 'Oh, this is it, this is good.' " The catchphrase emerged to lead the state of Montana's tourism industry out of the wreckage of the Great Recession. It rose free of the past. No one acknowledged Arnold Bolle, the forestry dean who first suggested that Montana sell getting lost to people on vacation. Advertising agencies bill themselves as forward-peering organizations, so MercuryCSC may not have noticed that Bolle had spun getting lost in a positive direction nearly fifty years before. The 2010 slogan even targeted the same audience Bolle had in mind when he addressed the Outfitters and Guides Association in 1967: the regional "drive market." "Get Lost" was supposed to attract "people from Billings and Salt Lake and Spokane who might dream of getting lost, or of losing themselves, in Montana." To everyone's surprise, the regional campaign escaped the mountain West region. Tourists and locals grabbed one of the three hundred thousand bumper stickers that flew out the door and slapped them on Chevy F150s, Subaru Outbacks, and at least one airport luggage vehicle in the Minneapolis airport. Fans of the sticker sent pictures of their "Get Lost" rides back to the state tourism office, which posted them on GetLostMT.com. The slogan worked, argues MercuryCSC on its website, because "Get Lost—in Montana" communicated a mixed message that attracted both outdoor enthusiasts and grouchy shut-ins. The sticker "was embraced by lovers and cynics alike." It could be read as an earnest expression of "Go out and explore this great place where we live and love," or it could signal territoriality and ambivalence. On alternating bumpers, "Get Lost—in Montana" meant welcome, have fun, or go to hell.[15]

Montana's "Get Lost" campaign traveled through internet culture, a sticker without stickiness. Its meaning floated according to the whims of individuals with their own ideas about getting lost. The slogan gestured toward a consumer future where social media dissolved the last vestiges of mass marketing. In 2016, MercuryCSC dropped out of the bidding for the state's tourism promotion. Looking back on "Get Lost—in Montana," CEO Welch wondered if techniques like bumper art still mattered. Instead of reaching out to people with billboards or leaflets, ad agencies were waiting for targets to come to them. Key demos announced themselves in search terms and click histories. If fingers googled "Montana" or "big sky" or "get lost," marketers "bombard[ed] potential customers with reminders and links through email and Facebook." In the "digital landscape," the advertising agencies used "geo-fencing" and "psychographics" to rig the pursuit of happiness, making entertainment hunters feel as though they navigated their own paths through the internet when, in virtuality, bots and

A "Get Lost" bumper sticker in its natural habitat. (Photograph by Tony Webster, 2016. Courtesy of Creative Commons, https://creativecommons.org/licenses/by-sa/2.0/legalcode)

algorithms strung them along by feeding their desires. For Montana, the mythic prey was known as "some guy from Connecticut." This key demographic, "a married male with a college degree who earns at least $80,000 a year," could begin a journey with a few keystrokes and wind up on vacation in a mountain lodge without ever really knowing how he got there: lost in Montana for real.[16]

The advertising business feasts on transpositions, chocolate-and-peanut-butter creations that bring unlike ideas or items into a partnership. Hetero male sexual longings, for example, have a history of being paired with products as diverse and as libido stifling as auto parts, socket wrenches, and light beer. If carnal desire could render motor oil alluring, imagine what getting lost in Montana could do to a tractor. In 2007, three years before the "Get Lost" bumper stickers became popular, Montana Tractors, a heavy-equipment manufacturer based in Arkansas, promoted its "breed of hard working, tough tractors with spirit, the spirit of Montana" with an ad that featured a woman feeding a horse a bale of hay from a green subcompact front loader. Performing the task in stylish work clothes, the woman avoided the classic vehicular advertising move of draping a scantily clad model over the hood of a sportscar, but the visual grammar recalled the strategy. The scene peddled a lifestyle and included an attractive woman, whose blond coif just happened to be positioned between the *t* and *a* in the word *Montana* floating in the background. Below, a tagline tempted viewers to "catch the spirit." In the foreground, two phrases—*Lose Yourself. Find Yourself.*—drew the eye toward the specs ("Available in 4WD compact models ranging from 23- to 49-horsepower . . ."). Even before "Get Lost—in Montana" became a touchstone, the advertising agency for a tractor company knew the combination of bewilderment and a rugged mountain state somehow added up to a "spirit" powerful enough to induce a hefty down payment on a small agricultural work vehicle. I do not want to exaggerate the effectiveness of this ad. Montana Tractors filed for bankruptcy in 2010. Yet an unseen force was at work, bringing these ideas together, and it's worth interrogating.[17]

Advertising professionals steered the tractor and the state of Montana toward the same end: some guy in Connecticut. This was the person they thought wanted to get lost. Why did a married man with a college degree earning at least $80,000 a year desire bewilderment? If anything, the landscape of postindustrial America seemed designed to make this person feel at home. The college degree indicated a level of comfort with the information economy. The gender and marital profile suggested privilege and status. In a society defined by growing economic inequality, this demo was keyed for accumulation. He would have the wherewithal to buy a vacation, a piece of land, a horse, and a subcompact front-loader. Why would the guy hope to get lost as well? Why did anyone think this stew of associations would convince anyone to buy anything?

By the time Montana Tractors and "Get Lost—in Montana" bumper stickers entered the mental space of American consumers, cultural depictions of white men on vacation suggested that, for them at least, getting lost was no longer shameful. Instead of revealing mental weakness and a dearth of frontier savvy, bewilderment displayed power. The tractor ad and the "Get Lost" bumper sticker shared a spatial grammar that privileged the male gaze. The perspective is easiest to spot in the tractor ad: look at the open expanse of grass with the tractor, hay, woman, and horse. The viewer sits in a refuge, a reading nook or an office cubicle, and scans a vista, claiming the privilege of seeing from safety. The observational perch, what psychologists call an isovist vantage point, enlivened the "Get Lost—in Montana" decals too. The sticker's double meaning, the invitation to go out and the warning to stay out, created a refuge for its owners. They could be embedded locals and carefree adventurers simultaneously. They could escape home and claim to be home, that age-old position American men liked to inhabit.

Seeing bewilderment in a positive light required an isovist position. One of America's earliest promoters of getting lost, Henry David Thoreau, for example, felt safe in the woods, in the dark, and in the snow because he could see what others could not. By living alone in a landscape with jumbled sight lines, he cultivated an outsider's perspective. He bore witness to the flaws in his neighbors' blinkered existence and tried to show them a path to redemption. Edward Abbey was also a privileged seer. From his perch as a National Park Service employee, he watched hordes of tourists descend on a natural treasure. The visitors huddled in cars and in campgrounds, clinging to their rolling sanctuaries so intently that few ventured into the desert they came to see. If only men stepped away from their vehicles, they might acquire a sublime perspective that would help them realize how trapped they had become.

Abbey labored in print to distance himself from conventional Americans, but his obsession with authenticity blinded him to the power male tourists claimed through their nonchalant befuddlement. Many vacationers shared Abbey's values. They too hoped to get back to nature, recover their masculinity, and exit their mundane yet stressful lives. They entered nature through consumption and relied on the assistance of service providers such as Abbey to unburden them. Their cluelessness was as much an act of rebellion as Abbey's criticism. The well-informed ranger and the baffled tourist were co-conspirators in the formation of a new version of the recreational wilderness that included the happily lost and dutiful minders.

The proud imbeciles championed by Robert Duffus and William Stockdale found consumer protection wherever they wandered. They fumbled through the backwoods of the Poconos or the side streets of Paris confident that a ranger or a porter would save them eventually. The advocates of self-bewilderment asserted a form of passive dominance. The pleasure of getting lost belonged to them. College-educated, married men with the resources to leave work, purchase transportation, and command service could enjoy bewilderment. The condition expanded their horizons. They got lost in landscapes only to discover that their refuges had followed them to the ends of the earth. Getting lost, even in jest, revealed a serious advantage: the power to venture into wildernesses and stay protected, safe from nature shock.

## SOS

The move to sell getting lost as a positive act of manly individualism did not lessen the tragedy when people actually became lost in the recreational wilderness. To grasp the scale of the getting-lost problem, the best place to look is in the national parks, where visitors scanned landscapes to view the wildlife and rangers peered into SUVs to count the visitors. In 2016, a reporter for the *Boston Globe*, following up on a story of vacationers getting lost in New Hampshire, tallied the National Park Service's search-and-rescue statistics for the decade between 2004 and 2014. In those ten years, 46,609 visitors needed emergency assistance. (To put this number in further perspective: the total number of visitors to national parks has climbed almost every year since 1945. In 1975, the number topped 200 million people per year for the first time. Visitations reached 300 million per year in 2015 and have stayed above that threshold since. A good rule of thumb is that 1 in 100,000 visitors to a national park will require search-and-rescue services.) In the 2004–14 decade, only a few thousand victims fit a definition of lost meaning they were lost to themselves as well as to others. Bewilderment was rare, but the major factors that led to emergency calls—including fatigue; errors in judgment; falls; insufficient equipment, clothing, or experience; and darkness—caused disorientation as well as injury and lateness. You were far more likely to be the source of your own misfortune in a national park than to be assaulted by uncontrollable nature. Acts of God—avalanches, wild animals, storms, rockfalls, lightning, and floods—prompted few search-and-rescue missions (all together, they accounted for around 8 percent). Off-road walking—*hiking,* in the recreational parlance—topped all other activities on the list of endeavors that might land you in trouble. Forty-two percent of all the people who required search and rescue were hiking. High-risk sports like climbing, skiing, canyoneering, or caving generated few missions. Going on a day hike in a national park and then becoming tired or making a wrong turn was the most likely circumstance to place you in harm's way.[18]

It also helped if you were a guy between the ages of twenty and forty. Adult males in that age span accounted for 52.8 percent of all search-and-rescue missions between 2004 and 2014.[19]

The statistics of getting lost in the recreational wilderness show beyond a doubt that individual space could be as baffling and as dangerous as relational space. The numbers, however, fail to capture nature shock, which was a private and subjective experience. Stories put flesh on the data, and the stories reveal how nature shock both changed and stayed the same from 1945 to the present moment.

In 1959, Laliah Barnes, a telegraph operator from Montreal, got lost in a snowstorm on a trail outside Jackson, New Hampshire, in the White Mountains. Barnes was an avid vacation hiker. She boasted over a decade of experience strolling in the woods, and she had spent the week before she wandered away exploring the trails around her resort. She felt confident going for a short jaunt alone on a sunny October Sunday afternoon. She wore a cotton sweater and a windbreaker and carried a candy bar to tide her over until dinner later at the hotel. The snowstorm hit midway through the hike. Barnes lost the trail and "went first in one direction, and then in another through a maze of trees." It was at that moment "I knew I was lost! And to make matters worse I realized that, with the darkness closing . . . it was going to be a bad night." She kept moving as the sun dipped, stomping her feet and rubbing her hands. Her body heat melted the snow on her thin clothing. The water refroze and stiffened the garments. Numb fingers and a frozen zipper kept the candy bar in the windbreaker pocket out of reach. In the pitch dark, she prayed at the edge of lucidity to fend off nature shock: "The prayers helped me keep my sanity." At first light, she broke for the trail, stumbling and falling as she searched for its faint outline in the snow. She prayed again and found the track. Rescuers met her halfway down. At first, they didn't recognize her. They thought she was another volunteer until she yelled, "Please help me I've been lost in the woods overnight." Being lost in the woods and looking for lost people in the woods were mirror undertakings.[20]

Like Barnes, Paul Snow talked to God when he became disoriented while hiking with a church group in Angeles National Forest. Forty-seven, out of shape, and inexperienced ("I'm not a woodsman," he said), he fell behind his campmates and walked down the wrong canyon during a vacation hike in 1970. Rescuers found him in that same canyon seven days later. Snow wandered back and forth. Asked why he didn't follow a stream downhill to safety, he responded, "I thought I was in the canyon that led to the campground, but I just couldn't find it." He could not reorient his mind around his actual surroundings because he was certain the camp belonged in that canyon. To stay alive and fight panic, he chewed roots and queried the Almighty. "I kept asking the Lord, Why? Why am I here?" In the end, he concluded, "If this is where You want me to be, it's in Your hands. But I wish You didn't have such a high estimation of my ability to take it." He attributed his survival to "the grace of God" and his extra weight, which the doctors said fueled his body. Snow lost twenty-five pounds during his canyon side trip, but he held onto his sanity and his sense of humor. His religious conversations marked the edge of nature shock.[21]

Linda Forney left her home in Pittsburgh in the summer of 1975 to visit New Orleans and other tourist hot spots, including the Grand Canyon. On the morning of August 1, she began a hike down to the Supai Village in Havasupai Canyon in the Grand Canyon National Park. She made a wrong turn and headed south into Havatagvitch Canyon instead. Dressed in blue jeans and a halter top, wearing "crepe-soled shoes," Forney left her backpack with her food behind. She brought her cockapoo along. As the heat increased in the canyon, she grew disoriented and thirsty. After a cold night, she located a spring, a "trickle from a crack in the rock." The water saved her. The temperature swung from one hundred degrees Fahrenheit in the day to fifty at night. Forney stayed near the spring to sleep and ventured out at daylight to find help. She never wandered far because "being without water was truly frightening." To stay in touch with reality she said the rosary and sang to herself. She wrote in an address book, keeping track of the days and writing recipes for dinners she would eat, "anything to keep busy." After a week, she quit scribbling for "it was too depressing to have to write" and began experiencing auditory hallucinations: "There was always a continuous buzz or hum at night." After she did not report back to work on August 13, a search was begun. A group of hikers found the dog, who had wandered away. Rescuers located Forney a few days later. She had lost twenty-one pounds in twenty days spent lost on vacation. A slight person to begin with, her weight dropped to eighty-five pounds. The *Arizona Republic* ran Forney's photograph on the front page of the newspaper. She looked hungrily at the camera, a blown-out crepe-soled shoe displayed in her hands.[22]

In 1989, Eloise Lindsay went backpacking in Table Rock State Park in South Carolina to "think about what to do next with her life." Twenty-two years old, Lindsay had graduated college six months before she entered the woods and got lost. She missed the main trail and became disoriented. Panicking, she plunged into the brush "when she sensed that she was being followed." "From the very beginning, before the search was initiated," reported Oconee County emergency preparedness director Walt Purcell, "she became frightened or paranoid that somebody was trying to run her down." Lindsay saw rescue helicopters circling for her, but she didn't want to build a fire or come out into the open to signal the pilots for fear that her stalkers would find her first. She fled search parties, thinking they were the men out to get her. Rescued after two weeks hiding and wandering lost in the park, Lindsay insisted that two men had chased her and wanted to do her harm. The authorities found no evidence of her pursuers, and they "had no plans to investigate further." Nature had traumatized Lindsay, at least in the eyes of the police and search-and-rescue professionals.[23]

A young man on a similar journey of self-discovery in scenic nature, Christopher Wearstler hiked into Olympic National Park in June 1997 on a solo camping trip. He became "disoriented on the third or fourth day" and decided to stay put until rescuers found him. Then he lost his camp when he went looking for water. He wandered in the woods for five days before he surprised a group of searchers sitting around a campfire, resting after a day spent out looking for him. Wearstler claimed "the sound of bagpipes and flutes" directed him to Elkhorn Ranger Station. Curt Sauer, the chief ranger of Olympic National Park, was dubious. "We don't have any [bagpipes or flutes] up here," he told a reporter, "so he was apparently beginning to hallucinate." Asked about Wearstler's condition, the chief ranger expressed his weariness at dealing with the likes of Wearstler. "He'll live to hike again."[24]

Nicolas Cendoya and Kyndall Jack walked into Trabuco Canyon in Cleveland National Forest, Orange County, California, on Easter Sunday 2013. They emerged five days later after rescuers expended nineteen hundred work hours and $160,000 to find them. A rescue volunteer fell and was badly injured. The local community was initially thrilled when the two were found alive, and the national media, including the television program *Good Morning America*, interviewed the teens and celebrated the miracle of their survival. The geography where the teens went missing was not particularly dramatic. The Cleveland National Forest was a suburban wilderness. Even when lost, the two could see the lights of Los Angeles, and they called and spoke with a 911 operator over a cell phone before its battery gave out. What attracted the news coverage were the reports that the two suffered wild hallucinations during their ordeal. Cendoya said that he saw a tiger and thought he was in a waking nightmare. "I can't even tell you when I woke up," he told reporters. "I was in lucid dream for days." He believed that the rescue helicopters were part of his visions. Jack "said that the wilderness got to her, making her imagine that animals were about to attack her and her companion." She thought a giant python was trying to swallow her alive and that her parents had been thrown in jail. The two were dehydrated and scared out of their minds. They may have also been ingesting crystal meth and cocaine. When word of the possible drug intake surfaced, sympathies waned, especially when police charged Cendoya with possession. Instead of achieving celebrity, he faced a three-year stay in California's penal system.[25]

Even though it ended badly for him, Cendoya appreciated his time in the wilderness. Nature shock caused him to reflect. He needed to work on himself, to become a better man. "So that's why when all this happened, I didn't cry, I didn't fear it. I just embraced everything. I just knew I would get through it. I knew this wasn't my time to die. I knew that I needed this, to become the person that I'm supposed to be."[26]

Neither Cendoya nor Jack nor the national forest that befuddled them fit the romantic ideal of the wilderness sublime. They took drugs instead of reading Thoreau or John Muir. A shopping mall glowed in the night just a few miles from their near-death experience. Yet getting lost in a wild enough place made them heroes for a news cycle. When the positive narrative collapsed and the cops found the stash, Cendoya knew to follow a wilderness plot. Nature shock opened a path to self-actualization. He found himself by losing himself. And then he entered rehab to secure a reduced sentence.

Kyndall Jack and her parents traveled a costlier but no less clichéd route in the aftermath of her wilderness rescue. They found themselves the targets of a civil lawsuit. A rescue volunteer had fallen a hundred feet down a canyonside during the search and broken his spine. He sued Jack and her parents for "negligently put[ting] rescuers in danger when she headed into the wilderness unprepared and intending to take hallucinogenic drugs." The family's lawyer argued that while Kyndall "was no angel," she "said she wasn't doing drugs out there." The trauma of getting lost caused her to see things and remember "fighting off animals and trying to 'light the sky' with a lighter to signal for help." Nature, not controlled substances, had shocked her. The family agreed to settle the suit nonetheless. Fighting the suit in court did not seem wise. The search-and-rescue volunteer was "the more sympathetic of the two figures in the case," the lawyer said, and Kyndall wanted to put the experience behind her. "It's had a very negative effect on her life," he said, "as you might have guessed already." The Jacks' home-owner's insurance paid $100,000 to help cover the volunteer's medical expenses.[27]

The statistics on getting lost in recreational nature leave out the meth, the gods, the paranoia, the pythons, and the bagpipes. Individual space in the post–World War II United States was as weird and unruly as any primeval forest. It could be just as psychologically haunting. It certainly wasn't neutered, manicured, or safe. Those who entered the modern wilderness did not leave their drugs, their criminality, or their sins behind. They packed grim realities in with them. Some hoped to rewrite their stories away from home in nature. Some sought inspiration and a new direction, a refuge to find themselves, a getaway to decide what they would become. The focus on self-making and choices announced the difference between relational and individual space. In relational space, who you were determined where you were, whereas in individual space, the input and the output reversed: where you were might change who you were.

Nature shock, however, also stifled choices. Stories that started out inno-cent or fun or postcollegiate turned desperate and crazy. The survivors who emerged tried to wrestle back their narratives, but they often had to share creative control with park rangers, search-and-rescue volunteers, newspaper reporters, family members, and neighbors. Onlookers questioned and criti-cized the lost. Survivors had to explain themselves and argue for being a heroic missing person rather than a jackass tourist or a druggy reprobate. Announcing your religious convictions calmed doubts. Talking to an invis-ible God raised fewer eyebrows than sensing phantom muggers, hearing flutes or night buzzes, or seeing a tiger. Recreational hikers went into nature to explore and to express their individuality. When the unforeseen struck them and they got lost, they learned that an invisible force had indeed followed them into the wilderness. Some encountered God while others fled stalkers, yet the most common confrontation with the imperceptible was with an impersonal infrastructure. Lost tourists discovered an underlay-ment of bureaucracy. Governments and NGOs staffed recreational wilder-nesses with rangers and volunteers. The service providers monitored refuges and retreats, and they had their own ideas about wilderness and personal autonomy. The rescuers and the rescued created individual space in recreational nature together, sometimes in harmony, sometimes in opposition.

## RETRIEVAL

Professional search and rescue (SAR) began in the United States when the Coast Guard officially adopted search-and-rescue operations as part of its core mission in 1837. The Forest Service and National Park Service sent rangers to look for lost people starting in the twentieth century. The earliest volunteer SAR groups formed to safeguard mountain playgrounds near urban centers. Rocky Mountain Rescue has been serving Boulder County, Colorado, since 1947. In January of that year, a failed lost-child search was one of a string of outdoor calamities that prompted the Boulder County Sheriff's Department to partner with volunteer mountain climbers to raise the level of search proficiency in the county's rugged terrain. The Yosemite National Park volunteer search-and-rescue team (YOSAR) was founded in the 1960s and took advantage of the climbing expertise that had gathered in the park's famous Camp Four to scale the massive rock walls of Half Dome and El Capitan. In 1965, Washington State's King County Sheriff's Department affiliated with the all-volunteer nonprofit KCSARA (King County Search & Rescue Association) to promote coordination, provide training, and encourage young people to prepare for wilderness vacations along with natural disasters and end-of-the-world scenarios. Wilderness educators in King County incorporated the "100% volunteer" KC ESAR (King County Explorer Search & Rescue) in 1954. The "first youth based search and rescue team in the nation," ESAR taught teenagers orienteering and survival skills, and search coordinators sent ESAR trainees into the field to assist during emergencies.[28]

The proliferation of volunteer SAR organizations coincided with a surge in the popularity of backcountry hiking. More Americans got lost hiking than while participating in any other outdoor sport, necessitating experts to find them. Going for a hike and searching for a lost hiker were basically the same activity, requiring the same gear, and the swelling ranks of backpackers fed SAR. Recreational hikers attended SAR conferences and participated in SAR training sessions and SAR courses. Local organizations gathered in larger umbrella groups like the National Association of Search and Rescue (NASAR), founded in 1972, and the National Association of Search and Rescue Coordinators (NASARC), organized in 1974.[29]

SAR volunteers and the boundary-pushing hikers, climbers, skiers, snowboarders, and BASE jumpers recalibrated the outer edges of actual jurisdictions controlled by federal and state governments. These new boundaries went up vertical rock walls as well as out back into the rough country auto tourists seldom visited. Mountain climbers in Yosemite National Park, for example, invented new routes, technologies, and training regimes following World War II. They scaled Half Dome and El Capitan using removable steel pitons crafted by Yvon Chouinard, the founder of Patagonia. Chouinard and legendary Yosemite climbers like Royal Robbins, Tom Frost, and Chuck Pratt advocated the minimal use of technological assistance. Instead of pounding or drilling permanent bolts into the rock, climbers with style slipped chocks and wedges into natural anchor points and removed the evidence that they were there after an ascent, packing out ropes, bivouacs, and trash. Such aesthetic climbers revolutionized the sport. They opened the way for the free climbers of the 1970s and 1980s, men and women who muscled up the rocks without any safety gear at all. The Yosemite climbers took mountaineering to places few park service employees could follow. If an accident befell a technical climber on a big wall, only another technical climber could possibly save them. Volunteer search-and-rescue outfits formed to fill the gap in knowledge and skill that opened between public servants and gravity athletes.[30]

The potential for traumatic injury defined spaces of extreme outdoor sport and search-and-rescue volunteerism. The risk takers and the responders entered danger zones—vertical faces, isolated chutes, exposed summits—in pursuit of authentic, unmediated, and noncommercialized experiences in nature. They labored to transcend the parking lots, the camping grounds, and the sanctioned trails monitored by rangers. They sought refuge from rules and surveillance, and they abetted one another's escape. The risk takers pushed to the edge of disaster, and the responders went after those who pushed too far. Together, they crafted individualistic spaces within state and federal preserves overrun by tourists. They hoped to escape park infrastructures, but they wound up extending the edge of supervision into hazardous spaces.

While they may have rebelled against the conventions of automotive tourism, neither the risk takers nor the responders saw themselves as irresponsible. Quite the opposite. They bragged about their superior ethics. Unlike the sedentary millions who drove into national parks and relied on the federal government to tell them where to go and how to behave, back-country enthusiasts invented and enforced their own codes for their spaces. Climbers in Yosemite policed and critiqued one another's styles. Since they bore the physical consequences of poor decisions, extreme athletes trained and studied before they set off. Experts instructed novices in the field, and newsletters, magazines, and guidebooks appeared to spread information, to sell gear, and to raise and adjudicate ethical questions.

Dennis E. Kelley began publishing *Search and Rescue* magazine out of his home in Montrose, California, in the fall of 1973. The initial issues were fanzine quality, mimeographed newsletters Kelley produced seasonally with a rotating cast of editors and contributors from Southern California's outdoor community. In 1974, *Search and Rescue* became the official publication of the National Association of SAR Coordinators. The magazine's production values and advertisements climbed throughout the 1970s. By 1977, glossy covers had replaced colored stock and Fabiano hiking boots and Mountain House freeze-dried foods bought professional ads that featured artistic renditions of Cross Country touring boots and smiling models grabbing packets of desiccated shrimp creole out of aluminum-frame backpacks. *Search and Rescue* reverted to its newsletter beginnings in 1982. Kelley explained to readers that he had become disenchanted with SAR and had to put the publication of the magazine "on hold because of severe funding and attitude problems." The magazine treaded water until 1984 when Kelley ended the run with a reprinted piece on drowning.[31]

Magazines like *Search and Rescue* and *Climbing*, an outdoor periodical also founded in the early 1970s, fostered community by linking readers with shared obsessions. Kelley's *Search and Rescue* was even more niche than *Climbing*. Fans of outdoor sports and wilderness culture might purchase *Climbing* to participate as voyeurs. *Search and Rescue* was pitched to insiders. Kelley listed the people who should subscribe. The magazine, he wrote, "is intended for the paid and volunteer, the coordinators and the members of":

Mountain Rescue
Ski Patrol
Civil Air Patrol
Explorer SAR
National Guard SAR
Air Force SAR

Coast Guard SAR
4×4 SAR
Automobile SAR
Motorcycle SAR
Scuba SAR
Posse SAR
Search Dog
Border Patrol SAR
Sheriff Aero Bureaus
Sheriff SAR
Fire Department SAR
Citizen Band SAR
Etc.

These groups needed a "common communications media," a place where rescuers could bone up on the latest technology, be made aware of meetings, seminars, and forums, and learn about "outstanding individuals" in the "SAR fraternity." Kelley's goal was informational uplift. By reading together, isolated SAR individuals and organizations would knit together and join in the unified effort "to upgrade this business for the victim's sake."[32]

The language of community and cooperation infused *Search and Rescue,* but the magazine revealed as many tensions as it resolved. Law enforcement and military officials sometimes eyed volunteers with suspicion, calling them "glory seekers" and "vigilantes." In the summer issue of 1975, Lois Clark McCoy, a frequent contributor, authored an editorial that attempted to quell turf battles and interagency mistrust. While it was "volunteers, both law enforcement and unaffiliated, who provide much of the manpower that actually get the job done," the responders sometimes failed to view one another as partners. Instead, groups and individuals competed: "We want to be the person, the group, the agency that finds the kid!" "We all know we must work together," she wrote, "but we're human and we're competitive." Paid emergency personnel in fire and police departments argued that volunteers took food off their tables, while volunteers with expertise in mountaineering or scuba diving grew leery when sheriff's departments or the National Park Service trained employees in those disciplines in order to replace the amateurs. In Los Angeles County, SAR activists worried about conflicts of interest when the sheriff's department deputized volunteers, a move that empowered SAR posse members to carry guns. In an interview with Kelley in 1975, LA County sheriff Peter J. Pitchess brushed aside this concern. "Yes," he responded, "we are aware [some persons may join to become gun carriers] and we are willing to risk it because your people police yourselves pretty well." Pitchess trusted the motives of the SAR leaders in the country, he praised their organizations, and he explained why law enforcement needed them: "There is going to be more and more people who are going to get lost, more and more people who are going to need rescuing, and there is a limit to how much tax payers can increase the burden of taxes. The only solution is for more and more citizen involvement." The popularity of outdoor recreation in nature preserves close to urban populations would keep the volunteers on the frontlines of locating and retrieving hurt and missing persons.[33]

Sheriff Pitchess argued in favor of volunteer SAR organizations being deputized and supervised by law enforcement. SAR belonged under the auspices of law enforcement, he said, because "rescuing people comes closer to a law enforcement function than it does to the fire function or to the civil defense or any other." Unlike firefighters and EMTs, the police "are always searching for people." In coalition with police departments, SAR organizations helped sports and surveillance communities spread into pockets of extreme geography, establishing the boundaries of cognitive, environmental, and social space.[34]

### WHO IS THE MAN?

SAR volunteers and police officers pursued human targets. Both looked for victims, but the cops hunted suspects as well. As deputized man hunters, what prevented SAR volunteers from performing law enforcement's job of going after people who escaped to the wilderness to avoid arrest or to enjoy illicit activities like smoking pot? Nothing, answered one contributor to *Search and Rescue*. In the summer of 1974, Dennis Kelley printed a short story by George Sibley entitled "The Rescue People." It was the only piece of fiction the magazine ran, and it was one of the few open critiques of SAR to appear. Sibley's satire followed the trials of a man named Harper Townsend. A cog in the tourist industry, Harper worked sixty hours a week at the fictional Trapper Mountain, a ski resort that catered to the station-wagon crowd in the summer. On Sundays, his day off, Harper drove his "old car" as far as it would take him into the backcountry to hike alone with a day pack filled with a flask of peppermint schnapps, a handful of raisins, matches, and a plastic tarp. One Sunday, he "had a little accident." He fell trying to scale a "short face of rock." He dropped fifteen feet to a ledge. The fall knocked the wind out of him, bruised his side, and cracked a few ribs. Hours passed as he recuperated and gingerly descended the rest of the face. He was physically fine but late. With the sun setting, Harper decided to build a fire and camp under his tarp. At daylight, he would hike out and explain to his boss what had happened.[35]

In the middle of the night, Harper was attacked by Trapper Mountain Search and Rescue. After he was reported missing by his girlfriend, who had expected him home by eight o'clock, the town's SAR volunteers, led by Harper's boss, scrambled to find the AWOL hiker. Townsend laughed at the mix-up. He tried to explain that he didn't need help and offered his saviors a nip of schnapps, "but all they wanted to do was rescue me, save me—and in the process convert me." They scolded him for the trouble he'd caused by going "off by yourself in places you shouldn't be, alone." Harper had to beg them not to carry him down to the parking lot "on their goddam stokes litter." "I'd rather have my bones bleach there [in the backcountry] as a monument to my stupidity," Harper said, "than live on their terms." Mountain SAR was not a civic good in this account, but rather "the foundation of fascism." Instead of "Search and Rescue," the badges should read "Surveillance and Restructuring."[36]

"The Rescue People" riled up readers of *Search and Rescue*. In the next issue, Kelley published three letters to the editor along with a note of his own. One letter denounced Sibley for his use of profanity. Another cheered the author for exposing "the mentality of some types." Jon Wartes, the leader of Explorer SAR in the Western Region (both search-and-rescue and law enforcement agencies sponsored Explorer programs for teenagers), noted that while "rumor has it that some people were unhappy with the fiction article," he and his wife, Wendy, "really enjoyed it—as did most of the ESAR leaders I've talked to." Kelley agreed in a parenthetical blurb attached to Wartes's letter. "The majority of SAR people I've talked to," he wrote, "tremendously enjoyed 'The Rescue People' by George Sibley." That Kelley broke in to voice his support indicated that he felt a response was warranted. The rumors had reached him. Sibley's jaded view of SAR had offended the law-and-order segment of his subscription base.[37]

Kelley went out of his way to inject an antiauthoritarian viewpoint into *Search and Rescue.* He had read the short story in another magazine and asked permission to reprint it. "The Rescue People" had first appeared in the March 1974 edition of the *Mountain Gazette,* an alternative outdoor magazine edited by Denver's Mike Moore. Sibley wrote lightly fictionalized stories about his hometown, Crested Butte, Colorado, for the *Gazette,* and Moore tapped climbers, travel writers, and environmentalists for offbeat articles. Edward Abbey wrote for the *Mountain Gazette.* Sibley's cantankerous rejection of fascist surveillance resonated with SAR activists less enthralled with organizational hierarchies and law enforcement partnerships than with the idea of helping individuals like themselves push their physical and spiritual limits in the wilderness. By promoting self-education, rigorous training, and personal responsibility, SAR volunteerism, for many activists, abetted backcountry adventure instead of stifling it. Many participants saw themselves as little better than and no different from the dirt bags and social misfits they found dangling from cliffs or buried in avalanches.[38]

Elements of SAR culture prized institutional independence and promoted rugged individualism. In the inaugural issue of *Search and Rescue,* Kelley interviewed Jon Wartes, training director for the Western Region Explorer SAR Advisory Committee and operations coordinator of the Seattle ESAR. An Explorer program introduced Wartes to SAR when he was fourteen. He did his time on monotonous gridline searches for missing persons and advanced to supervising teenagers. When someone turned up missing in the mountains of Washington, the county's sheriff's departments called out SAR teams from across the state. In 1973, Seattle ESAR had 400 members and could usually field 100 to 120 trainees when SAR coordinators needed them. They were brought in to do the boring routines regular SAR groups liked to avoid. "I don't think there is anything more demanding and tedious," reported Wartes, "than a gridline (sweep search) for a sustained period of time." The grunt work taught lessons about discipline and toughness: "The kind of guys who are going to suffer through the training and go out and do this kind of thing are the guys who are more or less self directive." Wartes valued competence and independence. He appreciated the helicopters provided by federal and state agencies, for instance, but he viewed government with suspicion. "Any time money passes hands," he noted, "so do obligations." As with the adult SAR units, ESAR survived on donations. Freed from bureaucratic entanglements, Wartes could focus on saving people rather than preserving an agency's reputation or budgetary bottom line. SAR units declared that they put victims first, and in the process, they cultivated and protected their individuality and autonomy.[39]

Midway through their interview, Kelley gave Wartes the opportunity to promote the social mission of ESAR: "Has ESAR been a real benefit to the community, not from an ESAR standpoint, but because it gets young people involved and off the streets?" Wartes redirected the question away from the communal ethos and society at large and, somewhat surprisingly, away from the inner lives of his students as well. Outdoor recreation advocates had been touting the character-building benefits of wilderness training since the nineteenth century. The Boy Scouts of America, an organization affiliated with many teen Explorer programs, insisted on a link between going outdoors and raising ethical males. Wartes fixed instead on individuals' command of the spaces around them. "I don't know if the benefits are so much social as they are personal. I'm speaking individually. Like guys have gone through our training, been out on operations, graduated from high school, then gone to Vietnam and written back that the skills they had like map and compass, getting from one place to another, have been very important." ESAR produced skillful navigators of dangerous environments. Not getting lost and triggering an emergency response was a sign of personal freedom and of being a responsible adult. Individuals expressed their freedom by increasing their navigational proficiency. ESAR exposed teens to SAR and gave them "a reason for continuing that kind of advanced training." The more skills rescuers acquired, the more autonomous they appeared. Training was an end in itself that built spatial libertarians.[40]

Search-and-rescue volunteers cultivated the skills of rugged individualism within a hierarchical command structure. The willingness of their surrender to authority was the key to explaining why so many put up with the movement's conflicting goals, and a primary reason why, besides taxpayer cost, most SAR groups remain fiercely nonprofit to this day. In Sibley's short story, the hero flees to the backcountry to escape his day job. Search-and-rescue volunteers did the same. When their beepers flared, they dropped their routines and plunged into the wilderness. "This is the pinnacle of a mountain rescuer's life," wrote Mark Scott-Nash in his memoir about his service in Boulder's Rocky Mountain Rescue: "being in the wilderness, whether playing on a planned trip, or unexpectedly called to save lives, interrupting their daily routines to eagerly jump into a rescue full of unknowns." The adrenaline rush of backcountry risk and the freedom of being in wild nature motivated everyone involved.[41]

Overbearing law enforcement threatened to shatter the searcher and victim comradery. Instead of seeing themselves in the people they rescued, some emergency technicians, officers, and agents perceived their targets as nonconformists and rule breakers. An early issue of *Search and Rescue* magazine included a questionnaire from a "Search and Rescue Mission Coordinator's Handbook" put out by the Colorado Search and Rescue Board, an umbrella organization for the state's local SAR outfits. Rescuers used the interview template to gather information from victims' friends and relatives. The queries ran the gamut from the clothes people had on to their military service and physical handicaps. The interviewers also asked about "personal habits." Did the victims smoke? Did they have a history of depression? How did they feel about authority and grown-ups in general? Had they ever been in trouble with the law? How did they feel about hippies? Were they a hippie? To find people, authorities felt the need to surveil and categorize them.[42]

The Colorado Search and Rescue Board believed that emergencies warranted invasions of privacy, but "man hunting" blurred the line between helpful identification and psychological distancing. For example, in the 1975 spring edition of *Search and Rescue,* Lois Clark McCoy interviewed Ab Taylor, the supervisory patrol agent in charge of the El Cajon Border Patrol Station near San Diego. An enthusiastic supporter of SAR, Taylor was frequently called out to assist the San Diego Mountain Rescue Team in finding missing persons. He was an expert tracker who had honed his skills in the desert chasing Mexican immigrants to the United States. "In the 1960s," Taylor explained, "almost every alien we caught was the result of tracking him from sun-up to sun-down all day through all types of terrain in spite of every trick he knew to disguise or hide his tracks." Man tracking, he was happy to report, was starting to catch on in SAR, but the crossover between SAR and law enforcement could go further: "There are areas in the interrogation of witnesses and in track identification that have hardly been explored." For Taylor, the undiscovered country was not a radical climbing pitch or a slick backcountry ski run, but rather the promise of applying the same surveillance and tracking techniques to the casualties of outdoor recreation that had proven effective on "aliens."[43]

Did search and rescue enhance individual liberty or criminalize those who sought freedom outside the lines of conventions and norms? For the most part, SAR advocates dodged this question by changing the subject. Instead of imagining Ab Taylor–trained pursuers tracking down hippies and radicals to eject them from the wilderness, SAR libertarians and law enforcement types pictured themselves rescuing lost children.

### BLESS THE CHILD

U.S. Border Patrol agents developed their tracking skills pursuing immigrants who entered the country illegally, yet when Ab Taylor switched his mental focus from his human-hunting day job to his human-hunting volunteer work, he did not imagine a "flood" of Mexican job seekers but rather a "poor little fella . . . curled up just like a baby rabbit in the grass." "Man-tracking was the best way to go," he reported, if the victims were "small children, retarded children, or senile adults." Like Taylor, Sheriff Pitchess from LA County emphasized the need to recruit SAR volunteers to save children. The sheriff's department, he asserted, must be able to search for missing persons at night: "If your kid were lost and the Sheriff Dept. searches all day until 7 PM, then says, 'We will be back tomorrow morning.' You'd get real mad! . . . That kid is lost up there and he's suffering more at nighttime than he is in the daytime." Lost children rallied searchers. Qualms about fascism and questions about freedom disappeared when the victim was a kid.[44]

In the same 1973 issue of *Search and Rescue* that featured Jon Wartes's interview, Kelley published a lengthy lost-child account written by Lena F. Reed. Two photos accompanied the story. They showed cops and SAR volunteers wearing cheesy mustaches, bell-bottoms, and big-collared windbreakers; the time frame was unmistakably the 1970s. Reed, however, chose to set the story of three-year-old Sandra Michelle Scalf's disappearance in the woods south of Tacoma in a mythic era. She did not mention the year, only that it was February, the depth of winter. As a result, the scenario, a lost child on a cold, dark night, had an elemental quality. It was more fairy tale than police procedural.[45]

The Pierce County Sheriff's Department fielded the call from Sandra's mother. The little girl had gone missing that afternoon. Temperatures were dropping into the twenties as the sun dipped. The sheriff declared an emergency and alerted the volunteer groups "at his disposal." The

"Explorer Scouts, Tacoma Mountain Rescue Association, Tacoma Citizen Band Radio Association, a helicopter crew from the Army's nearby Fort Lewis, Jeep and Four-Wheel-Drive clubs, and a Search Dog Club" rushed to the scene. They combed the countryside. Hearts sank when the pilot of the army helicopter spotted the girl's pink parka floating in a pond. A "veteran of fourteen years of mountain rescue work" reached the area where the pilot saw the parka. He found the girl jacketless but otherwise in good condition. "When they announced that the little girl was alive," Reed quoted one of the German shepherd handlers, "there wasn't a dry eye on the place." The miraculous recovery proved not only the value of volunteer search-and-rescue organizations working in coordination with local, state, and federal authorities but the emotional truth that "men can cry."[46]

Sandra Scalf was a more helpless lost child than her predecessors. After the American Revolution, agrarian children symbolized the first stirrings of individual space. Pamphlet writers and frontier historians told stories of their disorientation and nature shock. They showed communities rallying to search for missing children, restoring the power of surveillance, and reasserting the values of relational space, but they also portrayed very young wanderers as precocious individualists. If they kept their heads and remembered their parents' instructions, American children could navigate the wilderness on their own. They were born spatial libertarians. By the 1970s, no one believed this. Lost children were baby rabbits, and their disappearance summoned the full power of the state's emergency services and public's volunteer rescue organizations. Their innocence settled controversies and inspired interagency cooperation. When children became teenagers, they could sign up for Explorer SAR and begin the long years of training it took to become a certified backcountry expert. They could display their expertise and their independence by searching for and rescuing lost children.

A missing child could even bridge the cultural gap between law enforcement and hippies. On July 9, 1971, eight-year-old Douglas Legg went for a walk outside a campground in the Adirondack Mountains in upstate New York. Inspector Donald Ambler led the search for the boy. By July 21, the mission had ballooned to include four hundred volunteers on the ground as well as twenty-eight "rescue experts from California" and reserves from the U.S. Army and Marine Corps. An air force C-131 plane circled the mountains, photographing the terrain and scanning it with a sensor that detected heat waves from living bodies. The search area and effort were immense, and tension built as the days passed. Rescuers clung to hope, even though the SAR coordinators instructed them to expect the worst. "I just wish they wouldn't keep telling us 'Now remember, you're looking for a body,' " said Bill Allen, a local volunteer. "It drains everybody's enthusiasm."[47]

With the C-131 buzzing overhead, packs of bloodhounds baying in the woods, and legions of men pushing themselves to exhaustion to find a lost child, you would think the reporter from the *New York Times* would have had plenty of colorful material to relate besides the groovy appearance of some of the searchers. Yet twice in the course of one article he commented on the shocking sight of cops and hippies joining forces to find Legg. The lost boy came from a suburb near Syracuse University, and some students volunteered to help look for him. "Their long hair, bell bottoms and occasional beards," wrote the journalist, "contrasted with the crew-cuts and red jackets of some of the local men, many of whom carried knives on their belts." In another setting, the two groups may have formed lines to protest and attack one another, but for the greater cause of locating a wayward person, they "seemed to accept each other as they jounced along together in trucks and emerged from, or disappeared into, the forest." Watching the two groups emerge from the woods in unison was the bright spot of the ordeal. The search for Douglas Legg failed; his remains are missing to this day.[48]

The *Times* reporter could draw vivid distinctions because the long-hairs and the crew-cuts differed politically, culturally, and spatially. The SAR volunteers fought getting lost whereas the hippies celebrated it. They dropped out, cut loose, and smoked themselves dizzy. They developed a spatial slang to differentiate their expansive worldviews from their parents'. To them, far out and freak out were desirable states. They liked to get high and hoped to reach the astral plane. Being out of sight was good; being straight was not. Going with flows and on long, strange trips was okay; driving the family to Disneyland or Yellowstone was a bad trip. Still, as the search for Douglas Legg showed, the generation gap separating the searchers and the seekers could be spanned by the specter of a lost child.

The lost-child archetype established the border between positive loss and nature shock. In the post–World War II United States, outdoor enthusiasts and social dropouts sometimes said they wanted to get lost. They went on vacations in nature to locate spaces outside the mainstream where they could disconnect. But nature shock was not the destination they had in mind. Complete dislocation was where the lost children went, and hippies and cops worked together to haul them back.

Dennis Kelley outlined the contours of nature shock for his SAR readers. In 1973, he self-published a handbook for SAR volunteers titled *Mountain Search for the Lost Victim*. He serialized portions of the book in the early issues of *Search and Rescue*. Why do people become lost? he asked. "The motivation of the victim when lost is highly controversial." Subjects endure "a state of shock and panic." They "become semiconscious and operate in semihallucinary mode." The rescued ones reported "clouded visions" filled with dreams of "relatives and friends," "even in the daytime." Hungry victims conjured "grand feasts and meals." In these states of "semi-consciousness, it is believed that the victim becomes very basic in his needs and motivations." The lost became childlike. Kelley used the concept of childhood to define missing persons as victims. "It should be remembered," he wrote, "that it is often adults who place [children] involuntarily in strange and sometimes hostile environments." "One of the reasons," he went on, "we call the missing person a victim is because of the involuntary situation of the victim's plight."[49]

*Search and Rescue* magazine sometimes indulged in positive depictions of getting lost. Kelley ran advertisements for T-shirts that read, "Support Search and Rescue, Get Lost." The cover of the spring 1978 issue equated self-discovery with membership in the National Association of Search and Rescue. The headline read, "Find Yourself, Join NASAR." The front image, however, undercut the light sentiment of the slogan. It was a picture of a SAR volunteer, a grown man with a mustache, cradling a stunned child with a bloody nose. SAR activists and extreme outdoor recreationists talked about breaking free and getting lost, but neither wanted the experience that produced the terror in that child's eyes.[50]

## THE MEN IN THE MIRROR

Hidden behind the image of helicopter pilots, sheriff's deputies, and SAR teams getting outdoorsmen choked up after an iconic child rescue was the reality that most emergencies in the recreational outdoors involved males between the ages of twenty and forty-nine. Instead of hoisting innocent babes into helicopters after massive, multiday events, most lost-person SAR incidents resolved quickly, ending with male volunteers peering into the eyes of bewildered versions of themselves. Jon Wartes, the ESAR leader from Washington State, hinted at the ambiguous sentiments caused by these denouements. Kelley asked him about the wisdom of SAR units undergoing EMT training to provide medical care to victims they found in the backcountry. Wartes liked the idea of additional training for anything emergency related, but EMT expertise was not really applicable in the field. Searchers rarely met people in need of tracheotomies or pulmonary resuscitation. "Truthfully, if you were to encourage them to take it [EMT] because of the need, we haven't had any where near that much need. . . . A person is generally going to be dead or he's not in that much trouble." Rescuing adult male recreationists was nowhere near as romantic as plucking a three-year-old from a primeval forest, but the resemblance to themselves that greeted SAR volunteers when they found a dead body, or a healthy dude, confirmed the privilege of being a grown man in the wilderness. Men could present themselves as expert searchers, scanning mountain vistas for clues, tucked in the refuge of an information command post, or they could enjoy being wandering doofuses, losing themselves in nature to escape information overload, comfortable that if they met trouble, an interagency team of crack rescuers would come and locate them. And, beyond a suggested donation, no one would ask them to pay for the service.[51]

Large and long searches cost enormous sums of money with diminishing returns. Within twenty-four hours, the chances of finding a lost hiker dropped from 95 to 75 percent. Each day, the likelihood of survival slipped further. After seventy-two hours, hikers had a fifty-fifty chance of being found. Very few searches lasted as long as a day. Over 90 percent of the fifty thousand search-and-rescue incidents reported in the International Search and Rescue Database were resolved within a few hours. Arduous searches involving lost individuals who descended into nature shock and wandered for weeks tested SAR organizational coordination and skill, yet in truth wilderness rescue was a sprint rather than an endurance event. Success happened quickly, whereas failure dragged on for days, weeks, or forever, if a body was never found.[52]

If recreationists went missing in random places at random moments, finding them would have been next to impossible. It helped that lost people followed patterns—scripts that revealed the social biases of wilderness spaces even as mass communication and transportation opened access to national parks and wilderness areas. In 2009, researchers Travis

Heggie and Michael Amundson published a review of the U.S. National Park Service annual search-and-rescue reports from 1992 to 2007. They dug deeper into one year, 2005, to profile the age and gender of accident victims. Saving and rescuing guests was not and is not an official function of the park service. Congress never directed the agency to track people down and pack them out, and it does not earmark funds to pay for searches and extractions. The National Park Service (NPS) prioritizes safety nonetheless, placing human life above "all other management actions." The agency rescues visitors free of charge. From 1992 to 2007, the NPS recorded 65,439 SAR incidents involving 78,488 individuals. Forty-eight percent of the emergencies involved hikers. Boating entered the books as the next most dangerous activity, accounting for 21 percent of the calls. The rest of the incidents spread across a wide range of leisure pastimes from climbing (5 percent) to horseback riding (2 percent) to fishing (1 percent). Most emergencies involved adult men. In 2005, 60 percent of the emergencies happened to males of all ages, while adults, men and women in the prime of life, age twenty to thirty-nine, made up 55.6 percent of individuals involved in SAR events. The two groups seemingly most likely to struggle in space, the very young and the very old, accounted for only 16.8 percent of emergency mobilizations. The higher numbers of healthy adults who got lost testified to the ways conceptual geographies changed over time. The recreational wilderness flummoxed humans at the height of their hippocampal power while the agrarian woods and prairies tricked a more vulnerable population. Applying the 60 percent total male benchmark to total number of adults would yield 810 men ages twenty to thirty-nine, 33 percent of the total number of individuals involved in the 2,430 SAR incidents in 2005. Adult women made up 22 percent of the incidents. Heggie and Amundson totaled the cost of SAR operations from 1992 to 2007: it came to $58,572,164. "On average," they wrote, "there were 11.2 SAR incidents a day at an average of $895 per operation." They estimated that one in five of SAR emergencies would have ended in death had the NPS stuck to its mandate and let visitors fend for themselves. Despite the park service's best efforts, 2,659 outdoor enthusiasts perished. Over 13,000 other people would have died had the NPS not bothered. Search and rescue was an essential service that preserved the fun of going on vacation to a nature preserve. Without the volunteers, the parks would look grim.[53]

In 2012, geographer Jared Doke completed a master's thesis about SAR responses involving lost visitors in Yosemite National Park. The missing persons fell into two categories: the bewildered and the late. The bewildered could not locate their positions in space. They were lost to themselves. Forty-five percent of the missing persons reported feeling disoriented, a number Doke thought low since embarrassment suppressed self-reporting. The late failed to appear at a specific time and place. Friends or relatives reported their absence to the authorities. Getting bewildered could make someone late, as could an injury or a mistake in planning. In the eleven years Doke considered (2000–2011), YOSAR recorded 2,308 emergencies, from twisted ankles on fire roads to BASE-jumping catastrophes. Doke counted 213 lost-person searches. Sixty-two percent of the Yosemite lost incidents involved hikers. "Nearly two thirds of the searches," wrote Doke, "were for one subject and about two-thirds of these involved males." The mean age of a lost individual was thirty-six. Doke's findings echoed Heggie and Amundson's results in their general survey of SAR incidences in national parks as well as lost-person studies from Australia and Great Britain. Youngish to middle-aged men on foot proceeded to get lost and require a SAR intervention at higher rates than other genders or age groups, although national parks drew people from across ages and genders. A 2006 study of Yellowstone summer traffic found that males accounted for just 50 percent of all those entering the park.[54]

The top five list of mistakes that led people to get lost in Doke's Yosemite study were losing the trail, failure to communicate a plan with others, miscalculating time or distance, darkness, and leaving the trail intentionally. Snow and rain caused some hikers to get lost, as did steep terrain, animals, drugs, and errors in judgment. Losing the trail by accident constituted 16.9 percent of lost-person reports.[55]

To locate lost persons, psychologists studied why some victims lost their minds after they lost the trail. In *Analysis of Lost Person Behavior*, William G. Syrotuck related the descent into shock. After realizing their predicament, lost persons engaged in an assortment of stereotypical behaviors. Initially, they felt a compulsion to "break out." They crashed through brush and sprinted to higher ground. After they burned through their adrenaline, victims settled down and hatched plans that "may appear irrational to a calm observer." These plans might feature an obsessive component, such as climbing to the top of a specific peak or following a stream in the belief that "all streams led to civilization." As panic set in, some victims discarded equipment and even disrobed. They failed to make fires and shelters. Fear gripped some lost persons so fiercely that their sanity cracked, forcing searchers to think as bizarrely as they did to find them.[56]

SAR experts ventured into confused head spaces to "locate missing search subjects faster." Professional searchers considered emergency situations from every possible angle. They generated scenarios, gathered data, filled in charts, and drew up probability maps. To counter the spatial cluelessness missing persons often exhibited, search professionals approached space with hyper-awareness. They analyzed the terrain, measured the weather, and noted the cycles of the moon. They interrogated friends and family members to profile lost hikers. (Were they upset? Suicidal? Fond of hippies?) SAR experts adored information. Missing hikers got lost in mountains, forests, canyons, and deserts, but the certified professionals looked for them in the details.

Yet the minutiae could blind as well as reveal. Psychologists call the phenomenon of knowing too much *unpacking*. SAR experts enter uncertain situations and are called upon to evaluate the probability of finding a lost person in grid sections on maps. They look for clues to help them make best guesses. Yet in the process of gathering more information, they can grow attached to an original hypothesis. The more details they gather, the more convinced they become of their first theory, even if there's little evidence to support the initial selection of one search area over another. "Like the measured length of a coastline, which increases as a map becomes more detailed," wrote psychological theorists Amos Tversky and Derek J. Koehler in a 1994 article on unpacking, "the perceived likelihood of an event increases as its description becomes more specific." In 2012, Kenneth A. Hill, a specialist in lost-person behavior, investigated unpacking in SAR. In an experiment, he asked "32 adult males with search planning experience" to assign probabilities to five missing-person scenarios. He then fed his subjects additional details, and sure enough, the more information they received, the more convinced they became that the first scenario they chose was the correct one. The planners all experienced some level of "scenario lock," and Hill, to his surprise, found that the "most experienced planners in the sample (averaging 48 SAR incidents in the role of planner) were if anything more likely than less experienced planners to show unpacking effects." The more the experts zoomed in, the harder and longer they looked, the less likely they were to see the situation clearly. They could get lost in a collision of mental and geographic spaces just like their targets.[57]

Moreover, both SAR experts and missing tourists carried social presumptions about wilderness spaces into national parks. Masculinity, for example, clearly influenced navigation decisions and judgment calls. Males and females traveled to national parks in equal numbers, but men engaged in behaviors—hiking alone without a clear understanding of the trail network, the weather forecast, the traverse times and difficulty of routes, or the level of their own skill and physical condition—more likely to get them lost. Since the dawn of the industrial age, outdoor writers had informed American men, especially neurotic urbanites, that answers to their maladies lay in the recreational outdoors. The wilderness was their refuge. Men between the ages of twenty and forty-nine did not venture into danger thinking about nineteenth-century theories of the sublime. Most sallied forth into danger because they did not think about the underlying premises that governed their understanding of space at all. Walking in rugged environments without clear directions felt natural to a percentage of them.

The same desire to break free in wild nature that predicted adult male hikers would go missing on weekends motivated other adult male hikers to give up their weekends to go search for them. Both pursued unfettered individualism in the wilderness, and their libertarian tendencies camouflaged a truth about their autonomy: it grew from mutual dependence. Rescuers provided an amenity that tourists consumed while both pretended to run across one another by accident.

The lost and the rescuers created a new wilderness out of mountains of information and willful obliviousness. They trusted the ethos of moving faster and knowing more even as they sought to counteract it. A weekend hiker might seek relief from the onslaught of news and the hectic pace of the daily grind, but when he met trouble, he relied on data collectors, trackers who launched sweeps into areas divided into meticulous quadrants. Both may have been fooling themselves—unpacking showed that more details did not necessarily lead to successful rescues—but their relationship exposed the wilderness as a place where men could express their individual freedom in ignorance or expertise.

Nature and technology in individual space. (Photograph by Mitch Barrie, 2010. Courtesy of Creative Commons, https://creativecommons.org/licenses/by-sa/2.0/legalcode)

## WOMEN IN THE WILDERNESS

In 1975, Melvin Maddocks, a columnist for the *Christian Science Monitor,* rescued the getting-lost lifestyle piece. In "Vacation—The Art of Getting Lost," he invited readers (by deploying the second person) to imagine themselves floating on a lake in a remote vacation oasis: "Watching a train while lying on a raft in the middle of a Maine lake is as curiously comforting as stretching out on the floor as a boy while your train makes magic circles about you." For Maddocks, the art of getting lost involved cutting ties with transportation networks and information systems. In Maine, on the lake, he was far from commuter lines and telephone connections. Distance defeated "this system by turning trains and telephones into pure sights, pure sounds: a form of poetry." Recreational disconnection was an act of rebellion. "Vacations in the '70s," Maddocks wrote, "are what Americans have left of the counter-culture of the '60s. For a month one takes oneself out of context. One wears old, old clothes, goes barefoot, and lets whiskers grow as they will. One steps out of the kingdom of clocks. One selectively resigns—for a month—from the coming 21st century." The revolution would be fought away from the phone.[58]

The vacation beard sprouting on the faces of the lost man of leisure indicated that for Melvin and the readers of the *Christian Science Monitor,* the woods remained a space premised on masculinity. But the outdoors was never a male preserve. Women enjoyed lakes, mountains, and breaking free too, and they were present in the recreational wilderness from the start. While SAR remained an overwhelmingly male endeavor, women participated in the formation of SAR groups, and they have fought for positions on high-profile squads like YOSAR and Teton County, Wyoming's rescue team. Two women, Alice Holubar and Meg Kershaw, were early members of the Rocky Mountain Rescue Group in Boulder County, Colorado. Today, every team in the YOSAR organization includes several female experts.

Women rescuers appeared in human-interest newspaper stories. Sara Rathbun was one of two women on the sixty-seven-member California Urban Search and Rescue Task Force-2. The rescue team scrambled to search for survivors in urban disasters in the United States and throughout the world. Interviewed by LA's KQED, Rathbun admitted to facing pushback from SAR counterparts and rescue victims, especially in some countries where female rescue workers were unknown. But she found the work rewarding and thought herself better equipped than men to handle some crises: "I have more tools to deal with it than perhaps men do, because they are in a position where it is not socially acceptable for them to show as much emotion as it is for me." Women rescuers could form relationships, especially with children, tapping a long history of humans fighting disaster and disorientation with social bonds.[59]

Men and women enjoyed disconnecting from society just as they both took pride in the search-and-rescue work that went into locating people who disconnected too enthusiastically. However, unlike men, women recognized, and were forced to navigate, social relationships in emergency situations and wild spaces.

Despite and maybe because of its macho connotations, the modern wilderness attracted women seeking liberation. In 1980, Nancy LeMany wrote an account about hiking in the mountains of southwestern Colorado for the *Boston Globe.* The New England novice was not prepared for lugging a heavy pack for days at high elevations. At one point, she became trapped on an exposed ledge and asked her guides to call for a rescue team. "Get me the hell out of here!" she screamed. "Send in a helicopter! I'll use my MasterCharge!" The guides talked LeMany down, and by the end of the trek she regretted leaving the mountains. She lost her pride and a little blood, but she gained "the confidence and knowledge that we are capable of going beyond our physical limitations." LeMany demonstrated the give-and-take of consumer power in the wilderness. She could not hire a helicopter with a credit card, but she could employ a guide to show her the way to personal achievement. Like male hikers, she purchased a service that enhanced her autonomy.[60]

In 1995, Cheryl Strayed hiked portions of the eleven-hundred-mile wilderness path that runs the length of the Pacific coast by herself. In 2012, she published *Wild: From Lost to Found on the Pacific Crest Trail*, a best-selling memoir about her journey. She ventured off the trail several times and connected these instances of physical disorientation to the defining losses in the book: the hiking boot she accidentally pushed over a cliff and the grief she felt for her mother who had died from cancer years before. In a literary work of memory, forgiveness, and relationship repair, Strayed used the same women-as-wilderness-rookie setup LeMany deployed. Her heavy pack, which she called Monster, nearly ended her, yet as the miles rolled by, she grew stronger and more confident. The trail became her home, a refuge offering a perspective not unlike the Montana Tractor advertisement. She certainly wanted to lose herself and find herself by looking back on her troubled yet still promising life from a distance.

The most dramatic turn in the memoir happened when this perspective was nearly shattered by criminal aggression. Close to the conclusion of her adventure, Strayed happened upon two male bow hunters who were lost in the woods. The men noted her aloneness and threatened her safety. She escaped their clutches, but not their gaze. After one of the men surprised her at her campsite and commented on her appearance, Strayed "could hardly hear my own words for what felt like a great clanging in my head, which was the realization that my whole hike on the PCT could come to this. That no matter how tough or brave I'd been, how comfortable I'd come to be with being alone, I'd also been lucky, and that if my luck ran out now, it would be as if nothing before it had ever existed, that this one evening would annihilate all those brave days." For Strayed, the danger of the wilderness included other humans. Neither Abbey nor some guy from Connecticut felt this fear, for they looked out from refuges secure in the knowledge that as men in the wild they were not objects to be leered at or attacked.[61]

*Wild* and its author eventually wound up in Oprah Winfrey's warm embrace. Strayed visited with the "Queen of All Media" for an interview on July 22, 2012. The two sat among the trees in Oprah's front yard and talked about conquering fear, bearing burdens, and facing the challenge "of being in uncharted territory, in the wilderness, pitch-black, by yourself, female." *Wild* epitomized the healing power of losing oneself to find oneself, and Oprah thought the memoir so inspirational that she resurrected her book club to spread its message across her information empire.[62]

Oprah equated being alone and female with going blind and braving the wilderness. Each condition built on the other to escalate the danger for Strayed as well as to increase the magnitude of her victory at entering and exiting an uncharted space. The riskiness of her solo hike recalled Edward Abbey's macho idyll. For him, hazard defined wilderness, and post–World War II Americans need not travel far into the backcountry to experience the wild. Stepping away from the cars revealed the debilitating effects of modernity. Americans, especially men, had withered and softened. A short hike into the desert could kill them. And that would be a blessing, Abbey argued, for then they would rediscover their manhood on the brink of the unknown.

Neither Strayed nor Oprah imagined Abbey's antisocial wilderness. Strayed admitted to being afraid, but she created a second persona for the internal voice that told her that every bump in the night was a mountain lion out to eat her: "We all have those negative voices inside us—the ones that say, 'I'm too fat' or 'I'm not good enough'—and you just have to counter them and say, 'I'm not going to listen to that. I'm going to listen to this other thing.' When I was suffering, I'd say to myself, 'I'm uncomfortable right now, but I can do this.' And I could do it. I did it." In the memoir, Strayed surrounded herself with the memories of her mother, her family, and her former selves. She talked to them on the trail. She lashed them with anger, begged their forgiveness, and reconciled with their ghosts. She populated her wilderness, whereas Abbey emptied his. The intrusion of the hunters in the memoir's climactic scene reflected a final test of the therapeutic rehabilitation Strayed had achieved on the trail. In their interview, Oprah commented that "every time you encountered humans, I was more afraid for you than when you met up with the rattlesnake or the bear." Clueless men out to prove their virility in nature barged into Strayed's wilderness and threatened to drag her alone into their bleak landscape. That interpersonal scenario, rather than getting lost in geographic space, haunted Oprah and Strayed most.[63]

For women, gender realigned the social, mental, and geographic spaces of the extreme wilderness. Strayed explained to Oprah how the terrain of the mountains led to her emotional catharsis: "I had to accept the fact of the hour. The fact of the mile . . . each step led me to the next step, the next truth that was going to reveal itself. We all suffer." Men and women traveled into remote territories for similar reasons. They climbed mountains, skied near-vertical drops, and soloed for weeks in the backcountry to feel the exhilaration that came from maximum physical exertion. Men, however, could imagine a radical disconnection from society along with a gnarly interaction with nature. Women had a harder time ignoring the truth that relationships spiderwebbed the wilderness. Human beings conceived of spaces together, even individual ones. The extreme wilderness was no different from a village or a suburb in this respect. Wild places had to be imagined before they could be discovered and experienced. A jagged peak or a thousand-mile trail held no meaning until groups of people dressed them in narratives of adventure, risk, and self-discovery.[64]

Women told wilderness stories that laid these relationships bare. Bree Loewen worked for four years as a climbing guide in Mount Rainier National Park and has spent two decades as a volunteer and leader in Seattle Search and Rescue. She chronicled her service to her fellow mountaineers in two memoirs. She opens the first, which covered her seasons of employment in the National Park Service, with a harrowing account of nature shock. Loewen and her climbing partner, Cicely, set off on a short get-to-know-you winter hike on Rainier. The two, along with a third woman who was not present that day, were planning to climb Mount Denali in Alaska later that year. A storm hit the women before they could reach shelter, and they spent two nights in the snow with a pair of male climbers they stumbled into during the whiteout. Loewen wanted the Rainier training run and the upcoming Denali trip to cement her relationship with the other women: "I really wanted the Alaska climb to be a bonding experience. I wanted to forge a long-lasting climbing partnership with Cicely, to grow up and grow old with her and Alice." But Cicely started crying when the weather turned. She asked Bree to switch backpacks and to carry more weight because she was exhausted. Their second night in the blizzard, Cicely kicked Bree out of their snow cave, saying there wasn't enough room for her. On the third day, park service rangers and SAR volunteers found them and escorted Cicely, whose fingers were black with frostbite, to the parking lot where ambulances and news crews were waiting. Loewen never climbed with Cicely again, and she had to live down the infamy that, before she got hired as a climbing ranger on Mount Rainier, she got lost and had to be rescued by her future boss and coworkers.[65]

As a ranger and then as a SAR volunteer, Loewen wrestled with the social consequences of spatial disconnection. When climbers fell or hikers got lost, she scrambled to find babysitters for her young child and to justify the risk she undertook trying to save others in the recreational wilderness. Would people view her as a bad mother if she died on a mountain? "Why am I more worried about what other people think of me than the snowpack?" she wondered. A park ranger who also searched for lost tourists, Edward Abbey didn't give a fig about what other people thought of him, and he certainly didn't worry about how his wilderness commitments impacted his home life, which was as barren and chaotic as any badland. Loewen was made of tougher stuff. She recognized the bind, the "catch-22," as she labeled it, her gender put her in, yet she continued to plunge into dangerous spaces to save people who enjoyed the outdoors as she did. "I love the cold. I love the struggle, the realness, the ridiculousness, and the tenderness of it. . . . This is just what I do for love, just taking the time to be with someone who needs someone to be with them." Whether they reached the summit or got lost along the way, humans—a diverse crowd of them—created, enjoyed, and died in the extreme wilderness. No one walked in or out on his or her own. Some admitted as much. Loewen committed herself to watching over the lost and the injured, and she performed this service to humanity in the wilderness with a profound sense of being watched and judged.[66]

# Disconnect

IN 1999, STEPHEN KING PUBLISHED a novella about a nine-year-old girl getting lost on a section of the Appalachian Trail in southern Maine. Like Donn Fendler, Patricia MacFarland roamed the woods for over a week. Like him, she followed a stream, thinking it would take her to a town or a campground. She hiked to New Hampshire instead and wound up dozens of miles outside the search parameter established by search-and-rescue volunteers and law enforcement authorities. She passed into the same netherworld of exhaustion, starvation, and terror that Fendler experienced and began to hallucinate. Trisha rescued herself too, but she did so with the help of a literary device named Tom Gordon, a handsome baseball player whom she adored and who appeared to her as a vision in times of need. A Red Sox fan himself, King cheered for the real-life Tom "Flash" Gordon, a bullpen staple for the team between 1996 and 1999. You can almost see the germ for the book sprout in his head. What if a closing pitcher saved lives as well as leads?

Salvation came in three waves in *The Girl Who Loved Tom Gordon*. Trisha rescued herself, Gordon preserved victories against the New York Yankees and the Oakland Athletics, and an information network protected an innocent girl's soul from a malevolent force known as the "God of the lost," a ghoulish metaphysical stalker that attacked in the novella's climactic scene. The unreal Gordon comforts and instructs Trisha, and when she meets the God of the lost, he gives her the courage to stand her ground and smite the beast in the snout with a well-pitched Sony Walkman.[1]

The presence of a handheld listening device signaled that King's Trisha staggered through a different American wilderness than Donn Fendler. In 1939, Fendler got lost and resurfaced as a mass media sensation. He wandered out of the woods unaware that thousands of listeners and readers had been following him. Trisha's Walkman closed the distance between her and the news. She switched on the radio and heard reports of her disappearance. She found solace in Red Sox broadcasts as she sloshed through marshes, crashed through thickets, and huddled in the dark corners of her psyche. Though alone for the bulk of the story, she was never by herself.

In King's imagination the connection between the individual and the media held with the strength of an industrial cable. His protagonist couldn't shake free if she wanted, and cutting the line was the last thought on her mind. Her Walkman and the alternative reality it piped into her head rescued her before and after she entered the woods. Trisha's home life was a wreck. Her mother initiated the Saturday excursion to the Appalachian Trail in a desperate attempt to preserve family cohesion in the middle of her divorce from the children's father. Trisha went missing while her mom and her brother engaged in a screaming match. Popular culture diverted her attention from the interpersonal bonds unraveling around her; her earbuds muffled the sound of their dissolution. She was not truly lost until the battery light dimmed, and even then, the dead Walkman served as a blunt instrument of deliverance. Information mainlined to the brain vanquished nature shock's imaginary demons by conjuring imaginary relationships.

Stephen King contemplated a character needing to be rescued from at least three dangerous spaces—childhood, a broken home, and the wilderness. Trisha came from chaos, and she ventured into chaos. She found solace in the media. By the end of the twentieth century, information did more than connect people and places. It was a place itself, a retreat from a flood tide of hostility and disappointment that spilled all over the map. Urban decay, suburban rot, and rural decline spoiled points of departure. Shattered homes rattled nerves and damaged occupants. A fondness for them could no longer be assumed, revising the stories Americans told about their interior journeys. Instead of dragging their domestic ideals along with them, using newspapers and personal correspondence to leave home and be home, many travelers fled their families and tried to forget where they came from.

Not that they had welcome places to go. Destinations were as problematic as departures. The interstate highway system, for example, carried millions of tourists to Las Vegas or the Colorado Rockies. But the ribbons of speed fostered suspicion as well as freedom. For some, they bypassed the true America, and travelers had to get off them to eat real food, meet authentic people, and discover alternative ways of living. The same held for destinations packaged by the tourist industry. Niagara Falls was a dump and the Grand Canyon filled with crowds. Three years before King introduced Trisha and the phantasmagoric Tom Gordon, environmental historian William Cronon declared the wilderness a cultural construction. Even the most remote and detached places had been sullied, trammeled, and manipulated.[2]

And it got worse. In 1999, King imagined a wilderness conquered by a Walkman, but even a master of horror couldn't fathom the monstrous transformation the innovators at Apple, Motorola, and other tech companies were about to unleash. When they combined the Walkman, the cell phone, the digital camera, GPS, and the personal computer, the result melted space and minds. For the first time in history, civilians could travel in absolute space by observing a blue dot on a small screen. They could receive information, and they could broadcast it. They could indulge their sight-animal proclivities, submerging their eyes in image streams pouring from devices in torrents, spending their waking hours in the digital equivalent of peering out on savannahs from a defensive crouch. Smartphones offered mobile isovist perspectives. When threatened with dead air, discomfort, or boredom, they could pull out their phones and be somewhere else. Signal strength and battery power marked the only brakes on the spread of information. Indeed, the residents of the digital age could not even escape into their own persons. The back-and-forth of bits and bytes turned people into algorithms of preference. Individuals existed most vibrantly as backlogs of clicks, links, and purchases. Data histories defined contemporary mental spaces the way religious hierarchies, trading relationships, households, or back-to-nature movements oriented past cognitive geographies.[3]

The information overload prompted cries for reform. Commentators dreamed of spaces outside the media. "Lately, I fantasize about taking a holiday," wrote Canadian journalist Leah Eichler in 2012. "Not a destination holiday . . . I crave a break where I can go for an hour or two without checking one of my digital devices." Attentions bouncing all day from phones to televisions to computers distressed occupational experts. Multitasking workers were scattering their brains, and the information revolution was making them "dumber," less productive, and "suckers for irrelevancy."[4]

Stupidity left physical traces. In 2011, researchers at the University of London measured the hippocampi of cab driver trainees. They found that the region of the brain dedicated to memory and spatial cognition grew after the participants studied maps, memorized street layouts, and conceptualized regions, nodes, and landmarks to help them navigate without computers. The study suggested that an overreliance on satellite maps and GPS instructions might reverse the process, shrinking the part of the brain where synapses connected outside spaces with personal recollections.[5]

In 2014, reporter Curtis Silver sounded the alarm in, of all places, an online venue notable for its techie exuberance. Curtis covered the social media beat for The Next Web, a "future-poof tech media company" that served "Generation T (for technology)" with "remarkable stories and insights." In an article critical of GPS, he consulted a roster of experts appropriate to either a breakout panel at a Silicon Valley conference intended to disrupt industry norms or a four-people-walked-into-a-bar joke. The "Brain Coach" warned against overreliance on digital maps: "With GPS, our brains learn to rely on abstract direction command and trust it. This is not good to develop free critical thinking skills. No hard work, no mental growth; a dangerous cycle since the more we rely on a digital guide, the more we need to." The survival expert concurred with the coach. The phone navigation habit was "going to cost lives" when civilization fell. The volunteer search-and-rescue coordinator shared an instructive story from his first effort to locate a lost person in a forest. As he perused his GPS readout, he noticed that an old-timer was scanning the trees instead. "I asked him why he did not use GPS." He said, "Because I have never found a lost person on a GPS screen. They are always out there (he pointed to the woods)." Finally, the child therapist worried about the brains of the young: "Not only is technology destroying our creativity and brain cells, it is the perfect example of being lost, both literally and metaphorically. Technology sucks us in and the real question remains . . . how do we navigate our way out of this technological world and think independently?" To develop into high-functioning individuals, children needed to relearn how to get lost outside. The therapist illustrated her point with a personal anecdote. One day her son was let off at the wrong bus stop. Instead of using his cell phone to call her or pinpoint his location, he spent an hour walking around, taking pictures, and posting them on Instagram. He produced a slideshow "about being lost." His survival instincts had been replaced by an impulse to generate likes.[6]

Smartphones are making us dumber, atrophying our hippocampi, and turning us all into a Hollywood cliché: failed actors harboring ambitions to direct. We inhabit mental spaces packed with data, but instead of feeling joy in abundance we're overcome with loss. We've lost touch, lost connection, lost intimacy, lost childhood, lost nature, lost concentration, lost reality, lost community, and lost our minds. The information ecosystem has proliferated at a frightening rate, like a toxic algal bloom, swallowing pastimes, industries, and cultural landmarks. It has wiped cities clean of phone booths, deep-sixed record albums, cassette tapes, and compact disks, closed malls, imperiled the U.S. mail service, and reconfigured human biology.

We look up from our screens and ask, how did we get here? We arrived at this moment, this place, the same way we arrived at every other stop along the way. We traveled through spaces created by collective imagination, social power, and the natural environment. Human beings synchronized cognitive geographies to mark landscapes and reach destinations. They traveled in thought, within societies, and through material worlds. Together, these realms defined navigable space. Beyond them lay nature shock, where minds, relations, and coordinates unraveled.

Nature shock revealed the edges of American space and exposed its fictions: that authenticity, meaning, freedom, sanity, paradise, or invincibility resided there on the other side. None chose nature shock; it was a mistake, a tragedy. But one person's nature shock could be another person's home. Edges seen from one angle could appear central from another perspective. For most of North American history, humans crossed over spatial thresholds by establishing relationships. A person's position in a society determined where that individual stood geographically. Both Native Americans and Euro-American colonists imagined and navigated space through interpersonal connections. Isolation terrified everyone in the early modern period, and people switched cultures by choice or out of compulsion rather than endure separation. The invasions of North America triggered uncountable changes, but imagined spaces remained relational long into the nineteenth century.

White male heads of households wrote most of the documents of conquest, and their perspective dominated the records of the shocked. Yet white men never got lost by themselves. Woman, children, the elderly, enslaved persons, and Native Americans became disoriented along the edges of territorial expansion, and the heads of households' insistence on leaving home and being home spurred the creation of state-backed communication networks that spliced relationships across the North American continent. The whole point of white male mobility was to stay connected. Industrial communications extended interpersonal ties across the continent. Americans wrote to consolidate their country. They wrote to assert power and wield it in multiple places at once. They pursued wealth, land, livestock, and adventure on the road to maintain ideals of stationary domestic republics.

While a traveler like Samuel Nichols authored letters to communicate with a very specific spouse in Buffalo, New York, consumers of the U.S. mail, telegraph services, radio signals, and telephone networks learned to beckon a range of impersonal relationships. The intimate hierarchies and public oversight that held subordinates in place within households and communities crumbled as mobile networks took over surveillance for patriarchs and their deputies.

Surveillance became the work of impersonal organizations that erected and operated lines of communication. Male heads of households lost their exalted position as surveyors of independent domains and joined the crowds being watched. To escape supervision and the hectic pace of modernity, where relationships formed and dissolved willy-nilly, a cadre of nervous white male recreationists searched for pockets of calm wilderness in the late nineteenth and early twentieth centuries. At first, they read magazine articles to help them navigate unfamiliar and lightly supervised woods, deserts, and boundary waters, and then some yearned for more radical disconnections. They pondered getting lost as a destination, a bespoke experience one might pay tens of thousands of dollars to induce.

Agrarian heads of households wielding the power of industrial communication took an oversized role in the construction of American mindscapes in the nineteenth century. One of their most spectacular and troubling creations was the modern wilderness. Their fantasies of seeing while not being seen, of escaping relationships while being able to access service, defined the recreational outdoors. A legacy of affluence and authority runs through contemporary geographies and understandings of nature as existing out-there, in government-sponsored set-asides. The social relations of the past bent spaces to the specifications of a few people. While free to walk about with their handheld devices, the users of the future strolled through spaces fashioned by the influential dead.

Getting lost revealed the fingerprints of departed white men on American spaces, but it also revealed the limits of their grasp. Nature shock rattled people no matter their race, gender, rank, real estate holdings, or celebrity profile. Stepping outside of known territories not only horrified children and demented geriatrics, it brought burly mountaineers and snooty college professors to their knees. Getting truly, terribly lost was a crushing experience. No one sought it. Neighbors assembled to save bewildered people, and they manufactured histories afterward to protect themselves from nature shock. They placed getting lost behind them.

It's unsurprising that Stephen King picked a child as the main character in a horror story about getting lost. Bewildered kids have served as navigational mascots throughout North American history. Like Paul Gasford, Trisha MacFarland landmarked an era. He was a smaller version of an independent yeoman farmer; she was a mini consumer plugged into a network. Like Trisha, Gasford listened attentively. He navigated a wilderness through memories of his parents' advice and admonitions. Trisha, however, heeded the wisdom of an inner relief pitcher. Raised by popular culture, she attached and detached quickly as stars and fads streamed through her fancy and her earbuds. Gasford was stuck by comparison. After he hiked out of the woods, he could look forward to years of herding cows and mowing hay under the supervision of his parents and older siblings. He tasted freedom and proved his self-sufficiency, then he assumed his spot in a web of family and community.

Trisha's world not only turned faster, it spun new connections as it shredded old bonds. A divorce presaged her getting lost in Maine. Her father had left the home, and her mother and brother fought each other instead of looking out for her. Trisha retreated to a fantasy world of game telecasts and pop music. She curated a bubble of sound to cope with the rapid changeover of relationships in her life.

Her Walkman symbolized the paradox of intimacy kept at a distance, while the search-and-rescue groups out looking for her exuded transient dedication. No modern organization better exemplified the fleetingness and intensity of super-industrialized human relationships than volunteer SAR units. The unpaid members of SAR teams came and went. Many groups lacked permanent headquarters, and their budgets fluctuated with the generosity of donors. Adjuncts to local, state, and federal law enforcement departments, SAR organizations represented a fragmented and amorphous organizational future Alvin Toffler predicted in *Future Shock*. It was a mistake, he argued, to think that industrial-age trends toward larger and longer-lasting bureaucracies would continue. Instead, the future belonged to "ad-hocracies," swiftly created and dismantled working groups and task forces.[7]

In 1970, Toffler warned millions of readers about a "serious malady" he described as "the dizzying disorientation brought on by the premature arrival of the future." Future shock resembled nature shock in that you wanted neither. Nature shock ambushed humans when they ventured beyond the confines of memory and community surveillance. The future hurtling at you resembled horrifying plummets into unknown space: "Caught in the turbulent flow of change, called upon to make significant, rapid-fire life decisions, [one] feels not simply intellectual bewilderment, but disorientation at the level of personal values. As the pace of change quickens, this confusion is tinged with self-doubt, anxiety and fear." The victims of nature and future shock felt betrayed. Instead of the familiar landscapes they expected, they popped up in strange and unfamiliar environments ill prepared to puzzle their way out. They stumbled outside the boundaries of their experience and imagination.[8]

"Modular" relationships prepared the ground for future shock. Toffler described a future where humans built shoddy and shallow relationships on purpose. In "super-industrialized" economies, "associates" moved frequently to find gigs, and their transience discouraged enduring bonds to places, things, or people. Relationships were brief and serial. Neighbors, coworkers, and family members flew in and out of lives. Movement frustrated the formation of shared spaces. Impersonal surveillance networks performed the labor of keeping track and watching out. If children or the elderly wandered into trouble, they could rely on neither kith nor kin to save them because long-term relations were nowhere to be found.[9]

SAR organizations attached to wealthy mountain towns and national parks endured due to the dedication of boards, the support of umbrella state and national organizations, and the leadership of core personnel who recruited and trained a rotating cast of volunteers. Unlike formal bureaucracies, informal organizations constantly had to re-create themselves, with uneven results. "Volunteers can be hit-or-miss," admitted Bree Loewen. "Volunteerism can sometimes entail a strong desire to do a job that will most likely be marginally useless, or at best insignificantly helpful." Loewen felt an intense connection to SAR. She loved her fellow volunteers and the people she helped extract from the wilderness. Those she saved, however, did not always reciprocate. While the families of the dead climbers Seattle Mountain Rescue recovered invariably gave money to the organization, Loewen reported that "almost no one we rescue[d] alive donates money." Once the volunteer strike force pulled them from trouble, the victims ended the relationship. The transition from relational space to impersonal networks meant that volunteers literally roped in people who ventured over the edge only to watch them sever the connection once they returned to safety.[10]

Super-industrialized societies nurtured expectations that human connections could be made, and service providers could be summoned almost anywhere, even in remote wilderness areas. In 2001, for example, a hiker in Washington's Olympic National Park called a ranger and asked to be rescued by helicopter. The man could not claim to be injured, frostbitten, starved, or half eaten by a grizzly bear; he was late for a business meeting in Seattle. He graciously offered to pay for the service if someone would come pick him up. (He did not get the ride.)[11]

The man assumed that a dial-up solution could be found for his geographic dilemma. If the federal government refused to bail him out, there were private options. Money could buy a wilderness concierge to keep track of you and your appointments. Outfits like Black Tomato serviced clients who fancied connected disconnection. How did we end up here? Mobile media was the alpha and the omega, the problem and the solution. Adventurers could ditch their phones, get lost, and find themselves in the care of invisible minders who tracked their every move with satellite technology.

The rise of impersonal communication networks increased spatial confusion. Today, mobile users construct fabulous mental spaces that they carry with them on the subway and the city streets, into the exurbs and the wilderness. These bubbles of content are not only groundbreaking but bond breaking. Prior societies enforced mental spaces. Authorities used their power to impose common grounds by policing the borders of shared spaces to keep track of subordinates while excluding alternative visions of space. Built to mobilize hierarchical power, the communication networks unintentionally opened pathways for new connections. Spaces democratized as more people imagined and created more of them. Trisha's headphones were the vanguard of a cultural free range, where users surfed networks and rezoned the boundaries of communities and self-expression.

Of course, these new spaces came with serious fine print. The networks that promoted global communities and grassroots mobilization also surveilled customers and deployed their findings to influence imaginations. Choices that seemed free at the time looked coerced in hindsight. Virtual spaces hid expensive infrastructures as well as the energy costs of data transmission and storage while exposing personal data. Imagined spaces created unequal geographies few consumers acknowledged or understood. Bespoke mental spaces distracted from food deserts, gerrymandered voting districts, gentrified neighborhoods, and segregated schools. Amused by playlists and kitten memes, mobile users had to be woken up to the harsh realities surrounding them. The alarms often sounded in the echo chambers of social media, venues where real humans and purchased bots vied for reality.

The onslaught of misinformation and the rapidity of news cycles triggered the urge to escape to a wilderness for a relaxing session of curated derangement. The desire for restorative bewilderment reflected the historic power of space making. It promised a boundless service economy where wealthy clients performed rituals of disconnection in search of personal growth. Accessing a false edge where service appeared to, but didn't, fall off enriched the powerful. As they had done for centuries, they found meaning in the reaches of space. Exploring the edge gave them a new purchase on the navigable home spaces they shared with the less fortunate. Getting lost made them feel at peace with their power.

The history of actual edges tells the story of power along with others. Instead of comfort, truly detached people forsook their rational selves when they crossed over the edges of cognitive geography. They ripped off their clothes, tossed their supplies, and barreled through the prickly underbrush. They collapsed in whimpering heaps and hallucinated demons, bears, and ballplayers. The lucky ones who were saved remained unhinged for days. The episodes of unraveling exposed the stitching that held geographic, social, and mental spaces together. Cutting free was not an amenity. Disconnection ruined rather than liberated people, and it still can and does.[12]

Instead of taking us away, nature shock should take us back, to the unfinished projects of centuries of North Americans who altered environments to match the spaces in their heads. Getting lost circles back to history, where nature, power, and imagination created navigable environments, and it teaches that despite our smartphones, our online friends, and our ADHD, we are not that different from the generations that wandered before us. Rather than looking to a wilderness or some other wireless nirvana for freedom, sanity, or ultimate answers, we should look to each other and to the history that brought us here, to this weird, awful, and unpredictable place, together.

# NOTES

## INTRODUCTION

1. Black Tomato, "Get Lost with Black Tomato," accessed May 28, 2018, https:// www.blacktomato.com/us/get-lost/.

2. Ibid.; Michaela Trimble, "Would You Pay a Travel Service to Get You Lost?" *Vogue,* September 27, 2017, https://www.vogue.com/article/get-lost-adventure -travel.

3. Dana Gresh, *Get Lost: A Ten Session DVD Curriculum* (Pure Freedom, 2014). See also Jeff Wise, "Getting Lost, and Loving it: The Prospect of Becoming Disoriented Can Be the Most Exciting Aspect of Travel," *Psychology Today,* November 1, 2010, https://www.psychologytoday.com/us/blog/extreme- fear/201011/getting-lost-and-loving-it; and Scott C. Hammond, *Lessons of the Lost: Finding Hope and Resilience in Work, Life, and the Wilderness* (Bloomington, IN: iUniverse, 2013). See also Rebecca Solnit, *A Field Guide for Getting Lost* (New York: Penguin, 2005), 22.

4. Many authors have grappled with the transition from early modern social hierar- chies or communalism to modern individualism with various degrees of celebra- tion or handwringing. See John Mack Faragher, *Rereading Frederick Jackson Turner: "The Significance of the Frontier in American History," and Other Essays* (New Haven: Yale University Press, 1999), 31–60; E. P. Thompson, *The Making of the English Working Class* (New York: Vintage, 1966); Dror Wahrman, *The Making of the Modern Self: Identity and Culture in Eighteenth-Century England* (New Haven: Yale University Press, 2004); Stephen Greenblatt, *Renaissance Self- Fashioning: From More to Shakespeare* (Chicago: Chicago University Press, 2005); Duncan Kelly, *The Propriety of Liberty: Persons, Passions and Judgement in Modern Political Thought* (Princeton: Princeton University Press, 2011); John O. Lyons, *The Invention of the Self: The Hinge of Consciousness in the Eighteenth Century*

(Carbondale: Southern Illinois University Press, 1978); Thomas C. Heller, Morton Sosna, and David E. Wellbery, eds., *Reconstructing Individualism: Autonomy, Individuality, and the Self in Western Thought* (Stanford: Stanford University Press, 1986); Daniel Walker Howe, *Making the American Self* (1997; repr., New York: Oxford University Press, 2009); Susan J. Matt, *Homesickness: An American History* (New York: Oxford University Press, 2011); Larry Siedentop, *Inventing the Individual: The Origins of Western Liberalism* (Cambridge, MA: Harvard University Press, 2014); Urlich Beck and Elisabeth Beck-Gernsheim, *Individualization: Institutionalized Individualism and Its Social and Political Consequences* (London: Sage, 2002); David Reisman, *The Lonely Crowd: A Study of American Character*, rev. ed. (New Haven: Yale Note Bene, 2001); Robert D. Putnam, *Bowling: Alone: The Collapse and Revival of American Community* (New York: Touchstone, 2001); Brad Gregory, *The Unintended Reformation: How a Religious Revolution Secularized Society* (Cambridge, MA: Harvard University Press, 2012).

5. Barbara Tversky, "How to Get around by Mind and Body: Spatial Thought, Spatial Action," in *Evolution, Rationality, and Cognition: A Cognitive Science for the Twenty-First Century*, ed. Antonio Zilhao (New York: Routledge, 2005), 136. For animal navigation, see Bernd Heinrich, *The Homing Instinct: Meaning and Mystery in Animal Migration* (Boston: Mariner, 2014); and James L. Gould, *Nature's Compass: The Mystery of Animal Navigation* (Princeton: Princeton University Press, 2012).

6. For getting lost, see Paul A. Dudchenko, *Why People Get Lost: The Psychology and Neuroscience of Spatial Cognition* (Oxford: Oxford Scholarship Online, 2010); Collin Ellard, *You Are Here: Why We Can Find Our Way to the Moon but Get Lost in the Mall* (New York: Doubleday, 2010); Robert J. Koester, *Lost Person Behavior: A Search and Rescue Guide on Where to Look—Land, Air, and Water* (Charlottesville, VA: dbs Productions, 2008); Barbara Tversky, "Distortions in Memory for Maps," *Cognitive Psychology* 13 (1981): 407–33; William Syrotuck, *Analysis of Lost Person Behavior: An Aid to Search Planning* (Mechanicsburg, PA: Barkleigh Productions, 1976).

7. *Nature shock* is a play on *woods shock*, a term that has been around for over a century. The extreme crackups I look at, however, occurred in forests and other landscapes, such as prairies, plains, and swamps, necessitating a more expansive phrase. For woods shock, see Kenneth Hill, "The Psychology of the Lost," in, *Lost Person Behavior* (Ottawa: National SAR Secretariat, 1998), 12; John Edward Huth, *The Lost Art of Finding Our Way* (Cambridge, MA: Harvard University Press, 2013), 31–32; Laurence Gonzales, *Deep Survival: Who Lives, Who Dies, and Why* (New York: Norton, 2003), 165–66. See also Charles Darwin, "Origin of Certain Instincts," *Nature*, April 3, 1873, 418; Darwin's quote also appears in Dudchenko, *Why People Get Lost*, 2.

8. Henry Forde, "Sense of Direction," *Nature*, April 17, 1873, 463–64.

9. Ibid., 463.

10. Roderick Nash, *Wilderness and the American Mind*, 5th ed. (New Haven: Yale University Press, 2014); Michael Lewis, ed., *American Wilderness: A New History*

(New York: Oxford University Press, 2007); William Cronon, "The Trouble with Wilderness; or, Getting Back to the Wrong Nature," in *Uncommon Ground: Rethinking the Human Place in Nature,* ed. William Cronon (New York: Norton, 1995): 69–90; David Pogue Harrison, *Forests: The Shadow of Civilization* (Chicago: University of Chicago Press, 1992); Wilderness Act, Public Law 88-577 (16 U.S.C. 1131–36) 88th Cong., 2nd sess., September 3, 1964.

11. For hiking statistics, see Travis W. Heggie and Michael E. Amundson, "Dead Men Walking: Search and Rescue in US National Parks," *Wilderness & Environmental Medicine* 20, no. 3 (2009): 245.

12. For pedestrianism, see Silas Chamberlin, *On the Trail: A History of American Hiking* (New Haven: Yale University Press, 2016); Tim Ingold, *Being Alive: Essays on Movement, Knowledge, and Description* (New York: Routledge, 2011); Jo Lee Vergunst and Tim Ingold, eds., *Ways of Walking: Ethnography and the Practice on Foot* (New York: Routledge, 2008); Matthew Algeo, *Pedestrianism: When Watching People Walk Was America's Favorite Spectator Sport* (Chicago: Chicago Review, 2017); Geoff Nicholson, *The Lost Art of Walking: The History, Science, and Literature of Pedestrianism* (New York: Riverhead Books, 2009); Rebecca Solnit, *Wanderlust: A History of Walking* (New York: Penguin, 2000). On getting lost while hunting, see Syrotuck, *Analysis of Lost Person Behavior*; Kenneth A. Hill, "Spatial Competence of Elderly Hunters," *Environment and Behavior* 24, no. 6 (1992): 779–94. For the politics of guiding, see Annie Gilbert Coleman, "The Rise of the House of Leisure: Outdoor Guides, Practical Knowledge, and Industrialization," *Western Historical Quarterly* 42, no. 4 (2011): 436–57.

13. Excellent work is being done on the histories of the senses. Navigation, and thus disorientation, are multisensory. However, vision remains the sense under the most pressure while lost. The dominance of vision has everything to do with seeing's relationship with power. For a sampling of sensory history, see Jon T. Coleman, "Howls, Snarls, and Musket Shots: Saying 'This Is Mine' in Colonial New England," in *Colonial Mediascapes: Sensory Worlds of the Early Americas,* ed. Matt Cohen and Jeffrey Glover (Lincoln: University of Nebraska Press, 2014), 266–89; Sarah Keyes, " 'Like a Roaring Lion': The Overland Trail as a Sonic Conquest," *Journal of American History* 96, no. 1 (2009): 19–43; Mark M. Smith, *Sensing the Past: Seeing, Hearing, Smelling, Tasting, and Touching in History* (Berkeley: University of California Press, 2007); Richard Cullen Rath, *How Early America Sounded* (Ithaca: Cornell University Press, 2003). For vision and power, see Michel Foucault, *Discipline and Punish: The Birth of the Prison* (New York: Vintage, 1995); Dianne Harris and D. Fairchild Ruggles, "Landscape and Vision," in *Sites Unseen: Landscape and Vision,* ed. Dianne Harris and D. Fairchild Ruggles (Pittsburgh: University of Pittsburgh Press), 5–32; Dell Upton, "White and Black Landscapes in Eighteenth-Century Virginia," in *Material Life in America, 1600–1860,* ed. Robert St. George (Boston: Northeastern University Press, 1988), 357–69.

14. See Mark David Spence, *Dispossessing the Wilderness: Indian Removal and the Making of National Parks,* rev. ed. (New York: Oxford University Press, 2000); Karl Jacoby, *Crimes against Nature: Squatters, Poachers, Thieves, and the Hidden*

*History of American Conservation* (Berkeley: University of California Press, 2001); Alan Taylor, " 'Wasty Ways': Stories of American Settlement," *Environmental History* 3, no. 3 (1998): 291–310; Louis S. Warren, *Hunter's Game: Poachers and Conservationists in Twentieth-Century America* (New Haven: Yale University Press, 1997).

15. Aileen Fife, *Steam-Powered Knowledge: William Chambers and the Business of Publishing* (Chicago: University of Chicago Press, 2012); Cameron Blevins, "The Postal West: Spatial Integration and the American West, 1865–1902" (PhD diss., Stanford University, 2015).

16. For power and surveillance in landscapes, see Elizabeth Kryder-Reid, "Sites of Power and the Power of Sight: Vision in the California Mission Landscapes," in Harris and Ruggles, *Sites Unseen*, 181–212. For surveillance more generally, see Simone Browne, *Dark Matters: The Surveillance of Blackness* (Durham: Duke University Press, 2015); William G. Staples, *Everyday Surveillance: Vigilance and Visibility in Postmodern Life* (Lanham, MD: Rowman & Littlefield, 2000); Mike Davis, *City of Quartz: Excavating the Future of Los Angeles* (New York: Verso, 1990), 221–64.

17. For white male geographic power, see Owen J. Dwyer and John Paul Jones III, "White Socio-spatial Epistemology," *Social and Cultural Geography* 1, no. 2 (2000): 209–22.

18. For ocean navigation and human cognition, see Edwin Hutchins, *Cognition in the Wild* (Boston: MIT Press, 1995). For a frontier history rooted in water, see Andrew Lipman, *The Saltwater Frontier: Indians and the Contest for the American Coast* (New Haven: Yale University Press, 2015), 8–9.

19. Koester, *Lost Person Behavior*, 39–41.

20. For circling, see Jan L. Souman et al., "Walking Straight into Circles," *Current Biology* 19, no. 18 (2009): 1538–42. See also Edward K. Sadalla and Stephen G. Magel, "The Perception of Traversed Distance," *Environment and Behavior* 12, no. 1 (1980): 65–79.

21. See Richard White, *The Middle Ground: Indians, Empires, and Republics in the Great Lakes Region, 1650–1815* (Cambridge: Cambridge University Press, 1991); T. H. Breen, *The Marketplace of Revolution: How Consumer Politics Shaped American Independence* (New York: Oxford University Press, 2004); Pekka Hämäläinen, *The Comanche Empire* (New Haven: Yale University Press, 2009); and Pekka Hämäläinen, "Politics of Grass: European Expansion, Ecological Change, and Indigenous Power in the Southwest Borderlands," *William and Mary Quarterly* 67, no. 2 (2010): 173–208.

22. See Henri Lefebvre, *The Production of Space*, trans. D. Nicholson-Smith (Cambridge: Blackwell, 1991); Yi Fu Tuan, *Space and Place: The Perspective of Experience* (Minneapolis: University of Minnesota Press, 1977); James C. Scott, *Seeing Like a State: How Certain Schemes to Improve the Human Condition Have Failed* (New Haven: Yale University Press, 1998); Philip J. Ethington, "Placing the Past: 'Groundwork' for a Spatial Theory of History," *Rethinking History* 11, no. 4 (2007): 465–93; Richard White, "What Is Spatial History?" *Stanford Spatial History Lab*, February 2010, https://web.stanford.edu/group/spatialhistory/

cgi-bin/site/pub.php?id=29; Jo Guldi, "What Is the Spatial Turn?" *Spatial Humanities,* University of Virginia Library, accessed July 14, 2017, http://spatial .scholarslab.org/spatial-turn/; Barbara Tversky, "Distortions in Cognitive Maps," *Geoforum,* 23, no. 2 (1992): 131–38; J. B. Harley, *The New Nature of Maps: Essays in the History of Cartography* (Baltimore: Johns Hopkins University Press, 2002); Richard White, *Railroaded: The Transcontinentals and the Making of Modern America* (New York: Norton, 2011).

CHAPTER ONE. BRUTAL SYMMETRY

1. Gentleman of Elvas, *True Relation of the Hardships Suffered by the Governor Fernando de Soto and Certain Portuguese Gentlemen during the Discovery of the Province of Florida,* vol. 2, trans. and ed. James Alexander Robertson (Deland: Florida State Historical Society, 1933), in *The de Soto Chronicles: The Expedition of Hernando de Soto to North America in 1539–1543,* ed. Lawrence A. Clayton, Vernon James Knight Jr., and Edward C. Moore (Tuscaloosa: University of Alabama Press, 1993), 1:137.

2. See Andrés Reséndez, *A Land So Strange: The Epic Journey of Cabeza de Vaca* (New York: Basic, 2007); Tzvetan Todorov, *The Conquest of America: The Question of Other* (Norman: University of Oklahoma Press, 1999), 196–200.

3. Rolena Adorno and Patrick Charles Pautz, *Álvar Núñez Cabeza de Vaca: His Account, His Life, and the Expedition of Pánfilo de Narváez* (Lincoln: University of Nebraska Press, 1999), 19.

4. I adopt the term *Mississippian* with reservation. The inhabitants of the Southeast shared a set of beliefs and practices, not a regional, ethnic, or national identity. With the term, I am referring to a loose cultural affinity, a spatial mindset that recurred and varied in the chiefdoms (another vexing term) that defined the region's political territories and allegiances. The scholarship on the Mississippians is immense and contested. See Patricia Kay Galloway, ed., *The Southeastern Ceremonial Complex: Artifacts and Analysis* (Lincoln: University of Nebraska Press, 1989); Charles Hudson, *The Southeastern Indians* (Knoxville: University of Tennessee Press, 1976); John R. Swanton, *The Indians of the Southeastern United States* (Washington, DC: U.S. Government Printing Office, 1946). For the giant of Tazcaluza, see Charles Hudson, *Knights of Spain, Warriors of the Sun: Hernando de Soto and the South's Ancient Chiefdoms* (Athens: University of Georgia Press, 228). For a discussion of chiefdoms, see Timothy R. Pauketat, *Chiefdoms and Other Archeological Delusions* (Lanham, MD: Alta Mira, 2007); Robbie Ethridge and Sheri M. Shuck-Hall, eds., *Mapping the Mississippian Shatter Zone: The Colonial Indian Slave Trade and Regional Instability in the American South* (Lincoln: University of Nebraska Press, 2009), 3–10.

5. John R. Swanton, *Final Report of the United States De Soto Expedition Commission,* House Document no. 71, 76th Cong., 1st sess. (Washington, DC: U.S. Government Printing Office, 1939), reprinted in 1985 by Smithsonian Institution Press, with introduction by Jeffrey P. Brain (1).

6. See Robert S. Weddle, "Soto's Problem's of Orientation: Maps, Navigation, and Instruments in the Florida Expedition," in *The Hernando de Soto Expedition:*

*History, Historiography, and "Discovery" in the Southeast,* ed. Patricia Kay Galloway (Lincoln: University of Nebraska Press, 2006), 219–33.

7. For indigenous space, see Juliana Barr, "Geographies of Power: Mapping Indian Borders in the 'Borderlands' of the Early Southwest," *William and Mary Quarterly* 68, no. 1 (2011): 5–46.

8. For slavery in the Southeast, see Christina Snyder, *Slavery in Indian Country: The Changing Face of Captivity in Early America* (Cambridge, MA: Harvard University Press, 2010). For similarity as a basis for understanding Indian and European interactions, see Nancy Shoemaker, *A Strange Likeness: Becoming Red and White in Eighteenth-Century North America* (New York: Oxford University Press, 2004); and Daniel Richter, *Before the Revolution: America's Ancient Pasts* (Cambridge, MA: Harvard University Press, 2011), 11–37.

9. Archeologists argue each of these points: the origin and spread of Mississippian culture, the prevalence of centralized or decentralized settlement patterns and social structures, even the very existence of Mississippian culture. I am following in the tracks of the "historicists," scholars less interested in settling either/or questions and more interested in how Mississippian sites and regions changed over time and experienced dynamics of diffusion and hierarchy, settlement and migration. See John H. Blitz, "New Perspective in Mississippian Archaeology," *Journal of Archaeological Research* 18, no. 1 (2010): 1–39; Adam King, *Etowah: The Political History of a Chiefdom Capital* (Tuscaloosa: University of Alabama Press, 2003); Timothy R. Pauketat, *Ancient Cahokia and the Mississippians* (Cambridge: Cambridge University Press, 2004); James B. Stoltman, ed., *New Perspectives on Cahokia: Views from the Periphery* (Madison, WI: Prehistory, 1991).

10. For cycling, see David G. Anderson, "Chiefly Cycling and Large-Scale Abandonments as Viewed from the Savannah River Basin," in *Political Structure and Change in the Prehistoric Southeastern United States,* ed. John F. Scarry (Gainesville: University Press of Florida, 1996), 150–91.

11. For divisions, see Hudson, *Knights of Spain, Warriors of the Sun,* 3–11. For honor and gender in the Spanish borderlands, see Daniel S. Murphree, "Gendering the Borderlands: Conquistadores, Women, and Colonialism," *Sixteenth Century Journal* 43, no. 1 (2012): 47–69; Juliana Barr, *Peace Came in the Form of a Woman: Indians and Spaniards in the Texas Borderlands* (Chapel Hill: University of North Carolina Press, 2007), 12–3, 181–88; Scott K. Taylor, "Women, Honor, and Violence in a Castilian Town, 1600–1650," *Sixteenth Century Journal* 35, no. 4 (2004): 1079–97; Ramón A. Gutiérrez, *When Jesus Came, the Corn Mothers Went Away: Marriage, Sexuality, and Power in New Mexico, 1500–1846* (Stanford: Stanford University Press, 1991), 209–15; J. G. Peristiany, ed., *Honour and Shame: The Values of Mediterranean Society* (London: Weidenfeld & Nicolson, 1966).

12. For prospect and refuges, see Jay Appleton, *The Experience of Landscape* (London: John Wiley & Son, 1986); Collin Ellard, *You Are Here: Why We Can Find Our way to the Moon but Get Lost in the Mall* (New York: Doubleday, 2010), 144; for ocean

navigation, see John Edward Huth, *The Lost Art of Finding Our Way* (Cambridge, MA: Harvard University Press, 2013); Elvas, *True Relation*, 57.

13. Elvas, *True Relation*, 58.

14. Garcilaso de la Vega, *La Florida*, trans. Charmion Shelby, in Clayton, Knight, and Moore, *The de Soto Chronicles*, 2:113.

15. See Reséndez, *A Land So Strange*; the most extensive source on Ortiz is Garcilaso, *La Florida*, 100–112.

16. For the Mississippian cosmos, see Richard F. Townsend, Robert V. Sharp, and Garrick Alan Bailey, eds., *Hero, Hawk, and Open Hand: American Indian Art and the Ancient Midwest and South* (New Haven: Yale University Press, 2004); Cameron B. Wesson, "Mississippian Sacred Landscapes: The View from Alabama," in *Mississippian Towns and Sacred Spaces: Searching for an Architectural Grammar*, ed. R. Barry Lewis and Charles Stout (Tuscaloosa: University of Alabama Press, 1998), 93–122; Charles Hudson, *Conversations with the High Priest of Coosa* (Chapel Hill: University of North Carolina Press, 2003); Hudson, *The Southeastern Indians*, 120–83.

17. For an interpretation of Ortiz's ordeal as enslavement, see Snyder, *Slavery in Indian Country*, 35–45. For slavery as a form of social death, see Orlando Patterson, *Slavery and Social Death: A Comparative Study* (Cambridge, MA: Harvard University Press, 1982). For the Florida chiefdoms, see Jerald T. Milanich, *Florida's Indians: From Ancient Times to the Present* (Gainesville: University Press of Florida, 1998), 102–11; John Worth, *The Timucuan Chiefdoms of Spanish Florida*, vol. 1 (Gainesville: University Press of Florida, 1998).

18. For plazas, see R. Barry Lewis, Charles Stout, and Cameron B. Wesson, "The Design of Mississippian Towns," in Lewis and Stout, *Mississippian Towns and Sacred Spaces*, 11–16.

19. Garcilaso, *La Florida*, 105.

20. For the Uktena and Water Cougar, see Hudson, *The Southeastern Indians*, 141–44.

21. Garcilaso called the animal a lion in *La Florida*, 105; Elvas likened it to a wolf in *True Relation*, 61.

22. Garcilaso, *La Florida*, 105.

23. Luys Hernández de Biedma, *Relation of the Island of Florida*, trans. John E. Worth, in Clayton, Knight, and Moore, *The de Soto Chronicles*, 1:225.

24. Elvas, *True Relation*, 62.

25. Biedma, *Relation of the Island of Florida*, 225.

26. Elvas, *True Relation*, 47.

27. For the reading of and rationale behind the "Requerimiento," see Patricia Seed, *Ceremonies of Possession in Europe's Conquest of the New World, 1492–1640* (Cambridge: Cambridge University Press, 1995), 69–99. As Seed notes, officials drafted many requerimientos. I quote from the version she uses. See also Lewis Hanke, *History of Latin America* (Boston: Little, Brown, 1973), 1:93–5.

28. Elvas, *True Relation*, 76.
29. Seed, *Ceremonies of Possession* 69; Elvas, *True Relation*, 68.
30. Elvas, *True Relation*, 70.
31. Biedma, *Relation of the Island of Florida*, 225.
32. Elvas, *True Relation*, 65.
33. Biedma, *Relation of the Island of Florida*, 228–30. For assessments of the narratives' strengths and flaws as well as their intertextuality, see Ida Altman, "An Official's Report: The Hernandez de Biedma Account," Patricia Galloway, "The Incestuous Soto Narratives," Martin Malcom Elbl and Ivana Elbl, "The Gentleman of Elvas and His Publisher," Lee Dowling, "*La Florida del Inca*: Garcilaso's Literary Sources," and David Henige, " 'So Unbelievable It Has to be True': Inca Garcilaso in Two Worlds," all in Galloway, *The Hernando de Soto Expedition*, 3–180.
34. Elvas, *True Relation*, 74.
35. Ibid., 80.
36. Rodrigo Rangel, *Account of the Northern Conquest and Discovery of Hernando de Soto*, trans. John E. Worth, in Clayton, Knight, and Moore, *The de Soto Chronicles*, 1:273.
37. Garcilaso, *La Florida*, 248.
38. For Mississippian exchange networks, especially around Apalachee, see Claudine Payne and John F. Scarry, "Town Structure at the Edge of the Mississippian World," in Lewis and Stout, *Mississippian Towns and Sacred Spaces*, 47.
39. Elvas, *True Relation*, 74.
40. Ibid., 80.
41. James Mooney, *James Mooney's History, Myths, and Sacred Formulas of the Cherokees* (Ashville, NC: Historical Images, 1992), 333.
42. Hudson, *The Southeastern Indians*, 171.
43. Elvas, *True Relation*, 80; Biedma, *Relation of the Island of Florida*, 230.
44. Biedma, *Relations of the Island of Florida*, 230.
45. Ibid., 231, 233, 235.
46. Ibid., 236; Garcilaso, *La Florida*, 358.
47. Biedma, *Relation of the Island of Florida*, 236–37; Elvas, *True Relation*, 108.
48. Rangel, *Account of the Northern Conquest and Discovery*, 1:296.
49. Garcilaso, *La Florida*, 385.
50. Elvas, *True Relation*, 87, 96; Rangel, *Account of the Northern Conquest and Discovery*, 1:285.
51. Elvas, *True Relation*, 140–41.
52. Ibid., 137.
53. Biedma, *Relation of the Island of Florida*, 243.
54. Rangel, *Account of the Northern Conquest and Discovery*, 1:273, 289.
55. Cameron B. Wesson, "De Soto (probably) Never Slept Here: Archaeology, Memory, Myth, and Social Identity," *International Journal of Historical Archeology* 16, no. 2 (2012): 418–35.

CHAPTER TWO. HELPFUL WOODS AND VIOLENT WATERS

1. William Bradford, *Of Plymouth Plantation*, ed. Samuel Eliot Morison (New York: Knopf, 1952), 87. For the "patchwork" New England landscape, see William Cronon, *Changes in the Land: Indians, Colonists, and the Ecology of New England* (New York: Hill & Wang, 1983), 31.

2. William Wood, *New England's Prospect* (1634; repr., Boston: Prince Society, 1865), 76.

3. For early kidnappings and New England slavery, see Wendy Warren, *New England Bound: Slavery and Colonization in Early America* (New York: Liveright, 2016), 3–6.

4. Bradford, *Of Plymouth Plantation*, 62–63. For wilderness and Puritans, see John Canup, *Out of the Wilderness: The Emergence of American Identity in Colonial New England* (Middletown: Wesleyan University Press, 1990); Roderick Nash, *Wilderness and the American Mind*, 3rd ed. (New Haven: Yale University Press, 1982); Peter N. Carroll, *Puritanism and the Wilderness: The Intellectual Significance of the New England Frontier, 1629–1700* (New York: Columbia University Press, 1969); Perry Miller, *Errand into the Wilderness* (Cambridge, MA: Harvard University Press, 1956), 1–15; Alan Heimert, "Puritanism, the Wilderness, and the Frontier," *New England Quarterly* 26, no. 3 (1953): 361–82.

5. For population numbers, see Andrew Lipman, *The Saltwater Frontier: Indians and the Contest for the American Coast* (New Haven: Yale University Press, 2015), 25; for subsistence migrations and practices, see Cronon, *Changes in the Land*, 49–52; and Lipman, *The Saltwater Frontier*, 28–35. For Native American history in New England, see Lisa Brooks, *Our Beloved Kin: A New History of King Philip's War* (New Haven: Yale University Press, 2018); Neal Salisbury, *Manitou and Providence: Indians, Europeans, and the Making of New England, 1500–1643* (New York: Oxford University Press, 1982); David J. Silverman, *Faith and Boundaries: Colonists, Christianity, and Community among the Wampanoag Indians of Martha's Vineyard, 1600–1871* (Cambridge: Cambridge University Press, 2007); Jean M. O'Brien, *Dispossession by Degrees: Indian Land and Identity in Natick, Massachusetts, 1650–1790* (Lincoln: University of Nebraska Press, 2003); Ann Marie Plane, *Colonial Intimacies: Indian Marriage in Early New England* (Philadelphia: University of Pennsylvania Press, 2000).

6. Roger Williams, *A Key into the Language of America* (1643; repr., Bedford, MA: Applewood, 1936), 73.

7. For the berry hypothesis, see Cronon, *Changes in the Land*, 91. As was the case with the Mississippian chiefdoms, the complex politics of Native southern New England did not fit the analogy others used to describe their government. The term *monarchy* captures the impulse of some Algonquian leaders to consolidate power and keep it in their families. See Lipman, *The Saltwater Frontier*, 43–48.

8. For use rights, see Cronon, *Changes in the Land*, 58–59.

9. Williams, *A Key into the Language of America*, 73–74; for getting lost and promotion, see Wood, *New England's Prospect*, 80–81.

10. For the Indians' role in communication, see Katherine Grandjean, *American Passage: The Communications Frontier in Early New England* (Cambridge, MA: Harvard University Press, 2015). For livestock trouble, see Virginia Anderson, *Creatures of Empire: How Domestic Animals Transformed Early America* (New York: Oxford University Press, 2004).

11. For English population numbers, see Warren, *New England Bound*, 10; for a discussion of the decline of Native numbers, see Gloria L. Main, *Peoples of a Spacious Land: Families and Cultures in Colonial New England* (Cambridge, MA: Harvard University Press, 2001), 194; for the practice, legacy, and memory of Algonquian burning, see Timothy Dwight, *Travels in New England and New York* (New Haven: Timothy Dwight, 1821), 1:103; Stephen J. Pyne, *Fire in America: A Cultural History of Wildland and Rural Fire* (Seattle: University of Washington Press, 1982), 45–65.

12. For the Mississippian shatter zone, see Robbie Ethridge, *From Chicaza to Chickasaw: The European Invasion and the Transformation of the Mississippian World, 1540–1715* (Chapel Hill: University of North Carolina Press, 2013), 4. For exploration, see Richard Hakluyt, *Voyages and Discoveries: Principal Navigations, Voyages, Traffiques, and Discoveries of the English Nation* (New York: Penguin Classics, 1972); Peter C. Mancall, *Fatal Journey: The Final Expedition of Henry Hudson* (New York: Basic, 2010). For captivity, see Linda Colley, *Captives: The Story of Britain's Pursuit of Empire and How Its Soldiers and Civilians Were Held Captive by the Dream of Global Supremacy* (New York: Pantheon, 2003); and James Axtell, *The Invasion Within: The Contest of Cultures in Colonial North America* (New York: Oxford University Press, 1986).

13. For captivity and adoptions, see Brett Rushforth, *Bonds of Alliance: Indigenous and Atlantic Slaveries in New France* (Chapel Hill: Omohundro, 2012); Axtell, *The Invasion Within*. For the Hurons, see Pierre Esprit Radisson, *Voyages of Peter Esprit Radisson: Being an Account of his Travels and Experiences among the North American Indians, from 1652 to 1684* (Boston: Prince Society, 1885), 121.

14. For space as political project, see Henri Lefebvre, *The Production of Space* (New York: Wiley-Blackwell, 1992).

15. For the compact, see Bradford, *Of Plymouth Plantation*, 75–76; John Winthrop, "A Modell of Christian Charity," in *Collections of the Massachusetts Historical Society* (Boston: MHS, 1838), 31–48.

16. Bradford, *Of Plymouth Plantation*, 75; Winthrop, "A Modell of Christian Charity," 46–47.

17. Henry Martyn Dexter, ed., *Mourt's Relation; or, Journal of the Plantation at Plymouth* (Boston: John Kimball Wiggen, 1866), 148.

18. Ibid., 73–76.

19. For the musket episode, see ibid., 42–43; for the "positive, original, social compact," see John Quincy Adams, "Oration at Plymouth 1802," *Daily Republican*, December 22, 1802.

20. Dexter, *Mourt's Relation*, 40; Alexander Young, *Chronicles of the Pilgrim Fathers* (Boston: Charles C. Little & James Brown, 1841), 214.

21. For the 1623 division of land and various controversies involving Billington, see Bradford, *Of Plymouth Plantation*, 120, 147–58; *Governor Bradford's Letter Book* (Bedford, MA: Applewood Books, 2001), 13; for Elinor and Doane, see Nathaniel Shurtleff, ed., *Records of the Colony of New Plymouth in New England* (Boston: William White, 1855), 1:41–42.

22. I borrow the "Ponzi scheme" idea from Main, *Peoples of a Spacious Land*, 30.

23. Thomas Morton, *The New English Canaan of Thomas Morton* (Boston: Prince Society, 1883), 216. For another account of the murder in the woods, see William Hubbard, *A General History of New England* (Boston: Massachusetts Historical Society, 1815), 101,

24. W. L. Grant, *The Voyages of Samuel de Champlain, 1604–1618* (New York: Charles Scribner's Sons, 1907), 299–301.

25. Jeremy Belknap, *American Biography* (Boston: Isaiah Thomas & Ebenezer T. Andrews, 1794), 1:324–25.

26. Louis Hennepin, *A New Discovery of a Vast Country in America* (London: Henry Bonwiche, 1699), 1:231–32.

27. Ibid., 1:234.

28. Ibid.

29. For Ménard, see Nicolas Perrot, *Mémoire sur les moeurs, coustumes et relligion des sauvages de l'Amerique septentrionale* (Leipzig, Librairie A. Franck, 1864), 92; Chrysostom Verwyst, *Missionary Labors of Fathers Marquette, Menard and Allouez* (Milwaukee: Hoffman Bros., 1886), 174; Rev. Edward D. Neill, *The History of Houston County* (Minneapolis: Minnesota Historical Company, 1882), 3; Louise Phelps Kellogg, ed., *Early Narratives of the Northwest, 1634–1699* (New York: Scribner's, 1917), n25. For examples of a French hunter, an Indian slave child, and René-Robert Cavelier, Sieur de La Salle, getting lost at portages, see Kellogg, *Early Narratives*, 263, 347–48; Hennepin, *A New Discovery*, 83.

30. John M. Barry, *Roger Williams and the Creation of the American Soul: Church, State, and the Birth of Liberty* (New York: Viking, 2012); Edwin S. Gaustad, *Roger Williams* (Oxford: Oxford University Press, 2005); Edmund S. Morgan, *Roger Williams: The Church and the State* (New York: Norton, 1967).

31. Williams, *A Key into the Language of America*, 78, 70.

32. Ibid., 68–69, 71, 75, 74.

33. Wood, *New England's Prospect*, 80.

34. Benjamin Trumbull, *A Complete History of Connecticut* (New Haven: Maltby, Godsmith, & Samuel Wadsworth, 1818), 1:57.

35. Peggy Pascoe, *Relations of Rescue: The Search for Female Moral Authority in the American West, 1874–1939* (New York: Oxford University Press, 1993), 70. For adoption and enslavement, see Brett Rushforth, " 'A Little Flesh We Offer You': The Origins of Indian Slavery in New France," *William and Mary Quarterly* 60, no. 4 (2003): 777–808.

36. See J. H. Battle, ed., *History of Bucks County, Pennsylvania* (Philadelphia: A. Warner, 1887), 384.

37. John Winthrop, *Winthrop's Journal, "History of New England," 1630–1649* (New York: Scribner's, 1908), 1:142; Wood, *New England's Prospect,* 17, 80–81.

38. Wood, *New England's Prospect,* 81.

39. Winthrop, *Winthrop's Journal,* 1:68. This wigwam may have been the woman's menstrual hut. See also Lipman, *The Saltwater Frontier,* 115–16.

40. Winthrop, *Winthrop's Journal,* 1:64, 115; for more on Sagamores John and James, see Thomas Dudley, "Gov. Thomas Dudley's Letter to the Countess of Lincoln, March, 1631," *New Hampshire Historical Collections* 4 (1843): 226, https://digitalcommons.unl.edu.

41. Williams, *A Key into the Language of America,* 72, 172; Wood, *New England's Prospect,* 81.

42. Dudley, "Gov. Thomas Dudley's Letter," 244–45.

43. Wood, *New England's Prospect,* 7.

44. Ibid.

45. Winthrop, *Winthrop's Journal,* 1:111, 135; see also *Collections of the Rhode Island Historical Society* (Providence: Marshall, Brown, 1835), 3:19.

46. James D. Knowles, *Memoir of Roger Williams* (Boston: Lincoln, Edmands, 1834), 154–55; Williams, *A Key into the Language of America,* 69.

47. Knowles, *Memoir of Roger Williams,* 155–56.

48. Ibid., 157.

49. Winthrop, *Winthrop's Journal,* 2:29; see also Chandler Eastman Potter, *The History of Manchester, Formerly Derryfield, in New Hampshire* (Manchester: C. E. Potter, 1856), 109; John Josselyn, *Account of Two Voyages to New-England* (London: Giles Widdowes, 1674), 202–3.

50. Winthrop, *Winthrop's Journal,* 1:60.

51. Josselyn, *Account of Two Voyages to New-England,* 202–3.

52. Radisson, *Voyages,* 119.

53. Ibid.

54. Ibid., 121.

55. For Radisson, see Grace Lee Nute, *Caesars of the Wilderness: Médard Chouart, Sieur des Grosielliers and Pierre Esprit Radisson, 1618–1710* (1943; repr., St. Paul: Minnesota Historical Society, 1978), 39–57.

56. Radisson, *Voyages,* 62.

57. James Mooney, *James Mooney's History, Myths, and Sacred Formulas of the Cherokees* (Asheville, NC: Historical Images, 1992), 359.

58. John Gyles, *Memoirs of the Odd Adventures, and Strange Deliverances* (Boston: S. Kneeland & T. Green, 1736), 13–14.

59. For the regional rebellion the colonists called King Philip's War, see Brooks, *Our Beloved Kin;* Christine M. DeLucia, *Memory Lands: King Philip's War and the Place of Violence in the Northeast* (New Haven: Yale University Press, 2018); James D. Drake, *King Philip's War: Civil War in New England, 1675–1676* (Amherst: University of Massachusetts Press, 2000); Jill Lepore, *The Name of War: King Philip's War and the Origins of American Identity* (New York: Vintage, 1999).

60. Williams, *A Key into the Language of America*, 70.
61. Mary Rowlandson, *Sovereignty and Goodness of God* (Cambridge, MA: Samuel Green, 1682), 71.
62. Quotations from Isaiah 64:10 and Jeremiah 50:6, respectively.
63. Rowlandson, *Sovereignty and Goodness of God*, 33, 35.
64. Francis Higginson, *New England's Plantation* (London: Michael Sparke, 1630), 6, 11.
65. For Native survival and attempts to erase them from New England history, see Jean M. O'Brien, *Firsting and Lasting: Writing Indians out of Existence in New England* (Minneapolis: University of Minnesota Press, 2010); Lisa Brooks, *The Common Pot: The Recovery of Native Space in the Northeast* (Minneapolis: University of Minnesota Press, 2008).

CHAPTER THREE. CHILDREN OF THE REVOLUTION

1. *The True and Wonderful Story of Paul Gasford* (New York: Mahlon Day, 1826), 3. See also C. M. Woolsey, *History of the Town of Marlborough, Ulster County, New York* (Albany: J. B. Lyon, 1908), 388; J. Smyth Carter, *The Story of Dundas: Being a History of the County of Dundas from 1784 to 1904* (Iroquois, NY: St. Lawrence, 1905), 398. The family's name is spelled Glasford in both Woolsey and Carter.
2. I slip the Gasford/Glasford clan into an American context with reservations. They were actually a borderland family, living on the edges of Lake Ontario in Canada and the United States. The religious press turned young Paul into an archetype of American childhood when it converted his accident into instructional literature. For the history of American childhood, see Paula S. Fass, *The End of American Childhood: A History of Parenting from Life on the Frontier to the Managed Child* (Princeton: Princeton University Press, 2016); Steven Mintz, *Huck's Raft: A History of American Childhood* (Cambridge, MA: Harvard University Press, 2004).
3. *The True and Wonderful Story of Paul Gasford*, 13.
4. For the ingredients of getting lost, see Paul A. Dudchenko, "On Being Lost," in *Why People Get Lost: The Psychology and Neuroscience of Spatial Cognition* (Oxford: Oxford Scholarship Online, 2010), 5.
5. For love, see Andrew Cayton, *Love in the Time of Revolution: Transatlantic Literary Radicalism and Historical Change, 1793–1818* (Chapel Hill: University of North Carolina Press, 2013).
6. For the warning out of strangers, see Ruth Wallis Herndon, *Unwelcome Americans: Living on the Margin in Early New England* (Philadelphia: University of Pennsylvania Press, 2001); Cornelia H. Dayton and Sharon V. Salinger, "Was the Warning of Strangers Unique to Colonial New England?" in *Making Legal History: Essays in Honor of William E. Nelson*, ed. Daniel J. Hulsebosch and R. B. Bernstein (New York: NYU Press Scholarship Online, 2016), http://nyu.universitypressscholarship.com. For runaway ads, see David Waldstreicher, "Reading the Runaways: Self-Fashioning, Print Culture, and Confidence in Slavery in the Eighteenth-Century Mid-Atlantic," *William and Mary Quarterly* 56, no. 2 (1999): 243–72; Billy G. Smith and Richard Wojtowicz, *Blacks Who*

*Stole Themselves: Advertisements for Runaways in the "Pennsylvania Gazette,"*
*1728–1790* (Philadelphia: University of Pennsylvania Press, 1989).

7. Charles A. Bemis, *History of the Town of Marlborough: Cheshire County,*
*New Hampshire* (Boston, George H. Ellis, 1881), 304.

8. Ibid.

9. Laurel Thatcher Ulrich, *A Midwife's Tale: The Life of Martha Ballard, Based on Her*
*Diary, 1785–1812* (New York: Vintage, 1990), 9. For the spaciness of time, see
Phillip J. Ethington, "Placing the Past: 'Groundwork' for a Spatial Theory of
History," *Rethinking History* 11, no. 4 (2007): 465–93.

10. Ballard's diary can be word-searched at *Martha Ballard's Diary Online*, DoHistory
.org; see also Charles Elventon Nash, *The History of Augusta* (Augusta, ME:
Charles E. Nash, 1904), 292, 339, 343.

11. For Dismal Swamp enslaved, Maroon, and free persons of color communities,
see Marcus P. Nevius, *City of Refuge: Slavery and Petit Marronage in the Great*
*Dismal Swamp, 1763–1856* (Athens: University of Georgia Press, 2019); Sylviane
A. Diouf, *Slavery's Exiles: The Story of the American Maroons* (New York: NYU
Press, 2014), 209–29; Daniel O. Sayers, *A Desolate Place for a Defiant People:*
*The Archeology of Maroons, Indigenous Americans, and Enslaved Laborers in the*
*Great Dismal Swamp* (Gainesville: University Press of Florida for the Society of
Historical Archeology, 2014), 84–113; Ted Maris-Wolf, "Hidden in Plain Sight:
Maroon Life and Labor in Virginia's Great Dismal Swamp," *Slavery and*
*Abolition* 34, no. 3 (2013): 446–64; Warren E. Milteer Jr., "Life in a Great Dismal
Swamp Community: Free People of Color in Pre–Civil War Gates County,
North Carolina," *North Carolina Historical Review* 91, no. 2 (2014): 144–70. For
elderly slaves sent into the woods, see Moses Grandy, *A Narrative of the Life of*
*Moses Grandy: Formerly a Slave in the United States of America* (Boston: Oliver
Johnson, 1844), 32. For a digital exploration of the Great Dismal Swamp as
refuge, see Christy Hyman, *The Oak of Jerusalem: Flight, Refuge, and*
*Reconnaissance in the Great Dismal Swamp Region,* accessed August 10, 2018,
https://findauut.com/blackhistory-morethanamonth/15020/oak-jerusalem/.

12. For the shingles, see David Hunter Strother, "The Dismal Swamp," *Harper's*
*Monthly,* September 1856, 451.

13. Sayer, *A Desolate Place for a Defiant People,* 9–10.

14. See Charles Royster, *The Fabulous History of the Great Dismal Swamp Company: A*
*Story of George Washington's Times* (New York: Vintage, 2000); Bland Simpson,
*The Great Dismal: A Carolinian's Swamp Memoir* (Chapel Hill: University of
North Carolina Press, 1990).

15. John Spencer Bassett, ed., *The Writings of "Colonel William Byrd"* (New York:
Doubleday, 1901), 44. For southerners' lax hog surveillance, see Virginia
Anderson, *Creatures of Empire: How Domestic Animals Transformed Early America*
(Oxford: Oxford University Press, 2004), 107–40.

16. Bassett, *The Writings of "Colonel William Byrd,"* 46.

17. Ibid., 49.

18. See John Ferdinand D. Smyth, *A Tour of the United States* (London: G. Robinson,
1784), 2:100–102.

19. Though he heard that Maroons had raised families in the swamp in the past, Frederick Law Olmsted thought that era had passed by 1856. See Frederick Law Olmsted, *A Journey in the Seaboard Slave States, with Remarks on Their Economy* (New York: Mason Brothers, 1861), 159–60. For the visuality of slaveholding power and hidden landscapes of the enslaved, see Walter Johnson, *River of Dark Dreams: Slavery and Empire in the Cotton Kingdom* (Cambridge, MA: Belknap, 2013), 232. For the theory of landscapes of trauma and resistance during and after slavery, see Catherine McKittrick, *Demonic Grounds: Black Women and the Cartographies of Struggle* (Minneapolis: University of Minnesota Press, 2006).

20. *State Gazette of North Carolina* (Edenton), May 5, 1793; North Carolina Runaway Slave Advertisements Digital Collection, accessed October 23, 2019, http://libcdm1.uncg.edu/cdm/singleitem/collection/RAS/id/1121/rec/3.

21. *Virginia Gazette* (Williamsburg), October 6, 1768; *The Geography of Slavery in Virginia*, accessed June 16, 2018, http://www2.vcdh.virginia.edu/gos/index.html; *Herald of Freedom* (Edenton, NC), March 27, 1799; North Carolina Runaway Slave Advertisements Digital Collection, accessed June 18, 2018, http://libcdm1.uncg.edu/cdm/landingpage/collection/RAS.

22. *Wilmington (NC) Gazette*, June 13, 1799; North Carolina Runaway Slave Advertisements Digital Collection; *Virginia Gazette* (Williamsburg), December 13, 1770; *The Geography of Slavery*. For a discussion of the Buchanan ad, see Tom Costa, "What Can We Learn from a Digital Database of Runaway Slave Advertisements?" *International Social Science Review* 76, nos. 1–2 (2001): 36–43.

23. "Lost or Stolen," *Wilmington (NC) Journal*, October 29, 1860.

24. Ibid.

25. Josiah Fassett, "A Brief, but True Account of a Lost Child," Glenn Falls, NY, 1826, in *Readex: Early American Imprints, Series 1*, 3094.

26. Ibid.

27. Ibid.

28. Ibid.

29. For premodern nocturnal habits, see A. Roger Ekirch, *At Day's Close: Night in Times Past* (New York: Norton, 2005)

30. Minnie Kendall Loether, *History of Ritchie County* (Wheeling, WV: Wheeling News Litho, 1911), 165.

31. Henry Howe, *Historical Collections of Ohio* (Cincinnati: C. J. Krehbiel, 1902), 2:850–51.

32. John Milton Whiton, *Sketches of the History of New-Hampshire, from Its Settlement in 1623, to 1833* (Concord, NH: Marsh, Capen & Lyon, 1834), 161.

33. Henry C. Bradsby, *History of Bradford County, Pennsylvania* (Chicago: S. B. Nelson, 1891), 467.

34. Samuel Whaley, *History of the Township of Mount Pleasant, Wayne County, Pennsylvania* (New York: M. W. Dodd, 1856), 47.

35. Paul Maclean, *History of Carroll County, Iowa* (Chicago: S. J. Clarke), 1:92.

36. Andrew Jackson Sowell, *Early Settlers and Indian Fighters of Southwest Texas* (Austin: Ben C. Jones, 1900), 411; *History of Emmet County and Dickinson County,*

*Iowa* (Chicago: Pioneer, 1917), 1:191; Henry Howe, *History of Delaware County* (Cincinnati: C. J. Krehbiel, 1902), 2:602.

37. Sowell, *Early Settlers*, 411.

38. For Howe, see Mary Sayre Haverstock, Jeanette Mahony Vance, and Brian L. Meggitt, eds., *Artists in Ohio, 1787–1900: A Biographical Dictionary* (Kent: Kent State University Press, 2000), 431–32; Joseph P. Smith, "Henry Howe, the Historian," *Ohio Archaeological and Historical Publications* (Columbus: John L. Trauger, 1895), 4:311–37.

39. Howe, *Historical Collections of Ohio*, 132–33, 850, 723.

40. Ibid., 850.

41. For time expressed through place, see Ethington, "Placing the Past"; *History of Genesee County, Michigan: Its Prominent Men and Pioneers* (Philadelphia: Everts & Abbott, 1879), 203–4.

42. A. J. Coolidge and J. B. Mansfield, *History and Description of New England: New Hampshire* (Boston: Austin J. Coolidge, 1860) 544; *Collections of the Massachusetts Historical Society* (Boston: Historical Society, 1809), 10:84.

43. Reuben G. Thwaites, ed., *Collections of the State Historical Society of Wisconsin* (Madison, WI: Democrat, 1888), 11:430.

44. Kate M. Scott, ed., *History of Jefferson County, Pennsylvania* (Syracuse, NY: D. Mason, 1888), 32.

45. Ibid., 45.

46. Ibid., 34–35.

47. Walter Harriman, *History of Warner, New Hampshire* (Concord, NH: Republican, 1879), 542.

48. Ibid., 542.

49. Hiram Barrus, *History of the Town of Goshen, Hampshire County, Massachusetts* (Boston: By Author, 1881), 114.

50. *The History of Wyoming County, NY* (New York: F. W. Beers, 1880), 227.

51. *History of Cattaraugus, County, New York* (Philadelphia: L. H. Everts, 1879), 359.

52. *History of Noble County, Ohio* (Chicago: L. H. Watkins, 1887), 421.

53. L. F. Parker, *History of Poweshiek County, Iowa* (Chicago: S. J. Clarke, 1911), 1:93.

54. S. P. Bates, *History of Franklin County, Pennsylvania* (Chicago: Warner, Beers, 1887), 510.

55. Ibid.

56. Charles Ball, *Fifty Years in Chains; or, The Life of an American Slave* (New York: H. Dayton, 1859), 252–53, 260.

57. Smyth, *A Tour of the United States*, 2:100.

CHAPTER FOUR. HOMING

1. For Richard, see Jefferson Glass, *Reshaw: The Life and Times of John Baptiste Richard* (Glendo, WY: High Plains, 2014).

2. Francis Parkman, *The Oregon Trail: Sketches of Prairie and Rocky Mountain Life* (Boston: Little, Brown, 1904), 151–52. See also Shirley Ann Wilson Moore, *Sweet*

*Freedom's Plains: African Americans on the Overland Trails, 1841–1869* (Norman: University of Oklahoma Press, 2016), 151–52.

3. Parkman, *The Oregon Trail*, 153.

4. Ibid., 152.

5. Ibid; Francis Parkman, *The Journals of Francis Parkman* (New York: Kraus Reprint, 1969), 2:388.

6. See James L. Gould and Carol Grant Gould, *Nature's Compass: The Mysteries of Animal Navigation* (Princeton: Princeton University Press, 2012), 123–27; James L. Gould, "Animal Navigation: A Wake-up Call for Homing," *Current Biology* 19, no. 8 (2009): R338–39; Bernd Heinrich, *The Homing Instinct: Meaning and Mystery in Animal Navigation* (New York: Mariner, 2015).

7. I define agrarians as household producers who harvest animal and vegetable crops for subsistence and the market and who also lean on resources harvested from actual and customary commons (wild animals and plants) to survive. For agrarianism, see Stephen Stoll, *Ramp Hollow: The Ordeal of Appalachia* (New York: Hill & Wang, 2017), xiv; for power and politics of home and agrarian households, see Richard White, *The Republic for Which It Stands: The United States during Reconstruction and the Gilded Age, 1865–1896* (New York: Oxford University Press, 2017), 136–71; Honor Sachs, *Home Rule: Manhood and National Expansion on the Eighteenth-Century Kentucky Frontier* (New Haven: Yale University Press, 2015). For the discourses of American gender, domesticity, and territorial conquest, see Amy Kaplan, *The Anarchy of Empire in the Making of U.S. Culture* (Cambridge, MA: Harvard University Press, 2005); Amy S. Greenburg, *Manifest Manhood and the Antebellum American Empire* (New York: Cambridge University Press, 2005); Clark Shire, *The Threshold of Manifest Destiny: Gender and National Expansion in Florida* (Philadelphia: University of Pennsylvania Press, 2016).

8. For coverture, see Nancy Cott, *Public Vows: A History of Marriage and the Nation*, rev. ed. (Cambridge, MA: Harvard University Press, 2002), 11.

9. Parkman, *The Oregon Trail*, 11, 70, 124.

10. See Gary Wills, *Inventing America: Jefferson's Declaration of Independence* (Boston: Houghton Mifflin, 1978), 240–46.

11. See Kenneth A. Hill, "Spatial Competence of Elderly Hunters," *Environment and Behavior* 24, no. 6 (1992): 779–94; getting lost while hunting continues to this day. See "Search Crews Find Man Lost During Squirrel Hunt," *South Bend Tribune*, August 21, 2018, 2.

12. For Lakota sovereignty and American colonialism, see Jeffrey Ostler, *The Plains Sioux and U.S. Colonialism from Lewis and Clark to Wounded Knee* (Cambridge: Cambridge University Press, 2004); and Richard White, "The Winning of the West: The Expansion of the Western Sioux in the Eighteenth and Nineteenth Centuries," *Journal of American History* 65, no. 2 (1978): 319–43.

13. See Parkman, *The Oregon Trail*, 113.

14. For Crockett, see Paul Andrew Hutton's introduction to David Crockett, *A Narrative of the Life of David Crockett of Tennessee* (Lincoln, NE: Bison Books,

1987); and Michael Wallis, *David Crockett: The Lion of the West* (New York: Norton, 2012).

15. David Crockett, *A Narrative of the Life of David Crockett* (Philadelphia: Carey & Hart, 1834), 62–63.

16. Ibid., 63–64.

17. Ibid., 68.

18. Ibid.

19. Ibid.

20. George W. Nichols, Pittsburgh, PA, to Samuel Nichols, Clarksburg, VA, March 27, 1849, HM 48250–98, Huntington Library, San Marino, CA.

21. George W. Nichols, Pittsburgh, PA, to Sarah Ann Nichols, Buffalo, NY, April 21, 1849, HM 48250–298, Huntington Library.

22. A. A. Graham, *History of Fairfield and Perry Counties, Ohio: Their Past and Present* (Chicago: W. H. Beers, 1883), 249.

23. Ibid., 250, 227, 103.

24. Leonard Fletcher Parker, *History of Poweshiek County, Iowa: A Record of Settlement, Organization, Progress, and Achievement* (Chicago: S. J. Clarke, 1911), 1:322.

25. Henry C. Bradsby, *History of Bradford County, Pennsylvania* (Chicago: S. B. Nelson, 1891), 455.

26. Thaddeus S. Gilliland, *History of Van Wert County, Ohio* (Chicago: Richmond & Arnold, 1906), 415–16, 225.

27. Elisha Keyes, "Early Days in Jefferson County," in *Collections of the State Historical Society of Wisconsin*, ed. Rueben Thwaites (Madison, WI: Democrat, 1888), 11:430; Andrew Jackson Sowell, *Early Settlers and Indian Fighters of Southwest Texas* (Austin: Ben C. Jones, 1900), 235.

28. See Pekka Hämäläinen, *The Comanche Empire* (New Haven: Yale University Press, 2009), 264–69.

29. Sowell, *Early Settlers*, 235.

30. Henry David Thoreau, *Walden*, ed. Jeffery S. Cramer (New Haven: Yale University Press, 2004), 165–66.

31. Ibid., 166.

32. Ibid., 306.

33. Ibid., 164–65.

34. Henry David Thoreau, *The Maine Woods* (Boston: Ticknor & Fields, 1864), 63.

35. Ibid., 64. For Thoreau and Mount Katahdin, see Laura Dassow Walls, *Henry David Thoreau: A Life* (New York: University of Chicago Press, 2018); John J. Kucich, "Lost in the Maine Woods: Henry David Thoreau, Joseph Nicolar, and the Penobscot World," *Concord Saunterer* 19, no. 20 (2011–12): 22–52; Ronald Wesley Hoag, "The Mark of the Wilderness: Thoreau's Contact with Ktaadn," *Texas Studies in Literature and Language* 24, no. 1 (1982): 23–46; John G. Blair and Augustus Trowbridge, "Thoreau on Katahdin," *American Quarterly* 12, no. 4 (1960): 508–17.

36. Thoreau, *Walden*, 166.

37. Benjamin Drew, *A North-side View of Slavery: The Refugee* (Boston: John P. Jewett, 1856) 198–224.

38. Ibid., 213, 214.

39. Ibid., 215.

40. Ibid.

41. Ibid., 219.

42. See Terry G. Jordan and Matti E. Kaups, *The American Backwoods Frontier: An Ethical and Ecological Interpretation* (Baltimore: Johns Hopkins University Press, 1988); Stoll, *Ramp Hollow*, 87–88.

43. For prairie landscapes, see Courtney L. Wiersema, "A Fruitful Plain: Fertility on the Tallgrass Prairie, 1810–1860," *Environmental History* 16, no. 4 (2011): 678–99; John Mack Faragher, *Sugar Creek: Life on the Illinois Prairie* (New Haven: Yale University Press, 1986), 61–75.

44. *The History of Jasper County, Iowa* (Chicago: Western Historical, 1878), 13.

45. Paul MaClean, *History of Carroll County, Iowa* (Chicago: S. J. Clarke, 1912), 1:6.

46. Roderick A. Smith, *A History of Dickinson County, Iowa* (Des Moines: Kenyon, 1902), 96; *The History of Henry County, Iowa* (Chicago: Western Historical, 1879), 387; *The History of Iowa County, Iowa* (Des Moines: Union Historical, 1881), 245; J. F. Clyde and H. A. Dwelle, eds., *History of Mitchell and Worth Counties, Iowa* (Chicago: S. J. Clarke, 1918), 229.

47. Luther A. Brewer and Barthinius L. Wick, *History of Linn County Iowa* (Chicago: Pioneer, 1911), 1:9.

48. Ibid., 1:11–12, 52.

49. Parker, *History of Poweshiek County, Iowa*, 1:163.

50. The Mad Libs quality of many Iowa county histories comes from the fact that the Chicago publishing firm S. J. Clarke published a number of them with the same format and sales model: employ a local historian to fill in the details to prompt the families mentioned in the text to purchase their history. S. J. Clarke brought out histories of Poweshiek, Butler, Muscatine, Louisa, Calhoun, Linn, Carroll, Davenport, Scott, Clinton, Crawford, Webster, Iowa, Hamilton, Marion, and Warren Counties, among others.

51. Irving H. Hart, *History of Butler County, Iowa: A Record of Settlement, Organization, Progress, and Achievement* (Chicago: S. J. Clarke, 1914), 1:309.

52. Ibid., 1:310.

53. Ibid.

54. *The History of Cedar County, Iowa* (Chicago: Western Historical, 1878), 320.

55. Henry Franklin Andrews, *History of Audubon County* (Indianapolis B. F. Bowen, 1915), 107–8.

56. Ibid., 100–102.

57. Ibid., 102.

58. Lewis Albert Harding, *History of Decatur County, Indiana* (Chicago: B. F. Bowen, 1915), 289; Henry L. Kiner, *History of Henry County, Illinois* (Chicago: Pioneer, 1910), 1:769.

59. Ibid.

60. Kate M. Scott, ed. *History of Jefferson County, Pennsylvania* (Syracuse, NY: D. Mason, 1888), 632.

61. Ibid.

62. Rollin Lynde Hartt, "The Iowans," *Atlantic Monthly*, August 1900, 197.

63. Hartt, quoted in MaClean, *History of Carroll County, Iowa*, 1:iv; Hartt, "The Iowans,"197; *The History of Jasper County, Iowa*, 14.

64. Scott uses the phrase "prominent men and pioneers" in the subtitle of *History of Jefferson County, Pennsylvania*.

65. For communications in this period, see James Lundberg, *Horace Greeley's American Conflict: Politics, Print, and the Nation, 1831–1872* (Baltimore: Johns Hopkins University Press, 2019); Heather A. Haveman, *Magazines and the Making of America: Modernization, Community, and Print Culture* (Princeton: Princeton University Press, 2015); Daniel Walker Howe, *What Hath God Wrought: The Transformation of America, 1815–1848* (New York: Oxford University Press, 2007); Trish Loughran, *The Republic of Print: Print Culture in the Age of U.S. Nation Building* (New York: Columbia University Press, 2009); M. M. Warner, *Warner's History of Dakota County, Nebraska* (Dakota City, NE: Lyons Mirror, 1893), 121.

66. *History of Pottawattamie County, Iowa* (Chicago: O. L. Baskin, 1883), 61.

67. J. F. Clyde and H. A. Dwelle, eds., *History of Mitchell and Worth Counties, Iowa* (Chicago: S. J. Clarke, 1918), 1:311.

68. *History of Mills County, Iowa* (Des Moines: State Historical Company, 1881), 620.

69. T. K. Tyson, Western NE, to Jay A. Barrett, Lincoln, NE, October 24, 1899, HM 68389, Huntington Library.

CHAPTER FIVE. DEAD-CERTAIN MENTAL COMPASS

1. Samuel Nichols, Glasgow, MO, to Sarah Ann Nichols, Buffalo, NY, May 6, 1849, HM 48250–98, Huntington Library, San Marino, CA.

2. Luther Cleaves, Sacramento, CA, to Sarah Ann Nichols, Buffalo, NY, October 25, 1850, HM 48250–98, Huntington Library.

3. C. H. Gratiol, Sacramento, CA, to Sarah Ann Nichols, Buffalo, NY, July 14, 1851, HM 48250–98, Huntington Library.

4. For overland travel, see Shirley Ann Wilson Moore, *Sweet Freedom's Plains: African Americans on the Overland Trails, 1841–1869* (Norman: University of Oklahoma Press, 2016); Keith Heyer Meldahl, *Hard Road West: History and Geology along the Gold Rush Trail* (Chicago: University of Chicago Press, 2007); John D. Unruh Jr., *The Plains Across: The Overland Emigrants and the Trans-Mississippi West, 1840–60* (Champaign: University of Illinois Press, 1993); John Mack Faragher, *Women and Men on the Overland Trail* (New Haven: Yale University Press, 1979). For communication, see David M. Henkin, *The Postal Age: The Emergence of Modern Communications in Nineteenth-Century America* (Chicago: University of Chicago Press, 2007); Cameron Blevins, "The Postal West: Spatial Integration and the American West, 1865–1902" (PhD diss., Stanford University, 2015).

5. "Interesting from the Straits of Magellan," *Boston Daily Atlas*, February 15, 1850, 2.

6. Mark Twain, *Roughing It* (New York: Signet Classic, 2008), 3.

7. Ibid., 21.

8. Ibid., 81.

9. For the global context and international character of the gold rush, see David Igler, *The Great Ocean: Pacific Worlds from Captain Cook to the Gold Rush* (New York: Oxford University Press, 2013); Edward Dallam Melillo, *Stranger on Familiar Soil: Rediscovering the Chile-California Connection* (New Haven: Yale University Press, 2015); Susan Lee Johnson, *Roaring Camp: The Social World of the California Gold Rush* (New York: Norton, 2000); Malcolm J. Rohrbough, *Rush to Gold: The French and the California Gold Rush, 1848–1854* (New Haven: Yale University Press, 2013). For American views, see Brian Roberts, *American Alchemy: The California Gold Rush and Middle-Class Culture* (Chapel Hill: University of North Carolina Press, 2000); Malcolm J. Rohrbough, *Days of Gold: The California Gold Rush and the American Nation* (Berkeley: University of California Press, 1998). For Native Americans in California, see Benjamin Madley, *An American Genocide: The United States and the California Indian Catastrophe, 1846–1873* (New Haven: Yale University Press, 2016); and Albert L. Hurtado, *Indian Survival on the California Frontier* (New Haven: Yale University Press, 1990).

10. For the federal government and the West, see Richard White, *"It's Your Misfortune and None of Mine Own": A New History of the American West* (Norman: University of Oklahoma Press, 1993), 58.

11. Di Alessandro Arseni, "The Panama Route, 1848–1851," *Postal Gazette* 1, no. 2 (2006): 10–11. For western exploration, see Aaron Sachs, *The Humboldt Current: Nineteenth-Century Exploration and the Roots of American Environmentalism* (New York: Norton, 2007); William H. Geotzmann, *Exploration and Empire: The Explorer and the Scientist in the Winning of the American West* (Austin, TX: State Historical Assn., 1993).

12. See Pekka Hämäläinen, *The Comanche Empire* (New Haven: Yale University Press, 2009); Elliott West, *The Contested Plains: Indians, Goldseekers, and the Rush to Colorado* (Lawrence: University of Kansas Press, 1998).

13. For the transition from family, trade, and cross-cultural interrelation to sharply drawn racial and commercial separation, see Anne F. Hyde, *Empires, Nations, and Families: A History of the North American West, 1800–1860* (Lincoln: University of Nebraska Press, 2011).

14. "Letter C. O. Faxon, editor, from F. A. Percy, 24 June 1849," *Clarksville (TN) Jeffersonian*, September 4, 1849, Bieber Collection, Photostatic Copies, Rhode Island to Texas, box 20, Huntington Library.

15. Ibid.

16. Ibid.

17. "East Tennessee and California Gold Mining Company," *Knoxville Register*, May 8, 1849.

18. "From the Californians," *Knoxville Register,* September 15, 1849.

19. Frederick Marryat, *A Diary in America* (Paris: A. & W. Galignani, 1839), 162.

20. James C. Riggin to Rebecca Riggin, Missouri, June 26, 1850, Riggin/Pettyjohn Family Papers, Huntington Library. For animals on the trail, see Diana L. Ahmad, *Success Depends on the Animals: Emigrants, Livestock, and Wild Animals on the Overland Trails, 1840–1869* (Reno: University of Nevada Press, 2016).

21. "From the Californians," *Knoxville Register,* September 22, 1849; "Letters from the California Adventurers, No. 11," *Knoxville Register,* October 31, 1849.

22. For lateral extensive landscapes, see Robert Macfarlane, *Landmarks* (New York: Penguin, 2015), 16.

23. H. M. T. Powell, *The Santa Fe Trail to California* (San Francisco: Book Club of California, 1921), 47

24. Ibid., 47–49.

25. Ibid., 48.

26. Ibid., 85, 161.

27. For examples of the genre, see Horace Greeley, *An Overland Journey from New York to San Francisco* (New York: C. M. Saxton, Barker, 1860); Sarah Royce, *A Frontier Lady: Recollections of the Gold Rush and Early California* (New Haven: Yale University Press, 1932); Andel J, McCall, *The Great California Trail in 1849: Wayside Note of an Argonaut* (Bath, NY: Steuben Courier, 1882). For a detailed look at one of the oft-mentioned landmarks, see Merrill J. Mattes, "Chimney Rock on the Oregon Trail," *Nebraska History* 36 (1955): 1–26. For place-names and stopping with and observing the Latter-Day Saints, see Unruh, *The Plains Across,* 20, 302–37.

28. Murphy, Virginia Reed, Independence Rock, to Mary Catherine Keyes, Edwardsville, IL, July 12, 1846, photostat, Huntington Library.

29. Joseph Goldsborough Bruff, "Journal of an Overland Journey to California by Way of Oregon and Lassen Trails," transcript by Elliott Cues, 1898, Huntington Library.

30. James C. Riggin, Sacramento, CA, to Rebecca Riggin, Andrew Country, MO, September 3, 1850, Riggin/Pettyjohn Family Papers, Huntington Library.

31. Ibid.

32. Rev. Jermain Wesley Loguen, *Rev. J. W. Loguen, as a Slave and as a Freeman* (Syracuse, NY: J. G. Truair, 1859), 307. For slavery in Indiana and the Ohio River border, see Matthew Salafia, *Slavery's Borderland: Freedom and Bondage along the Ohio River* (Philadelphia: University of Pennsylvania Press, 2013).

33. For regionalism, see Edward L. Ayers, Patricia Nelson Limerick, Stephen Nissenbaum, and Peter S. Onuf, eds., *All of the Map: Rethinking American Regions* (Baltimore: Johns Hopkins University Press, 1995). For Loguen's abolitionist activism in Rochester, where he became known as the "underground railroad king," see Eric Foner, *Gateway to Freedom: The Hidden History of the Underground Railroad* (New York: Norton, 2016), 179–80; and Angela F. Murphy, *The Jerry Rescue: The Fugitive Slave Law, Northern Rights, and the American Sectional Crisis* (New York: Oxford University Press, 2016). For overviews of the lead-up to the Civil War, see Daniel Walker Howe, *What Hath God Wrought: The Transformation*

*of America, 1815–1848* (New York: Oxford University Press, 2007); David M. Potter, *The Impending Crisis: America Before the Civil War, 1848–1861* (New York: Harper Perennial, 2011).

34. The number of attempts and short-term absences was greater. John Hope Franklin and Loren Schweninger estimate that over fifty thousand enslaved persons left without permission each year. See John Hope Franklin and Loren Schweninger, *Runaway Slaves: Rebels on the Plantation* (New York: Oxford University Press, 1999), 282.

35. See Donna Lee Dickerson, *Course of Tolerance: Freedom of the Press in Nineteenth-Century America* (New York: Greenwood, 1990), 257–80; Susan Wyly-Jones, "The 1835 Anti-abolition Meetings in the South: A New Look at the Controversy over the Abolition Postal Campaign," *Civil War Studies* 47, no. 4 (2001): 289–309; Jennifer Rose Mercieca, "The Culture of Honor: How Slaveholders Responded to the Abolitionist Male Crisis of 1835," *Rhetoric and Public Affairs* 10, no. 1 (2007): 51–76.

36. Loguen, *Rev. J. W. Loguen*, 309–10.

37. Ibid., 311.

38. Sarah Logue's letter and Jermain Loguen's response were reprinted in Loguen, *Rev. J. W. Loguen*, 452–53.

39. L. A. Chamerovzow, ed., *Slave Life in Georgia: A Narrative of the Life, Sufferings, and Escape of John Brown* (London: By Editor, 1855), 76–77.

40. Henry Bibb, *Narrative of the Life and Adventures of Henry Bibb, an American Slave* (New York: By Author, 1849), 123–25.

41. Charles Ball, *Slavery in the United States: A Narrative of the Life and Adventures of Charles Ball* (New York: John S. Taylor, 1837), 430–43.

42. Chamerovzow, *Slave Life in Georgia*, 155.

43. Charles Whittlesey, "Two Months in the Copper Region," *National Magazine and Industrial Record* 2 (February, 1846): 820.

44. Ibid., 829.

45. Ibid., 833–34.

46. Ibid., 837, 833–34.

47. Ibid., 833, 821.

48. Ibid., 845.

49. Ibid., 846.

50. Ibid., 840–41.

51. Charles Whittlesey, *Ancient Mining on the Shores of Lake Superior* (Washington, DC: Smithsonian Institution Press, 1863), 13.

52. John Jeremiah Sullivan, *Pulphead: Essays* (New York: FSG, 2011), 127.

53. For Frémont's career, see Anne F. Hyde's introduction to John C. Frémont, *Frémont's First Impressions: The Original Report of His Exploring Expeditions of 1842–1844* (Lincoln: University of Nebraska Press, 2012).

54. Donald Jackson and Mary Lee Spence, eds. *The Expeditions of John Charles Frémont* (Champaign: University of Illinois Press, 1973) 1:100; John Charles Frémont and Jessie Benton Frémont, *Memoirs of My Life* (Chicago: Belford, Clarke, 1887), 1:76.

55. Frémont, *Memoirs*, 1:42.

56. Frémont, *Frémont's First Impressions*, 292–94.

57. Ibid., 294; Charles Preuss, *Exploring with Frémont*, trans. and ed. Erwin G. and Elizabeth K. Gudde (Norman: University of Oklahoma Press, 1958), 116–18.

58. Preuss, *Exploring with Frémont*, 116, 118.

59. Henry Washburn and Nathaniel Langford were veterans of the Civil War and Montana Territory political appointees. Washburn served as surveyor general of Montana in 1870. Langford was a tax collector and bank examiner with a fondness for vigilante justice. He became the first superintendent of Yellowstone National Park in 1872. Gustavus Doane was the army officer in charge of the survey's military escort. See Paul Schullery, *Searching for Yellowstone: Ecology and Wonder in the Last Wilderness* (Helena: Montana Historical Society, 2004), 51–53; Aubrey L. Haines, *Yellowstone National Park: Its Exploration and Establishment* (Washington, DC: General Printing Office, 1974).

60. Though I cite Everts's *Scribner's Monthly* article as a principal source, I relied on excellent research and sources gathered in Lee H. Whittlesey, ed., *Lost in Yellowstone: Truman Everts's "Thirty-Seven Days of Peril"* (Salt Lake City: University of Utah Press, 1995).

61. Truman Everts, "Thirty-Seven Days of Peril," *Scribner's Monthly*, November 1871, 1–4; for the expedition's interactions with the Crows, see N. P. Langford, "The Wonders of Yellowstone," *Scribner's Monthly*, May 1871, 5.

62. Everts, "Thirty-Seven Days of Peril," 17, 19.

63. Ibid.

64. Theodore Gerrish, *Life in the World's Wonderland: A Graphic Description of the Great Northwest* (Biddeford, ME: Press of the Biddleford Journal, 1887), 114.

65. Everts, "Thirty-Seven Days of Peril," 24. The sources for the sanity debate include "Letter from Mr. Everts," *Helena Daily Herald*, October 22, 1870; "The Finding of Hon. T. C. Everts," *Helena Daily Herald*, October 26, 1870; Olin D. Wheeler, *The Yellowstone National Park* (St. Paul, MN: Northern Pacific Railroad, 1901), 16; F. V. Hayden, *12th Annual Report of the United States Geological Survey*, pt. 2 (Washington, DC: U.S. Government Printing Office, 1883), 466; Whittlesey, *Lost in Yellowstone*, 56.

66. Everts, "Thirty-Seven Days of Peril," 26.

67. Whittlesey, *Lost in Yellowstone*, xvi, xxii. The age difference between the couple was extreme. The average age of first marriage for American women in 1890, the first year the U.S. Census collected marital data, was twenty-two. See U.S. Census Bureau, "Median Age at First Marriage: 1890 to Present," figure MS-2, accessed September 23, 2018, https://www.census.gov/data/tables/time-series/demo/families/marital.html. For the gossamer network, see Blevins, "The Postal West," iv.

CHAPTER SIX. KEEP YOUR HEAD

1. G. Nelson Allen, New Philadelphia, OH, to Emma Merritt, Burlington, NJ, December 21, 1858, HM 74421–23, Huntington Library, San Marino, CA.

2. Elizabeth Allen, Prairie du Chien, WI, to Emma Merritt, Burlington, NJ, January 4, 1860; G. Nelson Allen, Prairie du Chien, WI, to Emma Merritt, Burlington, NJ, January 12, 1860, all in HM 74421–23, Huntington Library.

3. Elizabeth Allen, Fort Des Moines, IA, to Emma Merritt, Burlington, NJ, April 17, 1860, HM 74421–23, Huntington Library.

4. Elizabeth Allen, Camden, DE, to Emma Merritt, Burlington, NJ, January 1, 1887, HM 74421–23, Huntington Library.

5. Ibid.

6. See Terence Young, *Heading Out: A History of American Camping* (Ithaca: Cornell University Press, 2017); Susan Sessions Rugh, *Are We There Yet? The Golden Age of American Family Vacations* (Lawrence: University of Kansas Press, 2008); Cindy Aron, *Working at Play: A History of Vacations in the United States* (New York: Oxford University Press, 1999); Phoebe Kropp, "Wilderness Wives and Dishwashing Husbands: Comfort and the Domestic Arts of Camping in America, 1880–1910," *Journal of Social History* 43, no. 1 (2009): 5–30; Annie Gilbert Coleman, *Ski Style: Sport and Culture in the Rockies* (Lawrence: University of Kansas Press, 2004); Marguerite Shaffer, *See America First: Tourism and National Identity, 1880–1940* (Washington, DC: Smithsonian Institution Press, 2001); Peter J. Schmitt, *Back to Nature: The Arcadian Myth in Urban America* (Baltimore: Johns Hopkins University Press, 1990); Earl Pomeroy, *In Search of the Golden West: The Tourist in Western America*, 2nd ed. (Norman, OK: Bison, 2010).

7. See Andrew Denning, *Skiing into Modernity: A Cultural and Environmental History* (Berkeley: University of California Press, 2014); Aaron Sachs, *Arcadian America: Death and Life of an Environmental Tradition* (New Haven: Yale University Press, 2013); Elizabeth R. McKinsey, *Niagara Falls: Icon of the American Sublime* (Cambridge: Cambridge University Press, 1985); Karl Jacoby, *Crimes against Nature: Squatters, Poachers, Thieves, and the Hidden History of American Conservation* (Berkeley: University of California Press, 2014); Mark David Spence, *Dispossessing the Wilderness: Indian Removal and the Making of the National Parks* (New York: Oxford University Press, 2000).

8. Paul Sutter, *Driven Wild: How the Fight against Automobiles Launched the Modern Wilderness Movement* (Seattle: University of Washington Press, 2005); William Cronon, *Nature's Metropolis: Chicago and the Great West* (New York: Norton, 1992); Gregg Mitman, "Hay Fever Holiday: Health, Leisure, and Place in Gilded-Age America," *Bulletin of the History of Medicine* 77, no. 3 (2003): 600–635.

9. Jessup was a prolific author. His outdoor works included, among many others, *Roughing It Smoothly: How to Avoid Vacation Pitfalls* (New York: G. P. Putnam's Sons, 1923); *A Manual of Walking* (New York: E. P. Dutton, 1936); and *The Boy's Book of Canoeing: All about Canoe Handling, Paddling, Poling, Sailing, and Camping* (New York: E. P. Dutton, 1926).

10. Elon Jessup, "Getting Lost in the Woods," *Outlook*, July 5, 1922, 414, 416.

11. "Elon H. Jessup, 73, Writer on Sports," *New York Times*, February 27, 1958, 27; Elon Jessup, "Catch 'Em Young: An Interview with Dr. George L. Meylan,

Professor," *Outlook*, April 25, 1923, 133; Elon Jessup, "Going Walking," *Outlook*, November 8, 1922, 439.

12. Elon Jessup, "Close-to-Home Mountain Climbing," *Outlook*, August 30, 1922, 718; Jessup, "Getting Lost in the Woods," 416.

13. Henry Howe, *Historical Collections of Ohio* (Cincinnati: C. J. Krehbiel, 1902), 2:133.

14. Jessup, "Getting Lost in the Woods," 415.

15. Edward Frank Allen, *A Guide to the National Parks of America* (New York: R. McBride, 1918), 86, 90.

16. Joel Tyler Headley, *The Adirondack; or, Life in the Woods* (New York: Baker & Scribner, 1849) 20, xi, 20, iii.

17. Henry Perry Smith, *The Modern Babes in the Woods; or, Summering in the Wilderness* (Hartford, CT: Columbian, 1872), 141; Charles Hallock, *The Sportsman's Gazetteer and General Guide* (New York: Orange Judd, 1883), 86; George O. Shields, *Camping and Camp Outfits: A Manual of Instruction for Young and Old Sportsmen* (Chicago: Rand, McNally, 1890), 137; O. E. Meinzer, preface to John Stafford Brown, *The Salton Sea Region, California: A Geographic, Geologic, and Hydrologic Reconnaissance with a Guide to Watering Places* (Washington, DC: U. S. Government Printing Office, 1923), xi.

18. See Stephen Hancock, *The Romantic Sublime and Middle-Class Subjectivity in the Victorian Novel* (New York: Routledge, 2005).

19. William Henry Harrison Murray, *Adventures in the Wilderness; or, Camp-Life in the Adirondacks* (Boston: Fields, Osgood, 1870), 22–23.

20. Ibid.

21. Ibid., 33.

22. Shields, *Camping and Camp Outfits*, 7; Horace Kephart, *Camping and Woodcraft: A Handbook for Vacation Campers and Travelers in the Wilderness* (New York: Macmillan, 1919), 1:24.

23. Dr. Eugene L. Swan, *Harper's Camping and Scouting: An Outdoor Guide for American Boys*, ed. George Bird Grinnell (New York: Harper Brothers, 1911), 337; Edward Breck, *The Way of the Woods: A Manual for Sportsmen in the Northeastern United States and Canada* (New York: Putnam's, 1908), 171.

24. For the gendered discourse of individualism, see Joan Wallach Scott, *Only Paradoxes to Offer: French Feminists and the Rights of Man* (Cambridge, MA: Harvard University Press, 1996), 5; Manly Hardy, "On Not Getting Lost in the Woods," *Forest and Stream*, November 18, 1905, 406.

25. Ernest Thompson Seton, "Woodcraft: Playing 'Injun,' " *Windsor Magazine: An Illustrated Monthly for Men and Women*, June–November 1905, 718–20. For repeats of the teepee line, see Charles S. Moody, "Lost in the Woods," *Forest and Stream*, January 13, 1906, 50; "Teepee Lost," *Wisconsin Presbyterian*, November 1914, 16; *Scouting for Girls: Official Handbook of the Girl Scouts* (New York: Girl Scouts, 1922), 284.

26. For Indians and modernity, see Philip J. Deloria, *Indians in Unexpected Places* (Lawrence: University of Kansas Press, 2004).

27. Vance Randolph, "Lost in the Ozarks: 'A Feller Caint Git Lost in Three Mile o' Timber,' " *Forest and Stream*, June 1928, 340.

28. Ibid., 340–41.

29. Ibid.

30. Ibid., 372.

31. See Robert Cochran, *Vance Randolph: An Ozark Life* (Urbana: University of Illinois Press, 1985).

32. Brooks Blevins, preface to Vance Randolph, *The Ozarks: An American Survival of a Primitive Society*, ed. Robert Cochran (Little Rock: University of Arkansas Press, 2017), ix.

33. Marijke Gijwijt-Hofstra and Roy Porter, eds., *Cultures of Neurasthenia from Beard to the First World War* (Amsterdam: Rodopi, 2001), 101.

34. Kephart, *Camping and Woodcraft*, 19, 60.

35. Ibid., 20.

36. Jeanette Augustus Marks, *Vacation Camping for Girls* (New York: D. Appleton, 1913), 178, 221–22, 22.

37. Ibid., 214.

38. *The Official Handbook for Boys*, 4th ed. (New York: Doubleday, Page, 1913), 67–70.

39. Ibid., v, 67.

40. The *Transcript* story is quoted in Donn Fendler, *Lost on a Mountain in Maine*, as told to Joseph B. Egan (New York: Harper, 1978), 98.

41. Ibid., 16, 21, 10, 26, 76.

42. "Searchers Admit Hope Faint for Boy Lost in Mountains," *Los Angeles Times*, July 22, 1939, 16; "Bloodhound Trails Boy to 400-Foot Cliff; Searchers Stop for Night at Katahdin Slide," *New York Times*, July 20, 1939, 4; "Follow Progress of Search: Trail of Boy Scout Lost at Brink of Precipice," *Daily Boston Globe*, July 20, 1939, 10; "New Search on Katahdin: Expert Climbers Called to Join Hunt for Boy as Hope Dims," *New York Times*, July 22, 1939, 11.

43. "Youth Actually Finds Himself After 8 Days Lost in Wilds," *Christian Science Monitor*, July 26, 1939, 9.

44. Ralph T. Jones, "Silhouettes: Scouts Training Builds Manhood," *Atlanta Constitution*, August 3, 1939, 8.

45. "Don Fendler Thanks Town That Aided Hunt," *New York Times*, August 2, 1939, 23; "Rye to Greet Donn Fendler," *New York Times*, September 10, 1939, 2; "Honors Don Fendler: Maine Guides Group Makes Him a Member for His Exploit," *New York Times*, August 3, 1939, 4; "More Honors for Donn," *Christian Science Monitor*, July 31, 1939, 10; "Maine Honors Donn Fendler: Mt. Katahdin Boy Hero Is Guest of Governor," *Daily Boston Globe*, August 3, 1939, 11; "Don Fendler to Get Medal in White House," *Daily Boston Globe*, October 11, 1940, 12; "Maine Indian Tribe Adopts Donn Fendler," *Daily Boston Globe*, February 3, 1941, 4; "Donn Fendler Fish Game Ass'n Roundup Guest," *Daily Boston Globe*, February 1, 1941, 16; "5000 Catholic Boy Scouts at Cathedral Service; Christian Courage, Sermon Keynote," *Daily Boston Globe*, February 10, 1941, 16.

46. Robert Aull, "1939 Survival Story Still Resonates in Maine: A North Carolina Boy's Wilderness Scare Recalls Donn Fendler's Eight-Day Ordeal on Katahdin," *Portland (ME) Press Herald,* March 22, 2001, A1.

47. Joseph B. Egan, "Donn Fendler's Story Coming," *Daily Boston Globe,* November 2, 1939, 1.

48. Fendler, *Lost on a Mountain in Maine,* 59.

49. "Pamela Lost 8 Days, Same as Donn Fendler," *Daily Boston Globe,* October 7, 1941, 6; James Stack, "Climb Every Mountain? Yes, He'll Try," *Daily Boston Globe,* August 15, 1970, 3.

50. "2 Lost Children Are Found Dead," *New York Times,* February 1, 1984, B5; Dera Bush, "Find Lost Boy Dead in Ice-Cooler," *New York Amsterdam News,* December 14, 1963, 29; "Lost Boy, 3, Found Dead of Exposure," *Daily Boston Globe,* January 26, 1959, 13; "2 of 3 Tots Lost in Blizzard Found Dead, Other Unharmed," *Washington Post,* March 25, 1952, 1.

51. "The Southland: Searchers Find Lost Boy's Body," *Los Angeles Times,* May 4, 1951, 20; "Missing Boy Found Dead in River," *Chicago Tribune,* July 26, 1965, 1; Mark I. Pinsky, "Patience Was Key in Desert Search," *Los Angeles Times,* October 22, 1984, OCA4; Mark I. Pinsky, "Search Stopped; Girl Believed Kidnapped," *Los Angeles Times,* October 22, 1954, OCA1; Mark I. Pinsky, "For Parents, There Is No Quitting," *Los Angeles Times,* October 18, 1985, OC1; Nieson Himmel, "Laura Bradbury Search Ends with Evidence of Death," *Los Angeles Times,* December 15, 1990, OCB1.

52. Pinsky, "For Parents, There Is No Quitting."

53. Ibid.

54. Tony Reaves, "Donn Fendler, Once a Boy 'Lost on a Mountain in Maine,' Dies at 90," *Bangor Daily News,* October 11, 2016; John Holyoke, "Fendler Still a Hero to Many 68 Years Later," *Bangor Daily News,* June 7, 2007, C1.

55. Uncle Dudley, "He Found Himself," *Daily Boston Globe,* July 27, 1939, 14.

CHAPTER SEVEN. MALE PATTERN TRAIL LOSS

1. Edward Abbey, *Desert Solitaire: A Season in the Wilderness* (New York: Ballantine Books, 1971), 48. For Abbey and the memoir that made him famous, see Paul Bryant, "The Structure and Unity of *Desert Solitaire,*" *Western American Literature* 28, no. 1 (1993): 3–19; Patricia Nelson Limerick, *Desert Passages: Encounters with the American Deserts* (Albuquerque: University of New Mexico Press, 1985); David Copland Morris, "Celebration and Irony: The Polyphonic Voice of Edward Abbey's *Desert Solitaire,*" *Western American Literature* 28, no. 1 (1993): 21–32; Richard Shelton, "Creeping Up on *Desert Solitaire,*" in *Resist Much, Obey Little: Some Notes on Edward Abbey,* ed. James Hepworth and Gregory McNamee (Tucson: Harbinger House, 1985), 89–104.

2. Abbey, *Desert Solitaire,* 48

3. Ibid., 11, 293, 291.

4. Ibid, 262.

5. Ibid., 267, 271. For Abbey's mysticism or lack thereof, see John R. Knott, "Edward Abbey and the Romance of Wilderness," *Western American Literature* 30, no. 4 (Winter 1996): 331–51.

6. Ibid., 96; Edward Abbey, *One Life at a Time, Please* (New York: Macmillan, 1988), 79.

7. See Tara Kathleen Kelly, *The Hunter Elite: Manly Sport, Hunting Narratives, and American Conservation, 1880–1925* (Lawrence: University of Kansas Press, 2018); Mischa Honeck, *Our Frontier Is the World: The Boy Scouts in the Age of American Ascendancy* (Ithaca: Cornell University Press, 2018); Benjamin Rene Jordan, *Modern Manhood and the Boy Scouts of America: Citizenship, Race, and the Environment, 1910–1930* (Chapel Hill: University of North Carolina Press, 2016); Gail Bederman, *Manliness and Civilization: A Cultural History of Gender and Race in the United States, 1880–1917* (Chicago: University of Chicago Press, 1995).

8. Tom Lewis, *Divided Highways: Building the Interstate Highways, Transforming American Life* (Ithaca: Cornell University Press, 2013).

9. Ginger Strand, *Killer on the Road: Violence and the American Interstate* (Austin: University of Texas Press, 2012).

10. A. W. Bolle, "The Future of Outdoor Recreation and the Place of Outfitters and Guides in Montana" (transcript of speech given at the Annual Meeting of Outfitters and Guides, Billings, MT, December 9, 1967); "Bolle Wants to Lose Tourists in Montana," *Sunday Missoulian*, December 10, 1967.

11. "The Art of Getting Lost," *Washington Post*, January 17, 1913, 6.

12. Robert L. Duffus, "An Old Innocent Abroad: The Art of Getting Lost," *New York Times*, October 4, 1964, 19.

13. William Stockdale, "Pointers for Getting Lost," *New York Times*, April 21, 1963, 12.

14. Ibid.

15. David Madison, "How Get Lost Got Lost," *Missoula Independent*, February 2–February 9, 2017, 14; MercuryCSC, "Get Lost (in Montana) Engaged Users Up 194%," accessed December 13, 2017, http://www.mercurycsc.com/get-lost-in-montana.

16. Madison, "How Get Lost Got Lost," 17.

17. Advertisement, "All on a Montana Tractor. Lose Yourself. Find Yourself.," accessed December 20, 2017, http://magissues.farmprogress.com/MDS/MS04Apr07/mds036.pdf.

18. Matt Rocheleau, "These 6 Charts Show the Most Common Reasons People Need Rescues in National Parks," *Boston Globe*, November 16, 2016, www.bostonglobe.com; Matt Rocheleau, "This Can Be a Dangerous Season for Hikers in N.H.," *Boston Globe*, November 14, 2016, www.bostonglobe.com.

19. Rocheleau, "These 6 Charts," www.bostonglobe.com.

20. Robert Carr, "Woman Lost on Mountain, Too Cold to Eat: She Had to Keep Walking All Night—or Die," *Boston Globe*, October 25, 1959, 52.

21. Dial Torgeson, "Rescued Hiker Tells of Ordeal during 7 Days in Mountains, "*Los Angeles Times*, May 25, 1970, 1.

22. John Schroeder, "Searchers Find Woman Lost 20 Days in Canyon," *Arizona Republic*, August 21, 1975, 1A, 8A. See also Charles R. "Butch" Farabee Jr., *Death, Daring, and Disaster: Search and Rescue in the National Parks* (Lanham, MD: Taylor Trade, 2005), 317–18.

23. "Lost Hiker Fled Rescuers, Fearing Harm," *Los Angeles Times*, November 22, 1989, 2.

24. "Hiker Missing 9 Days Starts to Hallucinate," *Santa Cruz (CA) Sentinel*, June 16, 1997, 7.

25. Lauren Williams, "Community Shows Outpouring of Support," *Daily Pilot* (Costa Mesa, CA), April 4, 2013, www.latimes.com; Sean Emery and Tony Saavedra, "Rescued Hiker Charged with Drug Possession," *Orange County Register*, May 2, 2013, www.ocregister.com; James Ney and David McCormack, "Hallucinating Teenage Hiker Who Spent Five Days Lost in Californian Wilderness and Whose Rescue Cost $160,000 Charged with Meth Possession," *MailOnline*, May 2, 2013, Nexis Uni.

26. Ney and McCormack, "Hallucinating Teenage Hiker."

27. Jeremiah Dobruck, "Injured Rescue Worker Settles Lawsuit," *Los Angeles Times*, January 17, 2015, B4.

28. For Rocky Mountain Rescue, see Mark Scott-Nash, *Playing for Real: Stories from Rocky Mountain Rescue* (Golden: Colorado Mountain Club, 2007), 120; "ESAR History," accessed December 5, 2017, www.kcesar.org. For histories of carnage and carnage prevention in the recreational outdoors, see Dee Molenaar, *Mountains Don't Care, but We Do: An Early History of Mountain Rescue in the Pacific Northwest and the Founding of the Mountain Rescue Association* (Seattle: Mountaineer Books, 2009); Joseph R. Evans, *Death, Despair, and Second Chances in Rocky Mountain National Park* (Denver: Johnson Books, 2010); Michael Ghiglieri and Thomas Myers, *Over the Edge: Death in the Grand Canyon* (Flagstaff: Puma, 2001); Lee H. Whittlesey, *Death in Yellowstone: Accidents and Foolhardiness in the First National Park* (Boulder: Roberts Rinehart, 1995).

29. See Silas Chamberlin, *On the Trail: A History of American Hiking* (New Haven: Yale University Press, 2016).

30. See Joseph E. Taylor III, *Pilgrims of the Vertical: Yosemite Rock Climbers and the Nature of Risk* (Cambridge, MA: Harvard University Press, 2010), 145–63.

31. Dennis Kelley, "Let It Be Said," *Search and Rescue*, Winter–Spring 1982–83, 6.

32. Dennis Kelley, "Editorial," *Search and Rescue*, Fall 1973, 2.

33. Hal Foss, "National SAR School Graduation Speech," *Search and Rescue*, Fall 1974, 15; Lois Clark McCoy, "We Gotta Have Heart," *Search and Rescue*, Summer 1975, 2; Dennis E. Kelley, "A Visit with Peter J. Pitchess, Los Angeles County Sheriff," *Search and Rescue*, Spring 1975, 4–7.

34. Kelley, "A Visit with Peter J. Pritchess," 7.

35. George Sibley, "The Rescue People," *Search and Rescue*, Summer 1974, 19.

36. Ibid., 20, 19.

37. "Letters to the Editor," *Search and Rescue*, Fall 1974, 44.

38. George Sibley, "The Rescue People," *Mountain Gazette*, March 1974, 14–15, 20–21; Edward Abbey, "Where's Tonto?" *Mountain Gazette*, December 1974, 5–7.

39. Dennis E. Kelley, "Jon Wartes," *Search and Rescue*, Fall 1973, 12–14.
40. Ibid.
41. Scott-Nash, *Playing for Real*, 120.
42. Lois Clark McCoy, "Land Search Organization," *Search and Rescue*, Fall 1974, 29.
43. Lois Clark McCoy, "Man-Tracking," *Search and Rescue*, Spring 1975, 22.
44. Ibid; Kelley, "A Visit with Peter J. Pitchess," 7.
45. Lena F. Reed, "A Little Girl Is Lost," *Search and Rescue*, Fall 1973, 19.
46. Ibid., 18, 25.
47. James F. Clarity, "400 Searching for Boy Lost in Adirondacks," *New York Times*, July 22, 1971, 35.
48. Ibid.
49. Dennis E. Kelley, "Mountain Search and Rescue for the Lost Victim: The Victim," *Search and Rescue*, Winter 1973, 37; Dennis E. Kelley, "Mountain Search for the Lost Victim: Introduction," *Search and Rescue*, Fall 1973, 31. See also Dennis E. Kelley, *Mountain Search for the Lost Victim* (Montrose, CA: Dennis E. Kelley, 1973), 2, 13.
50. Advertisement, *Search and Rescue*, Summer 1979, 12.
51. Kelley, "Jon Wartes," 14. In *Mountain Search for the Lost Victim*, Dennis Kelley claimed that the "most common lost victim is the teenage boy" (2). Later investigations with larger data samples have raised the age but kept the gender.
52. Elena Sava et al., "Evaluating Lost Person Models," *Transactions in GIS* 20, no. 1 (2016): 39–40; see also Robert J. Koester, *Lost Person Behavior: A Search and Rescue Guide on Where to Look—for Land, Air, and Water* (Charlottesville, VA: DBS Productions, 2008).
53. Travis W. Heggie and Michael E. Amundson, "Dead Men Walking: Search and Rescue in US National Parks," *Wilderness & Environmental Medicine* 20, no. 3 (2009): 244–49.
54. Jared Doke, "Analysis of Search Incidents and Lost Person Behavior in Yosemite National Park" (MA thesis, University of Kansas, 2012), 43, iii; Robert J. Koester and C. R. Twardy, "Washington State Missing Person Behavior," May 18, 2006, sarbayes.org; Charles R. Tweedy, Robert Koester, and Rob Gatt, *Missing Person Behaviour: An Australian Study*, June 2006, http://sarbayes.org/wp-content/uploads/2012/07/natsar.pdf; Dave Perkins, Pete Roberts, and Ged Feeney, *The U.K. Missing Person Behaviour Study*, March 2011, http://www.searchresearch.org.uk; Ariel Blotkamp, Bret H. Meldrum, Wayde Morse, and Steven J. Hollenhorst, *Yosemite National Park Visitor Study Summer 2009*, Park Studies Unit Visitor Services Project, Report 215, April 2010, nps.gov.
55. Doke, "Analysis of Search Incidents," 43–44.
56. William G. Syrotuck, *Analysis of Lost Person Behavior: An Aid to Search Planning* (Mechanicsburg, PA: Barkleigh, 2000).
57. Amos Tversky and Derek J. Koehler, "Support Theory: A Nonextensional Representation of Subjective Probability," *Psychological Review* 101, no. 4 (1994): 547–67, 565; Kenneth A. Hill, "Cognition in the Woods: Biases in Probability

Judgements by Search and Rescue Planners," *Judgement and Decision Making* 7, no. 4 (2012): 488–98, 493.

58. Melvin Maddocks, "Vacation—The Art of Getting Lost," *Christian Science Monitor*, August 7, 1975, 16.

59. "In the Beginning," Rocky Mountain Rescue History Blog, accessed December 4, 2017, http://www.rockymountainrescue.org/history-blog/; Yosemite Search and Rescue 2017 Teams, accessed December 4, 2017, https://www .friendsofyosar.org/team; "TCSAR Volunteers," accessed December 4, 2017, http://www.tetoncountysar.org/; Emily Green, "Elite L.A. Search and Rescue Team Member Hopes to Inspire Other Women," *The California Report: KQED News*, September 29, 2017, https://ww2.kqed.org/news/2017/09/29/elite-l-a -search-and-rescue-team-member-hopes-to-inspire-other-women/. For the emotional labor of SAR, see Jennifer Lois, *Heroic Efforts: The Emotional Culture of Search and Rescue Volunteers* (New York: New York University Press, 2003).

60. Nancy LeMany, "Adventure on High," *Boston Globe*, April 6, 1980, C1.

61. Cheryl Stayed, *Wild: From Lost to Found on the Pacific Crest Trail* (New York: Knopf, 2012), 286.

62. "Oprah Talks to Cheryl Strayed about Walking Her Way to Peace and Forgiveness," Oprah.com, July 22, 2012, http://www.oprah.com/omagazine/ cheryl-strayed-interview-with-oprah-wild/2.

63. Ibid.

64. Ibid.

65. Bree Loewen, *Pickets and Dead Men: Seasons on Rainier* (Seattle: Mountaineers Books, 2009), 14.

66. Bree Loewen, *Found: A Life in Mountain Rescue* (Seattle: Mountaineers Books, 2017), 60, 187. For Abbey's domesticity, see David Gessner, *All the Wild That Remains: Edward Abbey, Wallace Stegner, and the American West* (New York: Norton, 2016), 231–32.

EPILOGUE

1. Stephen King, *The Girl Who Loved Tom Gordon* (New York: Pocket Books, 1999), 243.

2. William Cronon, "The Trouble with Wilderness; or, Getting Back to the Wrong Nature," in *Uncommon Ground: Rethinking the Human Place in Nature*, ed. William Cronon (New York: Norton, 1995): 69–90.

3. See Gerard Goggin, "Making Voice Portable: The Early History of the Cell Phone," in *Foundations of Mobile Media Studies: Essential Texts on the Formation of a Field*, ed. Jason Farman (New York: Routledge, 2017), 1–20.

4. Leah Eichler, "Taking a Break from Digital Overload," *Globe and Mail* (Canada), November 10, 2012, 15; Bob Sullivan and Hugh Thompson, "Brain, Interrupted," *New York Times*, May 3, 2013; Adam Gorlick, "Media Multitaskers Pay Mental Price," *Stanford News*, August 24, 2009, https://news.stanford .edu/2009/08/24/multitask-research-study-082409/.

5. Mark Brown, "How Driving a Taxi Changes London Cabbies' Brains," *Wired,* December 9, 2011, https://www.wired.com/2011/12/london-taxi-driver -memory/.

6. Curtis Silver, "Get Lost: How Over Reliance on Digital Maps Could Lead Us Mentally Astray," *The Next Web,* July 23, 2014, https://thenextweb.com/ socialmedia/2014/07/23/get-lost-reliance-digital-maps-lead-us-mentally-astray/.

7. Alvin Toffler, *Future Shock* (1970; repr., New York: Bantam, 1984), 125.

8. Ibid., 11, 95.

9. Ibid., 15.

10. Bree Loewen, *Found: A Life in Mountain Rescue* (Seattle: Mountaineers Books, 2017), 81.

11. James Gorman, "The Call in the Wild: Cell Phones Hit the Trail," *New York Times,* August 30, 2001, http://www.nytimes.com/2001/08/30/technology/the -call-in-the-wild-cell-phones-hit-the-trail.html.

12. See Ken Nicholson, "Chad Cook: 'I Thought I Was Hallucinating and Asked (Rescuers), 'Are You Guys Real?' " *WRCBtv,* March 27 2017, updated April 20, 2017, http://www.wrcbtv.com/story/35006470/chad-cook-i-thought-i-was -hallucinating-and-asked-rescuers-are-you-guys-real.

Abbey, Edward, 242–45, 249, 254, 267, 282, 284
abolitionists, 154, 188, 190–91, 195
Adirondacks, 216, 220–22
agrarian communities and households: boundaries of, 10; defined, 313n7; in post-Revolutionary War America, 98, 111, 117, 120, 128–30, 132; and transcontinental travel, 136–39, 150, 152, 155, 159, 162, 163, 165, 169. *See also* farmers
Albee, James, 212, 213–14
Albert, J. J., 204
Algonquian Mining Company, 196
Algonquians, 54–57, 60, 64–65, 72, 77–79, 81, 84–85, 87, 89, 91–92, 305n7
Alimamos (member of de Soto's expedition), 45, 46
Allen, Bill, 272
Allen, Edward Frank, 221; *A Guide to the National Parks of America*, 219–20
Allen, Elizabeth, 212–14
Allen, G. Nelson, 211–14
Allison, J. D., 168
Ambler, Donald, 271–72
American Anti-slavery Society, 190
Amundson, Michael, 275, 276

Añasco, Juan de, 28, 34
Anderson, "General," 179, 181
Angeles National Forest, 256–57
Anhaica (Native American settlement), 34
animals: and de Soto expedition, 24, 28, 47; and disorientation, 176–77, 180–81, 184–86, 194, 203–5; in Great Dismal Swamp, 105; and homing experiences, 134, 138, 143–44, 149, 153, 159, 163–64, 169; in post-Revolutionary War America, 112–14, 116–17, 125, 128, 130, 132; as rescuers, 116; and search-and-rescue, 259, 276; and transcontinental travel, 180–81, 184–85, 203. *See also specific types of animals*
Apaches, 211
Apalachees, 31, 34–36, 37, 40
Appalachian Trail, 286
Arapahoes, 182–84
Arches National Monument, 242, 244
Arnold, George, 129
Ashcraft, Chester, 129
Ashcraft, Nathan, 129
Atahualpa, 28
Atwood, John, 124
Audubon County, Iowa, 161, 163

automobiles, 214, 242–43, 245, 246, 282.
    *See also* highways
autonomy: and disorientation, 200; of
    enslaved persons, 153, 155; and mental
    health and stability, 224–25, 228, 231,
    241; in post-Revolutionary War
    America, 98; of travelers, 65
Ayllón expedition, 19

backcountry: and homing experiences, 151;
    and mental health and stability, 225;
    in post-Revolutionary War America,
    130; and search-and-rescue, 266, 268,
    274, 282–83; and self-discovery, 245,
    254. *See also* wilderness
Badger, Benjamin, 127
Ball, Charles, 132, 194, 195
Ballard, Martha, 99–101, 102, 126
Ballard, Samuel, 161–63, 164
Barnes, John, 80–81
Barnes, Laliah, 256
Barnett, Joseph, 124–25
Barnett, Sarah, 125–26
Baronett, Jack, 209
Barrows, Lewis O., 235
Beard, Daniel Carter, 229, 244
Beebe, David, 119
Bennett, Ira, 117
Benton, Thomas Hart, 202
Benton Frémont, Jessie, 202, 204
bewilderment: in colonial America, 79, 81,
    89; and disorientation, 188, 206, 209;
    and homing experiences, 138–39, 151,
    162; and mental health and stability,
    217, 226, 231, 236; in post-Revolu-
    tionary War America, 109, 120; and
    self-discovery, 249, 253–55. *See also*
    disorientation
Bibb, Henry, 193–94, 195
Biedma, Luys Hernández de, 26, 27, 34–35,
    40, 42–43, 47
Billington, Elinor, 61, 63
Billington, Francis, 61, 62
Billington, John, Jr., 52–54, 55, 56, 58,
    61, 71
Billington, John, Sr., 61–64

bison, 181–84, 203
Bitterroot National Forest, 247
Bivens, Mr., 146
Black Hawk Purchase (1833), 157
Black Tomato (travel company), 1–2, 12,
    293
Blevins, Brooks, 228
bloodhounds, 194, 234, 237
Bobadilla, Dona Isabel de, 28
Bolle, Arnold, 247–48, 251
Bonwell family, 159–60
Border Patrol (U.S.), 269, 270
Boulder County, Colorado, 261
boundaries. *See* edges and boundaries
Boyden family, 74
Boy Scouts, 231–32, 235, 244, 268
Bradbury, Laura, 239–40
Bradbury, Patty & Michael, 239–40
Bradford, William, 52, 53, 56, 62, 70, 78
Bradford County, Pennsylvania, 146
Brayton, William, 119
Breck, Edward: *The Way of the Woods: A
    Manual for Sportsmen in the
    Northeastern United States and
    Canada*, 224
Brewer, Luther, 158
Brown, John "Fed," 192–93, 195
Brown, John Stafford: *The Salton Sea
    Region, California*, 221
Brown, Peter, 60
Brown, Sarah, 145
Bruff, Joseph Goldsborough, 185
Buchanan, James, 108, 131
buffalo, 181–84, 203
Burnside, James, 161
Bushnell, Daniel P., 196, 197
Byrd, William, 105

Cabeza de Vaca, Álvar Núñez, 13–14, 21, 33
Cahokia (Native American settlement), 17,
    38
California Urban Search and Rescue Task
    Force, 280
camping and campgrounds: and disorien-
    tation, 187, 205; and homing experi-
    ences, 161; and mental health and

stability, 211, 213–14, 219–20, 223, 229–30; and search-and-rescue, 256, 271; and self-discovery, 242–43, 254

Canonicus, 55

canyons, 256–57, 277

captives: in colonial America, 57–58, 66, 77, 85–88, 90; and de Soto expedition, 14, 23, 25, 26, 27, 32–33, 35, 40–41, 48

Carson, Kit, 202, 204

Caverly, Irvin "Buzz," 236

Cedar County, Iowa, 161

Cendoya, Nicolas, 258–59

Champlain, Samuel de, 64–69

Charles V (king of Spain), 28–29

Chauncy, Mr., 123

Cheney, Louisa, 121

Cherokees, 39, 58, 86

Cheyennes, 176

Chicaza (Native American settlement), 37, 43

Chickasaws, 58

Chickatabot, 76

Childersburg, Alabama, 50–51

children: in colonial America, 53, 57–58, 61, 67, 73, 77, 87–88; and de Soto expedition, 30, 33, 39, 48; and disorientation, 194, 210; and homing experiences, 136, 139, 142, 146–47, 149, 152, 160; and mental health and stability, 229, 237–40; nature shock experiences of, 8, 288, 290, 292; post-Revolutionary War era disappearances of, 93–102, 109–24; and search-and-rescue, 270–71, 273, 280

Chilton, Thomas, 140, 141

Chippewas, 123

Choctaws, 58

cholera, 171–72

Chouinard, Yvon, 262

Clark, Peter, 100, 101

Clarksville Company, 177

Cleaves, Luther, 172

Clemens, Orion, 173–74

Clemens, Samuel. See Twain, Mark

Cleveland, Ohio, 201

Cleveland National Forest, 258

coastlines, 19–21, 94, 97, 277

Coddington, Hannah, 145

Cofaqui (Native American settlement), 35, 36, 37, 38, 39, 40

Cofitachequi (Native American settlement), 35, 36, 37, 38, 39, 40

Colborn, Robert & John, 145

colonial America, 52–92; Champlain's expedition, 64–69; and King Philip's War, 87–92; portages in, 82–87; rescues of the lost in, 73–77; rivers as navigational aids in, 64–69; wilderness areas in, 58–64, 70–73

Colorado Search and Rescue Board, 269

Comanches, 148–49, 176, 177–78

communities: in colonial America, 59–60, 64; and de Soto expedition, 17, 20, 23, 25, 30, 32–33, 39, 41; and disorientation, 177–78, 195; and homing experiences, 146–48, 158–60, 163; and mental health and stability, 218; in post-Revolutionary War America, 97–98, 101–4, 107–8, 111, 114, 116–18, 121–22, 124–27, 130; and relational space, 2–3, 8, 10–11, 290–91, 294; and search-and-rescue, 263–64, 268

Compromise of 1850, 189

Condon, Henry, 232, 233

Conners, John H., 117

conquistadors, 13, 17, 29–30, 47–50. See also De Soto, Hernando

Cook, Ryan, 240

Coosa (Native American settlement), 37, 50–51

copper mining, 195–202

Corps of Topographical Engineers, 202, 203

Crawford, Andrew, 161

Creeks, 58

Crockett, David, 140–43

Cronon, William, 287

Crowley, Daniel, 237, 238

Crows, 208

Cushman, Robert, 59–60, 62

Dana, Sebattis, 225
darkness: and disorientation, 24, 60, 81, 194, 203, 208; and homing experiences, 145–46, 150–51, 160–61; and mental health and stability, 230; and nature shock, 24, 60, 81; in post-Revolutionary War America, 98, 100–101, 111–13, 116, 118, 120, 126, 130, 133; and search-and-rescue, 276; and self-discovery, 250, 255–56
Darwin, Charles, 3
Davila, Pedrárias, 28
Dean, Alexander, Jr., 109
Dean, Fanny, 109–11
Decatur County, Indiana, 163
dementia, 8, 101–2. *See also* mental health and stability
de Mons, Pierre Dugua, 64–69
Derosier, Baptiste, 204, 205
deserts: and disorientation, 5, 174, 185–86, 290; and homing experiences, 149; and mental health and stability, 226, 239; and search-and-rescue, 277, 282; and self-discovery, 242–43, 254
Des Groseilleirs, Médard Chouart, 85
De Soto, Hernando, 13–51; army of, 32, 38–39; and Christian spatial vision, 27–31; coasts vs. interiors explored by, 19–21; death of, 13, 45, 47, 50; enslavement of Native Americans by, 31–33; narratives of expedition, 15–16, 48–51; Peru expedition by, 27–28
Dibble, Clark, 121, 122
disconnection: of Maroon communities, 109; and nature shock, 285–95; for self-discovery, 10, 11–12; vacations as, 213–14, 215, 273, 279–80
Dismal Swamp, 102–9, 111, 132–33
disorientation, 171–210; by amateur travelers, 176–87; in copper mining region, 195–202; and fugitive slaves, 187–95; and gold rush, 171–210; and surveyors, 195–207; and vision, 299n13; and Yellowstone region, 207–10
Doane, Gustavus, 320n59

Doane, John, 63
Dodson, Jacob, 204, 205
Doke, Jared, 276
Donner Party, 184, 185
Dorr, Josiah R., 196
Doverspike, Lewis, 164
*Dred Scott* case (1857), 190
Drown, William, 115
Dudley, Roy, 234
Dudley, Thomas, 78
Duffus, Robert L., 249, 254
Duncan, Mrs., 128
Dye, E. J., 129–30

East Tennessee and California Gold Mining Company, 179
edges and boundaries: of agrarian communities, 10; in colonial America, 53; and de Soto expedition, 19, 23, 28, 32–33, 38; and disorientation, 183, 195, 199, 207, 210; and homing experiences, 139, 146–48, 152–53; and mental health and stability, 215, 218, 219, 234, 241; nature shock at, 8, 10–12, 289–90, 293–94; in post-Revolutionary War America, 101, 104–6, 107, 108, 132; and search-and-rescue, 256–57, 262; and self-discovery, 245
Egan, Joseph: *Lost on a Mountain in Maine*, 235–37
Eichler, Leah, 287–88
Ellis, Robert, 158
Elvas (member of de Soto's expedition), 30, 33–37, 40, 43, 45–46, 50, 303n21
Emmett County, Iowa, 117
Endecott, John, 76
enslaved persons: in colonial America, 58, 65, 73, 82, 84–86, 88; and de Soto expedition, 14, 19, 29, 31–33, 38, 46, 49; and disorientation, 187–93, 195; fugitive travels of, 152–55, 187–95, 319n34; and homing experiences, 135, 136, 138, 139, 154–55; Native Americans as, 14, 19, 29, 31–33, 38, 46, 49; in post-Revolutionary War

America, 98, 102–9, 131–32; and relational space, 4, 31–33, 102–9, 290; surveillance of, 8, 102–9, 131–32
Evans, Ebenezer, 117
Evans, Reese, 116–17
Everts, Truman, 207–10, 217, 320n67

families: in colonial America, 52, 55, 58, 61–63, 73–74, 84–88, 90–91; and de Soto expedition, 49; and disorientation, 177–78, 182, 190, 192–93, 195; and homing experiences, 140, 142–43, 145–49, 155–57, 159–64, 168; and mental health and stability, 211–14, 216, 218, 223, 229, 233, 235, 237; in post-Revolutionary War America, 93, 95, 97, 99, 101–2, 106–8, 111–16, 118–19, 121, 125, 128–30; and search-and-rescue, 282; and self-discovery, 244, 247
farmers: in colonial America, 63; and disorientation, 189, 196; and homing experiences, 153, 157, 163–65; and mental health and stability, 218; in post-Revolutionary War America, 105, 118, 123, 128–29. See also agrarian communities and households
Farney, John, 187, 191, 201
Fassett, Josiah, 109, 110–11
fear, 56, 64–66, 73, 84, 125, 205, 231, 258–59, 277
Federal Highway Act (1956), 246
Fendler, Donn, 232–38, 240–41
Fenton, Michigan, 121–22, 123
Feryada (member of de Soto's expedition), 45
Figueroa, Vasco Porcallo de, 29
finding yourself. See self-discovery
Finley, Polly, 141, 142
Fitt, Thomas, 107
Fitzpatrick, Thomas "Broken Hand," 204
food: in colonial America, 53–54, 70, 79–81, 83, 88; and de Soto expedition, 13, 16, 34, 36, 41, 43; and disorientation, 194, 196, 198–200; and homing

experiences, 144, 150, 167–68; and mental health and stability, 235; in post-Revolutionary War America, 123; and search-and-rescue, 257, 264. See also specific types of food
Ford, Henry, 216
Forde, Henry, 3–4, 5
forests: in colonial America, 54, 57, 64, 70–72, 74, 80, 89; and de Soto expedition, 20, 23–24, 27, 31, 39, 45; and disorientation, 192–94; and homing experiences, 140, 150, 153, 160, 162; and mental health and stability, 216–18, 223–24, 226–28; and nature shock, 5–6, 8, 10, 288; in post-Revolutionary War America, 100–101, 111–14, 119, 123–24, 126, 128; and search-and-rescue, 272, 277; and self-discovery, 250
Forest Service (U.S.), 247, 261
forgetting, 65, 98, 222. See also memories
Forney, Linda, 257
Fort Bernard, 134
Fowler, John, 144–46
Foxes, 156–57, 158
Franklin, John Hope, 319n34
freedom: and disorientation, 188–89, 195; and highway system, 287; and homing experiences, 137–39, 154; and mental health and stability, 220; in post-Revolutionary War America, 97, 104, 111, 126–27; and power, 11; and search-and-rescue, 268–70; seeking out, 5, 8, 289, 295; and self-discovery, 242, 244–45, 249
Frémont, John C., 202–5, 218
French exploration of North America, 57, 65–67, 73–74, 77, 83–86
frontier: and disorientation, 175; and homing experiences, 149, 166; in post-Revolutionary War America, 120, 122, 126, 130; and self-discovery, 244
Frost, Tom, 262
Fugate, Carol Ann, 247
Fugitive Slave Act (1850), 190

Gallegos, Baltasar de, 21, 26

Garcilaso de la Vega, 36, 37, 42, 44, 48, 49–50, 303n21

Gardiner, Christopher, 78

Gasford, Paul, 93–95, 96–97, 291, 309n2

Gaytán, Juan, 35, 42

gender: in colonial America, 58, 86; and homing experiences, 137, 143; and mental health and stability, 224–25, 229–30, 232; in post-Revolutionary War America, 126; and search-and-rescue, 275–76, 283–84; and self-discovery, 253. *See also* masculinity; women

geo-fencing, 251

geographic space, 139, 182, 278, 283

Gilliland, Thaddeus Stephens, 147

Glacier National Park, 219–20, 221

gold and gold rush: in colonial America, 62; and de Soto expedition, 27, 31, 34–35, 40–41; and disorientation, 171–210; and homing experiences, 138, 143–44, 168

Goodman, John, 60

Gordon, Tom, 285

GPS, 288

Graham, Elisha, 126

Graham, Sarah Barnett, 125–26

Grand Canyon, 257, 287

grasslands. *See* plains; prairies

Great Dismal Swamp, 102–9, 111, 132–33

Great Lakes, 37, 58, 69, 93, 196–97. *See also specific lakes*

Grinnell, George Bird, 223

Guachoya (Native American settlement), 37, 43

Guzmán, Francisco de, 45–46

Gyles, John, 87

Hale, Jimmy, 226–28

Hall, G. Stanley, 227

Hallock, Charles, 220–21

hallucinations, 137, 232, 259

Hancock County, Iowa, 212

Harding, Lewis Albert, 163

Hardy, Manly, 224–25

Harriman, Mrs., 127

Hart, Irving H., 160

Hartt, Rollin Lynde, 165, 166

Hastings, Thaddeus, 99, 101

Headley, Joel Tyler, 221; *The Adirondack; or, Life in the Woods,* 220

healthy last resort, 2

Heggie, Travis, 274–75, 276

helicopters, 239, 267, 273, 281, 293

Hemenway, Elias, 99

Hennipen, Louis, 68

herding, 97, 137, 181, 291

Higginson, Francis, 92

highways, 244, 246–48, 287

hiking: and mental health and stability, 214, 219, 226, 235, 239; and search-and-rescue, 261, 266, 278, 280–82; and self-discovery, 244, 255–58

Hill, Kenneth A., 277

hippies, 247, 269–73, 277

Hirrihigua, 22, 23–25, 48

Hollingsworth, Pamela, 237

Holubar, Alice, 280

homing experiences, 134–70; and agrarian communities and households, 136–39, 150, 152, 155, 159, 162, 163, 165, 169; and animals, 134, 138, 143–44, 149, 153, 159, 163–64, 169; and bewilderment, 138–39, 151, 162; and children, 136, 139, 142, 146–47, 149, 152, 160; in colonial America, 77; and communities, 146–48, 158–60, 163; and darkness, 145–46, 150–51, 160–61; and disorientation, 191; of enslaved persons, 135, 136, 138, 139, 154–55; and families, 140, 142–43, 145–49, 155–57, 159–64, 168; and hunting, 135, 138, 140–42, 146–47, 156, 161, 162, 164; and independence, 137, 141, 145, 155; and individual space, 140, 170; and landmarks, 135, 157, 159–60, 168; and memories, 135–36, 144, 159, 165–66; and nature shock, 135, 137–39, 144–45, 149; and relational space, 137, 150, 155, 170; and snowstorms, 151, 156–59, 161, 165, 167; and vision, 134, 136, 161

honor: and de Soto expedition, 18, 26, 42, 49–50; and disorientation, 190; and homing experiences, 147; in post-Revolutionary War America, 123

horses: in de Soto's expedition, 13, 25, 28, 32, 40–41, 43, 45, 47; and disorientation, 174, 177–81, 185, 187, 203–5, 207–8; and homing experiences, 134, 139, 148, 155, 157, 160, 162, 169; and mental health and stability, 211, 220; in post-Revolutionary War America, 116–17; and self-discovery, 252–53

Horton, Dexter, 121, 122

hospitality, 56, 65, 72, 81, 90

Howe, Henry, 119–20, 217; *Historical Collections of Ohio*, 119

Howell, Jay, 240

Hudson, Charles, 39

Hudson's Bay Company, 85

hunting: in colonial America, 54–55, 66, 72, 75, 81, 84, 85, 86; and de Soto expedition, 39; and disorientation, 181–82, 184, 199, 203–4, 207, 209; and homing experiences, 135, 138, 140–42, 146–47, 156, 161, 162, 164; and mental health and stability, 220, 223, 231; and nature shock, 4–5, 6; in post-Revolutionary War America, 110, 115; and search-and-rescue, 265, 282; and self-discovery, 244

Huntington Lake, 238

Hurons, 58, 64, 65, 83

Illinois country, 67–69

Incas, 27–28, 36

independence, 10–11; and disorientation, 171, 187, 193; and homing experiences, 137, 141, 145, 155; and mental health and stability, 236; in post-Revolutionary War America, 96, 98, 111, 122, 126–27, 132; and search-and-rescue, 267, 271; and self-discovery, 243

Indiana, 154, 163, 187–89, 195

individual space: and de Soto expedition, 15; and disorientation, 183, 202; and homing experiences, 140, 170; and mental health and stability, 213; and nature shock, 3–5, 7–8, 12; and search-and-rescue, 256, 260, 271, 279; and self-discovery, 245

information networks, 167–68, 172. *See also* mail service

insanity, 135, 198, 217, 233, 237. *See also* mental health and stability

International Search and Rescue Incident Database, 9, 274

Iowas, 156

Ipswich, Scott & Eliot, 74–75

Iroquois, 67, 68, 73–74, 83, 84

isovist perspective, 253–54, 287

Jack (fugitive enslaved person), 134–40

Jack, Kyndall, 258–60

Jackson, Andrew, 131, 147, 190

Jackson Township, Ohio, 147

James (king of England), 70

Jasper County, Iowa, 165–66

Jefferson, Thomas, 137

Jefferson County, Pennsylvania, 164

Jenkins, John, 161–62, 163

Jessup, Elon, 215–19, 321n9; "Getting Lost in the Woods," 215–16

Johnson, Galen, 121

Jones, Ralph T., 234–35

Joshua Tree National Monument, 239

Josselyn, John, 82

Kaboos, Robert, 238–39

Kansas-Nebraska Act (1854), 189

Kelley, Dennis E., 263, 265–67, 268, 273–74, 327n51; *Mountain Search for the Lost Victim*, 273

Kephart, Horace, 229; *Camping and Woodcraft: A Handbook for Vacation Campers and Travelers in the Wilderness*, 223

Kerlin, Maggie, 168

Kershaw, Meg, 280

Keyes, Elisha, 124

Kickapoos, 69, 73
Kilkenny, New Hampshire, 123
Kiner, Henry, 163
King, Stephen, 236, 291; *The Girl Who Loved Tom Gordon*, 285–87
King County Explorer Search & Rescue (KC ESAR), 261
King County Search & Rescue Association (KCSARA), 261
King Philip's War, 87–92
kinship, 2, 16, 20, 25, 29, 48. *See also* families; relational space
Kinsley, Daniel, 160
Koehler, Derek J., 277
Koester, Robert, 9

Lake Huron, 196
Lake Michigan, 69, 154
Lake Ontario, 64, 86, 93
Lake Superior, 196, 199–200
landmarks: in colonial America, 71, 82; and disorientation, 180, 182, 184, 191, 193, 197; and homing experiences, 135, 157, 159–60, 168; and mental health and stability, 216, 223, 231; and nature shock, 4, 6–7, 11, 288; in post-Revolutionary War America, 96–98, 104, 118, 120–24, 126–27, 131; and self-discovery, 250
landscapes: in colonial America, 53, 55, 72, 82, 92; and disorientation, 172, 180, 193–94, 207, 210; and homing experiences, 148, 152, 154, 156, 159; and mental health and stability, 219, 223; and nature shock, 5, 8, 11, 292; in post-Revolutionary War America, 98, 106–7, 120, 122–23; and self-discovery, 253–54
Langford, Nathaniel, 320n59
languages: in colonial America, 54, 70, 74, 77, 84; and de Soto expedition, 14, 19, 25, 27, 33, 35–37; and disorientation, 177, 197
Legg, Douglas, 271–72
LeMany, Nancy, 280–81
Lenape, 74

Lincoln, Abraham, 131, 173
Lindsay, Eloise, 257–58
Linn County, Iowa, 158
Little, John and Maria, 152–55, 156
Lobillo, Juan Ruiz, 45
Loewen, Bree, 283–84, 293
Logue, Sarah, 192, 193
Loguen, Jermain "Jarm," 187–93, 195, 201, 318n33
Longworth, Nicholas, 163
Los Angeles County, California, 264–65, 270, 280
lurking, 102–9

Mabila (Native American settlement), 42
Machias Corners, New York, 128–29
Maddocks, Melvin, 279
mail service: in colonial America, 76; and disorientation, 174, 175, 190–91; and homing experiences, 140, 143, 167
Maine Guides Association, 235
maize: in colonial America, 54, 56, 63, 67; and de Soto expedition, 17, 22, 25, 27, 33–34
Maliseets, 87
Manzano (member of de Soto's expedition), 45, 50–51
maps: and de Soto expedition, 15, 29, 51; and disorientation, 184, 191, 193, 196–98, 200, 202–7; and homing experiences, 162; and mental health and stability, 215–16, 223; and nature shock, 3, 10–12, 286; and search-and-rescue, 268, 277; and self-discovery, 246, 249–50
Marchant, Tom, 2
Marks, Jeanette Augustus: *Vacation Camping for Girls*, 229–31
Maroon communities, 102–9, 132–33, 311n19
Marryat, Frederick, 180
masculinity: and de Soto expedition, 18, 43, 48; and homing experiences, 148, 149; and mental health and stability, 234; in post-Revolutionary War America, 126; and search-and-rescue,

278, 280; and search and rescue methods, 278; and self-discovery, 243–44, 245, 254, 282

Massachusetts Bay Colony, 59, 63, 70, 72, 81

Massasoit, 55, 56

Mather, Increase, 88, 89, 90

Mayflower Compact, 59, 63

Mayo, John, 107

McCoy, Lois Clark, 264, 269

McHenry, William "Jerry," 190

McKenney, Robert & William, 112–13

McMoarn, Nelson, 233, 235

Meinzer, O. E., 221

memories: and disorientation, 191; and homing experiences, 135–36, 144, 159, 165–66; and mental health and stability, 211, 213, 218, 222; and nature shock, 3, 288, 291–92; in post-Revolutionary War America, 96, 98, 102, 114, 118–24; and search-and-rescue, 281–82; and self-discovery, 250

Ménard, Réne, 69

mental health and stability, 211–41; and autonomy, 224–25, 228, 231, 241; and bewilderment, 217, 226, 231, 236; and camping, 211, 213–14, 219–20, 223, 229–30; and children, 229, 237–40; and communities, 218; and darkness, 230; and edges and boundaries, 215, 218, 219, 234, 241; and families, 211–14, 216, 218, 223, 229, 233, 235, 237; and freedom, 220; and gender, 224–25, 229–30, 232; and hiking, 214, 219, 226, 235, 239; and independence, 236; and individual space, 213; and memories, 211, 213, 218, 222; and nature shock, 215, 224, 237, 241; and relational space, 216, 218–19; and relationships, 213, 219; and vacations, 213, 215, 219–24, 225, 235, 238, 240

mental spaces, 132, 253, 289, 293–95

MercuryCSC advertising agency, 250–51

Merrill, Eleazer & Hiram, 115

Metacom (King Philip), 88. See also King Philip's War

Metcalf, Lee, 247

Mexican-American War, 174

Miamis, 67, 68, 119

Miantonomi, 55

Miller, George, 148

Mills County, Iowa, 168, 169

Mississippians: fragmentation of, 58; and relational space, 22, 24–25, 31, 49; settlement patterns and social structures of, 16–19, 45, 302n9; trade network of, 37; use of term, 301n4

Missouri Compromise (1820), 189

Mocoso (Native American settlement), 25, 27, 31, 37, 48

modernity: and automobiles, 214, 242–43, 246, 282; retreats from, 10, 12, 213–14, 238, 290; and self-discovery, 228, 242; vacations as respite from, 238, 290; and wilderness, 214–15, 220, 225, 228, 260, 280, 290–91

Mohawks, 84, 85

Montana, tourism campaigns in, 250–53

Montana Outfitters and Guides Association, 248, 251

Montana Tractors, 252–53

Mooney, James, 38

Moore, Mike, 267

Moore family, 117

Mormons, 184

Morton, Captain, 173

Morton, Thomas, 63

Moscoso Alvarado, Luis de, 28, 45, 46

Moshier, William, 146

Mount Katahdin, Maine, 151–52, 232, 236

Mount Rainier National Park, 283

Mumford, Deborah & Sally, 116

Mumford, Jirah, 116

Mummie, Ludwig, 148, 149

Murray, William Henry Harrison, 221–23; *Adventures in the Wilderness; or, Camp-Life in the Adirondacks*, 222

Narragansetts, 55, 70, 80

Narváez, Pánfilo de, 13–14, 19, 21–22, 29, 48

Nash, Roderick: *The Wilderness in the American Mind*, 5

National Association of Search and Rescue (NASAR), 261, 273

National Association of Search and Rescue Coordinators (NASARC), 261, 263

National Park Service (NPS), 239, 254–55, 261, 264, 275, 283

Native Americans: in American West, 148–49; and Christian spatial vision, 29–30; and colonial America, 53–54, 57–58, 73–74, 76, 81, 84, 91; and copper region, 196, 200; and de Soto expedition, 16, 29, 39, 49–50; enslavement of, 31–33; in Great Dismal Swamp, 104–5; as guides in colonial America, 71–72, 78, 80–81; and homing experiences, 148–49, 157–58, 165, 168; and mental health and stability, 225, 228; and Narváez expedition, 13–14; nature shock experiences of, 5, 8–11, 225; relational space of, 21–26; and transcontinental travelers, 148–49, 157–58, 165, 168, 173, 176–78, 180, 185; and wilderness areas, 7, 9; in Yellowstone region, 208. *See also specific groups and individuals*

nature shock: in colonial America, 53, 57; defined, 3–4; and de Soto expedition, 10–13, 18, 39, 46; and disorientation, 176, 183, 185, 193, 195, 198, 201–2, 204, 206, 209; domestication of, 117–18; and future shock, 291–92; and homing experiences, 135, 137–39, 144–45, 149; and mental health and stability, 215, 224, 237, 241; in post-Revolutionary War America, 97–98, 102, 104, 111–14, 116–18, 120, 122, 125, 132; power as ingredient for, 6–7, 8; and search-and-rescue, 259–60, 271–74, 283; and self-discovery, 245, 255–57; source of, 3–4; vision's effect on, 7–8; wilderness areas as ingredients for, 5–6

Nausets, 53, 58

Navajos, 211

navigation: assistance with, 55, 65, 89; failure of, 12; as shared space, 3. *See also* disorientation; maps

neighbors: in colonial America, 61, 63, 76, 79, 82; and disorientation, 175, 182, 188; and homing experiences, 144–45, 147, 151–52, 159–60, 163, 166; in post-Revolutionary War America, 97, 99–102, 110–11, 115–19, 124–28; and search-and-rescue, 260; and self-discovery, 254

Newcomin, John, 63

Newhard, Eliza J., 159–60

Newton, Miriam, 99

Niagara Falls, 250, 287

Niantics, 55

Nichols, George, 143–44, 171–72

Nichols, Samuel, 171–73, 176, 218, 290

Nichols, Sarah, 172

Nicollet, Joseph, 203

Ninigret, 55

Nipissings, 69

Nipmucks, 87

Nixon, R. C., 109

Nolf, George, 164

Nolf, Henry, 164–65

North Carolina: community surveillance in, 102–9; de Soto expedition in, 13; Dismal Swamp in, 102–9, 111, 132–33; Little family's escape from slavery in, 152–53, 155

Northwest Ordinance (1787), 189

Nova Scotia, 66

NPS. *See* National Park Service

Ochuse (Native American settlement), 34, 35, 42, 47

Odawas, 123

Oglala Lakotas, 134, 135, 138–39

Ojibwes, 197, 201

Olmsted, Frederick Law, 311n19

Olympic National Park, 258, 293

Oregon Trail, 134–70

Ortiz, Juan, 21–27, 31, 33–35, 38, 40, 42, 47–48

Osorio, Don Antonio, 44
Overland Trail, 144
Oviedo y Valdés, Gonzalo Fernández de, 35, 36, 44, 45, 50; *Historia general y natural de las Indias*, 49
Ozarks, 226–28

Pacific Coast Trail, 281
panic: in colonial America, 52, 84; and de Soto expedition, 25; and homing experiences, 136; and nature shock, 6; in post-Revolutionary War America, 102, 113, 120; and search-and-rescue, 257–58, 273, 277; and transcontinental travel, 198, 206, 208, 217, 227, 230–31, 241
panthers, 24
Parker, Leonard Fletcher, 159
Parkman, Ebenezer, 123
Parkman, Francis, 134, 135–40
Peach, Arthur, 80–81
pedestrianism, 6, 39, 47, 57, 176. *See also* hiking
Pequots, 55, 81
Percy, F. A., 177
Perico, 34–41, 47
Pierce County Sheriff's Department, 270–71
Pike's Peak, 212
Pioneer Publishing Company, 158
Pitchess, Peter J., 265, 270
Pizarro, Francisco, 28
plains: and disorientation, 179–80, 182–84, 186, 203; and homing experiences, 134–36, 138–40, 143, 149, 156, 159, 168; and mental health and stability, 213. *See also* prairies
Plymouth Colony, 52–53, 55, 58, 60–62, 64, 72, 75, 80–81
Poire, Francis, 106
Ponce de León, 19
Portage County, Ohio, 114, 118, 119
portages, 57, 65–66, 69, 82–87
Port Barnett, 124–25
Posey, Mr., 192–93
positive bewilderment, 248–50, 272, 273

post-Revolutionary War America, 93–133; agrarian communities in, 98, 111, 117, 120, 128–30, 132; autonomy in, 98; bewilderment in, 109, 120; children disappearing in, 93–102, 109–24; communities in, 97–98, 101–4, 107–8, 111, 114, 116–18, 121–22, 124–27, 130; darkness in, 98–102; edges and boundaries in, 101, 104–6, 107, 108, 132; enslaved persons in, 98, 102–9, 131–32; families in, 93, 95, 97, 99, 101–2, 106–8, 111–16, 118–19, 121, 125, 128–30; freedom in, 97, 104, 111, 126–27; frontier in, 120, 122, 126, 130; independence in, 96, 98, 111, 122, 126–27, 132; landmarks in, 96–98, 104, 118, 120–24, 126–27, 131; memories and memorialization in, 96, 98, 102, 114, 118–24; nature shock in, 97–98, 102, 104, 111–14, 116–18, 120, 122, 125, 132; neighbors in, 97, 99–102, 110–11, 115–19, 124–28; power in, 98, 105; relationships in, 102–3, 107–9, 126, 128–29; surveillance in, 102–9, 113
Potawatomis, 156–57
Powell, H. M. T., 182, 183, 184
power: in colonial America, 55, 57, 71, 75, 86, 90–91; and de Soto expedition, 16, 20, 27, 29, 32, 47; and disorientation, 192, 198; and homing experiences, 136, 138–39; nature shock influenced by, 6–7, 8, 290, 294–95; in post-Revolutionary War America, 98, 105; and search-and-rescue, 271; and self-discovery, 244–45, 253–55
prairies: bison hunting on, 181–82; in colonial America, 67–68; and disorientation, 176–77, 179–82, 203; and homing experiences, 135, 136, 139–40, 154, 156–62, 165–67; and mental health and stability, 211–12; in post-Revolutionary War America, 102, 122, 126, 130–31; and search-and-rescue, 275; and self-discovery, 250

Pratt, Chuck, 262
Prescott, Joseph, 100, 101
Preuss, Charles, 204, 205–7
Pritchett, George A., 209
Protestants, 57, 59, 61, 66
Proue, Raphael, 204
Providence, Rhode Island, 70, 80
psychographics, 251
Purcell, Walt, 258
Puritans, 59, 63, 89, 91

Quizquiz (Native American settlement), 37

radio, 232, 235, 237–38, 243, 286
Radisson, Pierre Esprit (Peter), 83–86
railroads: and disorientation, 176, 180–83;
    in Great Dismal Swamp, 104; and
    homing experiences, 166; and mail
    service, 7; and modernity, 214; and
    nature shock, 11
Randolph, Vance, 226–28; *The Ozarks: An
    American Survival of a Primitive
    Society*, 228
Rangel, Rodrigo, 35, 36, 44, 45
Rathbun, Sara, 280
Read, Mercy, 129
recreational wilderness: and disorientation,
    210; and mental health and stability,
    232, 239–40; and search-and-rescue,
    275, 280, 284; and self-discovery,
    254–56
Reed, Lena F., 270–71
regionalism, 190
regional space, 176, 191
Reimer, Charles, 182–83
relational space: in colonial America, 54,
    58, 73, 76–77, 82, 84, 85, 91; and de
    Soto expedition, 14, 16, 18, 20–22,
    29–31, 40, 47–49; and disorientation,
    176, 178, 183, 185, 189–90, 192, 196,
    202, 206–7; and enslaved persons,
    31–33, 102–9; and homing experi-
    ences, 137–38, 150, 155, 170; and
    mental health and stability, 213, 216,
    218–19; and Native Americans,
    21–26; and nature shock, 3–8, 10–11,

290–93; in post-Revolutionary War
    America, 102–3, 107–9, 126, 128–29;
    and search-and-rescue, 256, 260, 271,
    278, 283
rescuers: and homing experiences, 167;
    and mental health and stability, 217,
    234; in post-Revolutionary War
    America, 125; and self-discovery, 245,
    248. *See also* search-and-rescue (SAR)
Rhode Island, 70, 80
Ribourde, Gabriel, 66–67, 68, 69, 73
Rice, William, 167
Richard, John Baptiste, 134, 135, 138
Riggin, James, 180–81, 185–87, 188
Riggin, Rebecca, 186–87
rivers and waterways: in colonial America,
    57, 64–69, 72–74, 78–83; and de Soto
    expedition, 13, 24, 39, 47–48; and
    disorientation, 171, 175, 180, 183, 185,
    191, 194, 203, 205; and homing expe-
    riences, 154, 161, 167; and mental
    health and stability, 233, 236, 239; as
    navigational aids, 64–69; in post-
    Revolutionary War America, 108, 125,
    128; and search-and-rescue, 257–58.
    *See also specific bodies of water by name*
Robbins, Royal, 262
Rocky Mountain Rescue, 261, 268, 280
Rodgers, John, 131
Rodriquez Lobillo, Juan, 28
romantic movement, 214
Roosevelt, Franklin, 235
Roosevelt, Theodore, 244
Rossetter, Robert, 239
Rothe, August, 148, 149
Rowlandson, Mary, 87–92

Sagamore John (Wonohaquaham), 75–76,
    79
St. Clair, Lucas, 240
San Diego Mountain Rescue Team, 269
SAR. *See* search-and-rescue
Satchell, Wilson, 130
Sauks, 69, 156–57, 158
Sauter, Jacob, 148, 149
Scalf, Sandra Michelle, 270–71

scenario lock, 277
Schroeder, Ricky, 240
Schuller, Robert, 240
Schweninger, Loren, 319n34
Scott, Kate M., 166
Scott-Nash, Mark, 268–69
search-and-rescue (SAR), 5, 255–78, 280.
    *See also specific groups*
*Search and Rescue* magazine, 263–64, 267,
    269, 270, 273
Seattle ESAR, 267, 283
Seattle Mountain Rescue, 293
Seed, Patricia, 303n27
self-discovery, 10, 11–12, 242–55
Semer, Catherine, 147
Semer, John H., 146–47
Senecas, 86, 125
Seton, Ernest Thompson, 225, 231, 244
shared space, 3, 23, 59, 292, 294
Shawnees, 119
Shields, George O., 221; *Camping and
    Camp Outfits,* 223
Shields, Susan, 158
Sibley, George, 265–66, 267
Sierra Madres Mountain Search and
    Rescue Association, 239
sight. *See* vision
Silver, Curtis, 288
Sioux, 69, 156, 176
S. J. Clarke (publishing company), 315n50
slavery. *See* enslaved persons
smallpox epidemic: (1619–20), 55; (1633),
    76, 79–80
smartphones, 288–89
Smith, Benjamin, 108
Smith, Henry Perry, 220
Smith, John Tirrell, 173
Snow, Paul, 256–57
snowstorms: in colonial America, 60, 74,
    81; and disorientation, 184–85, 205,
    208; and homing experiences, 151,
    156–59, 161, 165, 167; and mental
    health and stability, 220, 238–39; in
    post-Revolutionary War America, 117;
    and search-and-rescue, 256–57, 276,
    283; and self-discovery, 250, 254

South, Hazlett, 163
Southeastern Ceremonial Complex, 17, 23,
    37, 39
Sowell, Andrew, 117
spatial cognition, 3–4, 7, 11, 199, 213, 248,
    288
spatial libertarians, 268, 271
Standish, Miles, 61, 62
Starkweather, Charles, 247
steamboats, 175
Stearns, Jabez, 115–16
Steingrandt, Major, 182, 183
Stevens, De Cator, 192–93
Stewart, Thomas, 127
Stockdale, William, 249–50, 254
storms: and homing experiences, 134,
    137–38, 140, 152, 159–61, 167; and
    search-and-rescue, 283; and self-
    discovery, 255. *See also* snowstorms
Strayed, Cheryl, 281–83; *Wild: From Lost to
    Found on the Pacific Coast Trail,* 281
Sullivan, John Jeremiah, 201
surveillance: and disorientation, 175, 177;
    and enslaved persons, 102–9; and
    homing experiences, 169; and nature
    shock, 2, 4, 10, 290; in post-Revolu-
    tionary War America, 102–9, 113; and
    search-and-rescue, 262, 269, 271
surveyors, 195–207
Sutter, John, 204
swamps: in colonial America, 54–55, 57, 71,
    74, 80–81, 87, 89; and de Soto expedi-
    tion, 14, 21, 31–32; and disorientation,
    193–94, 199–200; and homing expe-
    riences, 153; and mental health and
    stability, 218; and nature shock, 5, 8,
    10; in post-Revolutionary War
    America, 102–8, 123, 126, 131–32
Swan, Eugene L., 223–24
Swanton, John R., 15, 50
Sylvestre, Gonzalo, 36
Syrotuck, William G.: *Analysis of Lost Person
    Behavior,* 276

Table Rock State Park, South Carolina,
    257–58

Tackett, Marine, 163
Tacoma Citizen Band Radio Association, 271
Tacoma Mountain Rescue Association, 271
Talbot, Theodore, 204
Tascaluza (Native American settlement), 37
Tatobem, 55
Taylor, Ab, 269, 270
Thoreau, Henry David, 149–52, 254; *Walden*, 149, 150
Thrall, James, 144
Tillotson, Mrs., 119
Timucuans, 31–33, 36
Tingley, Harry, 234
Toffler, Alvin: *Future Shock*, 292
Tonti, Henri de, 67, 68, 73
tourists: and disorientation, 210; and mental health and stability, 215, 219, 222, 226; and nature shock, 6, 287; and search-and-rescue, 257, 262, 278; and self-discovery, 242–43, 247–51, 254. *See also* vacations
Tovar, Nuño de, 28
Towns, Charles, 204, 205
Townsend, Harper, 265–66
trails: in colonial America, 70–72; and de Soto expedition, 15, 25; and disorientation, 174, 176–77, 180, 183–86, 188, 198; and homing experiences, 145, 157, 167–68; and mental health and stability, 212–13, 216, 220, 227, 231–33, 238; of Native Americans, 25; in post-Revolutionary War America, 94, 101, 110; and search-and-rescue, 256, 258, 276, 281–82; and self-discovery, 245
transcontinental travel, 171–210; by amateur travelers, 176–87; by copper miners, 195–202; by fugitive slaves, 187–95; by surveyors, 195–207; to Yellowstone region, 207–10
Treaty of Flint River (1837), 123
Treaty of Saginaw (1838), 123
Trumbull, Benjamin, 73
Tversky, Amos, 277
Tversky, Barbara, 3

Twain, Mark, 175; *Roughing It*, 173–74
Tyson, T. K., 168–69

Ulrich, Laurel Thatcher, 99, 101
Underground Railroad, 195
unpacking phenomenon, 277
Urriparacoxi (Native American settlement), 25
U.S. Forest Service, 247, 261
Uzachil (Native American settlement), 33
Uzita (Native American settlement), 20, 21–23, 25–27, 31, 34, 37, 42, 47

vacations: and mental health and stability, 213, 215, 219–24, 225, 235, 238, 240; and search-and-rescue, 257, 272, 275, 279; and self-discovery, 243, 249–53. *See also* tourists
Van Wert County, Ohio, 146–47
violence: in colonial America, 54, 56–57, 65–66, 68, 80; and de Soto expedition, 16, 20, 40, 42; and disorientation, 178, 187; and homing experiences, 149, 168
Virginia: community surveillance in, 102–9; Dismal Swamp in, 102–9, 111, 132–33; slavery in, 190
vision: in colonial America, 53, 59, 66, 87; and de Soto expedition, 19–20, 26, 28, 34, 39; and disorientation, 179, 191, 193–94, 299n13; and homing experiences, 134, 136, 161; and mental health and stability, 220, 233; nature shock affected by, 6, 7–8, 287; in post-Revolutionary War America, 93, 97, 102, 104, 106, 109–13; and search-and-rescue, 258, 274; and self-discovery, 253
Vizcaino, Joan, 45

Wabanaki, 87
Wahginnacut, 76
Waid, Mrs., 100
Walsh, Adam, 239
Wampanoags, 55, 87
Warren, Richard, 62

Warren Township, Iowa, 146
Wartes, Jon, 266, 267–68, 270, 274
Washburn, Henry, 320n59
Washburn-Langford-Doane expedition
    (1870), 207–10
waterways. *See* rivers and waterways
Wearstler, Christopher, 258
Weast, Abraham, 146
Welch, Jack, 250, 251
Wells Publishing Company, 235
Western Historical Company, 166
Western Reserve Historical Society, 201
Weynand, Herbert, 148
White Mountains, New Hampshire, 256
white supremacy, 189
Whiton, John Milton, 115
Whittlesey, Charles, 195–202, 217, 218
Wick, Barthinius, 158
Widney, John, 119
wilderness: defined and redefined, 5–6;
    extreme, 283–84; modern, 214–15,
    220, 225, 228, 260, 280, 290–91; and
    Native Americans, 7; recreational,
    210, 232, 239–40, 254–56, 275, 280,
    284; as respite from modernity, 213.
    *See also* recreational wilderness
Williams, Roger, 54, 55–56, 70–72, 80, 88;
    *A Key into the Language of America,*
    70, 77
Winchell, R., 121, 122
Winfrey, Oprah, 282–83
Winnebagos, 156, 158

Winslow, Edward, 62
winter: in colonial America, 52–54, 64, 70,
    74, 78–79, 81; and de Soto expedition,
    34, 42; and disorientation, 172, 174,
    176, 203; and homing experiences,
    147, 156–59, 161–62, 164, 167, 169; in
    post-Revolutionary War America, 105,
    117; and search-and-rescue, 270. *See
    also* snowstorms
Winthrop, John, 59, 70, 75–76, 78,
    79–80, 81
women: in colonial America, 58, 77, 88;
    and mental health and stability,
    224–25, 229–30, 232; in search and
    rescue groups, 280; wilderness self-
    discovery by, 279–84
Wonohaquaham (Sagamore John), 75–76,
    79
Wood, William, 52–53, 72–75, 77–79,
    81–82, 89; *New England's Prospect,*
    72
woods shock, 298n7. *See also* nature shock
Woodward, Cyrus, 100

Yeager, Jacob, 146
Yellowstone, 207–10, 250, 320n59
Yellowstone Lake, 207
Yosemite National Park, 261, 262–63, 276,
    280
Yûñwĭ Tsunsdi' (Little People), 38–39

Zenobe, Father, 67, 68